TREO *essentials*

MICHAEL MORRISON

QUE®
800 East 96th Street,
Indianapolis, Indiana 46240

Treo™ Essentials

International Standard Book Number: 0-7897-3328-5

Library of Congress Catalog Card Number: 2004116488

Printed in the United States of America

First Printing: August 2005

08 07 06 4 3

Trademarks

All terms mentioned in this book that are known to be trademarks or service marks have been appropriately capitalized. Que Publishing cannot attest to the accuracy of this information. Use of a term in this book should not be regarded as affecting the validity of any trademark or service mark.

Treo is a trademark of palmOne, Inc.

Warning and Disclaimer

Every effort has been made to make this book as complete and as accurate as possible, but no warranty or fitness is implied. The information provided is on an "as is" basis. The author and the publisher shall have neither liability nor responsibility to any person or entity with respect to any loss or damages arising from the information contained in this book.

Bulk Sales

Que Publishing offers excellent discounts on this book when ordered in quantity for bulk purchases or special sales. For more information, please contact

U.S. Corporate and Government Sales
1-800-382-3419
corpsales@pearsontechgroup.com

For sales outside of the U.S., please contact

International Sales
international@pearsoned.com

Associate Publisher
Greg Wiegand

Acquisitions Editor
Todd Green

Development Editor
Sean Dixon

Managing Editor
Charlotte M. Clapp

Project Editor
Tonya Simpson

Copy Editor
Lisa Lord

Indexer
Ken Johnson

Proofreader
Linda Seifert

Technical Editors
Greg Winton
James Alan Miller

Publishing Coordinator
Sharry Lee Gregory

Multimedia Developer
Dan Scherf

Book Designer
Anne Jones

Page Layout
Toi Davis

Contents at a Glance

Table of Contents

Contents at a Glance

Table of Contents

About the Author

Michael Morrison is a writer, developer, toy inventor, and author of a variety of computer technology books and interactive Web-based courses. In addition to his primary profession as a writer and freelance nerd for hire, Michael is the creative lead at Stalefish Labs, an entertainment company he co-founded with his wife, Masheed. The first commercial debut for Stalefish Labs is a traditional social/trivia game called Tall Tales: The Game of Legends and Creative One-Upmanship (http://www.talltalesgame.com/). When not glued to his computer, playing hockey, skateboarding, or watching movies with his wife, Michael enjoys hanging out by his koi pond while he surfs the wireless Web. You can visit Michael on the Web and discuss this book at http://www.michaelmorrison.com/.

Michael's previous books include *BlackBerry in a Snap*, *Special Edition Using Pocket PC 2002*, *The Unauthorized Guide to Pocket PC*, *Beginning Mobile Phone Game Programming*, and *Sams Teach Yourself Wireless Java in 21 Days*.

Dedication

To my Dad, for literally answering thousands of construction questions and for allowing me to pretend to be an architect as he patiently designed our new house.

And to my cousin, Randy Hood, who so generously gave of his time and considerable skill in drafting our house design.

A note to aspiring writers and architects: Pick one profession or the other, and never try to be both at once!

Acknowledgments

Thanks to Todd Green, Sean Dixon, and Lisa Lord for keeping me on track and preventing this book from taking two years to write! I also owe an enormous thanks to my wife, Masheed, who tolerates my night-owl writing schedule. And finally, a big thank you goes out to the many Treo users who shared ideas and insights on numerous Web sites and discussion forums I visited while working on this book.

We Want to Hear from You!

As the reader of this book, *you* are our most important critic and commentator. We value your opinion and want to know what we're doing right, what we could do better, what areas you'd like to see us publish in, and any other words of wisdom you're willing to pass our way.

As an associate publisher for Que Publishing, I welcome your comments. You can email or write me directly to let me know what you did or didn't like about this book—as well as what we can do to make our books better.

Please note that I cannot help you with technical problems related to the topic of this book. We do have a User Services group, however, where I will forward specific technical questions related to the book.

When you write, please be sure to include this book's title and author as well as your name, email address, and phone number. I will carefully review your comments and share them with the author and editors who worked on the book.

Email: feedback@quepublishing.com

Mail: Greg Wiegand
Associate Publisher
Que Publishing
800 East 96th Street
Indianapolis, IN 46240 USA

For more information about this book or another Que title, visit our website at `www.quepublishing.com`. Type the ISBN (excluding hyphens) or the title of a book in the Search field to find the page you're looking for.

Introduction

When I first started tinkering with Treo devices a few years ago, I had some reservations because of mixed feelings about handheld device convergence. I'm referring to the notion that many devices used regularly (phones, PDAs, music players, video games, and so forth) should be merged into a single all-purpose mobile computing device. This concept is important because it underlies the very design of the Treo line of devices. Treo devices represent one of the first mobile devices that truly serve as an all-in-one mobile computing solution.

So what brought on the mixed feelings? Well, the truth is that I kind of liked having a separate mobile phone and a separate gadget to check email, play music, and so on. I tend to carry my mobile phone in my pocket and I also tend to drop it a lot, so I like that most phones are small and often more rugged than their more full-featured counterparts. The idea of a larger, more fragile device has always been a turn-off to me—that is, until the latest generation of devices, including the Treo 650. The Treo 650 truly changed my perceptions of all-in-one mobile devices because I realized how nifty it can be having everything in one compact package.

Granted, the Treo 650 is still a bit chunkier than the tiny little Nokia phone I had been using, and I'm certain that it's more fragile, but the benefits proved to far outweigh my perceived negatives. I underestimated the significance of a larger screen that can be used to view full-blown HTML web pages, a dedicated MP3 player, and a digital camera and camcorder, all combined with a mobile phone. I have to be a little more careful with my Treo in terms of not dropping it or running over it with a bicycle or skateboard (I've done both in the past), but as I said, the tradeoff has been well worth it.

So this brings me to this book, which is intended to be an all-encompassing guide to your Treo. By all-encompassing, I mean that I've searched far and wide to include coverage of

IN THIS CHAPTER

- How This Book Is Structured
- What You'll Need

tricks, tips, and gotchas that you won't find in the manual for your device. I've read my share of books on computers and mobile devices, and I know when an author has taken the path of least resistance and created just a more user-friendly version of the manual. This book is user-friendly, but it's far from a rehashing of the manual. I like to tell people that anyone could write one of these books if given a device, Google access, and a few thousand hours!

If you're entirely new to the Treo family of devices, particularly the Treo 650, this book has plenty of introductory coverage to get you going. And if you've already spent some time getting to know your device, you'll also find loads of valuable information to help maximize the Treo experience. What's important is that I've tried to consider the practical issues that Treo users face, and when I stumbled across an interesting solution to a problem I encountered, I documented it. I hope you'll find that I've unearthed and addressed most, if not all, of the problems you've had while using your device.

It's important for me to share that I'm a Treo user just like you. I think sometimes people have a misconception that writers have hundreds of devices moving across their desks regularly. Although I have used several different handheld devices and own a handful of devices for testing mobile games that I develop, I use my Treo just like anyone else. I take pictures while on vacation, I get on the Web to track eBay auctions, I text-message friends late in the night, I listen to MP3 music, and I download and play games. My point is that I have a good idea of what kind of Treo book I'd want if I had the luxury of going out and buying one. I ended up having the luxury of getting to write a book instead. I hope you find the book to be as practical and informative as I set out to make it.

How This Book Is Structured

This book is organized into four parts, each of which explores a different facet of Treo devices:

- *Part I, "Getting Started with Your Treo"*—In this part, you get to know the Treo device platform and how it came to be. You install the Treo desktop software and learn how to perform all the essential tasks that make the Treo such an exciting device. You also find out how to customize and personalize your Treo to suit your own tastes.
- *Part II, "Managing Personal Information with Your Treo"*—In this part, you learn how to synchronize your Treo with a desktop or notebook computer as well as how to install new applications on your Treo. You also explore the details of some core Treo applications that work with personal information manager (PIM) data, such as contacts, appointments, tasks, and memos.

- *Part III, "Staying Connected with Your Treo"*—In this part, you explore your Treo's mobile phone features, including interesting features such as picture caller ID. You also learn how to set up email accounts on your device as well as send and receive text and multimedia messages. This part ends by taking a close look at the Treo Web browser and what is has to offer in browsing the wireless Web.
- *Part IV, "Your Treo as a Portable Entertainment Device"*—In this part, you experiment with your Treo as a portable entertainment device by first learning how to shoot and manage digital pictures and video. You then learn how to use your device as a portable MP3 music player. From there, you move on to exploring some popular Treo games, including a few multiplayer games that allow you to play networked via infrared, Bluetooth, or the wireless Internet. This part of the book also introduces you to global positioning system (GPS) navigation with your Treo and covers some handy third-party applications you might want to consider installing.

What You'll Need

All you really need for this book is a Treo device, preferably a Treo 650, and the desire to learn and explore. As with just about anything, you learn only by practice. So think of this book as laying the groundwork on which you build lasting knowledge by using and tinkering with your device. If you run into any problems along the way, I have a forum for this book on my Web site at http://www.michaelmorrison.com/. There you'll find other Treo users who are eager to discuss the book and share ideas. I regularly read and post in the forum, so it serves as a great way to interact with me if you have a question or suggestion. See you online!

GETTING STARTED WITH YOUR TREO

PART I

1

Meet Your Treo

IN THIS CHAPTER

- A Brief History of Palm Devices
- The Treo Device Family
- Getting to Know the Palm OS and Core Treo Applications
- Understanding the Treo 650 Memory System
- Up and Running with Your Treo

Your Treo device is a unique merger of a personal organizer, handheld computer, and mobile phone into a shape and size closer to a traditional mobile phone than a typical handheld computer. This chapter introduces you to your Treo by first laying the groundwork of how the device came to be, including the interesting history of the companies that played a role in evolving the original Palm Pilot device into the Treo. You then find out the major differences between the Treo 600 and 650 and take a quick tour of the Palm operating system used on Treo devices. The chapter concludes by exploring a limitation and workaround for the Treo 650's redesigned memory system as well as stepping you through the initial setup of your device.

A Brief History of Palm Devices

If you have any familiarity with the original Palm Pilot handheld devices, you can probably appreciate that the Palm family of devices has come a long way in a few years. The devices aren't all that have changed, however. The companies associated with Palm devices have morphed into and out of each other, making it confusing to figure out exactly who makes what. Given the rapid evolution of Palm devices and the major upheavals that have taken place in the companies that make them, it's worth a little history lesson on how today's Treo devices came to be. If you aren't too concerned with the history of Palm devices, feel free to skip ahead to the section "The Treo Device Family."

The Ever-changing Palm Company

The Palm story begins in January 1992 with the Palm Computing company, started by Jeff Hawkins, Donna Dubinsky, and Ed Colligan. Jeff Hawkins was the leading force behind Palm Computing and co-founded the company with the plan of developing a handheld device called the

Zoomer. With $1.3 million of venture capital funding at its disposal, Palm Computing set out to make the Zoomer a reality and released it in October 1993 on the heels of the ill-fated Apple Newton handheld. The Zoomer fared better than Apple's Newton, but it still failed to take the world by storm. So Palm went back to the drawing board and got to work on the Zoomer II.

In the process of redesigning the user interface and jazzing up the device to meet user demands, Palm lost some of its investment partners and ultimately had to scrap the Zoomer II. This led to refocusing its efforts on the software side of the handheld equation, with a goal of emerging as the major player in the handheld software industry. The problem was that handheld devices had yet to be established enough for a handheld software industry to exist. Out of necessity, Palm Computing decided to take a shot at developing an entirely new device for its software, and the Palm Pilot project, also known as Project Touchdown, began.

This time around, Hawkins hammered home his concept of elegant simplicity at all costs. The new device had to cost less than $300, fit in a shirt pocket, and be usable by the average person. To successfully establish a handheld market, Palm had to win over more than just computer hobbyists. The other big conceptual shift for the Palm Pilot that distinguished it from the Zoomer is that the Pilot was designed from the ground up as a computer accessory, not a computer replacement. This seemingly subtle design change allowed Pilot designers to throw out anything that didn't expressly serve to bolster the mobile computing experience. In other words, they opted not to include anything that could be done better on a desktop computer—let the mobile device do mobile things well, and leave the rest to the desktop.

NOTE You might be confused by seeing Palm devices referred to both as Pilots and PalmPilots. Which is it? Pilot was the original name for handhelds made by Palm, but Pilot Pen Corporation brought a lawsuit against Palm that forced a change in the name. As a result, Pilot become PalmPilot. Eventually, the PalmPilot name gave way to just Palm.

As the Pilot got closer to production, Palm Computing needed a new investor to pony up the cash to fund initial launch costs. Although Palm was looking for investors, it ended up getting a buy-out offer from U.S. Robotics, the dominant modem maker at the time. In August 1995, U.S. Robotics acquired Palm Computing for $44 million. Funding was now in place for Pilot production, and despite a few early technical hurdles, the first devices hit the street in April 1996. Both the Pilot 1000 and Pilot 5000 devices were released in 1996. It took less than a year for the Palm Pilot to take a 70% share of the handheld market and win numerous product awards. The Palm Pilot would eventually go on to become the fastest-selling computer product in history.

Although Palm Computing's relationship with U.S. Robotics was working, things changed quickly when 3Com Corporation acquired U.S. Robotics in 1997. It didn't take long for Palm's founders to bristle at being a subsidiary of a company with an imposing bureaucracy. In June 1998, Jeff Hawkins and Donna Dubinsky left Palm to form a new company that would later become Handspring, Inc. Shortly thereafter, all three original co-founders were reunited when Ed Colligan joined them at Handspring.

At Handspring, Hawkins, Dubinsky, and Colligan set out to repeat their success at Palm. Their initial focus was making a Palm-compatible device with more expandability than Palm Computing devices. Handspring released its first device, the Visor, in September 1999. The Visor was different from other Palm devices in that it used Universal Serial Bus (USB) to synchronize with desktop computers and included an expansion slot for adding optional components, such as extra memory, software modules, modems, cameras, and MP3 players. In addition to the Springboard Expansion Slot, the Visor line of handhelds was designed to be more hip and appealing to the average user than Palm's offerings. Not surprisingly, the Visor line took off and began to represent a challenge to Palm's handheld dominance.

NOTE The modern equivalent device for the original Palm Pilot 1000 and 5000 is the Zire 31.

NOTE Microsoft made a splash on the handheld front in 1998 when it announced a new handheld platform called Palm PC. Palm promptly filed suit, and Microsoft eventually agreed to change the name to Pocket PC. The Pocket PC name is still in use to describe handhelds that run on the Microsoft platform, although Microsoft's mobile operating system was later renamed Windows Mobile.

In early 2000, the Palm story took an important turn as 3Com decided to spin off Palm as an independent, publicly traded company called Palm Inc. Had 3Com made this decision a few years earlier, Handspring might never have come into existence, as Hawkins, Dubinksy, and Colligan would have likely stayed on. This turn of events didn't seem to matter, however, as things would come full circle anyway.

In October 2003, the Palm story took its last surprising turn when Palm Inc. agreed to acquire Handspring in a deal worth close to $169 million. Palm's three original founders (Hawkins, Dubinsky, and Colligan) were finally reunited with the company they first created. At the time of the Handspring acquisition, Handspring had shifted its focus to smartphones, which was likely the primary motivation for Palm's purchase. The last product made under the Handspring name was the Treo 600.

As part of the Handspring acquisition, a process that became known as "PalmSpring," Palm decided to separate its operating system division into a company called PalmSource, Inc. The idea is that Palm would continue to focus on making handheld devices, while PalmSource would focus on extending the reach of the Palm operating system, independently of Palm. But Palm didn't stop there. To help drive home the point that Palm was truly a new company, the name of the core company was changed to palmOne, Inc. To recap, the Palm operating system and associated Palm-branded devices are affiliated with the following two companies:

- *palmOne, Inc.*—On the Web at palmOne.com, NASDAQ ticker symbol PLMO
- *PalmSource, Inc.*—On the Web at PalmSource.com, NASDAQ ticker symbol PSRC

Just when it appeared that all the smoke had cleared in regard to palmOne and PalmSource, palmOne made yet another naming move by fully acquiring the Palm name

> **NOTE** In addition to palmOne and PalmSource, a third entity, Palm Trademark Holding Company, was created to own the Palm name and trademark. This holding company was owned 55% by PalmSource and 45% by palmOne but was acquired entirely by palmOne in mid-2005.

from PalmSource in May 2005. As part of the deal, palmOne decided to revert back to its original Palm name, although Treo devices have continued to sell under the palmOne name during the transition. The bottom line is that we'll eventually be back to where we started, and can simply refer to devices made by Palm as "Palm devices." That is, until palmOne/Palm/PalmSource decide to play musical chairs with their names again! For the sake of minimizing confusion, I refer to the palmOne/Palm company simply as Palm throughout the remainder of this book.

What matters in all this naming is that a clean division between the Palm operating system (OS) and Palm handheld devices makes it much easier for PalmSource to license the Palm OS to other device manufacturers and help extend the platform's reach. In fact, this has already taken place. Current Palm OS licensees include Sony, Samsung, Kyocera, Garmin, Fossil, Aceeca, AlphaSmart, Tapwave, and, of course, Palm.

The Evolution of Palm Devices

Although the Zoomer was the first device Jeff Hawkins pursued under the Palm name, it wasn't his first attempt at a pen-based handheld computer. His first stab at it came a few years earlier while working for the GRiD computer company. At GRiD, Hawkins worked on a product called the GRiDPad, a handheld device that used a pen for user input much like future Palm devices. In fact, the handwriting recognition software developed for the GRiDPad—called PalmPrint—was a precursor to the popular Graffiti handwriting recognition software that would later help seal the success of Palm Pilot devices.

The problem with the GRiDPad was that it weighed more than 4 pounds and had a retail price of $2,500—not exactly a consumer-oriented device, which was a problem. The GRiDPad was later resurrected as the Zoomer by Hawkins at his startup company, Palm Computing. But you've already heard that story, so you can fast-forward past the Zoomer and the original Palm Pilot 1000 and 5000 devices.

The following vertical timeline that gives you a quick glimpse at how the Palm family of devices evolved from the original Palm Pilot 1000 to the Treo 650 that is the primary focus of this book:

- March 1997—Palm Pilot Professional, Palm Pilot Personal
- March 1998—Palm III
- February 1999—Palm IIIx, Palm V
- May 1999—Palm VII
- September 1999—Handspring Visor

- October 1999—Palm Vx, Palm IIIe
- February 2000—Palm IIIc, Palm IIIxe
- August 2000—Palm VIIx, Palm m100, Handspring Prism
- March 2001—Palm m105, Palm m500, Palm m505, Handspring Visor Edge
- September 2001—Palm m125
- January 2002—Palm i705
- March 2002—Palm m130, Palm m515, Handspring Treo 180/180g
- May 2002—Handspring Treo 90, Handspring Treo 270
- August 2002—Handspring Treo 300
- October 2002—Palm Zire, Palm Tungsten T
- April 2003—Palm Zire (multimedia), Palm Tungsten C
- July 2003—Palm Tungsten T2
- October 2003—Palm Tungsten E, Palm Tungsten T3, Palm Zire 21
- November 2003—Handspring Treo 600
- April 2004—palmOne Zire 31, palmOne Zire 72
- October 2004—palmOne Tungsten T5, palmOne Treo 650

Although the distinction isn't noticeable until the last few entries in this list, there is a clear difference between Palm handhelds and Palm smartphones. The Treo devices (270, 300, 600, and 650) are the first Palm devices to merge mobile phone capabilities with traditional handheld (PDA, email, Web access, and so forth) capabilities. Every other Palm device to date falls under the more general "handheld" category, whereas the Treo devices are considered smartphones. In reality, all the devices are handhelds—you can think of a smartphone as a handheld with the addition of a mobile phone built into it.

The Current Palm Landscape

As you've learned, the Palm family of devices has come a long way since its journey began back in 1992. And I'm guessing that about now you're ready to put the history aside and start getting down to business with your Treo. Before you venture into the land of Treo smartphones, however, it's worth taking a quick look at what Palm currently has to offer in the way of handhelds. By knowing a little about the entire Palm family, you'll have a better idea of what kind of device the Treo is and how it fits into the overall Palm equation.

The Palm lineup of devices is currently divided into three families:

- Zire
- Tungsten
- Treo

The Zire and Tungsten handhelds originated with Palm and can be considered direct descendents of the original Palm Pilot handhelds. The Treo handhelds (smartphones, actually) arrived at Palm via the Handspring acquisition and are a different animal in that they add mobile phone functionality to the traditional Palm feature set. All the Palm devices share one thing in common—they are pocket organizers, or personal digital assistants (PDAs), meaning you can use them to manage contacts, tasks, and events. From there, each device takes a different path in addressing a specific need.

The Zire handhelds are Palm's consumer-level devices that target a lower price point yet still offer as many handheld features as possible. The Zire 21, the first Palm device under $100, is a bit stripped down compared to other devices in the lineup. The Zire 31 builds onto the Zire 21 by adding a color screen and support for MP3 music. The Zire 72 takes things a step further than the Zire 31 by adding a high-resolution color screen, music and video support, Office document compatibility, a digital camera, Short Message Service (SMS)/Multimedia Messaging System (MMS) messaging, and wireless Bluetooth connectivity.

> **NOTE** It's interesting to point out that Treo devices are the first Palm devices to ship without built-in support for the Graffiti handwriting recognition system. With a full QWERTY keyboard integrated into the design, Palm apparently figured that hardcore Palm users would learn to type and do without Graffiti. You can still add on a handwriting recognition system to your Treo if you find yourself missing Graffiti too much—see "Use Handwriting Recognition" in Chapter 15, "Improving Your Lifestyle with Your Treo," for more details.

The Tungsten handhelds are Palm's professional-level devices that offer a more consistent core group of features, such as a high-resolution color screen and Office document compatibility on all models. Most Tungsten models also support music and video playback and Bluetooth wireless connectivity. The Tungsten T5 even includes a 160MB flash drive, which allows it to double as a portable memory drive. The Tungsten family of devices represents some of the most powerful non-smartphone handheld devices on the market.

Finally, you arrive at Treo, which is what you're here for. You can think of the Treo family of devices as tricked-out Tungsten devices with a smartphone intelligently incorporated into the mix. I say "intelligently" because a lot of companies have rolled out "smartphones" by simply adding a wireless radio to a handheld without concern for the realities of how phones are used. Palm (or, more accurately, Handspring) carefully considered the manner in which mobile phones are used, as compared to handheld computers, and made a serious attempt at giving Treo devices more of a phone feel. The days of the chunky smartphone that doesn't fit in your pocket are over.

What makes Treo devices somewhat unique in the smartphone marketplace is that they manage to have a full QWERTY keyboard within a mobile phone footprint. Not only that, but they have a relatively large 320×320 color screen, which is much larger than most smartphones with a similar form-factor. Is the Treo family of devices perfect? No, and the reality is that no smartphone will ever be perfect. People use smartphones in such different ways that it's unlikely any single device will ever solve everyone's problems. But the Treo is one of the closest devices I've seen to date that successfully marries handheld computing with wireless mobile communication.

The Treo Device Family

The Treo product lineup currently consists of two models, the Treo 600 and Treo 650. The devices look a lot alike but there are some important differences you need to know. Because the devices are so similar, in many ways you can think of this book as covering both devices. However, the Treo 650 includes a few important changes and new features that are examined in detail as you work through the book. If you're reading this with a Treo 600 in your hand, just understand that the book is somewhat slanted toward the 650 because it's the newer model. Even so, much of the Treo experience is similar for both devices. Now it's time to learn more about these two devices!

The Treo 600 is one of Palm's first smartphones, and serves as a PDA, mobile phone, digital camera, email client, and Web browser, among other things. The Treo 600 is available in both Global System for Mobile Communications (GSM)/General Packet Radio Service (GPRS) and Code Division Multiple Access (CDMA) models through a variety of different wireless service providers. The Treo 600 includes a color screen (160×160), read-only support for Office documents, a digital camera, and a built-in QWERTY keyboard. As nice as the Treo 600 is, however, there are a few drawbacks. For one, if your device loses power, your data gets lost. This type of memory, known as *volatile memory*, can be a real pain if you forget to back up your device and the battery runs dry. Speaking of the battery, it isn't removable in the Treo 600, so there's no way to replace it or carry an extra.

> **NOTE**
> GSM, GPRS, and CDMA are all mobile phone standards that determine the specific manner in which voice and data communications are carried out over a wireless network. GSM and CDMA are considered second generation, or 2g, standards, and GPRS is considered a 2.5g standard. Third-generation (3g) mobile phone standards, such as W-CDMA and CDMA2000, are currently being deployed as well as a 2.75g standard known as EDGE (Enhanced Data Rates for Global Evolution). The standard your phone uses is largely determined by the wireless service provider you choose.

The Treo 650 directly addresses some of the more prominent issues raised by Treo 600 users. Following are the primary changes made in the Treo 650:

- Higher resolution color screen (320×320)
- Nonvolatile memory and a removable battery
- Bluetooth wireless connectivity

- Digital camera with support for video capture
- MP3 music player

The Treo 650 sports a much higher resolution screen than the Treo 600—320×320 resolution compared to 160×160. The nonvolatile memory in the Treo 650 is also significant because it eliminates the Treo 600's potential for data loss if your battery should run out of charge. In addition, the Treo 650 battery is removable, which means you can buy extra batteries and have a fully charged replacement if you want to make sure you never go without power.

Bluetooth wireless connectivity gives the 650 the capability to wirelessly connect with a headset, hands-free car kit, desktop or notebook computer, another Treo device, or any number of other interesting Bluetooth accessories. Although the digital camera in the Treo 650 is the same resolution (640×480, or 0.3 megapixel) as the Treo 600, you can use the camera in the 650 to shoot videos. And thankfully, Palm realized the importance of including MP3 support in the 650, so you can listen to digital music.

Table 1.1 sums up the major technical differences between the Treo 600 and Treo 650 smartphone devices.

Table 1.1 Comparing the Treo 600 and Treo 650 Smartphone Devices

Device	Treo 600	Treo 650
Palm OS	v5.2.1H	v5.4
Processor	TI 144MHz ARM	Intel 312MHz PXA270 XScale
Battery	Fixed lithium ion	Removable lithium ion
Screen	160×160	320×320
Available memory	24MB volatile	23MB nonvolatile
Wireless	GSM/GPRS or CDMA	GSM/GPRS, EDGE, or CDMA; Bluetooth
Video capture	No	Yes
Video playback	No	Yes
MP3 music	No	Yes

Now that you have an idea of how the Treo devices differ, in the following section, you shift gears a bit and take a look at the Palm OS that drives these smartphones. Although the Palm OS version is slightly different in the 600 and 650, it's generally the same OS.

Getting to Know the Palm OS and Core Treo Applications

The Palm OS has evolved quite a bit over the years and actually comes in several forms. The Palm OS version found on current Treo devices, version 5.x, is known as Palm Garnet and was rewritten from the ground up to support the newer generation of Palm devices. Palm OS 5 is unique in that it specifically targets Advanced Risc Machines (ARM)–based microprocessors, such as those made by Intel, Motorola, and Texas Instruments. Interestingly enough, ARM microprocessors are also used on Pocket PC devices, many of which are direct competitors of Treo devices.

> **NOTE** One other subtle but important design difference between the Treo 600 and Treo 650 involves the keyboard. The keys on the Treo 650 are slightly larger and flatter, which makes typing on the 650 considerably easier than on the 600. Additionally, the 650 adds the Phone/Send (green) and Power/End (red) buttons, which help make the 650 feel more like a true mobile phone.

Palm OS 5 is currently the most popular Palm OS, seeing that it's installed on every current Palm device, but it isn't the latest and greatest PalmSource has to offer. Palm OS 6.1, also known as Palm OS Cobalt, is a more powerful OS that has yet to appear on a physical device. I wouldn't be surprised to see Cobalt eventually show up on a Palm smartphone at some point in the future, but for now, Palm OS 5.4 on the Treo 650 is the latest Palm OS to actually appear on a device.

> **NOTE** Palm OS 5 does not run on the Motorola Dragonball processors found in older Palm devices, which means those devices can't be upgraded to OS 5.

Although manufacturers can customize specific Palm devices to include custom applications, some applications are considered core features of the Palm OS. Palm replaced several of these core applications with more advanced versions in its later devices, including the Treo devices. Following are the primary core applications built into the Treo devices:

- Calendar
- Contacts
- Tasks
- Memos
- Messaging
- VersaMail
- HotSync
- Phone
- Blazer Web browser
- Calc

- Camera/Camcorder
- RealPlayer

The next few sections introduce you to each of these applications and help give you a quick feel for how they work.

The Calendar Application

The Calendar application, also known as Date Book in other Palm devices, provides a calendar for scheduling appointments and generally managing your time. With the Calendar, you can schedule appointments (events) with a great deal of detail and set an alarm to remind you of the event. Several views are available in the Calendar application for zooming in and out of time frames, such as viewing a single day's appointments or an entire month of the year. Figure 1.1 shows the Calendar application in Month view where you can see a calendar month. To learn more about the Calendar application, see Chapter 6, "Getting Productive with the Calendar, Tasks, and Memos."

FIGURE 1.1

The Calendar application allows you to schedule appointments and events, and receive alarms to remind you of them.

The Contacts Application

Contact information on Treo devices is handled by the Contacts application, which is also known as Address in other Palm devices. The Contacts application keeps track of a database of contacts that can be categorized as you see fit. The Contacts application is extremely important to the overall usefulness of Treo devices because contacts are used as the basis for a variety of operations. For example, you can use a contact to send an email message, send a text message via SMS/MMS, and make a phone call. You can also wirelessly beam contacts back and forth between Palm devices.

Figure 1.2 shows the Contacts application with a contact in view. To learn how to squeeze the most out of the Contacts application, see Chapter 5, "Managing Treo Contacts."

FIGURE 1.2

The Contacts application serves as a database of categorized contact information for people with whom you communicate.

The Task Manager

Another integral part of any personal organizer is a task manager, and on Treo devices this function is carried out via the Tasks application, also known as the To Do List on some Palm devices. A *task* can be anything from a quick reminder to an important deadline for a project. Although not required, most tasks have an associated due date and priority. You can also categorize tasks to give them some additional organization. If a task has a due date, it appears in the Agenda view of the calendar for the day it's due.

Figure 1.3 shows the Tasks application with a task in view. For more details on how to create and manage tasks using the Tasks application, see Chapter 6.

The Memos Application

Treo devices support the software equivalent of a Post-It note via the Memos application, which allows you to enter simple text notes called *memos*. Memos created in the Memos application are limited solely to text, but they can be categorized to help organize them.

FIGURE 1.3

The Tasks application is where you enter reminders and schedule important deadlines.

Figure 1.4 shows a memo being created in the Memos application. To learn how to create and manage memos using the Memos application, check out Chapter 6.

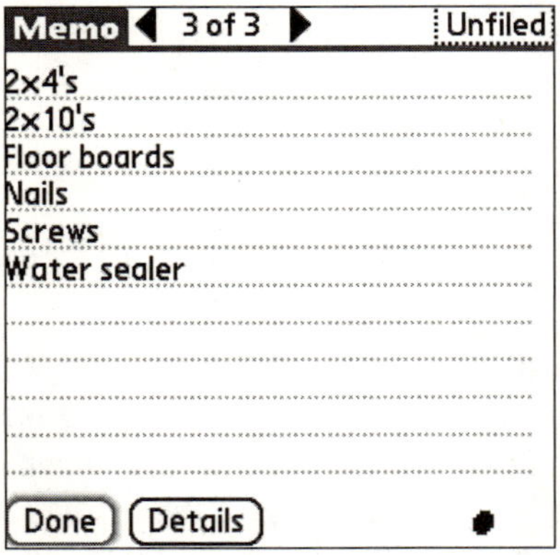

FIGURE 1.4

The Memos application allows you to create simple text notes (memos).

The Messaging Application

The Messaging application is what you use to send and receive text and multimedia messages using SMS/MMS. Unlike email messages, which must travel through a separate mail server of some sort, text and multimedia messages are handled solely by your wireless service provider, often using its own message servers. If you've ever sent text messages on a traditional mobile phone, you have an idea of how the Messaging application works on Treo devices. The main difference is that the built-in QWERTY keyboard makes the Treo a much more efficient messaging device than your average mobile phone.

Figure 1.5 shows a "conversation" taking place in the Messaging application. To find out more about text and multimedia messaging via the Messaging application, take a look at Chapter 9, "Communicating with Text and Multimedia Messages."

FIGURE 1.5

The Messaging application enables you to carry out a "conversation" with someone else who has a mobile phone with SMS/MMS support.

The VersaMail Application

Although text and multimedia messaging is handy, email is how most people carry out day-to-day written communication. The VersaMail application is Treo's email client and is flexible in allowing you to use different kinds of email accounts. For example, you can set up your own POP3 and IMAP email account or connect directly with an Exchange email server to access work email. In fact, you can use up to eight different email accounts with the VersaMail application. With the proper settings, which you learn how to use later in the book, you can even use VersaMail to access Web-based email accounts, such as Google's Gmail.

Figure 1.6 shows some received email messages in the VersaMail application. To learn all the ins and outs of Treo email with the VersaMail application, check out Chapter 8, "Staying in Touch with Email."

NOTE The Messaging application also enables you to send text and multimedia messages to an email address, but the application isn't a true email client. In other words, you can't use it to connect to a Post Office Protocol version 3 (POP3)/Internet Message Access Protocol (IMAP) email server to check your email messages. Also, SMS/MMS messages are sent using the voice component of your wireless service, not the data component used for email messaging.

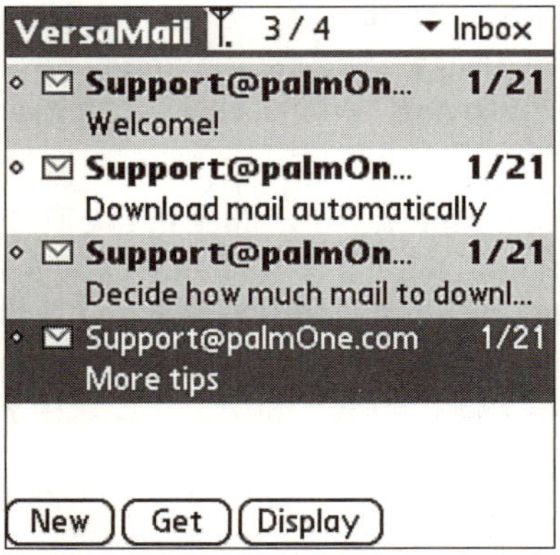

FIGURE 1.6

The VersaMail application acts as a full-featured email client on your Treo device.

The HotSync Application

The HotSync application is what enables you to connect to a desktop or notebook computer and synchronize data. For example, you can synchronize contacts, appointments, tasks, and notes between your Treo and primary computer. The HotSync application on your device works with a similar application on the PC side of the equation. The PC application is Palm Desktop, which comes in both Windows and Mac flavors. If you use Microsoft Outlook as your personal information manager (PIM) on a Windows PC, you can set up HotSync so that PIM data is synchronized through Outlook instead of Palm Desktop; Palm Desktop is still used to synchronize non-PIM data, such as photos and MP3 music. In addition to supporting synchronization, the HotSync application allows you to back up your Treo and install new applications.

> **NOTE** Just so you'll know, I use the term "PC" in its most generic form to literally mean "personal computer." Some people associate a PC with a Windows-based computer, but throughout this book I use the term PC to refer to any desktop or notebook computer, which can be running on Windows, Macintosh, Linux, or some other OS.

Figure 1.7 shows the HotSync application busy at work synchronizing with a desktop computer. To find out how to tweak synchronization to work exactly the way you want, take a look at Chapter 4, "Synchronizing with Your Desktop Computer."

The Treo Phone

The primary feature that sets the Treo devices apart from other Palm handhelds is the mobile phone functionality that effectively marries the familiar Palm organizer with a mobile phone. The Phone application is the Treo software component that makes the mobile phone feature possible. Not only does the Phone application provide a powerful mobile phone user interface, but it also offers a useful interface for quickly accessing other important Treo features. More specifically, the Phone application houses your "favorites," which are customizable buttons that serve as quick links to other applications and resources.

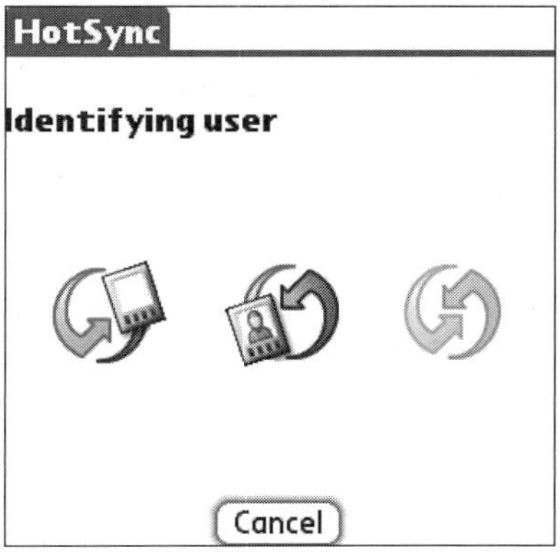

FIGURE 1.7

The HotSync application establishes a link between your Treo device and your desktop or notebook computer for synchronizing PIM data and sharing files.

Figure 1.8 shows the main Phone application screen with some of the favorite buttons visible along the bottom edge. To learn how to use the Phone application and customize the favorite buttons, check out Chapter 7, "Using Your Treo as a Mobile Phone."

FIGURE 1.8

The Phone application serves as the software portion of Treo's mobile phone functionality and offers some handy features, such as favorite buttons.

> **NOTE**
> WAP is a mobile version of the HTTP standard used to shuttle web pages back and forth between Web servers and browsers. Mobile web pages delivered via WAP are typically much simpler in design than their HTTP counterparts, which allows them to be downloaded more quickly and viewed more easily on mobile devices.

The Blazer Web Browser

The Blazer Web browser, Treo's link to the World Wide Web, enables you to view Wireless Application Protocol (WAP) pages tailored for mobile devices as well as normal web pages delivered via Hypertext Transfer Protocol (HTTP). This means you can visit any website using the Blazer Web browser, although there are practical screen real-estate limitations when you consider that few web pages are designed to fit on a 320×320 screen (Treo 650). Aside from screen size limitations, the Blazer browser is surprisingly full-featured, supporting such browser features as frames, cookies, JavaScript, and cascading style sheets (CSS).

Figure 1.9 shows the Blazer Web browser with a weather page from the Sprint PCS mobile website in view. To find out exactly how to browse the Web with Blazer and get the most out of the mobile Web experience, see Chapter 10, "Browsing the Wireless Web."

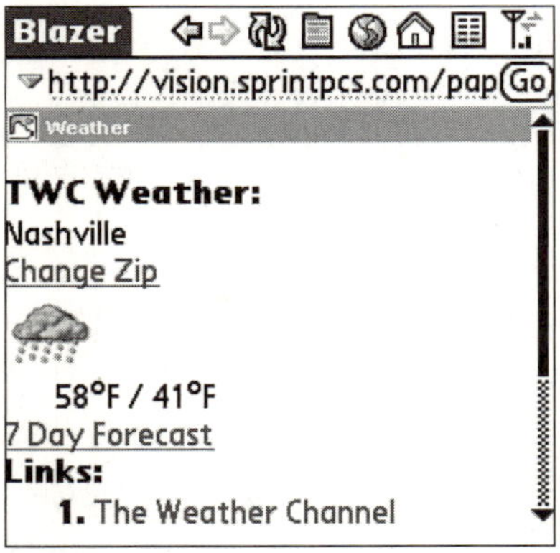

FIGURE 1.9

The Blazer application serves as a fully functional Web browser that enables you to surf the wireless Web on your Treo device.

The Calculator

The Calc application provides a software calculator for carrying out familiar mathematical functions, along with several more advanced functions, such as finance, logic, statistics, and unit conversion. Even if you find yourself needing the Calc application only to figure a tip or crunch the numbers on a discount price while shopping, it's still handy to have around.

Figure 1.10 shows the Calc application converting an amount in square feet to acres. Check out "Use the Calculator" in Chapter 2, "Performing the Treo Essentials," for more details on how to use the Calc application.

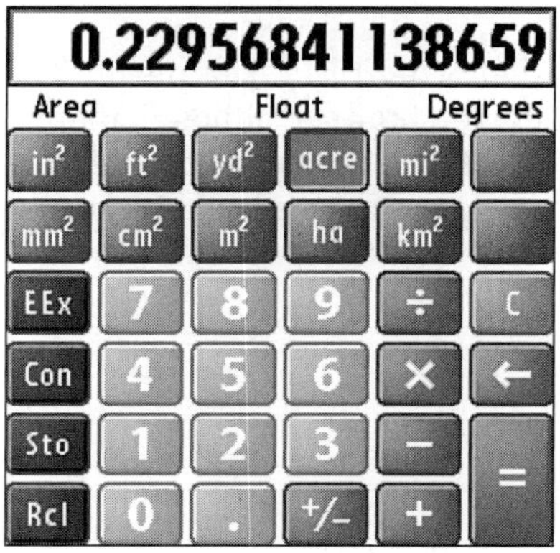

FIGURE 1.10

The Calc application supports common mathematical calculations and numerous advanced features, such as unit conversion.

The Treo Camera and Camcorder

The Treo 600 includes a digital camera with 0.3 megapixel resolution, which allows you to shoot pictures up to 640×480 in resolution. Although this resolution is admittedly quite low by most digital camera standards, it isn't all that bad for a phone camera. Unfortunately, the Treo 650 didn't increase the digital camera resolution, but it did add support for shooting videos. The application that makes digital photography and videos possible is Camera/Camcorder. You see individual icons for Camera and Camcorder, which makes them appear to be separate applications, but they are actually different modes of the same application. Another mode in the "camera" application is Pics&Videos, which enables you to browse through the pictures and videos that you've shot with your device. You can use this mode to beam pictures and videos to another Palm device, upload them to your PC, send them via an MMS or email message, or store them to a memory card.

Figure 1.11 shows the Camera/Camcorder application busy at work capturing a picture of my koi pond. To learn how to shoot your own pictures and videos with this application, take a look at Chapter 12, "Taking and Sharing Digital Pictures and Videos."

FIGURE 1.11

With the Camera/Camcorder application, you can use your Treo device as a digital camera and camcorder.

The RealPlayer Application

The last major piece of the Treo application puzzle is the RealPlayer media player for playing digital music (only on the Treo 650). Unfortunately, the RealPlayer version that ships on the Treo 650 is somewhat limited in that it can play music only in the MP3 and RealMedia formats. Media files in these formats typically have `.mp3` and `.rm` file extensions, respectively. This limitation means that you can't play songs purchased from a digital music service, such as Apple's iTunes or Microsoft's MSN Music, because those sites rely on other music formats that aren't supported by the Treo's RealPlayer. Although this is certainly a limitation, you are entirely free to rip songs from your own CDs in the MP3 format and play them on your Treo device.

Figure 1.12 shows a song in MP3 format playing in the RealPlayer application. To explore digital music and learn how to play it on your Treo device, check out Chapter 13, "Listening to Digital Music."

This discussion wraps up the quick tour of the Palm OS and core Treo applications. You're almost ready to get your Treo up and running and connect it to your PC. But before doing that, it's worth visiting an important topic that serves as an important distinction between the Treo 600 and 650 devices: the memory system.

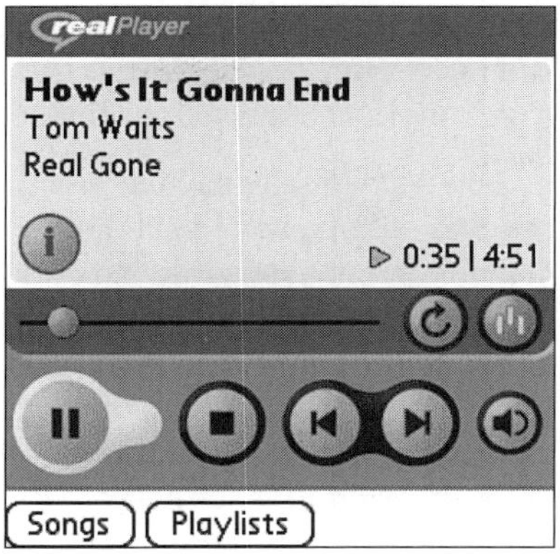

FIGURE 1.12

The RealPlayer application is a digital media player that allows you to play digital music in the popular MP3 and RealMedia formats.

Understanding the Treo 650 Memory System

I already explained that the Treo 650 uses a nonvolatile memory system that is different from the volatile memory approach the Treo 600 takes. What I didn't explain is how this change affects the Treo 650 on a practical level, which ultimately led Palm to offer free memory cards to Treo 650 users. Maybe the word "free" got your attention. Although I can't promise that the offer is still available, continue reading to find out how you might be able to snag a free memory card for your Treo 650. In the process, you'll learn some important information about how your device works.

The Treo 600 relies solely on random access memory (RAM) for storing device data and applications that you install. The core Palm applications are stored in read-only memory (ROM) and, therefore, are protected from being lost, but everything else is subject to being lost on a whim if the device should somehow lose battery power. Granted, you'd have to completely forget about charging your device and ignore its low-battery warnings for this to happen, but it's entirely possible. The volatile memory in the Treo 600 makes the device a little like a pet, in that you have to feed it regularly (charge the battery) or it will die (lose the memory). Pets are great, but I don't need that kind of responsibility in my handheld communicator!

Palm realized the memory problem with the Treo 600 and set out to solve it in the Treo 650. The result is the *Non-Volatile File System (NVFS)*, which uses Flash memory, a form of rewritable memory that retains its content without power. Although the 650's new NVFS memory system solved the volatility problem, it introduced a new problem of its own: storage inefficiency. The internal design of the NVFS required a minimum memory

> **NOTE** The Flash memory–based NVFS is also used in the Palm Tungsten T5 handheld device to give it nonvolatile memory.

allocation of 512 bytes for any discrete piece of information, even if it's far less than 512 bytes. In practical terms, this means that a 32-byte memo takes up 512 byes, which is obviously a serious waste of space.

If the Treo 600 was equally as inefficient in its memory management as the Treo 650, no one would ever know the difference. But the 600's memory management system doesn't have the 512-byte minimum allocation size; a 32-byte memo on the Treo 600 really takes up only 32 bytes. You're probably starting to see where the problem lies. A considerable number of Treo 600 users, possibly even you, made the logical upgrade path to the Treo 650, only to find out that their data suddenly ballooned in size. More important, some users found that their existing data wouldn't even fit on their Treo 650. Sure, it's great knowing that you won't lose your data if your battery dies, but that doesn't help much if you can't even fit your data onto your shiny new Treo 650!

The NVFS memory inefficiency problem wouldn't be that big a deal if Palm had included more internal memory in the Treo 650. The 650 has 23MB of usable nonvolatile memory (22MB in the multilingual version of the device) as well as 10MB of true RAM used as a buffer for the NVFS. The nonvolatile memory is further reduced by the Documents To Go application, which is installed when you first synchronize your device with your PC; see Appendix B, "Conserving Memory on Your Treo 650," for information on how to move applications to a memory card to reduce internal memory overhead. If the nonvolatile memory had simply been increased to, say, 64MB or 128MB, the increased memory requirements of the NVFS wouldn't be an issue.

> **NOTE** On average, Treo 650 users have reported that most applications require about 30% more memory than they did on the Treo 600. Using average assumptions for PIM data (contacts, calendar, tasks and memos), the Treo 650 requires approximately an extra 800KB to store PIM data, compared to the Treo 600's storage requirements.

One other interesting limitation of the NVFS has to do with the internal 10MB RAM buffer. The NVFS is designed so that large chunks of data are read from it into the RAM buffer, where they are then made available to applications. The problem is that you have a maximum of 10MB of true RAM available at any given time. This means that even if you install a hefty 1GB or 2GB memory card, you might encounter an "out of memory" error if you attempt to open a piece of data larger than 10MB. This doesn't apply to all data, as some applications don't open all the contents of a file at once. For example, the RealPlayer application enables you to play MP3 songs that are larger than 10MB.

Now the good news. The engineers at Palm realized their mistake with the Treo 650 NVFS memory system and developed a new version of it that uses smaller blocks of memory (32 bytes instead of 512 bytes). This newer memory system is still nonvolatile, yet it has the efficiency of the Treo 600 memory system, giving you the best of both worlds.

The new memory system is available as a software update for some Treo models. Check the Treo 650 Updater page at http://www.palmone.com/us/support/downloads/treo650updater/ to see whether an update is available for your Treo.

If for some reason an update isn't yet available for your device, all is not lost. In a goodwill effort to compensate Treo 650 users for the NVFS memory problem, Palm has an alternative campaign to offer Treo 650 users free 128MB memory cards. It isn't clear how long this offer will last, but visit the following link to see whether you're eligible for a free 128MB memory card: http://web.palmone.com/support/sd.jhtml.

NOTE Palm's move to the NVFS memory system in the Treo 650 has been interpreted by some as a first step toward shifting to a Treo with an internal hard disk drive for nonvolatile storage, similar to popular digital music players such as Apple's iPod.

Up and Running with Your Treo

If you're like me, you're probably ready to put the theory and background information aside and start using your Treo device. Fortunately, your Treo is just about ready to roll out of the box. The only thing you must do is charge the battery. I also highly recommend installing the Palm Desktop software so that you can start synchronizing data, installing applications, and moving files back and forth between your Treo and your PC.

Following are the general steps you should take to get started using your Treo:

1. Charge the device.
2. Set up the device.
3. Install the Palm Desktop software.
4. Synchronize with your PC.
5. Turn the device on and off.

Your Treo device includes instructions on how to initially charge the device. Unlike the Treo 600, the Treo 650 uses a removable battery, so you need to install the battery in the device before you begin charging it. The initial charging might take up to four hours, but it's an important part of the setup process.

After the device is charged up and ready to go, you can turn it on and proceed with the setup. This setup procedure is simple and

NOTE You will more than likely find yourself in one of three scenarios in regard to the Treo 650 memory issue. Ideally, you are fortunate enough to have a newer Treo 650 that already includes the memory system update. If that's not the case, you might find that a software update is available for your device. And finally, the worst case is that you snag a free memory card from Palm while you await a software update for your device. The two web pages mentioned previously should help clarify your status and options.

really involves simply calibrating the touch screen and setting the date and time. Press the red Power/End button (Treo 650) to turn the device on, after which you are prompted to calibrate the screen by touching several targets with the stylus. This is an important step in setting up your device, so make sure to touch the targets accurately with the stylus (see Figure 1.13) .

Figure 1.13

The screen on the Treo 650 is calibrated by touching the stylus on several targets.

After calibrating the screen, you are prompted to confirm an option that automatically sets the date and time on your device by using the phone. If you choose to use this feature, the date and time are automatically set each time you access the mobile phone network with your device. You'll probably want to use this useful feature, but if for some reason you'd rather have control of the date and time on your device, tap the check box with the stylus to disable the option. If you disable the option, a few fields appear where you specify your location, date, and time (see Figure 1.14).

> **Note**
> The available locations are limited to fairly large cities, so yours might not be listed. For example, Chicago is the closest location to me even though I live in Nashville—what's important is choosing a location in your same time zone.

After setting the date and time, you are prompted to take a Quick Tour (or Tutorial on the Treo 600) of your device. If this is your first experience with a Treo device, I highly recommend taking the Quick Tour. I realize that you bought this book to learn about your device, but the Quick Tour is unique in that it shows you how to do some Treo basics in the context of the device itself.

FIGURE 1.14

You have the option of allowing your mobile phone network to automatically set your Treo's time or setting it manually yourself.

Install the Palm Desktop Software

The Palm Desktop software is by no means required for you to start using your Treo, but it does serve an important purpose in allowing you to install additional applications and synchronize data with your PC. For example, if you use Microsoft Outlook as your desktop PIM, you'll no doubt want to pull all your contacts, appointments, tasks, and notes into your Treo. Even if you don't use Microsoft Outlook, you can still take advantage of the Palm Desktop software on your PC to make PIM data management on your Treo much more efficient.

To install the Palm Desktop software, place the installation CD that came with your Treo in your computer's CD-ROM drive. If you're using a Windows PC, the setup program starts automatically. If you're using a Macintosh, you need to double-click the CD-ROM icon on your desktop to get the setup program started. The setup program is specific to each wireless service provider, but Figure 1.15 shows roughly what you can expect; this figure shows the setup program on a Windows PC for a Treo 650 using Sprint.

> **TIP** If you're upgrading from another Palm device, make sure to provide the same username to your Treo so that it can synchronize with your old Palm data.

The Palm Desktop software installation proceeds much like the installation of any other desktop application. At some point during the installation, you are prompted to enter a HotSync username, which is used to establish a named link from your Treo to your PC. This name can be your first name, your full name, or some other name that you want to use to identify yourself for the purposes of synchronizing your Treo device. Figure 1.16 shows how you specify the HotSync username during the Palm Desktop software installation.

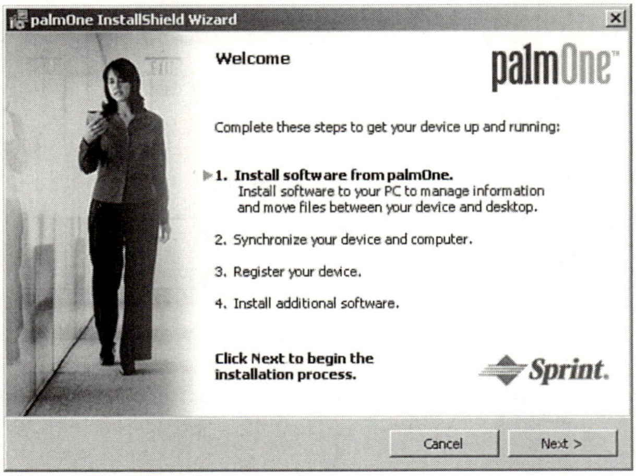

FIGURE 1.15

The setup program for the Palm Desktop software steps you through the installation process.

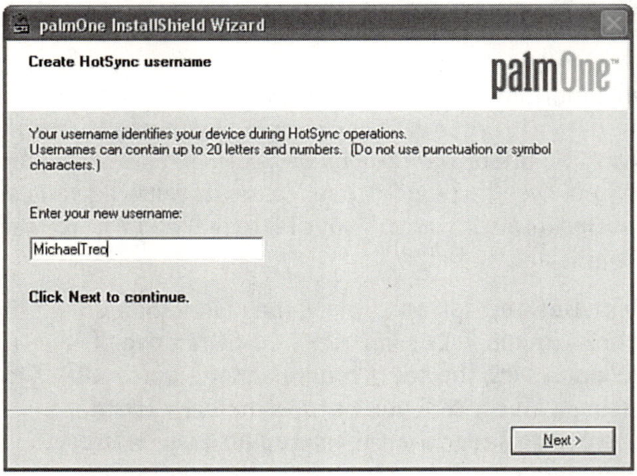

FIGURE 1.16

The HotSync username is used to establish a connection between your Treo device and your PC.

Another important step in the Palm Desktop software installation is specifying what software you'd like to use for synchronization. This decision comes down to whether you use Microsoft Outlook as the PIM on your PC. If so, go with the option that includes synchronizing with Microsoft Outlook. If not, choose the option that uses only the Palm

Desktop software for synchronization. Figure 1.17 shows how these options are displayed in a typical Windows installation.

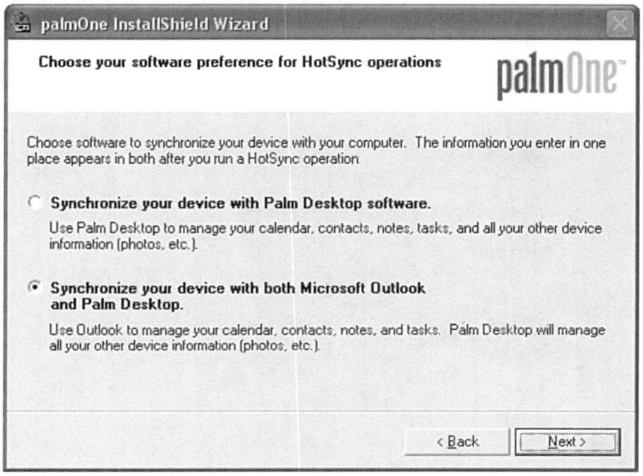

FIGURE 1.17

Use the synchronization options to choose between using the Palm Desktop software by itself or using it with Microsoft Outlook.

The Palm Desktop software installation finishes by leading you to synchronize your Treo device with your PC.

Synchronize with Your PC

You have the option of skipping the synchronization process if you'd rather worry about synchronizing later. Incidentally, Chapter 4, "Synchronizing with Your Desktop Computer," covers synchronization in much more detail. For now, however, it's not a bad idea to go ahead and synchronize, especially if you have Microsoft Outlook data (contacts, appointments, tasks, and so on) that you'd like to access on your Treo. Figure 1.18 shows the step in the Palm Desktop software installation that gives you an opportunity to synchronize your device.

If you elect to synchronize your Treo, you must initiate the synchronization by plugging your device into your PC. Plug the device into a USB port on your computer using the Multi-connector that came with the device, and then press the HotSync button on the connector. A HotSync window opens and shows the status as the synchronization takes place (see Figure 1.19).

TIP Synchronization isn't the only way to move PIM data to your Treo device. If you have an older Palm device that you are upgrading from, you can easily beam PIM data from that device to your Treo. See the chapter relating to the specific PIM data type to find more information on how this is done. For example, the "Send and Receive Contacts Wirelessly" section in Chapter 5, "Managing Treo Contacts," explains how to beam contacts with another Palm device.

Although Palm Desktop is the application used to configure synchronization settings, HotSync is the actual application that carries out the synchronization.

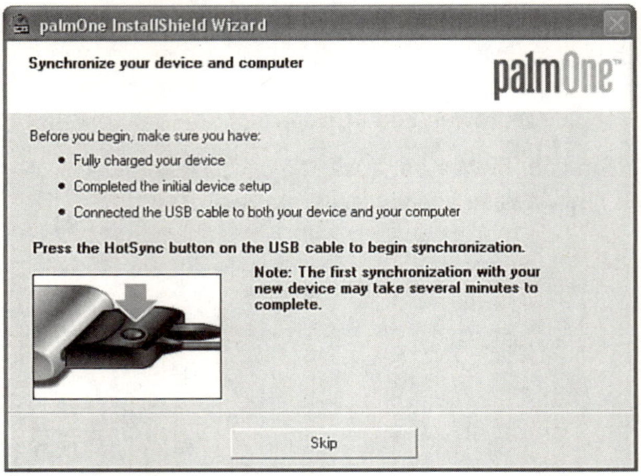

FIGURE 1.18

Synchronizing your Treo at this point isn't imperative, but it's not a bad idea if you have Microsoft Outlook PIM data that you want on your device.

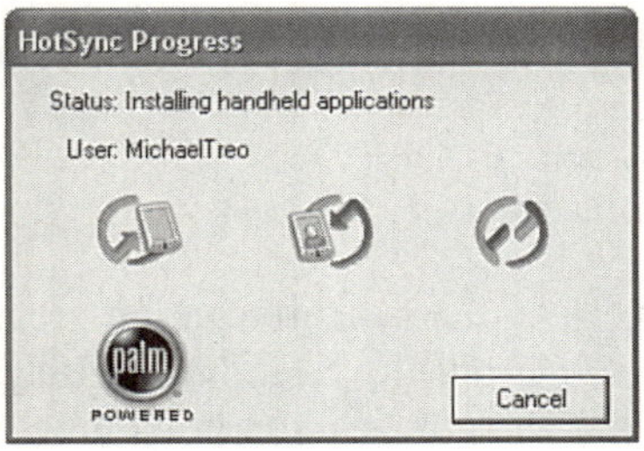

FIGURE 1.19

The HotSync application provides a status window that gives you detailed information about synchronization as it takes place.

With the Palm Desktop software successfully installed, you're now ready to fire up your Treo and start using it. I realize that I've spent the majority of a chapter without even asking you to pick up your device, but from here on I can assure you that the remainder of the book focuses on doing interesting things with your Treo.

Turn Your Treo On and Off

The Treo 650 includes the familiar Send and End buttons you find on a traditional mobile phone. The End button on the 650 is actually called Power/End and serves a dual purpose as a power button and an End button for the Treo phone. To turn your device on and off, just press the Power/End button.

When you first turn your device on, a feature called Keyguard is used to lock the keys in case you've accidentally pressed the Power/End button. This feature prevents you from inadvertently pressing additional keys that might cause data loss or, even worse, the embarrassing situation of calling someone without realizing it. This has happened to me, so I know of what I speak! Most mobile phones put the responsibility of locking the keys on you, the user, but the Treo assumes the role of locking the keys every time you turn the device off. To unlock the keys after powering on your device, just press the Center button on the five-way navigator centered just below the screen. After Keyguard is turned off to unlock the keys, you're free to use your device however you want.

The Treo 650 is somewhat different from most mobile phones in that it allows you to turn the mobile phone radio on and off independently of the device's power. If you've just turned your device on and have yet to use the phone or any Internet features, there's a good chance the mobile radio isn't turned on. You can easily check whether the mobile radio is on by looking in the upper-right corner of the screen for a signal strength indicator. This indicator appears just to the left of the battery indicator and shows a small antenna and bars to indicate the signal strength. If you don't see a signal indicator, odds are your device's mobile radio is off.

To turn on the mobile radio, hold down the Power/End button for a few seconds, after which a special tone sounds and a screen appears to indicate that the mobile phone radio has been activated. More important, the signal strength indicator appears in the upper-right corner of the screen and shows you how good the current wireless signal is (see Figure 1.20).

TIP If you have trouble getting your desktop/notebook computer to recognize your Treo for synchronization, check to see which USB port you're using on your PC. Some PCs use an internal USB hub for the USB ports on the front of the PC, which can sometimes cause problems. If your device is plugged into a front port and isn't working, try plugging it into a rear port. The same rule applies to docking stations for notebook computers; try the port on the actual notebook if the docking station port is giving you trouble. For the record, my Treo syncs fine on a front USB port of my computer, so this might be an isolated problem.

NOTE Note that email isn't automatically synchronized with your device, even if you elect to synchronize with Microsoft Outlook. You must go in and set up each email account as part of the VersaMail synchronization option. Email synchronization is covered in detail in Chapter 4, "Synchronizing with Your Desktop Computer."

FIGURE 1.20

The signal strength indicator provides a quick and easy way to tell whether the mobile phone radio is turned on.

The reason for allowing you to turn the mobile radio on and off independently of the device is that you might want to work with applications on your device while offline. In fact, taking your device offline is a good idea if you don't need the mobile radio to receive phone calls because the radio puts a considerable strain on the battery. Granted, the Treo is designed to be used as a wireless mobile communicator, so you can certainly leave the mobile radio on all the time if you want. However, you might find it handy to turn the radio off while on an airplane so that you can keep working on your device while adhering to the strict airline policies on mobile phone usage.

> **NOTE** The Bluetooth wireless connectivity feature on the Treo 650 also puts a noticeable strain on the battery when it's in use, albeit less than the mobile phone radio. Bluetooth is turned off by default, as shown by the small gray indicator icon to the left of the signal strength indicator (refer to Figure 1.20). To find out how to turn on Bluetooth and wirelessly connect to headsets, hands-free car kits, other Palm devices, and your PC, see Chapter 11, "Communicating Wirelessly with Bluetooth."

Getting back to the mobile radio and your device's battery, it's important to understand that the battery life is largely in your control. You'll probably want to leave the mobile radio on most of the day to make and receive phone calls, not to mention surf the Web, check email, and so on. However, if you get in the habit of turning off the mobile radio when you truly don't need it, you'll find that each battery charge carries you much further than if you leave the radio on all the time. This is especially true if you're in an area with no wireless coverage—the radio expends a lot of battery charge continuously searching for a base station.

To turn off the mobile radio, hold down the Power/End button for a few seconds until you hear a special tone and see a screen that indicates the mobile radio is powering down. To turn your device off but leave the mobile radio on so that you can receive phone calls, just press the Power/End button without holding it down. The screen turns off, but you won't hear any kind of special tone or screen, which means the mobile radio is still on.

Summary

Admittedly, this chapter spent a fair amount of time covering background information that doesn't necessarily translate into practical Treo skills. However, becoming a truly proficient user of any computing device involves understanding a little about the history of the device and where it's headed. This is particularly true of smartphones, which represent a slice of the computer industry that's still in a great deal of flux. The Treo family of devices is as much evolutionary as it is revolutionary, and understanding their lineage helps you see why. At any rate, you're now ready to dive in and get busy putting your Treo to work. The next chapter guides you through performing some essential tasks that demonstrate many of the features that make the Treo a unique device.

Performing the Treo Essentials

Odds are you're itching to get busy doing interesting things with your Treo device. Rather than wait and show you how to carry out important tasks with your Treo as each chapter unfolds, I thought it might help to give you a quick primer and let you hit the ground running. So this chapter begins by exploring the basics of the Treo user interface, and then moves on to showing you exactly how to perform several of the most common functions you'll likely be carrying out on a regular basis: making phone calls, sending text messages, visiting web pages, taking digital pictures, searching your Treo for text, and so forth. Later chapters dig into all these topics in more detail, but this chapter gets you busy using your device for practical, everyday tasks.

IN THIS CHAPTER

- Navigate the Treo User Interface
- Make a Phone Call
- Send a Text Message
- Visit a Web Page
- Take a Digital Picture
- Use the Calculator
- Search Your Treo for Text
- Reset Your Treo
- Preserve the Treo Battery

Navigate the Treo User Interface

The engineers at Palm went to a great deal of effort to design the Treo user interface so that it's ruthlessly efficient at allowing you to carry out common tasks with minimal effort. Everyday tasks such as making a phone call and replying to an email message were studied in detail, with the end result being a reduction in the number of actions required on your part to carry out these tasks. For example, dialing a recent number on your Treo requires as few as three button presses via the five-way navigator. These efficiency gains in the Treo user interface are subtle, but they dramatically affect the device's usability. The following sections examine the basics of navigating around the Treo user interface and uncover some of these efficiencies.

Traverse Screens and Controls

Although you might have an affinity for using the stylus, eventually you will come to appreciate the usefulness of the five-way navigator. With this control, you can move throughout the Treo user interface with your thumb while holding the device in the same hand. In other words, you can do just about anything on your Treo with one hand. Granted, I wouldn't recommend typing text with one hand unless you have a physical limitation, but most people are accustomed to using a mobile phone with one hand. The five-way navigator enables you to carry this usability pattern over to your Treo.

The five-way navigator actually consists of five different buttons in one control: Left, Right, Up, Down, and Center. The first four buttons serve primarily as directional navigational controls, and the Center button functions as a selection button for making choices. You can generally think of the five-way navigator buttons as serving as a crude mouse, with four of the buttons accounting for mouse directions and the Center button corresponding to entering mouse clicks. Of course, you can also use the stylus as a useful alternative to the five-way navigator. You'll likely find your own unique approach to navigating your Treo that involves a combination of the five-way navigator and the stylus.

Many screens on the Treo present a sequence of controls, such as a group of command buttons. To move between these controls with the five-way navigator, just press the Up, Down, Left, and Right buttons to move to the control in the desired direction. Many screens are laid out so that you can move vertically to activate different groups of controls and then move horizontally within each group. Figure 2.1 shows the Day view in the Calendar application, which is a good example of how the directional buttons on the five-way navigator are used to navigate through an application.

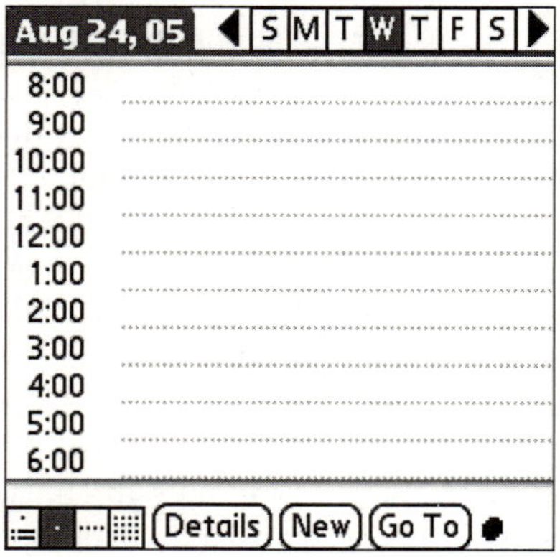

FIGURE 2.1

The weekday selection control at the top of the screen, along with the hour list and command buttons along the bottom, demonstrate the flexible user interface in the Calendar application.

In the Calendar application shown in Figure 2.1, you can press the Left and Right buttons on the five-way navigator to change the weekday along the top of the screen. Pressing the Down button shifts the focus to the hour list, which you can use to select specific hours of the day to schedule appointments. By pressing the Center button to activate the hour list, you can then move within the specific hours of the day by pressing Up and Down. Press the Center button again, followed by the Down button, and you can access any of the command buttons along the bottom of the screen by using the Left and Right buttons, of course. If you experiment with the five-way navigator in applications such as Calendar, you'll see a deliberate rhyme and reason to how the Treo's user interface flows.

By default, the hour list in the Calendar application shows exactly enough hours of the day to fit on one screen. Some lists in your Treo don't have enough room to show their entire contents, in which case you must scroll to see more of the list. The Up and Down buttons on the five-way navigator are used to scroll up and down within a list. In many lists, you can also scroll a page of data at a time by holding down the Option key with your left thumb while pressing the Up or Down button with your right thumb. In lists where the default action of the Up and Down buttons is to scroll the entire list, use the Center button with the Up and Down buttons to scroll between individual items in the list.

TIP You can use the stylus to interact with controls on any Treo screen. For example, to scroll a list with the stylus, just tap the arrows at the ends of the list. You can also tap and drag the slider in the middle of a scroll bar for exact scroll positioning.

Just as the Up and Down buttons are useful for navigating lists where information flows vertically, the Left and Right buttons are important in allowing you to navigate left and right through text entry controls. For example, the Memos application (see Figure 2.2) basically serves as a way to create and organize simple text notes. When entering a memo, you'll likely need to back up and change or delete text, and you can use the Left and Right buttons to move around within a memo's text. Of course, the Up and Down buttons still come into play for navigating up and down through memo text, but for quick corrections, the Left and Right buttons are invaluable.

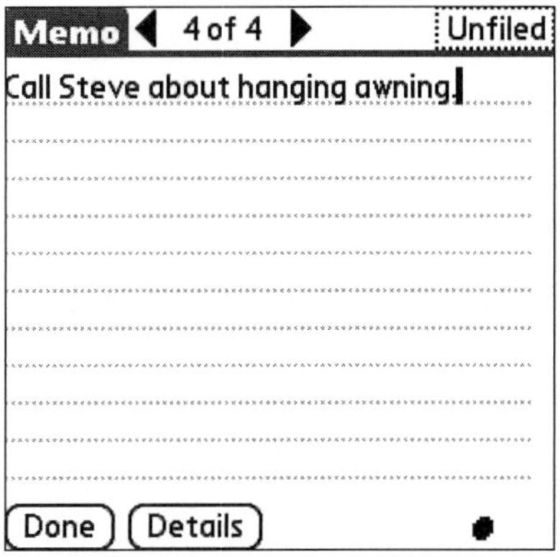

FIGURE 2.2

The text edit control in the Memos application is a good example of where the Left and Right buttons come into play for navigating through text as you enter it.

TIP You can often jump directly to the command buttons along the bottom of a screen by pressing the Right button on the five-way navigator.

A critical concept to understand when navigating through the Treo user interface is *highlighting*, which indicates that a control has the input focus and is ready for action. In other words, a highlighted control is ready for a press of the Center button to carry out some action. This action varies depending on the type of control. For example, pressing the Center button while a command button on the screen is highlighted results in the command being issued. On the other hand, pressing the Center button while a list is highlighted activates the list so that you can edit individual list items. You can easily tell whether a control is highlighted because it has a noticeable blue glow around it; for lists, the blue "glow" comes in the form of horizontal blue bars above and below the list. Figure 2.3 shows how these two horizontal bars frame the email list in the VersaMail application.

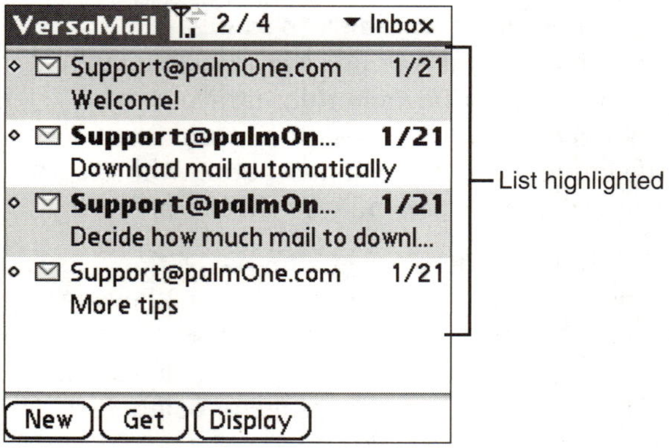

FIGURE 2.3

The email list in the VersaMail application is highlighted with horizontal bars above and below the list.

When a list is highlighted, you must push the Center button to activate the list and access the items within it. The highlight bars disappear, and one of the items in the list gains the input focus. To deactivate the list and return to the other controls on the screen, press the Left button. The highlight bars return to the list, indicating that you can press the Up and Down buttons to navigate to other controls on the screen.

Highlights don't always come in the form of a blue glow around an item. Phone numbers, email addresses, and links on web pages are highlighted by being shown in reverse text. For a web page that normally displays black text on a white background, the highlight around a Web link appears with white text on a black background. Press the Center button to activate a phone, an email, or a link highlight. This results in the phone number being dialed, a new email message being created, or a Web link being traversed.

Speaking of reverse text indicating highlighting, this is exactly how text is highlighted in a text edit field. I'm sure you've selected text in a desktop application and cut and pasted it into another application. The selection concept on the Treo is the same—you block off a selection of text, which then becomes highlighted. Some text edit fields don't immediately allow you to edit them; instead, they show the entire text contents highlighted. Simply press the Center button to begin editing the text. Press the Center button again when you're finished editing the text.

Unfortunately, selecting a block of text on Treo devices can be accomplished only via the stylus. In other words, there's no way to select a block of text with the five-way navigator without the aid of third-party software. This is a strange limitation, but I have to admit that the stylus provides a more effective way to select text. To select a block of text with the stylus, just tap and drag the stylus across the text. To highlight a word, double-tap the stylus on the word. To highlight an entire line of text, triple-tap the stylus anywhere on the line. Quadruple-tap the stylus to...just kidding on that one! Triple-tapping is as fancy as the stylus shortcut moves get.

> **NOTE** Speaking of cut and paste, the Treo 600 and 650 devices have a 1KB limit on how much text can be copied or cut to the Clipboard for pasting. With some third-party applications, such as FieldPlus by Ansel Rognlie, you can overcome this limitation with a much larger Clipboard buffer. FieldPlus also adds the capability of selecting a block of text with the five-way navigator, which is unfortunately a feature lacking in the Treo user interface. To download FieldPlus, visit a site with Treo software downloads, such as http://mytreo.net.

Access Menus

Although menus aren't readily visible in Treo applications, they are nevertheless a vital part of the Treo user interface. The Menu button, located slightly above and to the right of the five-way navigator on the Treo 650, gives you access to the menus in the current application. Just press the Menu button to open the application's menus. Figure 2.4 shows the menus available in the Phone application.

> **NOTE** The Palm OS is designed so that the most commonly used commands are available via onscreen buttons, and lesser used commands are accessed via menus.

After opening a menu with a press of the Menu button or a tap of the stylus on an application's title bar, you can navigate through the menus. Use the Left and Right buttons on the five-way navigator to move through the different menus, and then use the Up and Down buttons to move up and down a particular menu and select a menu command. To issue the command, press the Center button. Of course, you can also use the stylus to tap a menu and then tap the menu command you'd like to issue. If you change your mind and decide not to issue a command from the menus, just press the Menu button again to exit the menus and close them.

FIGURE 2.4

The three menus in the Phone application—Record, Edit, and Options—provide access to a variety of phone commands and options.

TIP You can also tap the stylus in an application's title bar to access the menus. However, not every application has a visible title bar (Calc and Camera, for example), which means you have to resort to the Menu button from time to time, even if you're a big fan of the stylus.

NOTE Similar to menu shortcuts, the Phone application also supports Quick Keys, which are keys you associate with a favorite, such as a frequently dialed contact or a frequently visited website. While in the Phone application, you can immediately issue a Quick Key command by holding down the appropriate key. To find out how to create custom Quick Keys, see "Create and Manage Favorites" in Chapter 7, "Using Your Treo as a Mobile Phone."

You might notice that most menus have shortcuts listed next to some of the more commonly used commands. You can use these shortcuts to quickly issue a command with a two-key combination involving the Menu button and one other key, the shortcut key. For example, in Figure 2.4 you can see that three menu commands have shortcuts, as indicated by the forward slash icon and a letter beside the command. To issue the New Contact command at any point while using the Phone application, simply press the Menu button followed by the N key. If the menu is already open, just press the N key to issue the command.

Another user interface control closely related to menus is the *pick list*, which allows you to select from a list of possible values. Like a menu, a pick list drops down to reveal additional information when opened. More specifically, only one item is visible in the list until you activate it; then the list opens and provides access to all the items in the list. You can easily spot pick lists because they always have a small down arrow displayed next to their current selections. Figures 2.5 and 2.6 show a pick list as it's selected and opened to reveal cities in the World Clock application.

After opening a pick list, you can use the Up and Down buttons to scroll within the list and highlight items. When you find the item you want, press the Center button to select it and close the pick list. To close the pick list without changing the selection, press the Left or Right button. You can also use the stylus to scroll a pick list by tapping the arrows at the top and bottom of the list. To select an item in the pick list, just tap the item with the stylus.

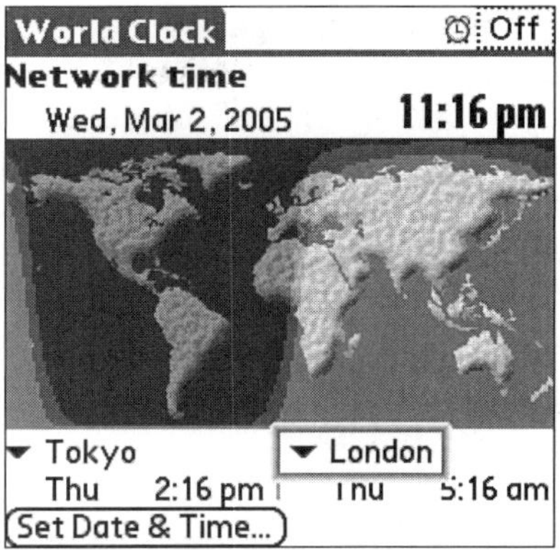

FIGURE 2.5

A pick list in the World Clock application is first selected, in which case it's highlighted to show that it has the input focus.

FIGURE 2.6

Pressing the Center button activates the pick list, causing it to open and reveal more items that can be selected.

Launch Applications

I'm sure you noticed that the Menu button isn't the only button that accompanies the five-way navigator and the Phone/Send and Power/End buttons. There are, in fact, three other buttons in the same "navigation" area of the Treo keyboard, and they all relate to launching applications. The Application button, located just above and to the left of the five-way navigator, is used to access various application screens. Figure 2.7 shows the main application screen, which displays all the applications available on your device.

TIP

To quickly move around within a pick list, press a letter key on the keyboard. The pick list immediately highlights the first item on the list beginning with that letter. You can continue spelling out the name of a pick list item by quickly typing additional letters. If you pause for a couple of seconds and then press another letter, the selection process starts over with the new letter.

You might notice in the figure that the word *All* appears near the top of the screen and is, in fact, a pick list. You can use this pick list to change the category of applications displayed onscreen. *All* appears by default because it's the one selection that displays all applications. Press the Up button followed by the Center button to access and open the application category pick list. Figure 2.8 shows the application categories available in this pick list, some of which might be empty on your device.

By selecting any category other than All, you are effectively filtering the applications displayed on the application screen according to a particular category. An optional and often quicker way to move between application categories is to press the Application button repeatedly; doing so cycles through the application categories that contain applications. This is why I mentioned that some categories might be empty initially, in which case they are skipped over when you press the Application button to cycle through the categories. You might notice a small memory card icon at the bottom of the pick list—selecting this "category" results in displaying only the applications stored on the memory card.

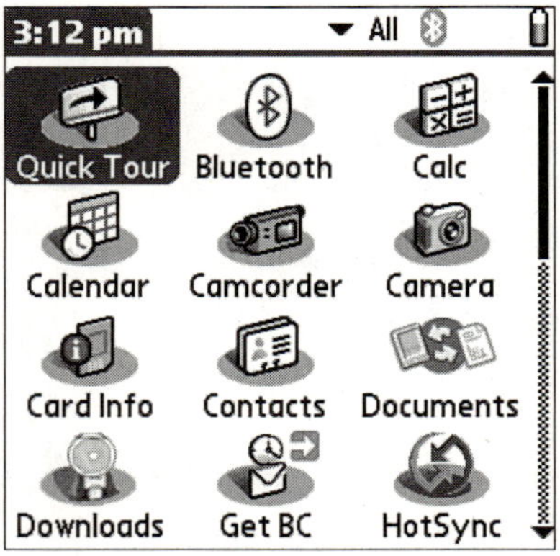

FIGURE 2.7

The main application screen shows all the applications available on your device, including core applications and applications that you've installed.

To launch an application from the application screen, just use the five-way navigator to highlight the application, and then press the Center button to launch it. Or use the stylus to scroll up and down via the scrollbar on the right edge of the screen, and tap the application to launch it.

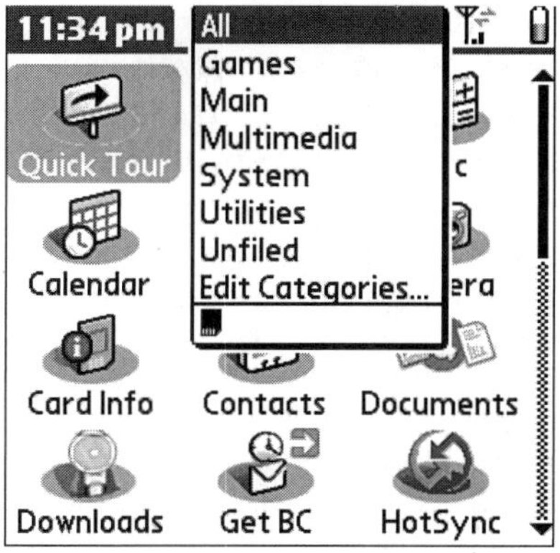

FIGURE 2.8

The application category pick list allows you to filter the applications that are displayed according to a specific category.

Although the Application button provides a way to access all the applications on your device, the other buttons can be used as shortcuts to commonly used applications. For example, the Calendar button, located just below the Application button, launches the Calendar application when pressed. Similarly, the Messaging button just below the Menu button launches the Messaging application. Some buttons also offer an optional application launch when you press the button preceded by the Option key. Following are buttons and button combinations, along with the applications they launch or, in some cases, the actions they take:

- *Phone/Send*—Launch Phone application, Phone "send"
- *Option + Phone/Send*—Launch Blazer Web browser
- *Power/End*—Turn power on and off, Phone "end"
- *Option + Power/End*—Turn on Keyguard
- *Calendar*—Launch Calendar application
- *Option + Calendar*—Launch World Clock application
- *Messaging*—Launch Messaging application
- *Option + Messaging*—Launch VersaMail application

> **TIP**
> You can quickly highlight an application on the application screen by typing the first letter or two of the application name. For example, to launch the Tasks application, press the T key, followed by the A key; the T key is probably enough to get to the Tasks application in most cases. If you want to type and highlight a different application, just pause for a moment and then resume typing the first letters of its name.

You'll find these buttons indispensable in quickly moving between applications on your Treo. You might also find that you use some applications more than others, in which case you might want to tweak the applications that these buttons launch. You learn how to customize the application buttons in Chapter 3, "Customizing and Personalizing Your Treo."

Enter Text with the Keyboard

Probably the most notable feature of the Treo family of devices is the full QWERTY keyboard it sports. Few smartphones include a full keyboard, and most of the handhelds that include keyboards are large and clunky. The Treo is one of the few devices to successfully merge a full keyboard into a mobile phone form-factor. Given that this keyboard is one of the highlights of the Treo device, it's worth taking a moment to learn a bit more about it.

> **NOTE** The Treo keyboard includes a backlight that automatically turns on and off with the screen.

Like a normal computer keyboard, the Treo keyboard allows you to enter lowercase letters by default. If you want to tinker with typing and using the keyboard, launch the Memos application and quickly create a new memo by following these steps:

1. If you aren't already viewing the main application screen, press the **Application** button to open it.
2. Press the **M** key to jump to the Memos application, or scroll to it by using the five-way navigator.
3. Press the **Center** button to launch the Memos application.
4. Press the **Right** button to highlight the New button on the screen, and press the **Center** button to create a new memo.
5. You can now type to create a new memo.

The main reason I'm having you create a memo is because it's a great place to explore using the keyboard to enter text. For example, to enter uppercase characters, press the Shift/Find or Right Shift key followed by the letter key. Unlike a desktop or notebook computer keyboard, you don't have to hold down the Shift/Find or Right Shift keys to enter an uppercase letter—just press the Shift key and then press the letter key. If you want to enter several uppercase letters, you can turn on Caps Lock by pressing the Shift/Find or Right Shift key twice. To turn Caps Lock off, just press either key again. A small arrow with a line through it appears in the lower-right corner to indicate when Caps Lock is turned on (see Figure 2.9).

I'm sure you've already noticed that just about every key on the Treo keyboard has an additional number, punctuation, or symbol printed above and to the right of the letter on the key. This additional character is entered by pressing the Option key before pressing the letter key. So to enter a dollar sign ($), press the Option key followed by the H key. Like the two Shift keys, the Option key doesn't have to be held down—just press it before pressing the letter key.

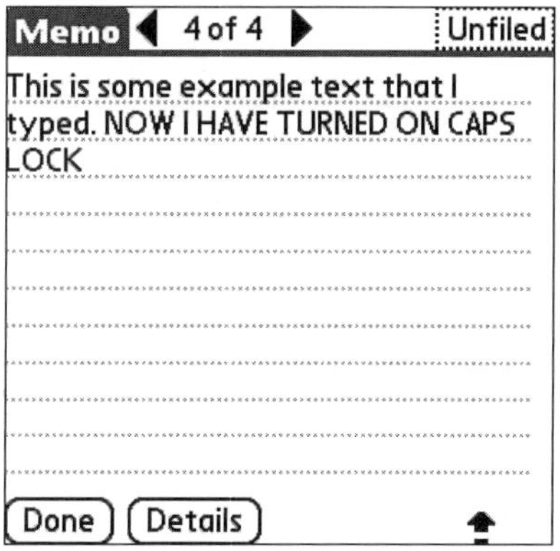

FIGURE 2.9

When you turn on Caps Lock while editing text, a small arrow with a line through it appears in the lower-right corner.

Also similar to the Shift key, the Option Lock feature locks in the Option key for entering numbers, punctuation, and symbols. To turn on Option Lock, press the Option key twice. When Option Lock is turned on, a small oval icon with a line under it appears in the lower-right corner of the screen (see Figure 2.10). To turn off Option Lock, press the Option key again.

> **NOTE** Because typically you want to start a sentence with a capital letter, the Treo automatically enables the Shift key when you start a new sentence. This means you can type away without having to worry about capitalizing the beginning of each sentence.

In addition to using the Shift keys and Option key to access different characters on the keyboard, one other technique offers access to more obscure characters and symbols. I'm referring to the Alt key, located just to the right of the Space key on the keyboard. The Alt key enables you to select from several different characters and symbols associated with each key. For example, type the letter *c* by pressing the C key, and then press the Alt key. Scroll through the selection list that appears with the Up and Down buttons to choose from several symbols related to the letter *c*, such as the copyright symbol (©) and the cent symbol (¢). Figure 2.11 shows the copyright symbol as it's selected from a list of characters associated with the letter *c*.

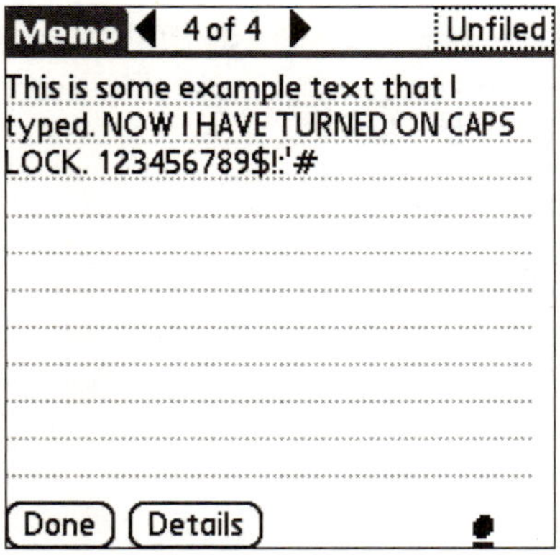

FIGURE 2.10

When you turn on Option Lock while editing text, a small oval icon with a line under it appears in the lower-right corner.

> **NOTE**
> The Option Lock feature is sometimes turned on automatically in data entry fields that expect numbers. For example, the phone number entry fields for a new contact in the Contacts application automatically turn on Option Lock because the fields expect numeric input.

To accept a selection from the alternate character selection list, press the Center button or tap the character in the list. If you change your mind and decide not to choose an alternate character, press the Left or Right button.

It's important to understand that you can use the Alt key to access alternate characters for a particular key at any time, not just when you first type a character. For example, use the five-way navigator to position the text entry cursor just to the right of any character in a body of text, and press the Alt key. A selection list appears with alternate characters that correspond to the character next to the cursor.

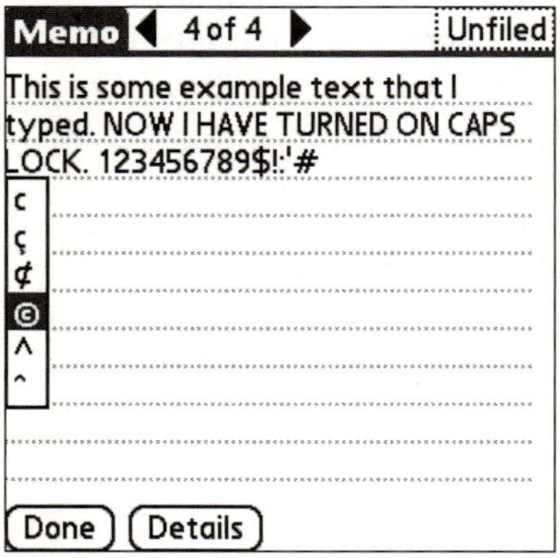

FIGURE 2.11

You use the Alt key to select an alternate character from a list of choices when entering text.

Making Sense of the Indicator Light

The indicator light near the upper-left corner of your Treo (just beside the earpiece) is an important part of the Treo user interface because it conveys information about your network access and battery status. More specifically, the indicator light changes from off to flashing green to flashing amber to indicate the wireless network's availability. The light also comes into play when charging your device, except in this case the light glows solid instead of flashing. When charging your Treo, a solid red light indicates that the battery is charging, and a solid green light indicates that the battery has a full charge. If you're attempting to charge your device and the indicator light is off, there's likely a problem with the connection or the power source.

To recap the exact meaning of the indicator light, take a look at the following list:

- *Flashing green*—Connected to wireless phone/data network.
- *Flashing amber*—Outside the wireless phone/data network coverage area.
- *Solid red*—Battery is charging.
- *Flashing red rapidly*—Battery is very low.
- *Solid green*—Battery is fully charged.
- *Solid amber*—Active application is running, but the screen is off.
- *Off*—Disconnected from wireless phone/data network, or battery is not charging.

> **NOTE** If you're moving to the Treo from an earlier Palm device that relied heavily on the Graffiti handwriting recognition feature, you've probably already realized that no Treo devices include Graffiti because they all have full QWERTY keyboards. Even so, third-party applications, such as Graffiti Anywhere (http://www.escande.org/palm/GrfAnywhere/) and Jot (http://www.shopcic.com/product_details/jot_details.asp), enable you to install Graffiti on your Treo as an add-on.

> **NOTE** If the battery is completely drained, the indicator light might not come on for a few moments when you begin charging it.

Some users have noted that the flashing green indicator light sometimes flashes at different rates. Unfortunately, there isn't currently any consensus among users on what this flashing rate change indicates, and Palm has offered no answers on the matter. Possibilities range from the flashing rate indicating how much charge is left on the battery to perhaps indicating that you have new voicemail messages or missed calls. The problem is that a soft reset of the device typically does away with the rapid flashing, which leads you to believe that maybe it isn't indicative of anything. Even without the mystery flashing rate, the indicator light is useful in quickly diagnosing your wireless network availability and battery charge status.

TIP If you'd like to exert some control over the indicator light on your Treo, you might want to consider using a third-party application, such as LEDOff or Butler. Some people get annoyed by the indicator light at night, and these applications allow you to turn it off. Butler is actually capable of doing much more than just providing control over the indicator light. To find out more, check out Butler at Hobbyist Software (http://www.hobbyistsoftware.com/) or LEDOff at FreewarePalm (http://www.freewarepalm.com/utilities/ledoff.shtml).

Make a Phone Call

Making a call on your Treo device is easy and can actually be carried out in a variety of ways. Because I don't want to assume that you've synchronized contacts from a desktop PIM application, such as Microsoft Outlook, I'm going to focus on showing you how to dial a number as opposed to dialing via a contact. Follow these steps to make a phone call on your Treo:

1. If the mobile radio isn't turned on, hold down the **Power/End** button until you hear a tone and a screen appears that indicates you're being connected to the wireless network.
2. After you are connected to the network, press the **Phone/Send** button to launch the Phone application.
3. Dial the phone number by pressing number keys on the keyboard (Option Lock is on by default) or by tapping numbers on the onscreen Dial Pad with the stylus (see Figure 2.12).
4. Press the **Phone/Send** button again to dial the number. The number is dialed and you are connected on the call (see Figure 2.13).
5. To end the call, press the **Power/End** button or tap the **Hang Up All** button on the screen.

FIGURE 2.12

You dial a number in the Phone application by pressing number keys on the keyboard or tapping the numbers on the onscreen Dial Pad.

Notice in Figure 2.13 that several options are available when you're on a call. You can easily tap a button on the screen to switch to the speakerphone, put the call on hold, access the Dial Pad, or mute the microphone. You can just as easily use the five-way navigator to navigate between these buttons and issue phone commands. You can also originate another phone call and conference the calls together, but that's a more advanced topic for Chapter 7, "Using Your Treo as a Mobile Phone."

NOTE A soft reset is the Treo equivalent of a system reboot on a desktop computer when you shut down the computer and restart it. This is in contrast to a system reset and a hard reset, which are increasingly serious in terms of how they affect your device. All three types of resets are covered later in the chapter in the section "Reset Your Treo."

In addition to making a call, if you're new to your mobile phone service, you might need to access phone information on your device to help remember your mobile phone number. Follow these steps to look up the phone number for your Treo:

1. If the mobile radio isn't turned on, hold down the **Power/End** button until you hear a tone and a screen appears that indicates you're being connected to the wireless network.
2. After you are connected to the network, press the **Phone/Send** button to launch the Phone application.

FIGURE 2.13

After you're connected on a call, you can switch to the speakerphone, put the call on hold, access the Dial Pad, or mute the microphone.

3. Press the **Menu** button to open the menus for the Phone application.
4. Press the **Right** button twice to activate the Options menu, and then scroll down and select **Phone Info**. The Phone Info screen that appears displays a variety of information about your device, including its phone number (see Figure 2.14).

TIP You might find that you need to adjust the phone's volume while you're on a call. Just press up or down on the Volume button on the left side of your Treo to adjust the call volume.

I explained how to dial a phone number, but I didn't clarify what to do to answer an incoming call. I'm sure you've already guessed, but the Phone/Send button is all you have to press to answer an incoming call.

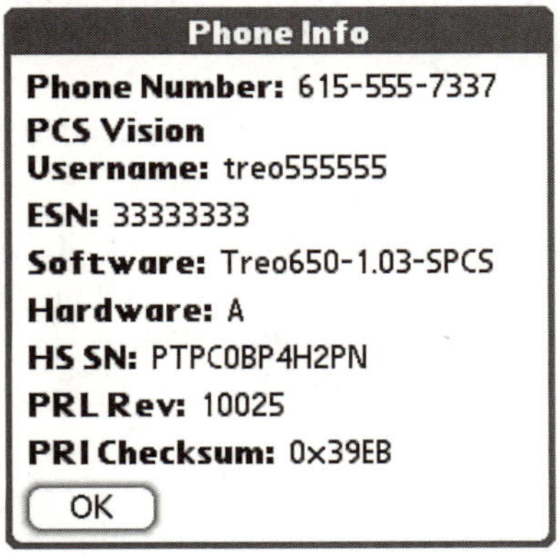

FIGURE 2.14

The Phone Info screen includes a lot of information you probably don't care to know, but it also happens to show your mobile phone number.

TIP No one appreciates a noisy mobile phone ringing in a theater or some other place where noise is undesirable. Treo devices are one of the only mobile phones that include a hardware ringer switch to instantly turn off the phone's ringer. The switch is on the top of the phone near the expansion card slot. Just slide it over to the right, and your phone's ringer won't bother you during a movie. Chapter 7, "Using Your Treo as a Mobile Phone," explores different settings for how your phone vibrates (or not) in lieu of the muted ringer.

Now that you have a phone call under your belt, you can move on to sending a text message.

Send a Text Message

The full QWERTY keyboard on the Treo devices opens up all kinds of interesting possibilities for text messaging. Granted, hardcore text message users have become quite adept at cranking out messages on tiny phone keypads with only a few keys. With the Treo, however, you can start using your smartphone as more of a true text communicator. To send an SMS (Short Message Service) text message on your Treo, follow these steps:

1. If the mobile radio isn't turned on, hold down the **Power/End** button until you hear a tone and a screen appears that indicates you're being connected to the wireless network.
2. After you are connected to the network, press the **Messaging** button (to the lower right of the five-way navigator) to launch the Messaging application.
3. Tap the **New** button to begin creating a new message. The Compose screen opens, as shown in Figure 2.15.

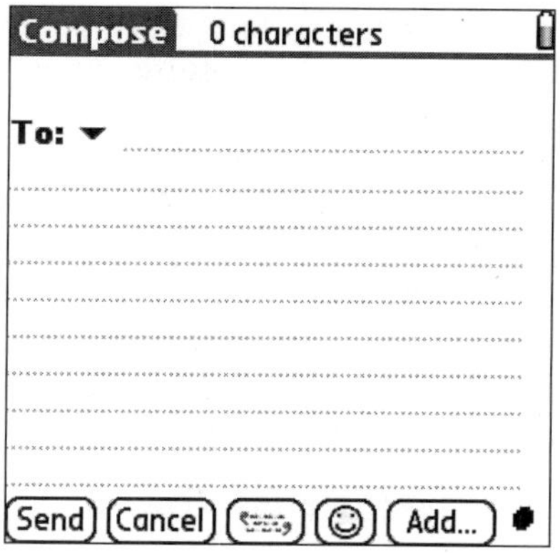

FIGURE 2.15

Use the Compose screen in the Messaging application to enter a text message.

4. Press the number keys on the keyboard to enter the phone number of the text message's recipient next to the To: label. If you want to send a text message to an email address instead, you can enter the address in the To: field.
5. Press the **Down** button on the five-way navigator to move to the message body and begin entering the message text (see Figure 2.16).

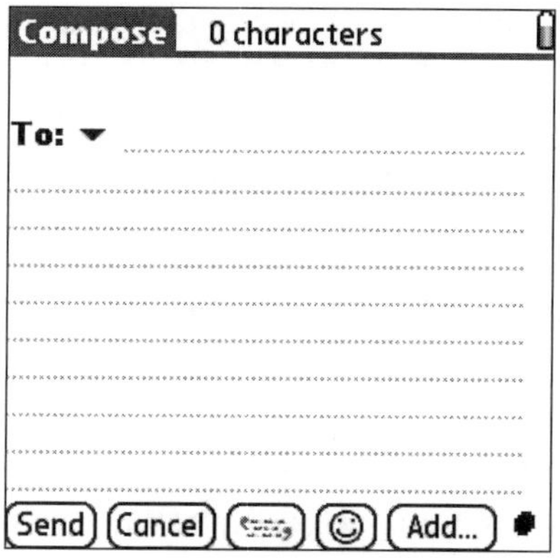

FIGURE 2.16

Entering text for a text message simply involves typing text in the body of the message in the Compose screen.

6. When you're ready to send the message, tap the **Send** button near the bottom of the screen. After a few seconds, the message is sent to the recipient.

You probably noticed some additional buttons along the bottom of the Compose screen that I neglected to mention in the previous steps on how to send a text message. You can use these buttons to do some useful things, such as insert QuickText, which consists of commonly used phrases that you can select and insert to save time. You can also select emoticons (smilies) to insert in a message. To add pizzazz to your text messages, you can turn them into multimedia messages by adding a voice memo, digital picture, or video clip. All these topics are tackled in detail in Chapter 9, "Communicating with Text and Multimedia Messages."

NOTE SMS text messages are limited to only 160 characters, so the idea is to keep them short and sweet. However, if you find yourself rambling past the 160-character limit, don't fret because the Treo's Messaging application automatically breaks longer messages into 160-character chunks that are sent as separate messages.

Visit a Web Page

Accessing the wireless Web is truly one of the most exciting facets of any smartphone, and the Treo makes this prospect particularly compelling, given its relatively high screen resolution (320×320). Blazer is the standard Web browser on Treo devices, and it does a good job of allowing you to view both mobile-specific and general websites designed for full-sized computers. To visit a web page by using the Blazer Web browser on your Treo, follow these steps:

1. If the mobile radio isn't turned on, hold down the **Power/End** button until you hear a tone and a screen appears that indicates you're being connected to the wireless network.
2. After you are connected to the network, press the **Option** key followed by the **Phone/Send** button to launch the Blazer Web browser. The web page for your wireless service provider will likely open by default.
3. To visit a different page, press the **Menu** button, scroll over once to the Go menu, and then scroll to select the **Go to Web Page** menu item. Press the **Center** button to issue the menu command and open the Go to Web Page screen, as shown in Figure 2.17.
4. Enter the URL of the web page you want to visit by typing it on the keyboard. You can use the helper boxes just above the text entry area for common parts of the URL, such as the `www.` at the beginning and the `.com` at the end.
5. When you're finished entering the URL, tap the OK button to accept it and open the page in the browser. Figure 2.18 shows the splash page for my website (http://www.michaelmorrison.com/) open in Blazer.

TIP As a shortcut for entering the URL of a web page you'd like to visit, tap the Earth icon in the Blazer toolbar to open the Go to Web Page screen, or just tap the address bar of the Blazer browser and enter the URL directly in it. If you enter the URL directly in the address bar, tap the Go button to open the page.

FIGURE 2.17

The Go to Web Page screen enables you to enter a URL for a web page to visit, and it includes several helper boxes for entering common URL components.

FIGURE 2.18

The web page you specified opens in the Blazer Web browser and displays as best it can, given the limited screen size.

Although the layout is different when you view the page in a normal desktop Web browser, the content is still visible in a reasonable format in Treo's Blazer browser. Some pages scale down better than others, but most pages are at least readable on your Treo. Just keep in mind that the Blazer browser tends to stack Web content vertically down the screen even if its original layout is horizontal. Figure 2.19 shows my page on a normal desktop Web browser, which illustrates what I'm talking about because the image and text appear horizontally as they were intended. (Compare this layout to the one shown in Figure 2.18.)

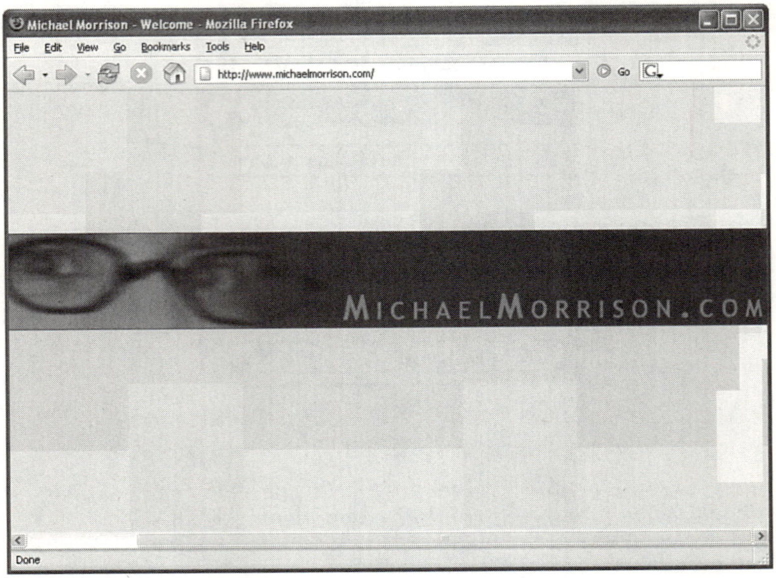

FIGURE 2.19

This full-size web page is oriented properly in the desktop Firefox Web browser.

> **TIP** The Blazer Web browser also supports a Wide Page view, which doesn't stack the content on a wide page vertically as in the default Optimized view. Instead, you must scroll left and right in the browser to view the full width of the page. To toggle between Optimized and Wide Page view, tap the toolbar icon that looks like a miniature Blazer screen (located to the left of the Earth icon). You'll find that Wide Page view is often preferable on pages with a layout you're accustomed to viewing a certain way.

The toolbar along the top of the Blazer screen allows you to perform common Web-browsing tasks, such as navigating backward or forward a page, refreshing the page, changing the page view (Wide Page or Optimized), jumping to the Home page, and accessing bookmarks. The Blazer browser is a powerful little Web browser with lots of handy features that are covered in detail in Chapter 10, "Browsing the Wireless Web."

Take a Digital Picture

What started as somewhat of a gimmick has turned into a truly useful feature that many people can't do without, including me. I'm referring to the digital cameras included in many mobile phones, including the Treo smartphone. With the digital camera in the Treo, you can take digital pictures up to VGA resolution, which is 640×480, or 0.3 megapixels. Granted, this resolution isn't so great by digital camera standards, but it's not bad at all by mobile phone standards. Keep in mind that not everyone has unlimited data on his or her service plan, in which case sending hefty high-resolution images would put a serious strain on your phone bill.

Although you can certainly take pictures on your Treo device without a memory card, if you get serious about it, I'd recommend buying a card at some point to beef up the storage capabilities. For now, however, you just want to learn how the camera works and take a few pictures to get your feet wet. To take a digital picture with your Treo, follow these steps:

> **NOTE** The Treo 650 adds support for capturing video with the onboard digital camera. Capturing video is practically the same process as shooting a still picture; you just operate the camera in video mode instead of camera mode. Chapter 12, "Taking and Sharing Digital Pictures and Videos," tells you everything you need to know about shooting and sharing pictures and videos with your Treo.

1. Press the **Application** button to open the main application screen.
2. Press the **C** key to jump near the Camera application, and then navigate with the five-way navigator to select the **Camera** application.
3. Press the **Center** button to launch the Camera application. The digital camera immediately turns on, and the screen becomes the virtual lens for the camera (see Figure 2.20). The camera lens is located on the back of the device in the upper-left corner—aim the lens at the target you want to photograph.

FIGURE 2.20

A large portion of the screen in the Camera application serves as a virtual camera lens for the digital camera.

4. Zoom in and out on the picture by pressing the Up and Down buttons on the five-way navigator. (There are only two zoom levels.)
5. When you're ready to take a picture, just press the **Center** button. You hear a shutter sound and the picture is displayed, along with a series of buttons at the bottom of the screen for deciding what to do with the picture (see Figure 2.21) .

FIGURE 2.21

The picture preview screen in the Camera application gives you an opportunity to decide what to do with a freshly taken picture.

6. To save the picture, tap the **Save** button on the toolbar, which is the first button with a floppy disk icon. If you want to delete the picture and try again, tap the **Delete** button, which has a trash-can icon.

7. To view a picture after you've taken it, tap the **Pics&Videos** button in the lower left of the Camera screen, which has four small squares to indicate several pictures. Figure 2.22 shows the Pics&Videos screen, which provides access to all the pictures and videos stored on your device.

TIP You might notice a little round mirror positioned adjacent to the camera lens on the back of your device. This mirror enables you to aim the camera at yourself for taking self-portraits or pictures of yourself with friends and family. Just make sure you can see yourself in the mirror when you snap the picture!

You can do all kinds of interesting things with a picture after you've taken it, such as sending it as part of a multimedia message, organizing it into a photo album, and viewing it as part of a slide show. All these topics are covered in detail in Chapter 12, "Taking and Sharing Digital Pictures and Videos."

FIGURE 2.22

The Pics&Videos screen serves as a file viewer for pictures and videos and allows you to organize, edit, and send them to others.

Use the Calculator

The Calc application on the Treo serves as a calculator that does much more than just basic math functions. The Calc application includes several advanced modes for performing conversions between different units of measure as well as scientific, financial, and statistical calculations. Following are the different modes the Treo calculator supports, along with what functions they offer:

> **TIP** If you want to keep your pictures as small as possible, change to a lower resolution by tapping the resolution pick list in the lower-right area of the Camera application, and select 320×240 instead of 640×480.

- *Basic*—Common math functions, such as addition, subtraction, multiplication, division, square root, and memory
- *Math*—Advanced math functions, such as exponents, roots, logarithms, as well as flexible memory storage
- *Trig*—Trigonometric functions, such as sine, cosine, and tangent, as well as flexible memory storage
- *Finance*—Financial functions typically found on a financial calculator, such as amortization, as well as flexible memory storage
- *Logic*—Logical operations, such as And, Or, Not, and Xor, as well as conversions between different bases and flexible memory storage
- *Statistics*—Statistical functions, such as sum and factorial, as well as a handy random number generator and flexible memory storage

- *Weight/Tmp*—Unit conversion for weight and temperature in metric and English as well as flexible memory storage
- *Length*—Unit conversion for length in metric and English as well as flexible memory storage
- *Area*—Unit conversion for area in metric, English, and traditional as well as flexible memory storage
- *Volume*—Unit conversion for volume in metric and English as well as flexible memory storage

To use the calculator, follow these steps:

1. Press the **Application** button to open the main application screen.
2. Press the **C** key to jump near the Calc application, and then navigate with the five-way navigator (if necessary) to select the application. Press the **Center** button to launch the calculator, which appears in Basic mode (see Figure 2.23).

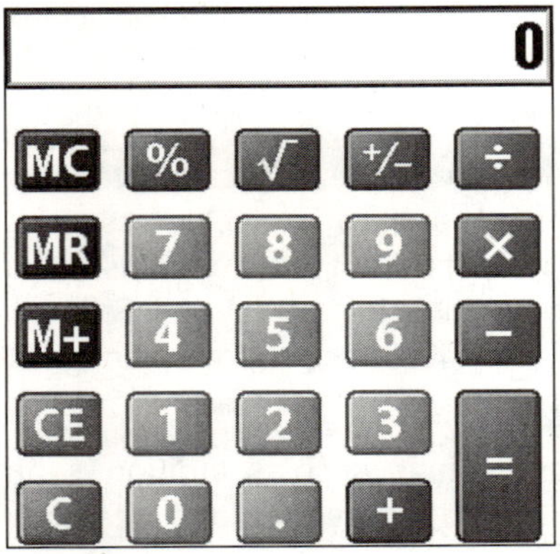

FIGURE 2.23

In Basic mode, the Calc application appears as a simple calculator with familiar buttons for performing basic calculations.

3. To perform a calculation, tap a number on the screen using the stylus or enter it on the keyboard; Option Lock is automatically turned on so that you don't have to press the Option key on the keyboard.
4. Specify the math function by tapping it on the screen or pressing the key on the keyboard—the **W** (addition), **S** (subtraction), **Z** (multiplication), and **Q** (division) keys contain the four basic math functions.

5. Enter the second number for the calculation, and then tap the **Equals** button on the screen or press the **Enter** key on the keyboard. The result is displayed on the screen.

6. Switch to an advanced mode by pressing the **Right** button on the five-way navigator. To cycle through the different advanced modes, press the **Right** button; to return to Basic mode at any time, press the **Left** button. Figure 2.24 shows the calculator in Length mode.

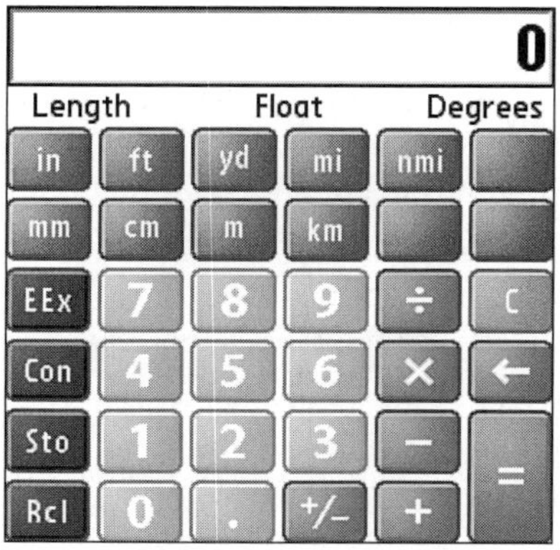

FIGURE 2.24

In Length mode, you can use the calculator to convert between metric and English units of length.

The Calc application has several menus for fine-tuning the specific mode you're using. For example, most of the advanced modes allow you to specify the number of decimal places to display in the calculator. To change this setting, follow these steps:

1. Enter the number of decimal places, and then press the **Menu** button.
2. Navigate to the **Pref** menu, and scroll down to select **Fixed(x)** from the menu.
3. Press the **Center** button to accept the change.
4. If you want to return to a format that shows all the decimal places in a number, select **Float** from the Pref menu.

The numeric notations on the Pref menu actually correspond to floating-point (Float), fixed-point (Fixed(x)), scientific (Sci(x)), and engineering notation (Eng(x)). The last three notations have an *x* in their names because these modes expect you to enter a number indicating the number of decimal places to display for each notation.

The Pref menu also enables you to switch between degrees (Degrees), radians (Radians), and gradians (Grads). Radians express angles in terms of the math constant pi, and gradians are a European form of degrees; there are 400 grads in a circle, as compared to 360 degrees.

The Pref menu is the same in all the advanced modes except Logic mode, in which case the menu changes so that you can change the base and width of numbers. More specifically, you can choose between binary (Bin), octal (Oct), signed decimal (SDec), unsigned decimal (UDec), and hexadecimal bases (Hex). The storage width of a number can be set to 8 Bit, 16 Bit, or 32 Bit.

The last detail to cover for the Calc application is the History feature, which displays a list of recent calculations you've performed. To access the history, press the Menu button and select Show History on the Edit menu. A history of your recent calculations is displayed, as shown in Figure 2.25. In this example, I divided 5280 by 4, and then converted the result from feet to miles.

FIGURE 2.25

The History feature of the Calc application displays a list of recent calculations.

You can copy the history to paste into other applications, such as an email or a text message, to share with someone by selecting Copy History from the Edit menu. To clear the history, select Clear History from the Edit menu. The Edit menu also includes a Copy Total command for copying the current calculation results. Finally, the Paste command on the Edit menu allows you to paste in a number you've copied from another application.

Search Your Treo for Text

As you continue to use your Treo for a while and amass a fair amount of data, you'll undoubtedly run into a situation where you need to search your device for information. Fortunately, the Treo includes a built-in text search feature called Find used to search the entire device for a string of text. Follow these steps to use the Find feature to find text on your device:

1. Press the **Option** key followed by the **Shift/Find** key to open the Find screen (see Figure 2.26).

FIGURE 2.26

In the Find screen, you can enter a string of text to search for on your device.

2. Enter the exact text for which you'd like to search, and tap the **OK** button to carry out the search. The search results appear in a larger Find screen (see Figure 2.27). In this example, the memo named "2x4's" is a match because it contains the search term "nails."
3. If you don't see an interesting match, tap the **Find More** button to continue searching your device. When you see an interesting match in the Find screen, tap it in the list to open it.

The Find feature searches the database of each application on your device for an exact match of the text you specify. Although the match must be exact, the text does not have to appear as individual words. So if you search for the text *sam*, possible matches could include *Sam*antha, *sam*ple, and flot*sam*.

FIGURE 2.27

The Find screen expands to show the search results, which you can interact with by tapping a specific result.

Reset Your Treo

It's a sad truth that Treo devices are like every computer, in that they can get unstable from time to time and require a reboot. The likelihood of your device getting unstable has to do with how many applications you install and how much of a strain you put on its memory, among other things. Even the most conscientious user who is careful not to overload his or her device is still capable of running into a shaky system at some point, which makes a reset a good idea.

You can perform three different kinds of resets on your Treo. Here I've listed them in increasing order of severity:

- Soft reset
- System reset
- Hard reset

The next few sections examine these types of resets in more detail. If you find yourself contemplating a reset, make sure you try them in the same order that I explain them here. Or let me put it more bluntly—resort to a hard reset only when you're desperate and out of options because it blitzes your device's memory!

Perform a Soft Reset

A soft reset is the Treo equivalent of rebooting your desktop or notebook computer, and it's a good idea to do one from time to time if you notice your device behaving strangely. There aren't any risks to performing a soft reset, as it preserves data as long as you aren't in the middle of editing a new piece of data (contact, memo, and so forth). Just make sure you don't have a specific piece of data open in an application when you perform a soft reset. Following are the steps for a soft reset:

> **NOTE** A soft reset is supposed to safely close applications so that you don't lose any data, but it's safer not to leave anything open.

1. Press the battery door release button on the back of your device, and slide the battery door downward to remove the door. Be careful not to remove the battery, just the battery door.
2. To the left of the battery, you'll see a small recessed hole that contains the device's Reset button. Press the **Reset** button by gently pushing the stylus down into the recessed hole until you feel a tiny click.
3. Replace the battery door as your device restarts.

After you perform a soft reset, your device restarts and returns you to the main Phone screen.

Perform a System Reset

A *system reset* is a step more serious than a soft reset because it immediately restarts your device without necessarily closing applications safely. A system reset is also different from a soft reset in that it restarts your device without loading any system extras, which means you get a bare-bones restart that allows you to potentially uninstall malicious applications. In this way, you can think of a system reset as being similar to rebooting in safe mode on a Windows PC. If you need to perform a system reset, keep in mind that you always want to perform a soft reset following the system reset so that you finish with a normal (full) restart. To perform a system reset, follow these steps:

1. Press the battery door release button on the back of your device, and slide the battery door downward to remove it.
2. Press and hold the **Up** button on the five-way navigator. While holding down the **Up** button, gently press the **Reset** button on the back of the device with the stylus.
3. Continue to hold the **Up** button until the circular Palm Powered logo appears onscreen, and then release the button.
4. Replace the battery door as your device restarts.
5. Solve the problem that required the system reset, and then perform a soft reset.

Understand that the purpose of performing a system reset is to solve a problem that can't be fixed with a soft reset, such as an application that has somehow entered an infinite loop and locked up your device. Whether or not you need to uninstall the offending application, it's important that you perform a soft reset at some point following a system reset. You won't be able to turn on the mobile radio until you do so, not to mention that a host of other important device features are disabled after a system reset.

Perform a Hard Reset

Read on with caution. Seriously, a *hard reset* is recommended only in the direst of circumstances or when you're getting rid of your device and want to erase all third-party applications and all data from your device, effectively restoring it to its factory state. Even though a hard reset is aggressive, if you've synchronized your device recently, you can restore data by synchronizing after performing a hard reset. A hard reset can be useful if you encounter a problem that can't be solved with a soft or system reset. And as I mentioned already, a hard reset is extremely valuable for wiping your device should you sell it or turn it in to your company at some point. To perform a hard reset, follow these steps:

1. Press the battery door release button on the back of your device, and slide the battery door downward to remove it.
2. Press and hold the **Power/End** button on the five-way navigator. While holding down the **Power/End** button, gently press the **Reset** button on the back of the device with the stylus.
3. Continue to hold the **Power/End** button until the circular Palm Powered logo appears onscreen, and then release the button.
4. A prompt appears asking whether you want to erase all the data on the device. Press the **Up** button to confirm that you want to continue with the hard reset.
5. A language screen might be displayed next, in which case you must select your language; this language should match the language you selected during the Palm Desktop software installation.
6. Replace the battery door as your device restarts.

After the hard reset, your device is completely clean, as though you just bought it and took it out of the box. Use the Palm Desktop software to reinstall applications and synchronize any data.

Preserve the Treo Battery

An important aspect of using any mobile device is learning how to manage battery power carefully. Treo devices are efficient, but their battery life depends a great deal on how you use them. In other words, the amount of device usage you get out of each battery charge has as much, if not more, to do with you as it does the device itself. So it's worth examining some strategies to help maximize battery life on your Treo.

First, the Treo battery is designed to provide about 6 hours of talk time when using the device as a mobile phone or about 300 hours of standby time if the phone is doing nothing more than waiting for calls. Using the device for other things can add to or take away from this usage range. For example, Bluetooth puts a significant drain on the battery, so it's worth considering whether you want to leave features such as Bluetooth turned on all the time.

The first step you can take toward maximizing the Treo battery is to charge it regularly. Unlike some older battery technologies, the lithium ion battery in your Treo performs better when topped off regularly, as opposed to letting it run down entirely before each charge. So charging your device every night is generally a good idea. You can also get into the habit of connecting it and allowing it to charge when you're at your desk. Because the Multi-connector used to synchronize your device includes a plug for the AC charger, you can combine charging the device and synchronizing it into a single step.

Although charging the battery regularly ensures that your battery has a good charge, it doesn't address the issue of making the charge last as long as possible. Following are some suggestions for squeezing the most out of each battery charge:

- Use wireless features only when necessary. All the device features that require turning on the wireless radio put a significant drain on the battery. This includes the Phone, Messaging, Blazer Web browser, and VersaMail applications. Keep in mind that you can work in some of these applications offline to preserve the battery.
- Bluetooth is another wireless feature that takes a toll on the battery. If you use Bluetooth, consider turning it on and off as needed, as opposed to leaving it turned on all the time. As an example, if you use Bluetooth with a headset, you could leave Bluetooth on during business hours and then turn it off after work when you receive fewer calls. Chapter 11, "Communicating Wirelessly with Bluetooth," explores the Bluetooth feature of your Treo in detail.
- The screen is another fairly big power hog, and its capability to drain the battery depends largely on how bright it is. So you can save some battery consumption by adjusting the screen brightness down to a dimmer level. This is particularly useful if you're using your Treo in a dimly lit area that doesn't require as much backlighting to see the screen. Chapter 3, "Customizing and Personalizing Your Treo," shows you how to adjust the screen brightness in the "Adjust the Brightness and Screen Settings" section.

> **NOTE** Obviously, I'm not suggesting that you don't use the phone feature on your Treo. It's just important to understand that the wireless radio puts a big hit on the battery charge, so if you're in a situation where you can live without the phone, by all means turn the wireless radio off and save the battery. Remember, to turn the wireless radio on and off, just hold down the red Power/End button.

- Another screen-related power-saving feature is the Auto-off setting, which controls how long your device must sit dormant before turning off the screen. You can decrease this setting down to as low as 30 seconds, although I tend to find it annoying if my device turns off after such a short time. On the other hand, if you're trying to squeeze every bit of power out of your battery, it's not a bad idea. You learn how to alter this setting in Chapter 3 in the "Tweak the Power Preferences" section.
- Although not on par with the wireless radio or Bluetooth radio in terms of battery consumption, the infrared port on your device requires power to be constantly available for receiving beamed data. If you don't receive beamed data via the infrared port often, you might consider turning it off. This topic is also covered in the "Tweak the Power Preferences" section of Chapter 3.
- You might not think about it, but the sound volume on the Treo has an impact on the battery, albeit somewhat small because most sounds play only briefly. However, music played in the RealPlayer application can certainly put a drain on the battery, especially if you listen to it with the device's speaker, as opposed to headphones. Consider turning the speaker volume down lower in general, and use headphones when listening to music to help conserve the battery. The RealPlayer application is covered in Chapter 13, "Listening to Digital Music."

Even if you follow all these tips to help prolong each charge of your battery, you might be in a situation, such as traveling, where you have absolutely no access to an AC charger to recharge your Treo. Don't despair because some interesting options that don't involve a fixed power source are available. I'm referring to Treo chargers that use traditional batteries to charge your Treo battery. For example, a company called Seido makes an Emergency Charger for the Treo 650 that allows you to use a 9-volt battery to charge your device. A single 9-volt battery can charge your Treo battery to 40% to 50% of its full capacity, which isn't bad. This affordable charger is available from the TreoCentral Store at http://store.treocentral.com/—just search for "seido emergency charger."

> **NOTE**
> Palm also makes a car charger for charging your Treo device using the cigarette lighter plug found in most automobiles. This charger is available online at Palm's Palm Store at http://store.palmone.com/.

If you prefer using AA batteries instead of 9-volt batteries to charge your Treo, you might want to look into BoxWave's Battery Adapter, which uses four AA batteries to charge your device. This adaptor also requires BoxWave's miniSync cable, which is a dual charger/synchronization cable. BoxWave also makes an interesting product called VersaCharger that serves as both an AC charger and a car charger in one compact unit. To learn more about BoxWave's charging products for the Treo 650, visit the Treo 650 section of its website at http://www.boxwave.com/products/easyfinder/products-for-palmone-treo-650_442.htm.

Summary

I hope you're now feeling a bit more at home with your Treo. This chapter has covered a great deal of territory in introducing you to most of the Treo's key applications and features. In reality, however, you only scratched the surface. The remainder of the book dials in much more closely on each aspect of Treo devices and guides you through getting the most out of them. The next chapter is particularly interesting because it focuses on customizing and personalizing your device to suit your own style and mobile workflow.

3

Customizing and Personalizing Your Treo

Smartphones and handheld computers are unique among electronic devices, in that you typically carry them with you everywhere you go. Similar to a wallet or purse, the contents of a smartphone are different for every person. You'll probably want to personalize your Treo so that it reflects your own personal style and image. Or maybe you just want to personalize it to include your owner information in case it's lost and you want to make sure it can be returned to you. If style isn't a good enough reason for you to tweak settings on your Treo, maybe a more utilitarian approach will interest you—you can customize many features on your Treo to satisfy the way you work and use the device. This chapter shows you how to do all these things.

IN THIS CHAPTER

- Make the Most of Keyguard
- Secure Your Treo with a Password
- Set Owner Information
- Tweak the Power Preferences
- Adjust the Brightness and Screen Settings
- Select Wallpaper for the Phone
- Customize the Application Buttons
- Choose, Create, and Download Ring and Alert Tones
- Take Control of Your Treo's Volume
- A Few Other Interesting Treo Customizations

Make the Most of Keyguard

The debate continues to rage on about the benefits of flip phones versus nonflip phones, which leave the keys exposed. Flip phones have the enormous benefit of protecting keys from accidental key presses. Of course, the drawback is that you have to flip open the phone every time you want to use it. The problem is that often you'd like to quickly look at the screen without having to flip open the phone. I won't claim to have an answer to the flip versus nonflip debate, but Palm clearly took a side when it designed the Treo family of devices as nonflip devices.

Because Treo devices are nonflip, you have to consider protecting the keys from accidental key presses. Fortunately, the Treo includes a standard feature for solving this problem. I'm referring to Keyguard, which is a feature that locks out the keyboard whenever you turn off your device. Keyguard locks out not only the keys, but also the touchscreen. When Keyguard is turned on, only a certain key sequence unlocks the keyboard and touchscreen. More specifically, you have to

> **TIP**
> To lock the keyboard and touchscreen without turning off your Treo, press the Option key followed by the Power/End button.

> **NOTE**
> Speaking of locking the Treo keyboard, a few devices have been reported with keyboards that barely work. The culprit turned out to be a faulty P key that sticks and locks up the entire keyboard. If your keyboard ever stops working or works only intermittently, contact your wireless service provider and find out if you can get a replacement. In the meantime, try fiddling with the P key to see whether that solves the problem.

> **TIP**
> If you find yourself constantly having to unlock the keyboard because your device is turning off during brief periods of idle time, try setting the Auto-Keyguard option to turn on after a 5- or 30-second delay, instead of turning on immediately upon powering off.

press the Power/End button followed by the Center button to power on the device and unlock the keyboard and touchscreen.

Most Treo devices are configured at the factory to automatically turn on Keyguard when you power off your device or when it powers itself off after a period of sitting idle. This Auto-Keyguard feature is worth checking in case it isn't turned on for your device or you want to alter the way it works. To fine-tune the Auto-Keyguard feature, follow these steps:

1. Press the **Application** button to open the main application screen.
2. Press the **P** key to jump near the Prefs application, and then navigate with the five-way navigator to select the **Prefs** application.
3. Press the **Center** button to launch the Prefs application. The **Preferences** screen appears and displays several options for tweaking device settings.
4. Navigate to **Keyguard** on the Preferences screen under the General heading, and press the **Center** button to open the Keyguard Preferences screen, shown in Figure 3.1.
5. To activate the Auto-Keyguard feature, set the **Auto-Keyguard** option to something other than Disabled. The remaining options allow you to fine-tune locking the keyboard when you power off the device. If you want to avoid an automatic key lock when your device sits idle for a few seconds and automatically powers off, select **5 Seconds After Power Off** or **30 Seconds After Power Off**. Otherwise, set the option to **When Power Is Turned Off**.

You might have noticed a related setting in the Keyguard Preferences screen for controlling how and when the touchscreen is disabled. For example, you can set the touchscreen so that it's automatically disabled when a phone call comes in or when you're on a call. The idea behind these settings is to prevent you from accidentally answering a call by touching the screen and to prevent your face from accidentally being interpreted as a stylus tap if it brushes against the touchscreen during a call. Both settings can be useful if you find yourself accidentally hitting the touchscreen when managing phone calls. On the other hand, disabling the touchscreen while on a call prevents you from accessing onscreen buttons via the stylus, which can be a bit limiting if you like using the stylus.

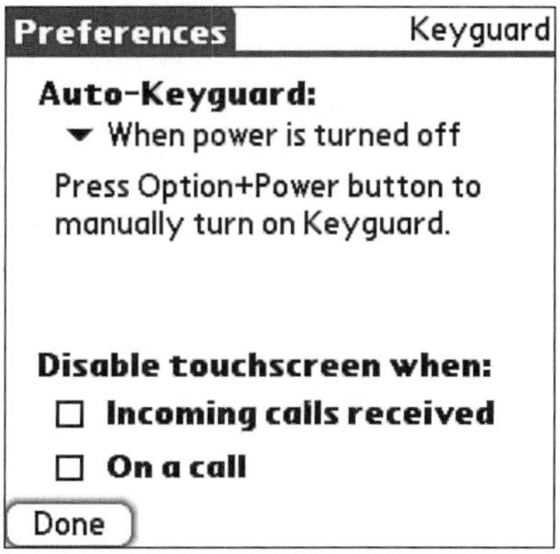

FIGURE 3.1

The Keyguard Preferences screen includes an option for setting the Auto-Keyguard feature.

If you enable Keyguard and you elect to lock the touchscreen when an incoming call arrives, the Phone/Send and Power/End buttons are still activated on an incoming call. In other words, Keyguard doesn't lock out the two phone buttons, which makes sense, given that you wouldn't want to have to unlock the keyboard to answer or ignore an incoming call.

If you'd like even more control over disabling keys on your Treo, you might consider using the third-party application TreoGuard, by geakware software. This application enables you to customize key locking, including the volume keys, which you might find handy. TreoGuard has other useful features, such as allowing you to automatically turn the wireless radio on and off at certain times of the day to conserve battery power. To learn more about TreoGuard, visit the geakware website at http://www.geakware.com/treoguard/.

> **TIP** Some people find that the backlight on the keyboard gets annoying and is an unnecessary drain on the battery. A handy little third-party application called KB LightsOff allows you to turn off the keyboard independently of the screen. To find out more about KB LightsOff, visit its website at http://www.lilapps.com/.

Secure Your Treo with a Password

Although the word "lock" was used quite a bit in the preceding section on the Treo keyboard, you don't lock the keyboard or touchscreen for security purposes. However, there *is* a way to lock your device for security purposes, and you should strongly consider taking advantage of this feature. I'm referring to a device password, which can be

> **NOTE**
>
> In addition to the keyboard/touchscreen lock and the password lock, your Treo recognizes one other type of lock. I'm referring to the phone lock, which allows you to lock out access to the wireless radio on your device. Chapter 7, "Using Your Treo as a Mobile Phone," explains exactly how to lock the phone part of your Treo.

used to prevent access to your device. The idea is that you create a password for your device and then lock the device; no one can use your device without entering the password.

Your Treo takes the password notion a bit further than most mobile devices by also allowing you to flag certain pieces of data as private, in which case the device password is required to view or edit the data. This is a useful way to separate the general security of device access from the specific security of data access. You can configure the security settings to completely hide private data until the password is entered or to just mask the data. The difference in these settings is subtle but important because private data doesn't even appear to exist until you enter the password.

Regardless of how far you want to take the private data security issue, I encourage you to at least experiment with using a password to secure your device against unwanted access. Here are the steps you need to follow to establish a device password:

1. Press the **Application** button to open the main application screen.
2. Press the **S** key to jump near the Security application, and then navigate with the five-way navigator to select the **Security** application.
3. Press the **Center** button to launch the Security application. The Security screen appears (see Figure 3.2) and displays a password option, an Auto Lock option, and a setting for determining how private records are displayed.

FIGURE 3.2

The Security screen includes options for establishing a device password and locking the device.

4. Tap the **Password** box to create a password for your device. The Password screen appears, prompting you to enter a password and a hint for remembering the password (see Figure 3.3).

FIGURE 3.3

The Password screen prompts you to enter a password and a hint to help you remember the password later.

5. Enter the password and hint, and then tap the **OK** button. A password verification screen appears and prompts you to enter the password again. Enter the password again and tap **OK** to finalize the password setting.

The password is now set, but it won't actually go into effect until you lock your device. In other words, your device must be locked explicitly to take advantage of password protection, unless you want to use the Auto Lock feature. Auto Lock enables you to set your device so that it locks itself automatically under certain circumstances, such as when the device is powered off, at a predetermined time, or after a predetermined amount of idle time. To set the Auto Lock feature for your Treo, follow these steps in the Security screen:

1. Tap the **Auto Lock Device** box to access the Auto Lock settings. Before you are shown the settings, you must enter the password for the device (see Figure 3.4). Tap the **OK** button after entering the password.

FIGURE 3.4

You must enter the device password before accessing Auto Lock settings.

TIP

I find that having to enter a password every time I turn my device on is a bit of overkill, yet I don't like having to remember to lock it. So I recommend setting the Auto Lock feature to activate after a certain amount of idle time or based on a certain time of day when you're typically finished using the device, such as 8:00 p.m. Keep in mind that the idle approach is generally safer than the time-of-day approach because your device will likely stay unlocked until the specific time of day rolls around.

2. After successfully entering the device password, the Lock Device screen appears with several options for the Auto Lock feature (see Figure 3.5). The different Auto Lock settings have to do with how and when you want your device to lock and require a password for re-entry. The default value of Never results in the device never auto-locking, and the On Power Off setting results in the device being locked every time it's turned off or powered off when idle. The next two options allow you to auto-lock your device based on time—either an exact time of day or an elapsed amount of time that the device sits idle. Any of these settings can work for you, but I find the After a Preset Delay setting to be my favorite; I set the delay to 30 minutes, as shown in Figure 3.5. After selecting your setting for the Auto Lock feature, tap the **OK** button to accept the change.

3. Back in the Security screen, if you'd like to test the device lock, tap the **Lock & Turn Off** button. A screen appears prompting you to confirm that you want to lock and turn off your device. Tap the **Off & Lock** button to proceed to lock your device and turn it off.

4. Now turn your device back on by pressing the **Power/End** button followed by the **Center** button if the keyboard is locked. You then see the System Lockout screen, which prompts you for the device password before allowing you into the device (see Figure 3.6). Enter the password and tap the **OK** button to access your Treo.

FIGURE 3.5

The Lock Device screen offers several approaches for auto-locking your device.

FIGURE 3.6

The System Lockout screen prevents device access unless you enter the device password.

Now that you've learned most of what the Security screen has to offer, I might as well tidy things up and finish telling you about the only remaining option. This option, called Current Privacy, enables you to specify how private data is displayed on your device. This private data, also known as *private records*, can be anything you want—you can flag any record on your device as being private. In doing so, you're saying that you want access to the data to be limited and require the device password to be entered to view or edit the data.

NOTE You might have noticed that most of the System Lockout screen is blank. Although the bottom area is reserved for the password entry field, the remainder of the screen shows the owner information for your device. Because you haven't entered this information yet, that area is likely blank. Entering this information is important should someone find your lost device and want to return it to you; remember, he or she won't be able to get into the device because it's locked! The next section, "Set Owner Information," shows you exactly how to set the owner information.

NOTE Entering the device password to access private records is independent of entering the password to unlock your device. In other words, you must enter the password to unlock the device and then enter it again to access private records. This feature is an added security precaution in case you unlock your device for someone to use but still don't want that person to be able to access private records.

The Current Privacy option has three possible values: Show Records, Mask Records, or Hide Records. With the Show Records setting, private records can be viewed but can't be edited until the device password is entered. The Mask Records setting results in the records being visible only in the sense that you know they exist; any content associated with the records is masked so that you can't see it. The last setting, Hide Records, results in private records being invisible until you change the security option to one of the other settings.

One interesting note about the Current Privacy option is that it applies to all the data on your device. In other words, you can't selectively mask private data for one application and hide private data for another. All data marked as private falls under the single setting you apply to the Current Privacy option. You learn more about flagging individual pieces of data as private when you explore individual applications in more detail. For example, in Chapter 5, "Managing Treo Contacts," you learn how to mark a contact as private.

Set Owner Information

Although entering owner information might not seem all that important right now, it's a critical step in personalizing your Treo. If you suffer the unfortunate fate of losing your coveted Treo, the owner information might be all that connects the device to you. Granted, you can always try the trick of calling your own smartphone, but even this might not work if you have set the device so that it automatically locks and prevents access. The simplest and safest way to help improve the odds of recovering a lost Treo is to enter your contact information so that it's displayed prominently when the device is locked. To set the owner information, follow these steps:

1. Press the **Application** button to open the main application screen.
2. Press the **P** key to jump near the Prefs application, and then navigate with the five-way navigator to select the **Prefs** application.
3. Press the **Center** button to launch the Prefs application. The Preferences screen appears and displays several options for tweaking device settings.
4. Navigate to **Owner** on the Preferences screen under the Personal heading, and press the **Center** button to open the owner preferences. You can use the Owner

Preferences screen to view and edit the owner information for your device. The owner information is likely empty on your device if you've never set it before.

5. You can enter as much or as little owner information as you'd like, but make sure to enter enough information for someone to be able to get in touch with you if he or she finds your device. Figure 3.7 shows an example of how you might enter owner information for your Treo. When you're finished entering the owner information, tap the **Done** button to confirm the changes.
6. Make sure to test the owner information and make sure it all fits on the screen when the device is locked. To do so, simply lock your device by opening the Security application and tapping the **Lock & Turn Off** button. You then have to tap **Off & Lock** to confirm the device lock. Now power on your device, and you should see the new owner information in the System Lockout screen (see Figure 3.8).

NOTE

If you have a password set for your device, you have to enter it to access the owner information. This is because the owner information is considered a private record and, therefore, is password-protected. To enter the password and access the owner information, tap the Unlock button in the Owner Preferences screen, enter the password, and then tap the OK button.

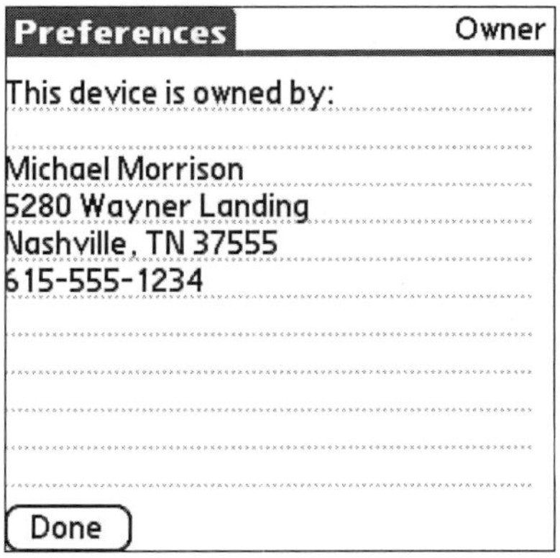

FIGURE 3.7

Use the Owner Preferences screen to enter owner information that can be used to contact you if your lost Treo is found.

With your owner information nailed down, you're ready to move on and customize the power settings for your Treo so that you can max out each battery charge.

FIGURE 3.8

The new owner information is displayed in the System Lockout screen so that someone who finds your lost device can get in touch with you.

Tweak the Power Preferences

Your Treo includes a couple of power settings for maximizing each battery charge based on how you use your device. More specifically, if you don't mind your device turning off after a short period of idle time, a change to the Auto-off feature can help save some battery charge. And if you don't use the infrared receiver much to receive beamed data, you might consider turning it off as well. You can always turn it on if someone needs to beam you something. Of course, if you beam information back and forth on a regular basis, it's well worth the small battery drain the infrared receiver incurs.

The power settings for your device are entirely personal, and you may or may not decide to deviate from the default settings. To tweak the power preferences, follow these steps:

1. Press the **Application** button to open the main application screen.
2. Press the **P** key to jump near the Prefs application, and then navigate with the five-way navigator to select the **Prefs** application.
3. Press the **Center** button to launch the Prefs application. The Preferences screen appears and displays several options for tweaking device settings.
4. Navigate to **Power** on the Preferences screen under the General heading, and press the **Center** button to open the power preferences. The Power Preferences screen provides access to a couple of power options for your device, as shown in Figure 3.9.

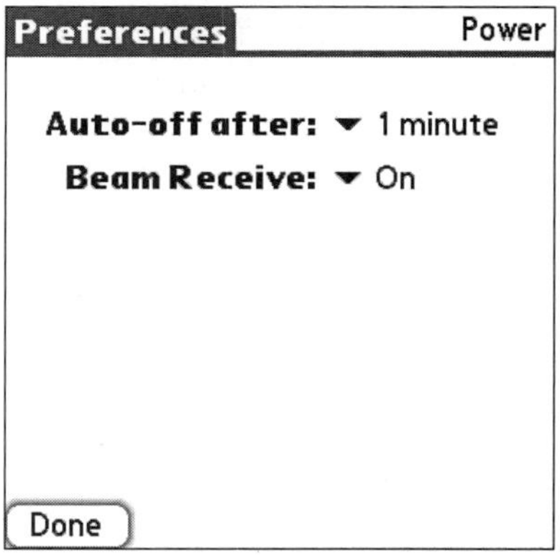

FIGURE 3.9

The Power Preferences screen presents two power settings that you can customize to help reduce the drain on the battery.

5. Because the screen eats up a fair amount of battery life, decreasing the Auto-off time can help reduce the toll on the battery. Options for the Auto-off After setting include 30 Seconds, 1 Minute, 2 Minutes, and 3 Minutes. If you don't find the 30 Seconds option too annoying, it's the optimal setting for maximizing battery life.
6. To turn off the infrared receiver, select **Off** for the Beam Receive setting. If you decide to make this change, just remember that you'll need to manually turn on the infrared receiver when you want to receive beamed information from someone. However, you can always beam information to someone, regardless of the Beam Receive setting.
7. Tap the **Done** button to accept the changes to the power preferences.

> **NOTE** The one scenario in which you might want to shy away from setting a short Auto-off time period is if you have your device set so that it automatically locks when it powers off. You'll probably grow tired of re-entering the device password every time the device shuts off after a 30-second idle period. In this case, you might want to extend the time period to 1, 2, or 3 minutes to help minimize unnecessary password entries.

You might be a little surprised that there aren't more power preferences to set for your device. However, keep in mind that a lot of power management boils down to using your Treo efficiently, as opposed to relying on the device to force you into certain habits. To brush up on some practical ways to take battery life management into your own hands, see "Preserve the Treo Battery" back in Chapter 2, "Performing the Treo Essentials."

Adjust the Brightness and Screen Settings

Another handy way to prolong the life of your Treo battery is to reduce the screen brightness. Of course, this option isn't always practical. Being able to use your device is certainly more important than trying to preserve its battery. However, if you're in a dimly lit place and can get away with a dimmer setting for the screen, by all means turn down the brightness and save some battery charge. To quickly adjust the screen brightness up or down, follow these steps:

1. Press the **Option** key followed by the **P** key. The Adjust Brightness screen appears, as shown in Figure 3.10.

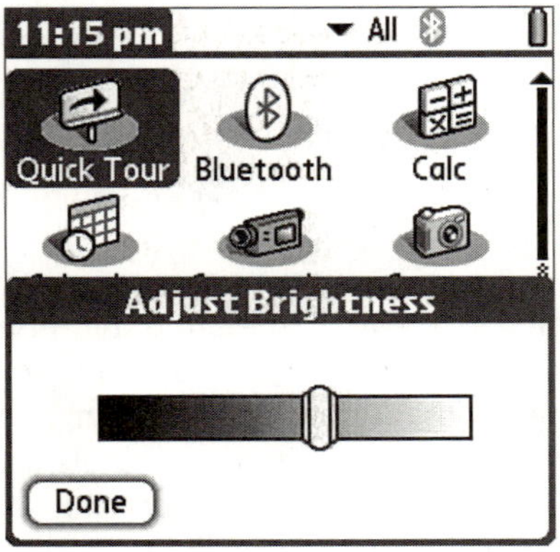

FIGURE 3.10

The Adjust Brightness screen displays a slider control for increasing and decreasing the screen brightness.

> **TIP** If you want to quickly dim the screen brightness and you don't need to choose an exact setting, try pressing the Option key followed by the Right Shift key. The screen dims to a preset brightness level. To restore the screen to the previous brightness level, just press the same key combination again.

2. To adjust the screen brightness, just press the **Left** and **Right** buttons on the five-way navigator.
3. Tap the **Done** button to accept the changes to the screen brightness.

The brightness level is not the only customization you can make to the Treo screen. Another important tweak you might want to consider is the default font size, which is changed on an application-by-application basis. More specifically, you can specify the font size for the Calendar, Contacts, Memos, Messaging, and Tasks applications. However, I have to admit that I use the phrase "font size" rather loosely. In reality, you get to choose between only two different sizes and whether you want the font displayed in a regular or bold typeface for each size. This results in a total of four font options for each application. As an example, follow these steps to change the font size for the Contacts applications:

1. Press the **Application** button to open the main application screen.
2. Press the **C** key to jump near the Contacts application, and then navigate with the five-way navigator to select the **Contacts** application.
3. Press the **Center** button to launch the Contacts application.
4. Press the **Menu** button and scroll over twice to the **Options** menu. The first menu item, Font, should already be selected, so press the **Center** button to issue the menu command and open the Select Font screen, shown in Figure 3.11.

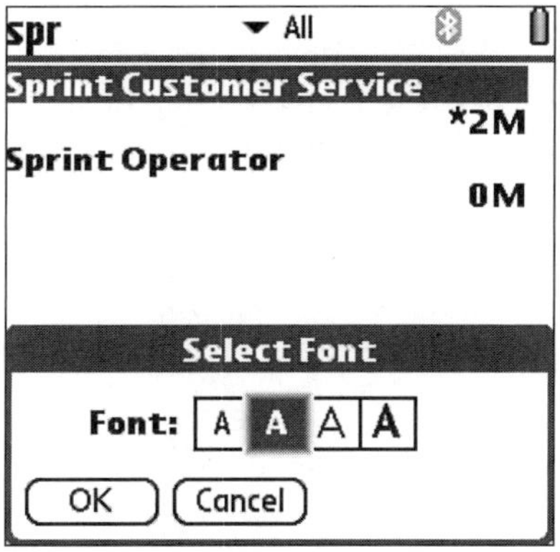

FIGURE 3.11

In the Select Font screen, you can change an application font to one of four different sizes and weights.

5. Press the **Up** button to highlight the currently selected font/weight. To select a different font/weight, press the **Left** or **Right** button until you reach the desired setting.
6. Tap the **OK** button to confirm the font change for the application.

Don't forget that font changes apply only to the application in which you made the change. To alter the font setting for other applications, you need to open each individual application and repeat the previous steps.

TIP While I'm on the subject of the Treo screen, it's worth pointing out that you might need to recalibrate the touchscreen at some point. You'll know if this is necessary because the stylus taps won't seem to accurately reflect where you touch the screen. The "Up and Running with Your Treo" section in Chapter 1, "Meet Your Treo," addressed touchscreen calibration when setting up your device initially, but you can initiate a touchscreen recalibration by tapping Touchscreen in the main Preferences screen.

The last screen customization worth looking into is more decorative than practical, yet it's still something you'll want to consider changing. I'm referring to the color theme for your Treo, which is much like the desktop themes that are popular on desktop and notebook computers. The Treo is a much simpler device than a full-size computer, however, and therefore the color theme setting for your device is simple. In fact, Treo themes are responsible only for establishing the colors used on your device, nothing more.

You select a theme by name with no regard for any other details, such as fonts or wallpaper. To change the color theme for your device, follow these steps:

1. Press the **Application** button to open the main application screen.
2. Press the **P** key to jump near the Prefs application, and then navigate with the five-way navigator to select the **Prefs** application.
3. Press the **Center** button to launch the Prefs application. The Preferences screen appears with several options for tweaking device settings.
4. Navigate to **Color Theme** on the Preferences screen under the Personal heading, and press the **Center** button to open the color theme preferences. The Color Theme Preferences screen consists of a long list containing theme names (see Figure 3.12).

FIGURE 3.12

You can to select a different color theme for your Treo from a large list of predefined themes in the Color Theme Preferences screen.

5. To select a new color theme, press the **Up** button followed by the **Center** button to activate the theme list, and then press the **Up** and **Down** buttons to move between themes. You can also just tap each theme with the stylus. The cool thing about the color theme list is that you see the change immediately when you select a theme in the list.
6. Tap the **Done** button to confirm the color theme change for your device.

TIP If you forget the initial theme setting and would like to restore the default color theme, just choose Original as the theme.

In case you're wondering, it is indeed possible to change the wallpaper for your device. However, wallpaper is unique on Treo devices because it applies only to the Phone application.

NOTE What I said about wallpaper applying only to the phone isn't entirely true. You can also set a background image for the Agenda view of the Calendar application. You learn how to set this background image in Chapter 6, "Getting Productive with the Calendar, Tasks, and Memos."

Select Wallpaper for the Phone

Although you don't dig deeply into the Phone application until Chapter 7, "Using Your Treo as a Mobile Phone," changing the phone's wallpaper is too cool of a personalization to wait until Chapter 7. Keep in mind that wallpaper applies only to the phone, and even then you have to specifically set the phone so that it displays the wallpaper instead of the familiar Dial Pad view. So before changing the wallpaper, follow these steps to change the phone's view so that it displays the current wallpaper instead of the Dial Pad:

1. Press the **Phone/Send** button to launch the Phone application.
2. Press the **Menu** button and scroll over twice to the **Options** menu. The first menu item, General Preferences, should already be selected, so press the **Center** button to issue the menu command and open the General Preferences screen.
3. Tap the **Show Dial Pad** setting and change it to **Show Wallpaper**. The small preview image next to the setting changes to show the wallpaper (see Figure 3.13).
4. Test the wallpaper by tapping the **OK** button and returning to the phone. The wallpaper should now appear instead of the Dial Pad. To view the Dial Pad, just start dialing a number by using the number keys on the keyboard.

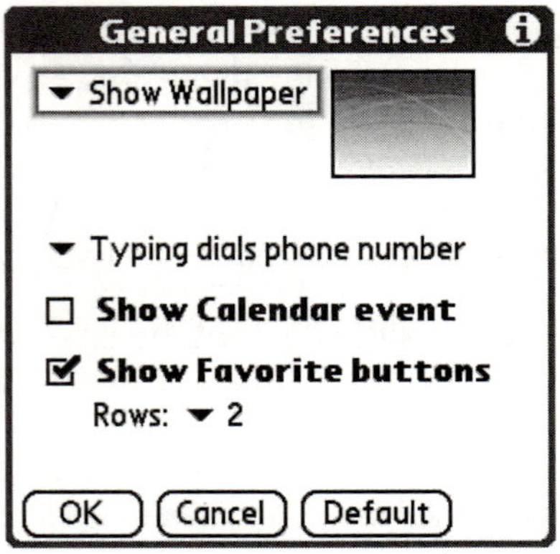

FIGURE 3.13

You use the General Preferences screen in the Phone application to change the phone's view to show wallpaper instead of the Dial Pad.

Changing the phone's view to show wallpaper instead of the Dial Pad is neat, but I'm sure what you really wanted is to change the wallpaper to an image of your own choosing. This change is much easier than you might have thought. In fact, if you have a picture you've taken recently with the Treo's digital camera, I encourage you to try using it as wallpaper. Just follow these steps:

1. In the Phone application, press the **Menu** button and scroll over twice to the **Options** menu. The first menu item, General Preferences, should already be selected, so press the **Center** button to issue the menu command and open the General Preferences screen.
2. Next to the Show Wallpaper setting is a small preview image of the wallpaper. Tap this image to select a new image for the wallpaper from the Select Picture screen, as shown in Figure 3.14.
3. After selecting a wallpaper image, test the wallpaper by tapping the **OK** button in the General Preferences screen and returning to the phone. The wallpaper now appears instead of the Dial Pad (see Figure 3.15). To view the Dial Pad, just start dialing a number by using the number keys on the keyboard.

FIGURE 3.14

The Select Picture screen shows all the pictures stored on your device and allows you to select one of them for wallpaper.

FIGURE 3.15

The new wallpaper now appears on the main phone screen.

The wallpaper for the phone isn't the only image customization you can make for your Treo, but it's certainly the easiest. You can also customize the splash screen that appears when you turn the mobile radio on and off on your device. However, this customization isn't as simple as tapping to select an image. In fact, you have to install new splash screens for the phone as you would install a full-blown application, using the Palm Desktop software. To find out more about how to install custom phone splash screens, visit the Dialer Patches page on the Shadowmite website at http://shadowmite.com/p-f.html.

Customize the Application Buttons

Just above the main keyboard on the Treo you'll find a series of application buttons that give you speedy access to some of the more commonly used standard applications. For example, the Calendar button launches the Calendar application, and the Messaging button launches the Messaging application. You can use the Option key with these buttons to launch additional applications. The "Launch Applications" section in Chapter 2, "Performing the Treo Essentials," detailed exactly which of these buttons and combinations launch which applications. However, you don't need to flip back to that chapter because you can access this information directly on your device. In fact, you can customize the application buttons to launch any application you want. To do so, follow these steps:

> **NOTE** Shadowmite is the user name for a Treo developer and hacker who has contributed quite a lot to the Treo community in the way of Treo tricks, hacks, and patches. The Shadowmite website (http://shadowmite.com/) contains lots of useful information and resources, but approach some of it with caution, as it involves tinkering with advanced device features.

> **TIP** If you find that you've made too many changes to the application buttons and you want to restore them to their default settings, just tap the Default button in the Buttons Preferences screen.

1. Press the **Application** button to open the main application screen.
2. Press the **P** key to jump near the Prefs application, and then navigate with the five-way navigator to select the **Prefs** application.
3. Press the **Center** button to launch the Prefs application. The Preferences screen opens with several options for tweaking device settings.
4. Navigate to **Buttons** on the Preferences screen under the Personal heading, and press the **Center** button to open the application button preferences. The Buttons Preferences screen consist of two columns of settings that show the applications launched by each button as well as the Option key plus the button (see Figure 3.16). In addition to customizing the buttons, you can use this screen to help remember the functions of application buttons.
5. To change an application button setting, just tap the application next to the button and change it to a different application. For example, I use the Contacts application much more than World Clock, so I set the Option + Calendar button combination to launch the Contacts application, as shown in Figure 3.17.
6. Tap the **Done** button to confirm the application button changes for your device.

You might have noticed a HotSync button in the Buttons Preferences screen in the lower-right corner. What could the HotSync synchronization application have to do with application button customization? The relationship between the HotSync application and the application buttons has to do with the HotSync button on the Treo Multi-connector cable used to connect your device to a desktop computer. The

Multi-connector has a button that acts as an application button for the HotSync application. Typically, you press this button to launch the HotSync application and synchronize your device, but you can change this button to launch any application you choose.

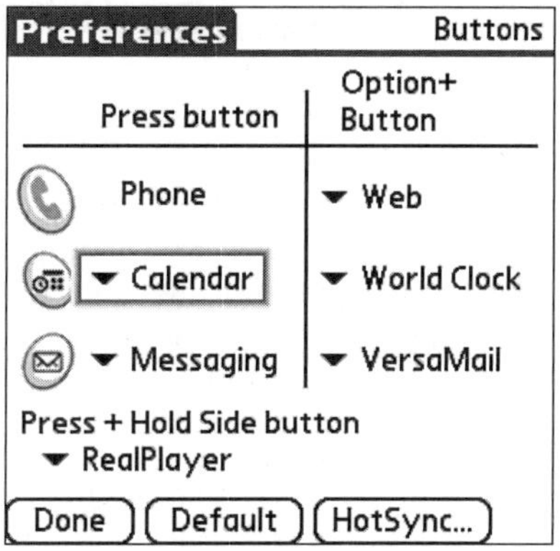

FIGURE 3.16

The Buttons Preferences screen enables you to customize the applications launched by the buttons.

FIGURE 3.17

The World Clock application is changed to the Contacts application for the Option + Calendar button combination.

I'm not entirely sure why you would want to change the application button on the Multi-connector cable to launch a different application, but the option is there if you choose to use it. To change the application this button launches, tap the HotSync button in the Buttons Preferences screen, and then change the Cable setting to an application of your choosing. After tapping OK to accept the change, you can press the HotSync button on the Multi-connector to launch the application.

Choose, Create, and Download Ring and Alert Tones

One of the first things most people want to tinker with when they get a new phone is the primary ring tone. And unfortunately, most of us have to suffer through this tinkering when that person's phone rings in public with a loud and obnoxious ring tone. I'm not a big fan of loud and annoying ring tones, even if they sound neat when you first set them, but that's another issue. By all means, feel free to set your Treo to ring however you want; just try not to forget that often you aren't the only person who has to listen to your phone ring.

Seeing as how Treo devices are much more than phones, the concept of a ring tone is much broader when it comes to your Treo. There are tones that apply to many events other than phone calls. In fact, the Phone, Calendar, and Messaging applications have their own distinct set of tones that can be customized to your liking. As an example, the Phone application supports the following different tones:

- *Known Caller*—An incoming call from someone listed as a contact or favorite
- *Unknown Caller*—An incoming call from someone not listed as a contact or favorite
- *Roaming*—An incoming call when you are roaming outside your home mobile network
- *Voicemail*—An incoming voicemail message arriving
- *Service*—A service warning, such as moving into or out of your home mobile network

As you can see, you can use these specific tones to determine the nature of an incoming call based solely on the ring tone. To customize these tones for the Phone application, follow these steps:

1. Press the **Phone/Send** button to launch the Phone application.
2. Press the **Menu** button and scroll over twice to the **Options** menu. Navigate down to the second menu item, **Sound Preferences**, and press the **Center** button to issue the menu command and view the Sound & Alerts Preferences screen.
3. Make sure **Phone** is selected as the current Application, and then tap the **Tones** box. The different tones supported by the Phone application are displayed, along with the specific settings for each tone (see Figure 3.18).

FIGURE 3.18

In the Sound & Alerts Preferences screen, you can access each tone supported by the Phone application.

4. To change one of the tones, tap the pick list to the right of the tone. For example, to change the Known Caller Tone setting from Alarm Flute to Blues 12 Bar, select **Blues 12 Bar** in the pick list (see Figure 3.19). You hear a preview of the ring tone when you select it, which makes it easier to choose a new tone. By the way, if you'd like to record your own custom voice tone, keep the Sound & Alerts Preferences screen open and continue reading!

Changing tones for applications is certainly useful, but using your own custom tones is more interesting. You can create your own voice tones or download musical tones online. You create a custom voice tone by recording it directly into your device's microphone. So, as an example, you could create a "tone" of your own voice saying "Incoming call!" To create your own custom voice tone, follow these steps:

1. From the Sound & Alerts Preferences screen in the Phone application, tap the **Manage** button in the lower-right corner. The Manage Sound screen appears, as shown in Figure 3.20, and displays a list of the tones available on your device.
2. You can tap any of the tones in the list to listen to them (or navigate through the list with the **Up** and **Down** buttons and press the **Center** button to listen to a tone).

NOTE

You might have noticed the No Sound option in the main tone list. This tone is completely silent, which seems strange until you consider that it can be used to quiet a certain event tone. Although you might find a need for the No Sound tone in the Phone, Calendar, or Messaging applications, it primarily comes into play for silencing the caller ID ring tone of a contact. You might not realize that you can assign unique ring tones to contacts. For example, maybe you have friends who call too much, and you don't want to be bothered with an audible ring every time they call. Just set their caller ID ring tone to No Sound, and the problem is solved. You learn how to set caller ID ring tones in the "Assign a Caller ID Ring Tone and Picture" section in Chapter 5, "Managing Treo Contacts."

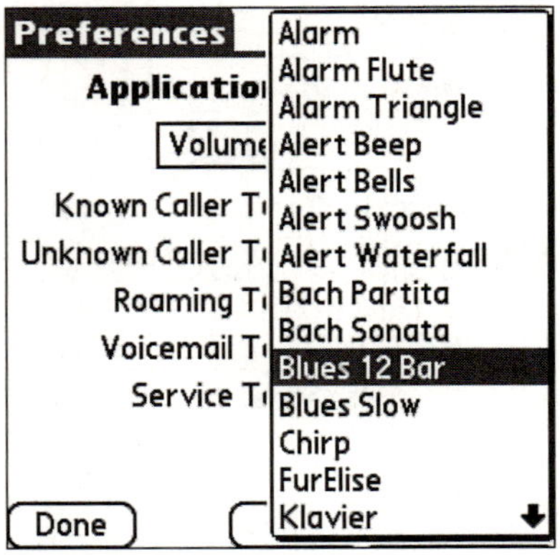

FIGURE 3.19

Changing a ring tone is as easy as selecting the new tone from a pick list.

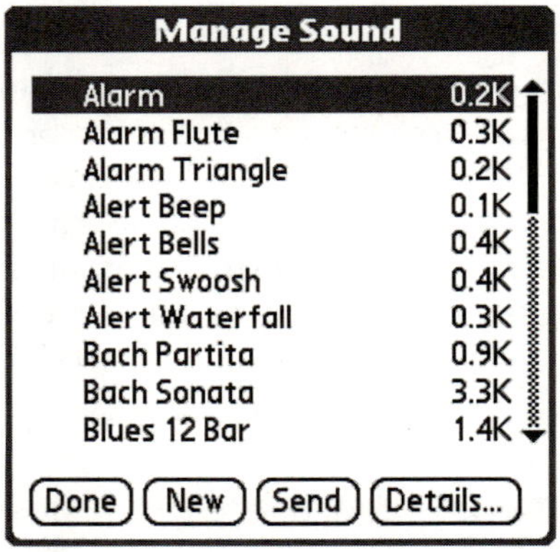

FIGURE 3.20

You can view all the tones on your device and record new tones in the Manage Sound screen.

3. To record a new tone, tap the **New** button. The Recorder screen appears, as shown in Figure 3.21.
4. You can see in the figure that the Recorder screen includes a huge Record button (red dot). Tap the button to begin recording a new sound. When you're finished, quickly tap the button again.

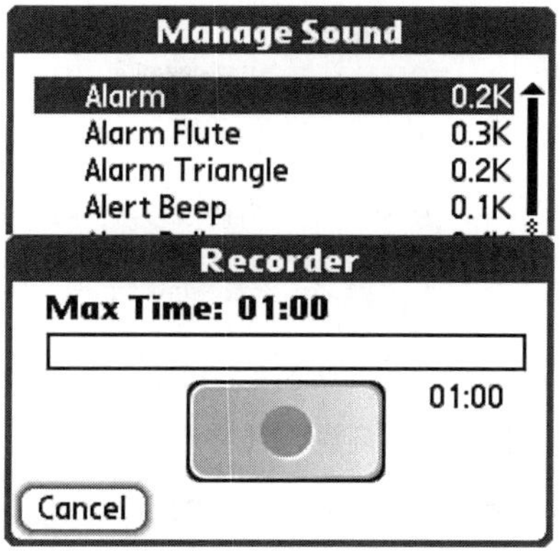

FIGURE 3.21

The Recorder screen allows you to record a digital sound that can be used as a device tone.

5. After you record a sound, the Recorder screen changes to the Playback screen. You then have a chance to play the sound, re-record the sound, cancel the recording, or accept the recorded sound. If you need to re-record the sound, tap the **Re-record** button and try again. When you're satisfied with the sound, tap the **Done** button to accept it.

6. The last step in creating a new tone (sound) is to give the tone a name, which you do in the Edit Tone screen shown in Figure 3.22. Make sure to enter a name that clearly describes the tone so that you can identify it in the pick list of tones. Tap the **OK** button to finish creating the tone and return to the Manage Sound screen.

Creating a voice tone is fun, but maybe you aren't terribly excited about listening to yourself every time your phone rings. If so, you might want to consider downloading additional musical tones to beef up the default tones already stored on your device. Fortunately, lots of websites offer MIDI tones for download. Unfortunately, many of those sites are extremely aggressive with pop-up ads and other adware annoyances. So I took the liberty of assembling a small list of MIDI tone websites as resources for finding and downloading new tones. Here goes:

NOTE

Voice tones are stored in a different format than normal Musical Instrument Digital Interface (MIDI) musical tones. For some reason, Palm limited caller ID ring tones to MIDI tones, so voice tones won't work as caller ID tones. To learn how to set caller ID ring tones to MIDI tones for specific contacts, please refer to Chapter 5, "Managing Treo Contacts."

TIP

The Edit Tone screen also includes a Delete button used to delete tones. If you need to delete a tone after creating it, select the tone in the Manage Sound screen, and tap the Details button to open the Edit Tone screen. Then tap the Delete button followed by Yes to confirm the deletion.

NOTE In addition to downloading MIDI tones from the Web, you can also email MIDI tones, beam them back and forth between other Palm devices, and transmit and receive them wirelessly via Bluetooth.

- *TreoBits Ring Tones*—http://portal.treobits.com/index.php?ind=ringtones
- *MIDI Database*—http://www.mididb.com/
- *MIDIRingTones*—http://www.midiringtones.com/
- *Mike Oldfield's Tubular.net Ring Tones*—http://tubular.net/midi/

FIGURE 3.22

The Edit Tone screen prompts you to specify the name of the newly created tone.

TIP Voice and MIDI tones aren't the only types of sounds you can use as event tones on your Treo. The Treo 650 also supports Wave sounds, which are popular on Windows systems. You can download a Wave file (.wav file extension) from a website or email it to your device and integrate it as a tone. Your Treo automatically recognizes a Wave file as a sound and prompts you to store it in the tones database when you download it.

By all means, feel free to carry on the search for MIDI tones further than this list, but you should be able to find a few useful tones from these sites. As an example, I found a tone for the theme song of the old television show *Quincy*, which is one of my favorites. After you find a tone, you can download it directly onto your device. In other words, you need to use your device to browse to the sites I just mentioned, and then tap the link for a specific MIDI tone to download it to your device. In reality, I recommend using your desktop or notebook PC to first browse the sites and listen to MIDI tones because it's usually much easier to get around the sites on a larger screen. However, after you isolate a tone, follow these steps to download it to your device:

1. Press the **Option** key followed by the **Phone/Send** button to launch the Blazer Web browser. If you've changed the Option + Phone/Send application button combination, you can also navigate to the Blazer Web application on the application screen and launch it.

2. Tap the address bar on the Blazer Web browser, and enter the address of the MIDI website containing a tone you'd like to download. Tap the **Go** button to open the site.

3. If necessary, navigate to the page on the site that contains the MIDI tone you want to download. Tap the link for the MIDI tone to begin downloading it. Figure 3.23 shows the `Quincy.mid` link highlighted as I begin downloading the file. Your device might display a warning prompt to make sure you want to download the file—tap **Yes** or **OK** to confirm that you want to proceed.

4. The Download screen prompts you to clarify where you want the file to be stored (see Figure 3.24). Make sure the Save To setting is set to **Sounds**, and tap the **Yes** button to continue.

> **TIP** If you have trouble finding the equals sign (=) when entering the TreoBits Ring Tone Web address, it's located as an alternate character for the pound symbol (#). So press Option+B to insert the pound symbol, and then press the Alt key to access a pick list containing the equals sign.

FIGURE 3.23

The first step in downloading a MIDI tone to your device is to follow the link to the MIDI file on a website.

5. Next, you are prompted for what you want to do after the download finishes—you can save the file or save and open the file. Go ahead and select **Save and Open** so that you can make sure the file is what you wanted (see Figure 3.25).

6. Before the new MIDI tone is actually stored to your device, you must give it a name. The Confirm Name screen prompts you to enter a name for the tone (see Figure 3.26). The tone may or may not have a meaningful name by default, so make sure to name it appropriately so that you can quickly identify it in the main tone list.

FIGURE 3.24

The Download screen prompts you to specify where to store the MIDI file on your device.

FIGURE 3.25

After downloading a MIDI file, you can specify that you'd like to both save and open the file.

7. The tone is downloaded, which should take only a few seconds because most MIDI files are relatively small. The MIDI tone download process ends with the Manage Sound screen, which shows the new tone as part of the main tone list. From here, you can tap the tone to listen to it, or tap **Details** to change its name or delete it. Tap the **Done** button to exit the Manage Sound screen. Keep in mind that you need to return to the sound preferences for each application you'd like to associate the tone with.

As I mentioned earlier, the Calendar and Messaging applications also support custom tones for events related to those specific applications. Chapters 6, "Getting Productive with the Calendar, Tasks, and Memos," and 9, "Communicating with Text and Multimedia Messages," explore these applications in more detail, including the application events with which you can associate tones.

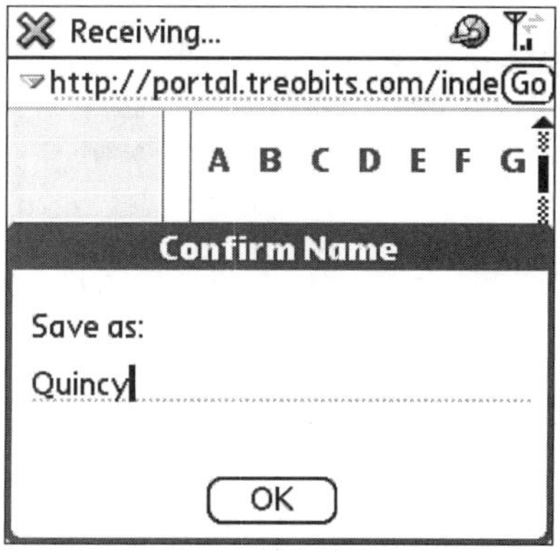

FIGURE 3.26

Naming a downloaded MIDI tone is the last step in making the tone ready for use on your device.

Take Control of Your Treo's Volume

You've probably already figured out that the Volume button on the left of your Treo provides a quick way to adjust the device volume. If you haven't used this button yet, try pressing the top and bottom of it to adjust the device volume up and down, as shown in Figure 3.27. Press the Side button just below the Volume button to accept the volume change.

Although the Volume button provides a relatively fine degree of control over your device's volume, another hardware control affects the volume more dramatically. I'm referring to the ringer switch located on the top of the device just to the right of the infrared port. The ringer switch acts as a mute button, allowing you to completely turn the device's speaker on and off with the flip of a switch. The ringer switch is an easy way to mute your Treo quickly when you're in a movie or some other place where a noisy device would be an unwelcome nuisance.

> **NOTE** I didn't cover the topic of creating your own MIDI tones because it's a fairly involved process that requires some knowledge of music. If you're interested in learning how to create MIDI music, you'll want to look into MIDI-composing software for your PC, such as Myriad's Melody Assistant. To learn more about Melody Assistant, visit the Myriad website at http://www.myriad-online.com/.

Although the Volume button and ringer switch are certainly useful, I don't consider them to be Treo customizations. There are some volume customizations that you can make, however. To do so, you must revisit the familiar Sound & Alerts Preferences screen from the previous section. Follow these steps to tweak the volume settings of your Treo:

1. Press the **Phone/Send** button to launch the Phone application.

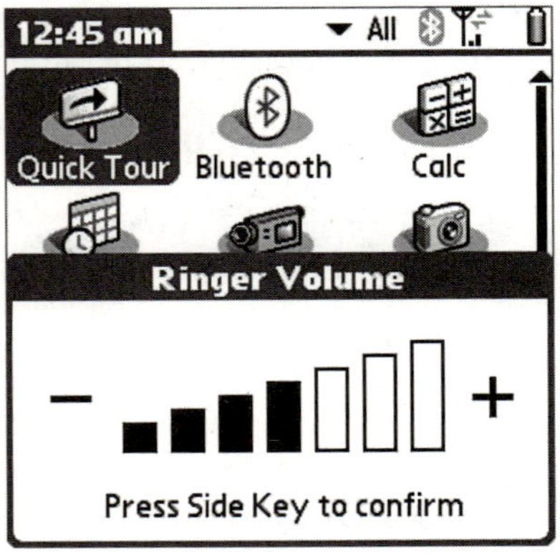

FIGURE 3.27

The Volume button on the left side of your Treo allows you to adjust the device volume quickly.

2. Press the **Menu** button and scroll over twice to the **Options** menu. Navigate down to the second menu item, **Sound Preferences**, and press the **Center** button to issue the menu command and view the Sound & Alerts Preferences screen.

3. Tap the **Application** option and select **General** from the pick list. The general sound preferences appear, as shown in Figure 3.28. These preferences distinguish between the overall system volume level and the volume level of games, with the idea being that you might not want game sounds to be as loud as normal system sounds.

4. If you'd like to change the relative volume level of the system and games, change the values for the **System Volume** and **Game Volume** settings. The possible values for these settings can range from Off (minimum volume) to 4 (maximum volume).

5. When you're finished with the general sound preferences, tap the **Application** option and select **Phone** as the application. Then make sure the **Volume** box is highlighted, not Tones. You'll notice a few settings related to the ringer switch, as

NOTE

The Calendar and Messaging applications have the same volume and vibration options as the Phone application. The values of these settings vary from application to application. To access the volume and vibration settings for the Calendar and Messaging applications, just select each application from the Application pick list in the Sound & Alerts Preferences screen.

shown in Figure 3.29. More specifically, the Sound Mode On settings go into effect when the ringer switch is on, and the Sound Mode Off settings apply when the switch is off (device muted). The main thing to note about these settings is how the default values result in the device vibrating only when the sound is off. You can easily change these settings so that the device never vibrates or always vibrates. You can also change the Alert Volume setting to raise or lower the volume of all alerts when the sound is on.

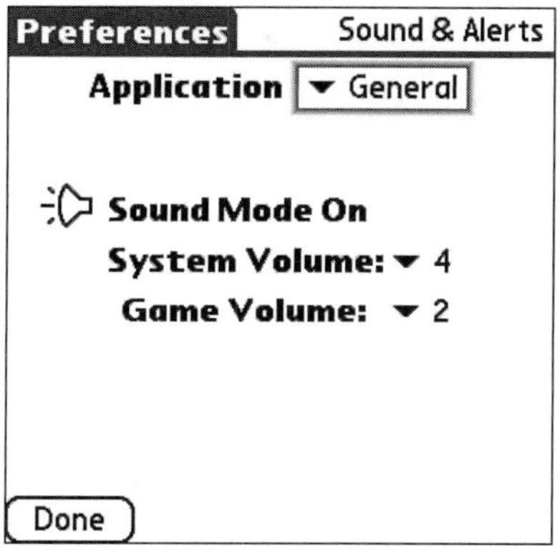

FIGURE 3.28

Using the general sound preferences, you can alter the volume level of the system separately from the volume level of games.

6. When you're finished altering the phone volume settings, tap the **Done** button to finish and exit the preferences.

You probably didn't realize you have so much flexibility in adjusting and customizing the volume for your Treo. The good news is that the default settings might work well for you if you aren't sure about making changes. You can always return to this discussion and change the settings later if you decide that you don't like the volume and vibration settings for a certain application.

NOTE The Calendar and Messaging applications have the same volume and vibration options as the Phone application. The values of these settings vary from application to application. To access the volume and vibration settings for the Calendar and Messaging applications, just select each application from the Application pick list in the Sound & Alerts Preferences screen.

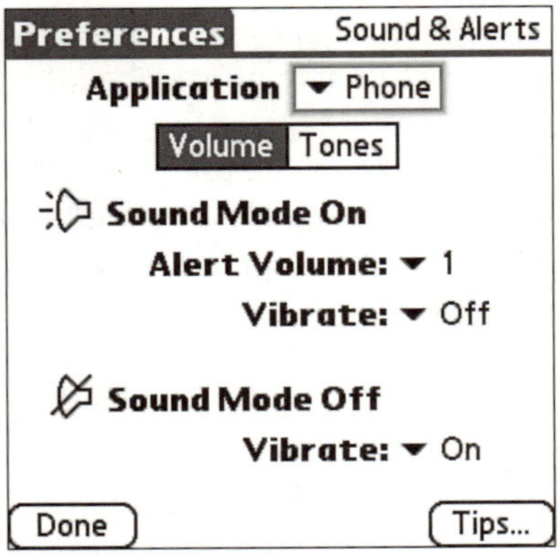

FIGURE 3.29

With the phone volume settings, you can specify the volume level and vibration settings for your device based on the ringer switch.

A Few Other Interesting Treo Customizations

You might be surprised that not every Treo customization has to do with tweaking software settings. In fact, I've run across a few interesting customizations that have nothing to do with the Treo OS or applications. These customizations involve making subtle changes to the physical device to help prolong its life or improve its usability.

You've probably already considered a case of some sort to help protect your Treo. Everyone has an opinion as to what kind of case is ideal for protecting a device yet allowing quick access. I won't attempt to weigh in on the case debate simply because it's such a personal choice. What I will weigh in on, however, is an issue somewhat related to cases: screen protectors.

A Treo *screen protector* is a thin clear film that you apply over the surface of your device's screen to help prevent scratches and, in some cases, eliminate glare. You have a few different options for Treo screen protectors, such as a transparency sheet that you cut to fit or a commercial screen protector with an antiglare coating. If you're the kind of person who enjoys tinkering and solving your own problems, you might want to try a nonadhesive transparency sheet before spending the money on a commercial screen protector. If you decide to consider a commercial screen protector, following are some options to consider:

- *TreoCentral Screen Protector*—http://store.treocentral.com/content/accessories/15-43—28.htm
- *Martin Fields Screen Protector*—http://www.overlayplus.com/

- *BoxWave ClearTouch Anti-Glare*—
http://www.boxwave.com/products/cleartouch/cleartouch-screen-protector-palmone-treo-650_442.htm

All these screen protector options will likely serve you well in terms of extending the life of your Treo's touchscreen and helping keep it clean.

Another interesting customization I heard mentioned by a Treo user involves the pesky little plug that connects the AC charger into the Multi-connector cable (or directly into your device). The plug on the AC charger is very small and square, making it difficult to tell which way it should be oriented when plugging it into the Multi-connector or your device. A little raised arrow on one side of the plug identifies the side of the plug that should face upward. The customization involves placing a small dab of white correction fluid or light-colored paint on the arrow to make it more easily visible. This allows you to quickly determine the correct orientation of the plug without having to pull out your magnifying glass!

> **TIP** While you're at it, the paint dab idea isn't bad to use on USB plugs as well. Few of my USB cable ends are easy to read in terms of quickly figuring out which side should be facing up.

Summary

Although you might certainly find settings and features for your Treo that you continue to refine and change over time, this chapter gives you a head start toward making your device suit you better. Whether it's fine-tuning the Keyguard feature, locking down your device with a password, or customizing the application buttons to fit your work style, you found out in this chapter that the Treo can be molded to meet each person's unique needs. You continue fine-tuning your device throughout the remainder of the book as you explore various Treo applications in more detail.

Part II of this book, "Managing Personal Information with Your Treo," focuses on desktop synchronization and managing contacts, events, alarms, tasks, and memos.

Managing Personal Information with Your Treo

Part II

Synchronizing with Your Desktop Computer

Admittedly, synchronizing your Treo device with a desktop computer sounds like a simple topic. However, several subtle issues come up when you start delving into synchronization. What I'm getting at is that this chapter is fairly hefty, so I'll just forgo any additional pleasantries and allow you to get started!

IN THIS CHAPTER

- Understand the Treo-to-PC Connection
- Synchronize with Microsoft Outlook
- Use the Palm Desktop Application
- Fine-Tune HotSync Manager
- Install and Remove Applications
- View Application Information
- Categorize Applications
- Add a Memory Card
- Back Up Your Treo to a Memory Card
- Manage Files

Understand the Treo-to-PC Connection

Unlike some handheld devices, which are packed full of desktop features in the hopes that some users might forgo a notebook computer for a handheld, Treo devices aren't intended to replace a traditional computer. Treo devices are designed for phone and data services that work together with your desktop or notebook computer to provide features that are truly useful in mobile scenarios. It just isn't realistic to think that a device with a mobile phone footprint can possibly play the role of a full-blown computer. I mention this fact because it helps explain why the connection between your Treo and your desktop computer is so important.

You have a few options when it comes to connecting your Treo to your desktop or notebook PC, but more than likely you'll start out using the multi-connector cable that came with your device. This cable connects your device to a USB port on your computer and includes a HotSync button directly on the connector. It's also possible to connect with a computer via Infrared, Bluetooth, or even Wi-Fi if you add a Wi-Fi expansion card (available from Palm). However, I'd like to focus on the trusty USB connection for now because it's the simplest way to connect your Treo to your computer.

You must have the Palm Desktop software installed on your computer to connect your device and exchange information. You have the option of synchronizing data solely through the

Palm Desktop software or through a combination of the Palm Desktop software and Microsoft Outlook. If you use Outlook as your personal information manager (PIM), you'll likely want to synchronize with it. The Palm Desktop software installation prompts you to specify how you plan to synchronize.

You learn more about the difference between synchronizing with the Palm Desktop software and Microsoft Outlook in a moment. For now, focus on the software components that make it possible to synchronize Treo data with your desktop computer.

What Is a Conduit?

One challenge in synchronizing data from one computer to another one is accounting for people wanting to add applications. It would be no good if you could synchronize data for only a handful of built-in applications and nothing else. To solve this problem, Palm established the concept of a *conduit*, which is a software component responsible for shuttling data back and forth between your Treo and your desktop computer. Each application that can be synchronized has its own conduit that governs how the application's data is synchronized.

> **NOTE** Some third-party application publishers offer conduits to support synchronization with desktop applications that aren't supported by default in the Palm Desktop software. For example, mNotes by CommonTime (http://www.commontime.com/) allows you to synchronize your Treo with Lotus Notes.

A conduit is a piece of desktop software, so it doesn't directly affect your device until it comes time to synchronize. The HotSync Manager, which is the desktop application that actually carries out the synchronization process, manages and oversees conduits. Fortunately for you, conduits are largely invisible from the end user's perspective. When you download and install a new application, the conduit for the application is automatically installed so that you can synchronize the application.

Even though conduits are more or less invisible to you under normal circumstances, it's important to understand what they are because you will inevitably encounter references to them. If nothing else, you might want to fine-tune synchronization settings for an application, in which case you might have to deal with the application's conduit. In most cases, however, conduits cruise along doing their job without you even knowing they are there.

The Palm Desktop Software and Outlook

The Palm Desktop software actually consists of several desktop applications that make it possible to synchronize your Treo with your desktop computer. You will use some and possibly all of these applications to synchronize applications and data on a regular basis. Following are the management and synchronization applications included in the Palm Desktop software:

- HotSync Manager
- Palm Desktop
- palmOne Quick Install

HotSync Manager is the application that is actually responsible for carrying out the synchronization of applications and data between your device and your desktop computer. HotSync Manager must be running in the background on your desktop computer to respond to synchronization requests from your device. For this reason, HotSync Manager is configured to carry out the synchronization process through a certain connection, such as a USB connection, a network connection, or an Infrared connection. HotSync Manager operates independently of the Palm Desktop application, although it does prevent you from using Palm Desktop during synchronization.

> **NOTE** Keep in mind that you aren't required to synchronize your device with a desktop computer if you don't want to, in which case you can forgo using both Palm Desktop and Outlook. Just know that you won't be able to install applications to your device via your desktop computer, which is a significant limitation.

The Palm Desktop application acts in many ways like a PIM, such as Microsoft Outlook, except that it's geared toward managing data for your Treo device. If you don't use Microsoft Outlook or another popular PIM that you can get a conduit for, you'll likely want to use Palm Desktop. If you regularly use Microsoft Outlook, configuring the Palm Desktop software so that PIM data is synchronized with Outlook rather than the Palm Desktop application is a good idea. Although you must declare Palm Desktop or Outlook as your PIM synchronization choice when initially setting up the Palm Desktop software, you can change between the two later without too much trouble; see "Fine-Tune HotSync Manager" a little later in this chapter.

The palmOne Quick Install application is used to install applications and files to your Treo device from your desktop computer. The act of installing an application or file is technically part of the synchronization process that HotSync Manager carries out, but specifying which applications and files to install is delegated to palmOne Quick Install. In other words, if you want to install a new application from your desktop computer to your Treo, you must first specify that you want to install the application via palmOne Quick Install; double-clicking an application file on your desktop computer is all it takes to prep the application for installation with palmOne Quick Install. The application is then queued up and ready for installation, which doesn't actually occur until you synchronize your device with the desktop computer.

Synchronize with Microsoft Outlook

If you selected Microsoft Outlook as the synchronization option when installing the Palm Desktop software, any synchronization you perform automatically uses Outlook as the basis for PIM data on your desktop computer. Figure 4.1 shows HotSync Manager busy at work synchronizing Outlook PIM data.

FIGURE 4.1

HotSync Manager is busy synchronizing PIM data between my Treo and desktop PC.

> **NOTE** Even though you can't synchronize email between your Treo and a Macintosh computer, you can still configure email accounts on your Treo to send and receive email directly on your device.

Although the synchronization of PIM data between your device and Outlook is mostly automatic, there are a couple of caveats for synchronizing email. First, email synchronization is handled through a desktop software component called VersaMail, which unfortunately is available only for Windows computers. So if you have a Macintosh computer, you won't be able to synchronize email between your device and your Mac via VersaMail—you might want to look into a third-party Mac email synchronization solution. However, this isn't as big of a limitation as it might seem because you might not be truly synchronizing email, even if you're using a Windows computer.

> **NOTE** If you are a Mac user and would prefer sticking with Apple's Address Book and iCal applications for your PIM data, you should look into Apple's iSync synchronization application, which supports synchronizing your Treo with these Mac applications. To learn more about iSync, visit the iSync Web site at http://www.apple.com/isync/.

VersaMail is designed for synchronization with Microsoft Exchange Server, which is a common email server many businesses use. If your email is running on Exchange Server or Internet Message Access Protocol (IMAP), you will have true synchronization and your email on your device will match your email in Outlook on your desktop PC. This is because Exchange Server and IMAP email systems handle all email management directly on the server, allowing Outlook and VersaMail to simply check in and see what's new.

If you use some other email protocol that isn't running on Exchange Server or IMAP, such as the incredibly popular Post Office Protocol (POP)/Simple Mail Transfer Protocol (SMTP) email, things change dramatically. In this case, no synchronization takes place at all. Instead, VersaMail is simply using your desktop computer to establish a network connection and check your email account for new messages. In other words, VersaMail is checking your email with no regard for Outlook, and in this situation, it's entirely possible for Outlook and VersaMail to get out of sync. For example, when you read a message and delete it in Outlook, it's still sitting in your Inbox in VersaMail. Granted, it's handy to be able to check email with VersaMail even for POP/SMTP email, but it's a bit misleading for the Treo documentation to refer to the process as "synchronization."

The point to this discussion is that when you first synchronize your device and your desktop computer via Outlook, everything but email synchronizes. You must go into VersaMail and configure your email accounts to have your email synchronized to your device. Even then, the synchronization can take place only with Exchange Server or IMAP. Otherwise, you're configuring VersaMail to send and receive messages just like any other email client, and you must take care to keep Outlook and VersaMail synchronized manually. You learn a great deal more about how to set up email accounts for VersaMail in Chapter 8, "Staying in Touch with Email."

> **TIP** Because POP/SMTP email clients typically inform the email server to delete mail messages after they are retrieved, make sure that VersaMail checks messages but doesn't delete them from the server if you plan to use an account with both VersaMail and Outlook. Otherwise, VersaMail might "steal" messages from the server, preventing Outlook from ever seeing them. The default setting for VersaMail does not involve deleting messages off the server, which is good to keep unless you don't plan to use another client (Outlook) to access the email account. Check the preferences for VersaMail for more details on this setting.

Use the Palm Desktop Application

The Palm Desktop application serves as a desktop PIM for entering and managing data that's synchronized with your Treo. You can use Palm Desktop to create PIM records and then synchronize them with your device. Beyond basic PIM data, Palm Desktop also enables you to move media files back and forth between your device and desktop computer as well as launching the palmOne Quick Install application and accessing VersaMail accounts. Following are the default applications and data types you can manage with Palm Desktop:

- Calendar
- Contacts
- Tasks
- Memos
- Media
- Quick Install
- VersaMail

The first four applications are the standard PIM applications on your Treo that take care of managing calendar events and appointments, contacts, tasks, and memos. The Media support in Palm Desktop is what makes it possible to share pictures, videos, and music between your Treo and your desktop computer. Quick Install is simply a link to the palmOne Quick Install application for installing new applications onto your device. And finally, VersaMail allows you to create and manage email accounts for synchronization via VersaMail.

The next few sections explore these features of Palm Desktop in more detail. Keep in mind that the PIM applications on the Treo side of the equation are covered in more detail in upcoming chapters—the focus right now is on learning how to manage applications and data on the desktop side for synchronization.

Schedule Calendar Events

If you haven't already done so, launch the Palm Desktop application on your computer. Calendar is the first Treo application you see referenced in Palm Desktop, as is evident by its icon in the upper-left corner of the application window. If Calendar isn't already selected, click this icon. The remainder of the Palm Desktop window changes to the desktop calendar, as shown in Figure 4.2.

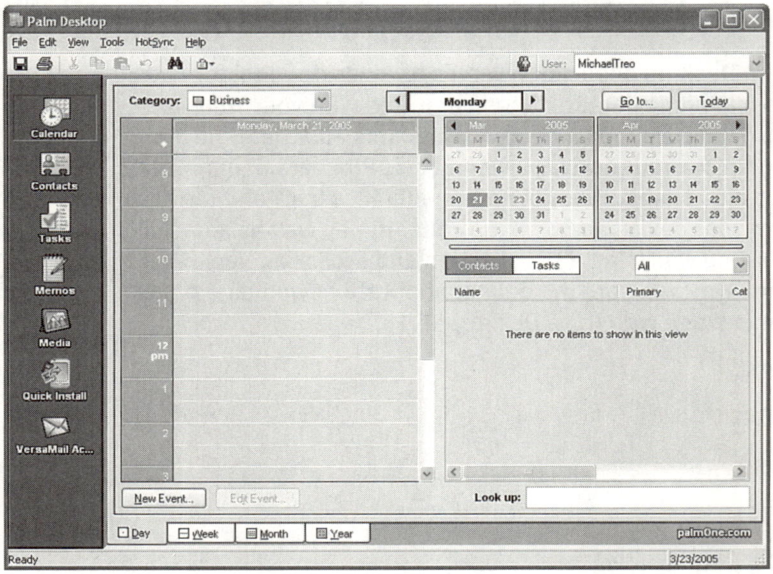

FIGURE 4.2

You can use the desktop calendar in the Palm Desktop application to create and manage calendar data for your device.

Because I'm starting out clean with no previous PIM data, the desktop calendar shows no events. You'll notice an event list on the left side of the desktop calendar and on the right, a small calendar view of the current month and the upcoming month. Below the small calendars is a list that can be changed to show either contacts or tasks. Along the top of the desktop calendar is the Category list for filtering events, along with a day navigation control and buttons for jumping to another day or returning to today. Along the bottom are tabs for selecting different views on the calendar, such as Day, Week, Month, and Year.

To create a new event in the desktop calendar, follow these steps:

1. Click the New Event button. The New Event dialog box, shown in Figure 4.3, opens.

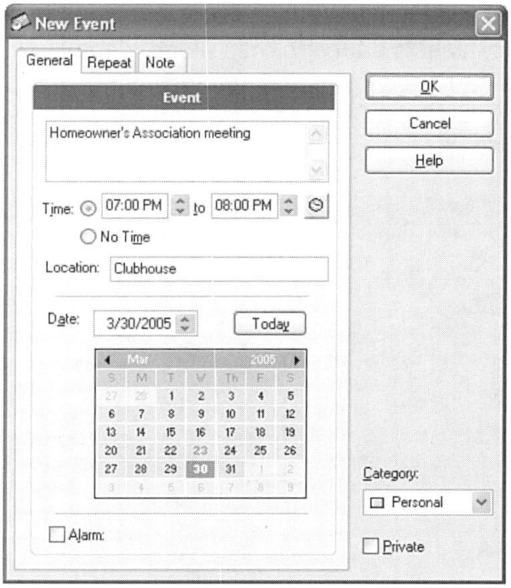

FIGURE 4.3

The New Event dialog box prompts you to enter the details for a new event.

2. Enter the event details, including a description, the start and end time, the location, the date, and whether you want an alarm to notify you of the event. You can also categorize the event by choosing a category in the Category pick list in the lower-right corner.
3. If you'd like to create an event that repeats, click the Repeat tab and specify the details of how the event repeats.
4. You can add a note to the event by clicking the Note tab and entering a text note that you'd like to associate with the event.
5. When you're finished editing the new event, click the OK button to create it. The new event is added to the calendar, but you won't see it in the event list unless you navigate to the day of the event. Click the day of the event on the small calendar in the main Palm Desktop window, and

> **TIP** To flag an event as private, click to enable the Private check box. Other types of PIM data can be flagged as private using the same technique.

> **TIP** To delete an event, select it in the event list and press the Delete key. Optionally, you can right-click the event and select Delete from the shortcut menu.

make sure you aren't filtering out the event's category in the Category pick list. The event now appears in the event list, as shown in Figure 4.4.

The next time you synchronize your device with the Palm Desktop, the new event is added to the Calendar application on your device. Similarly, events you created on your device appear in the desktop calendar in Palm Desktop. Any changes you make to events in the Palm Desktop application carry over to your device upon synchronization.

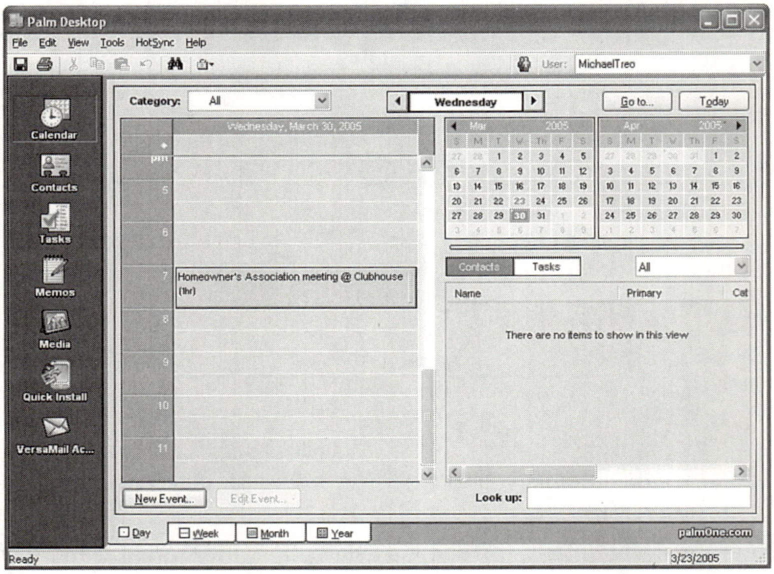

FIGURE 4.4

The newly created event is now visible in the desktop calendar of the Palm Desktop application.

Organize Contacts

The Contacts application appears just below Calendar in Palm Desktop. To activate the desktop contact manager, click its icon. The Palm Desktop window changes to the desktop contact manager, as shown in Figure 4.5.

The desktop contact manager looks somewhat similar to the desktop calendar, in that it has a Category list at the top and multiple tabs at the bottom. The List tab at the bottom is probably the most important tab because it enables you to view contacts in a compact list. The other tabs offer different approaches to viewing contacts, including a photo view that displays a picture of each contact.

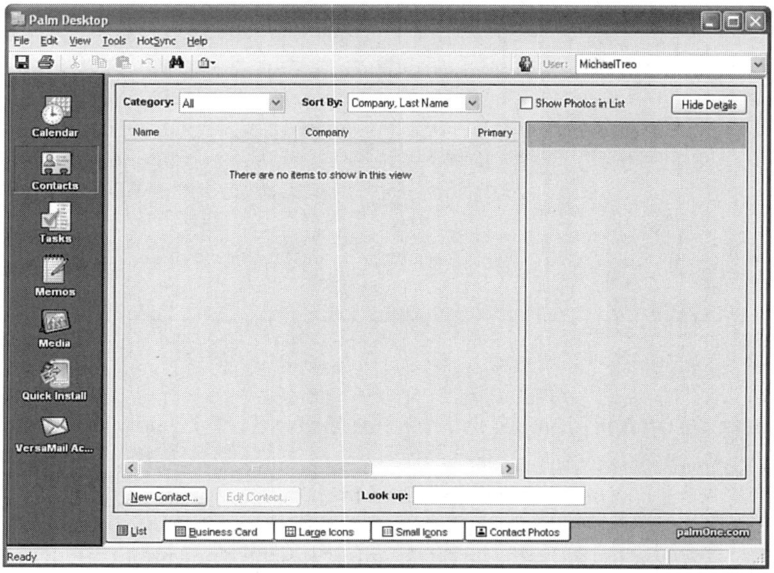

FIGURE 4.5

With the desktop contact manager in the Palm Desktop application, you can create and manage contacts for your device.

To create a new contact in the desktop contact manager, follow these steps:

1. Click the New Contact button. The New Contact dialog box, shown in Figure 4.6, opens.
2. Enter as many contact details as you want, including name, contact information, chat and Web addresses, mailing addresses, birthday, and even a contact photo. You can also categorize the contact by choosing a category in the Category pick list in the lower-right corner.
3. To add a note to the contact, click the Note tab and enter a text note you'd like to associate with the contact. For example, you might want to enter the names of the contact's spouse and children.
4. When you're finished editing the new contact, click the OK button to create it. The new contact is added to the desktop contact manager and appears in the contact list; make sure you aren't filtering out the contact's category in the Category pick list.

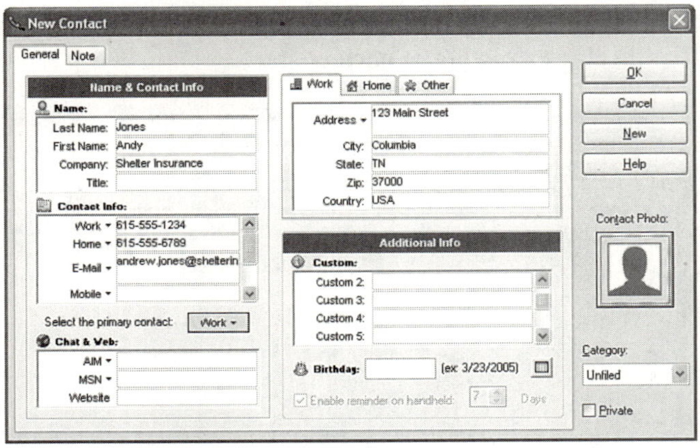

FIGURE 4.6

The New Contact dialog box prompts you to enter the details for a new contact.

> **TIP** The contact photo is used in the Phone application on your Treo to serve as a photo caller ID when the person calls you. The easiest way to set the contact photo is to edit the contact on your device and take a picture of the person with your Treo camera. In other words, you'll probably want to leave the contact photo blank when creating contacts in the desktop contact manager. However, if you happen to have pictures of contacts on your desktop computer, by all means set the contact photo. You can let the photos automatically resize to the smaller contact photo size (144×144), or you can manually resize them yourself to 144×144 by using an image editor before setting the photo in the contact.

The new contact is added to the contacts on your device the next time you synchronize. Future changes made to the contact on your device or in the Palm Desktop application are automatically updated on the other when you synchronize.

Work with Tasks

The Tasks application is linked through Palm Desktop via the desktop task manager, which is accessed by clicking the Tasks icon just below Contacts. The Palm Desktop window changes to the desktop task manager, shown in Figure 4.7.

The look and feel of the desktop task manager should be familiar now that you've seen the desktop calendar and contact manager. Similar category and sorting options appear along the top of the window, and a single tab appears at the bottom along with a couple of buttons.

To create a new task in the desktop task manager, follow these steps:

1. Click the New Task button. The New Task dialog box, shown in Figure 4.8, opens.
2. Enter the task details, including a description, the priority level (1 is the most urgent and 5 is the least urgent), the due date, and whether you want an alarm to notify you of the task's due date. You can also categorize the task by choosing a category in the Category pick list in the lower-right corner.

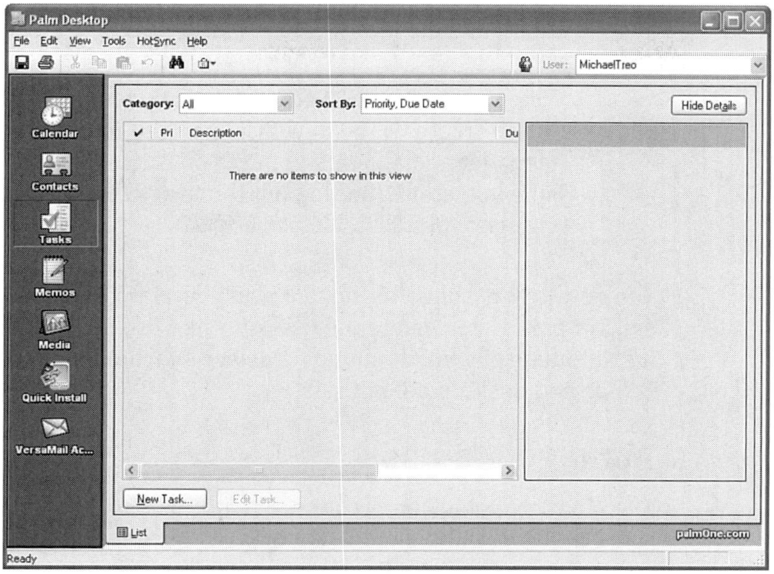

FIGURE 4.7

The desktop task manager in the Palm Desktop application allows you to create and manage tasks for your device.

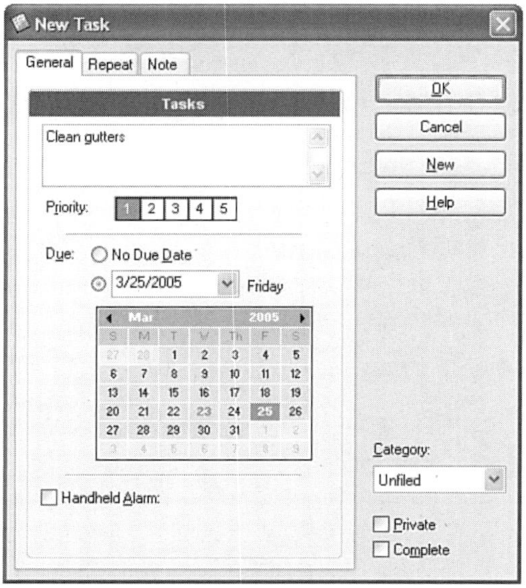

FIGURE 4.8

The New Task dialog box prompts you to enter the details for a new task.

TIP To delete a contact, select it in the contact list and press the Delete key. Optionally, you can right-click the contact and select Delete from the shortcut menu. This same approach works for deleting other types of PIM data in the Palm Desktop application.

TIP To flag a task as completed, click to enable the Complete check box.

3. To add a note to the task, click the Note tab and enter a text note that you'd like to associate with the task.

4. When you're finished editing the new task, click the **OK** button to create it. The new task is added to the desktop task manager and appears in the task list (see Figure 4.9); make sure you aren't filtering out the task's category in the Category pick list.

The new task is added to the tasks on your device the next time you synchronize. If you delete the task or otherwise modify it in the future, it's automatically updated upon a device synchronization to keep your device and desktop data in sync.

Manage Memos

The Memos application is connected to the Palm Desktop application through the desktop memo manager, which is accessed by clicking the Memos icon just below Tasks. The Palm Desktop window changes to the desktop memo manager, shown in Figure 4.10.

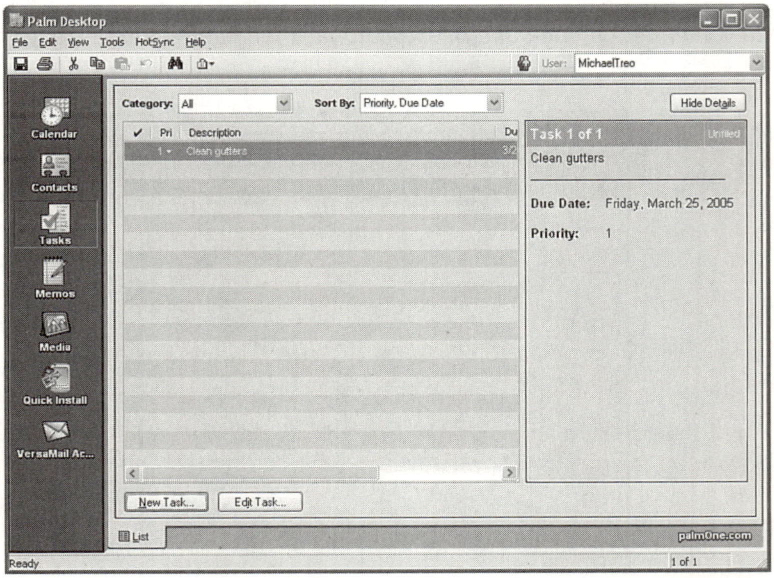

FIGURE 4.9

The newly created task is now visible in the desktop task manager of the Palm Desktop application.

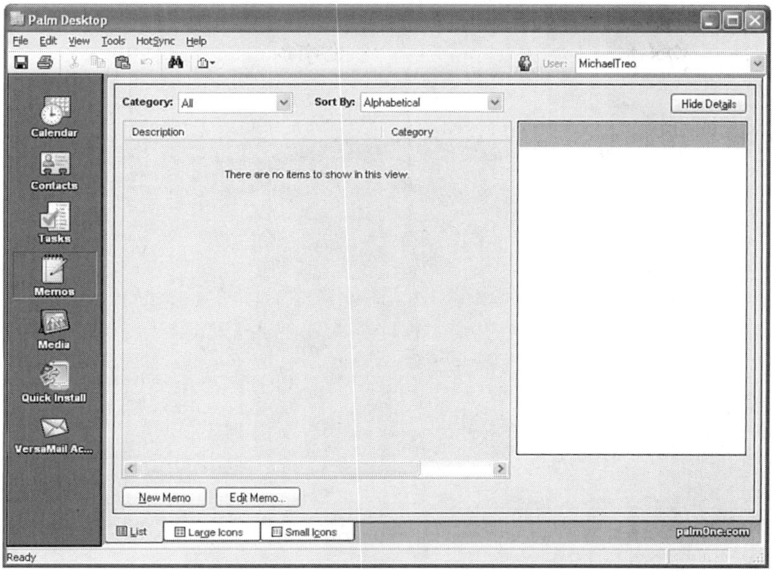

FIGURE 4.10

The desktop task manager in the Palm Desktop application enables you to take control of memos for your device.

I realize this discussion is starting to get a bit redundant, as the Palm Desktop PIM features are very similar. However, for the sake of completeness, I'll continue to wrap up this little desktop PIM tour by showing you a quick look at the desktop memo manager. The familiar category and sorting options appear along the top of the window, and a few tabs appear at the bottom along with a couple of buttons.

To create a new memo in the desktop memo manager, follow these steps:

1. Click the New Memo button. The Palm Desktop window changes to display a text entry field where you enter the memo (see Figure 4.11).
2. Enter the text of the memo in the text entry field. The memo is created and updated in the memo list as you enter the text. In other words, you don't do anything special to finish creating the memo.
3. If you would like to categorize the memo, click the Edit Memo button and select the category from the Category pick list that appears in the Edit Memo dialog box. Click the OK button to accept the changes.

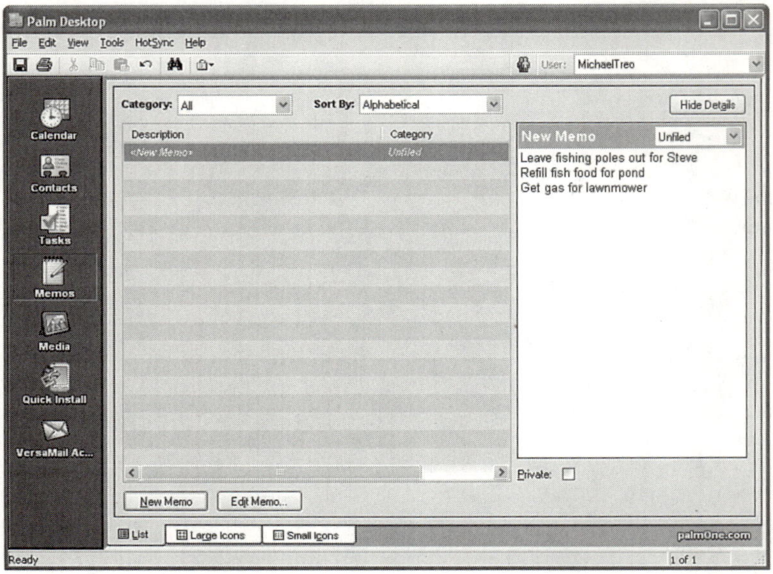

FIGURE 4.11

The Palm Desktop application window provides a text entry field for entering a new memo.

The new memo is added to the memos on your device the next time you synchronize. If you delete the memo or otherwise modify it later, it automatically updates upon a device synchronization to keep your device and desktop data in sync.

Import and Export Data

You might find it helpful at some point to import or export data with the Palm Desktop application. For example, if you've been using a PIM that Treo doesn't support, you might be able to export data from it and import into Palm Desktop to prevent having to re-enter everything manually. The import and export features in Palm Desktop are carried out based on a certain type of PIM data, such as events or contacts. More specifically, you select the PIM application in Palm Desktop, and then carry out an import or export operation on that application's data.

Data can be imported in several different formats that depend on the specific data being imported. First, you need to reference the application from which you are exporting data to see what formats are available. Then match up that data type with Palm Desktop to import the data. As an example, Palm Desktop accepts the following file types for importing contact data:

- Comma-separated text
- Tab-separated text
- Address archive
- vCard file

Understanding the details of these data formats isn't as important as finding a format that's compatible with the application from which you are exporting data. Comma- and tab-separated text are fairly common data formats used regularly to shuttle data from one database to another. For example, Microsoft Excel is capable of exporting an Excel spreadsheet as comma-separated text. I doubt you store your contacts in an Excel spreadsheet, but you get the idea.

> **TIP** Most PIM applications, such as Microsoft Outlook, include flexible export features that enable you to export PIM data in a variety of different formats, including those supported by Palm Desktop.

To import a data file into the Palm Desktop application, follow these steps:

1. Click to select the PIM application in Palm Desktop.
2. Click the File menu, followed by Import. The Import dialog box opens and prompts you to browse for the data file and select the import file type (see Figure 4.12). In this example, I've selected a comma-separated text file containing exported contact data.

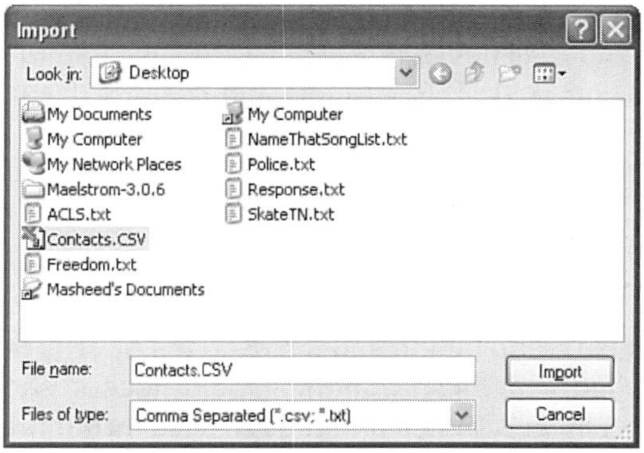

FIGURE 4.12

The Import dialog box in Palm Desktop prompts you to browse to the data file to be imported.

3. After selecting the file type and browsing to select the data file, click the Import button to import the data. The Specify Import Fields dialog box opens and prompts you to map Treo contact data fields with those in the import data file (see Figure 4.13).

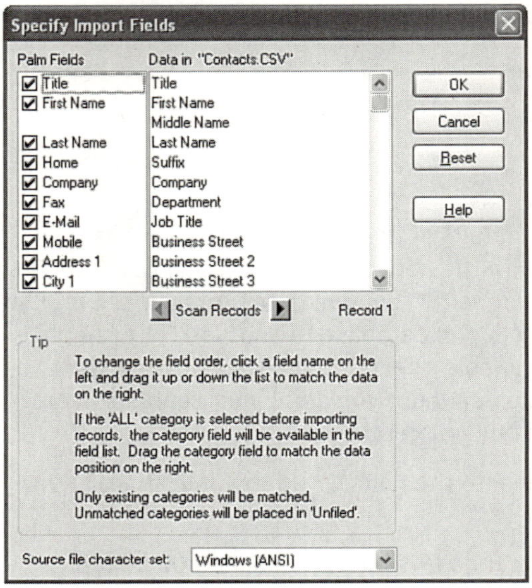

FIGURE 4.13

The Specify Import Fields dialog box prompts you to carefully map Treo data fields to fields in the data file to be imported.

4. The Specify Import Fields dialog box is extremely important because it determines exactly how data is imported. Palm Desktop doesn't magically know how to correlate data fields in the import file to those on your Treo, so you must help it along. Most of the mapping is obvious, but some fields might not map at all. For example, there is no field in Treo contacts for Suffix, which in Outlook stores the suffix (Mr., Mrs., and so forth) for a contact. You have to make sure this field isn't mapped to a Treo field; it simply isn't imported.

5. When you finish mapping the data fields in the Specify Import Fields dialog box, click the **OK** button to finish with the import process. The data is added to Palm Desktop, where you can then fine-tune it and synchronize it with your device.

You'll probably find that you're more likely to import PIM data than export data, but you still might need to export data on occasion. An advantage of Palm Desktop's export feature is that you can export individual records or all the records for a particular type of data.

Following are the steps required to export PIM data from Palm Desktop:

1. Click to select the PIM application in Palm Desktop.
2. If you want to export individual records, select those records in the data list in Palm Desktop.
3. Click the File menu, followed by Export. The Export As dialog box opens and prompts you to specify the export data file and file type (see Figure 4.14). Near the bottom of the dialog box, select All or Currently Selected Records to specify what records you want to export. In this example, I'm exporting a single task.
4. After specifying the export file and file type, click the **Export** button to export the data. The data is exported and stored in the file you specified.

> **TIP**
> If you're exporting a contact or contacts to an application that supports the vCard contact type, select Export vCard instead of Export from the File menu. Similarly, if you're exporting events and you want the output to be in the vCal format, select Export vCal instead of Export from the File menu.

FIGURE 4.14

The Export As dialog box in Palm Desktop prompts you to specify the export data file and records to be exported.

Importing and exporting data in the Palm Desktop application is the fastest way to migrate PIM data to and from your Treo if you don't have the luxury of synchronizing directly with Microsoft Outlook. I highly recommend considering at least importing data into Palm Desktop to ease the pain of initially setting up your device, assuming you have PIM data stored in an application capable of exporting in a suitable format.

Fine-Tune HotSync Manager

You learned earlier in the chapter that HotSync Manager is responsible for actually carrying out the synchronization process between your Treo and desktop computer. By default, HotSync Manager is installed to run in the background and constantly wait for a synchronization request from your device. You can change this default behavior if you don't like the idea of the HotSync Manager running all the time.

To specify exactly when HotSync Manager should run on a Windows computer, follow these steps:

1. Right-click the HotSync Manager icon in your desktop computer's taskbar, and click Setup on the menu. The Setup dialog box, shown in Figure 4.15, opens.

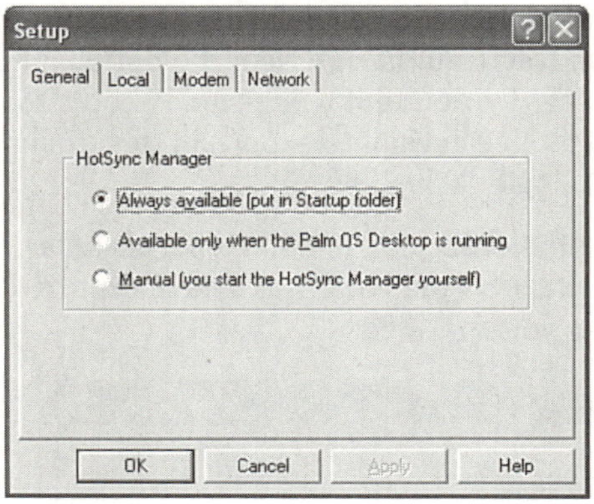

FIGURE 4.15

The Setup dialog box for HotSync Manager allows you to specify exactly how HotSync Manager should run.

2. The default tab, General, shows the options available for running HotSync Manager. These options include Always Available, Available Only When the Palm OS Desktop Is Running, and Manual. The first setting is the default and indicates that HotSync Manager runs all the time. The second option makes HotSync Manager available only when the Palm Desktop application is running. And the Manual setting means that you must manually launch HotSync Manager yourself to synchronize.

3. When you're satisfied with the setting, click the **OK** button to accept the change and close the Setup dialog box. You need to restart your computer if you're changing the setting to or from Always Available.

On a Macintosh computer, the steps for changing how HotSync Manager runs are similar:

1. Open the palmOne folder on your desktop computer, and then double-click the HotSync Manager icon.

2. The Enable HotSync Software at System Startup check box determines whether HotSync Manager runs all the time. If you'd prefer manually running HotSync Manager yourself, click to clear the check box.

3. Restart your computer.

Another important setting related to HotSync Manager has to do with how the synchronization process is carried out for each data type. More specifically, you can specify that your Treo or desktop computer completely overwrites the other when synchronizing. For example, if you've entered a few contacts in your Treo and later decide to import your entire contact list from Outlook via synchronization, you might choose to allow Outlook to overwrite your Treo contacts, as opposed to synchronizing and blending device and desktop contact data.

You change the synchronization details for PIM data according to each specific data type. In addition to settings for overwriting data in each direction, there is also an option to do nothing, which means you are no longer synchronizing a particular data type. It's worth pointing out that you usually leave the default setting of synchronizing in both directions for all data types, but this is one of those little tricks that might come in handy at some point.

To change the synchronization settings for a data type in HotSync Manager on a Windows computer, follow these steps:

1. If HotSync Manager isn't already running, launch it.
2. Right-click the HotSync Manager icon in the taskbar, and click Custom on the menu. The Custom dialog box opens, as shown in Figure 4.16.

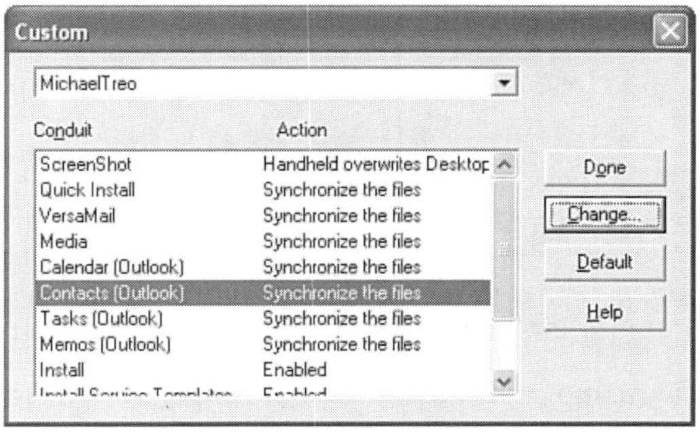

FIGURE 4.16

The Custom dialog box for HotSync Manager provides access to the different data types available for synchronization.

3. Make sure your user name is selected in the pick list at the top of the dialog box, and then click to select a data type in the Conduit list.
4. Click the Change button to edit the synchronization settings for the data type. What you're really doing is editing the conduit for the data type. Figure 4.17 shows the Change HotSync Action dialog box, where you can change the conduit's synchronization setting.

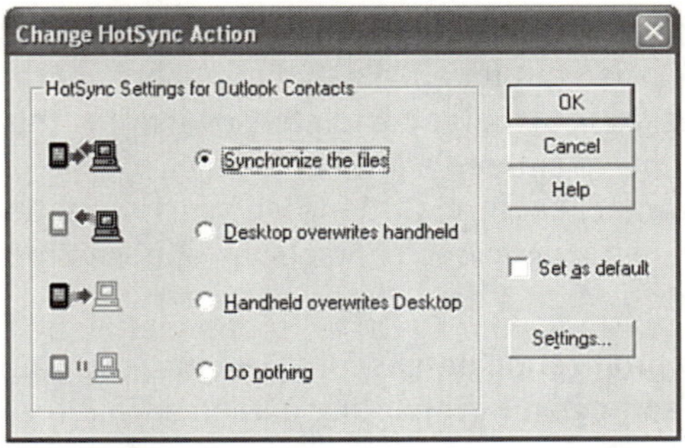

FIGURE 4.17

The Change HotSync Action dialog box for HotSync Manager enables you to change the synchronization settings for an individual data type.

5. Click to select the synchronization option you'd like to use for the conduit. For normal synchronization, click Synchronize the Files. To have the synchronization overwrite data in one direction or another, click Desktop Overwrites Handheld or Handheld Overwrites Desktop. And finally, to disable synchronization for the data type, click Do Nothing.
6. When you're satisfied with the synchronization settings, click the **OK** button to accept them and close the dialog box. Then click **Done** to close the Custom dialog box.

To access these settings on a Macintosh computer, you must go through the Palm Desktop application:

1. If HotSync Manager isn't already running, launch it. Then launch Palm Desktop.
2. Click the HotSync menu, followed by Conduit Settings. The Conduit Settings dialog box opens and displays information similar to the Windows Custom dialog box shown in Figure 4.16.
3. Make sure your user name is selected in the pick list at the top of the window, and then click to select a data type in the Conduit list.
4. Click the Conduit Settings button to edit the synchronization settings for the data type. What you're really doing is editing the conduit for the data type. The Change HotSync Action dialog box opens and allows you to change the conduit's synchronization setting.
5. Click to select the synchronization option you'd like to use for the conduit. For normal synchronization, click Synchronize the Files. To have the synchronization overwrite data in one direction or another, click Macintosh Overwrites Handheld

or Handheld Overwrites Macintosh. And finally, to disable synchronization for the data type, click Do Nothing.

6. When you're satisfied with the synchronization settings, click the **OK** button to accept them and close the dialog box. Then close the Conduit Settings dialog box.

If you ever decide to change your synchronization method from Microsoft Outlook to Palm Desktop, or vice versa, the HotSync Manager synchronization settings can be useful. In this case, you'll have up-to-date data on your device that you'll want to synchronize back to the new application; if so, it might make sense to change the synchronization settings temporarily so that your device overwrites the computer for the first synchronization. You can set it back to the normal synchronization setting from then on.

TIP Make sure to synchronize your device just before changing the synchronization method. Because your device is completely in sync with your desktop before switching desktop applications, you can successfully synchronize with the new application, and everything will be up to date.

To change the synchronization method from Outlook to Palm Desktop (or the reverse), you must insert the Palm Desktop software CD-ROM into your computer and allow the setup program to run as though you're going to reinstall the Palm Desktop software. However, at the beginning of the installation procedure, you'll see the Change Synchronization Method option. Choose this option and follow the instructions for changing the synchronization method. After the changeover is completed, you can then focus on synchronizing data from your device to the new application.

Install and Remove Applications

Your Treo is a device that can be improved quite a bit by installing additional software. Although your device comes with several useful applications that are built in and ready to use, tons of third-party Palm OS applications, such as business software, games, and much more, are available. And the thriving Palm development community regularly offers new and innovative Treo applications for download and purchase. You will likely find yourself installing and removing applications on a fairly regular basis.

Most Treo applications are packaged into files with a `.prc` extension. These files are ready to be installed to your device by using the palmOne Quick Install application. If you download an application online, the `.prc` file might be packaged into a compressed file with a `.zip` (Windows) or `.sit` (Macintosh) file extension. If so, you need to use a utility to uncompress the `.prc` file so that you can install it by using palmOne Quick Install.

NOTE You can also install Palm database files to your Treo. These files have an extension of .pdb.

Install from a Windows Computer

To install a Treo application from a Windows computer, follow these steps:

1. Navigate to the .prc file on your computer, and double-click it to launch the palmOne Quick Install application. Optionally, you can launch palmOne Quick Install and drag-and-drop the .prc file onto it. If palmOne Quick Install isn't already open, you're prompted to confirm the addition of the application for installation. Make sure your user name is selected in this confirmation window, and then click OK to confirm.
2. The palmOne Quick Install window opens (see Figure 4.18). The window is divided into two areas: one for the handheld memory and one for the memory card. You can drag an application back and forth between these areas if you'd prefer to install the application to the memory card instead of the main application memory.

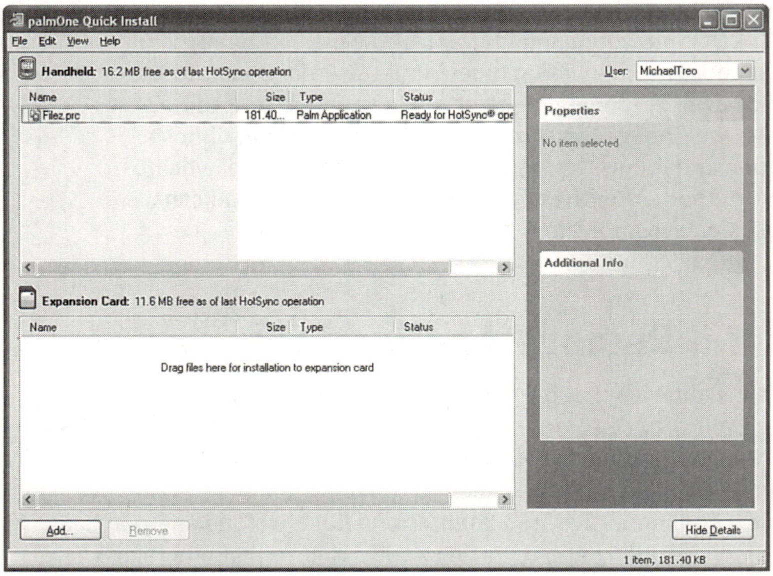

FIGURE 4.18

The palmOne Quick Install window shows a list of all the applications ready to be installed.

3. If you have additional files or applications to install, drag them onto the palmOne Quick Install window or click the Add button to add them.

4. Connect your Treo to the desktop computer with the multi-connector cable, and press the **HotSync** button to synchronize. The application is then installed on your device.

After the application is installed, you can begin using it on your device immediately.

Install from a Macintosh Computer

Installing an application to your Treo from a Macintosh computer is similar to installing from a Windows PC:

1. Launch the Palm Desktop application.
2. Click the HotSync menu, followed by Install Handheld Files. In the window that opens, make sure your user name is selected in the User Name pick list.
3. Click the Add To List button and locate the `.prc` file for the application you want to install. Click the Add File button to add the file for installation.
4. Connect your Treo to the desktop computer with the multi-connector cable, and press the HotSync button to synchronize. The application is then installed on your device.

The application is now installed on your device and ready to be run.

Install Directly from the Wireless Web

A more direct approach than installing an application from a desktop computer involves installing an application directly from the Web. For example, you can navigate to a website that has an application available for download, and then download and install it directly through the Blazer Web browser on your device. The drawback to this approach is that you can use it only to install applications that are available for download directly as `.prc` files. In other words, you can't download `.zip` or `.sit` files unless you also install a utility on your Treo to uncompress files. Even so, some applications are offered online as uncompressed `.prc` files.

Follow these steps to install an application directly onto your device from the Web:

1. Press the Option key followed by the Phone/Send button to launch the Blazer Web browser. You can also navigate to the Web application on the application screen and launch it if you've changed the Option + Phone/Send application button combination.
2. Tap the address bar on the Blazer Web browser, and enter the address of the website containing an application you'd like to download. Tap the Go button to open the site.

3. If necessary, navigate to the page containing the application you want to download. Tap the link for the application's .prc file to begin downloading it. Your device might display a warning prompt to make sure you want to download the file—tap Yes or OK to confirm that you want to proceed.

4. The Download screen prompts you to clarify where you want the file to be stored (see Figure 4.19). Make sure the Save To setting is set to Applications, and tap the Yes button to continue.

FIGURE 4.19

The Download screen prompts you to specify where the application file is to be stored on your device.

5. Next, you are prompted for what you want to do after the download finishes—you can save the file or save and open the file. Go ahead and select Save and Open so that you can make sure the file is what you wanted.

6. Before the new application is actually installed as an application to your device, you must accept it. The Transfer screen prompts you to accept the application. Tap Yes to accept the application.

7. The application is then installed, which should only take a few seconds because the file has already been downloaded.

The application is now installed and ready to be used on your device, just as though you had installed it from a desktop computer.

It's worth pointing out that there are other installation options similar to installing applications over the Web. I'm referring to Infrared, Bluetooth, and even email application installation. The only requirement to install an application is to receive a `.prc` file. You can send a `.prc` file through any of these mechanisms, which means you can install an application through them as well. It might seem strange thinking that you can beam an entire application to someone via Infrared, but it's entirely possible, even if it's a bit slow. Bluetooth makes more sense in terms of having a better transfer speed.

Remove an Application

No doubt you'll need to remove some applications from time to time, which is as easy as installing applications. You can also remove data files associated with applications. To remove an application or a data file from your device, follow these steps:

1. Press the Application button to open the main application screen.
2. Press the Menu button, navigate down to the Delete menu item, and press the Center button to issue the menu command. The Delete screen appears, showing a list of applications and data files that can be removed from the device (see Figure 4.20).
3. To remove an application or a data file from the phone's memory, scroll to select the item in the list, and then tap the Delete button. You are prompted to confirm the deletion—tap the Yes button to follow through and delete the application or data file.
4. You can use the Delete screen to delete applications and application data from the phone's memory or a memory card, if you have one installed. To switch between the two, tap the Delete From pick list and select the device. You learn more about memory cards later in this chapter in the "Add a Memory Card" section.
5. After removing an application from your device, it's a good idea to synchronize with your desktop computer so that the application is also removed from the Backup folder on your computer.

> **NOTE** The standard copy and delete features on your Treo are geared more toward applications and application data than they are to files. In other words, you can't use these features to access your Treo at the file level. For example, you can't copy or delete images or MP3 music files. If you want more of a true file manager, you have to resort to a third-party application, such as FileZ. You learn more about file management on your Treo a bit later in this chapter in the "Manage Files" section.

One problem with removing applications from your device is that they aren't automatically removed from your desktop computer's Backup folder. This folder, created as part of the synchronization process, contains all the applications that have been installed on your device, even those you have removed. Under normal circumstances, you never see these applications again, but if there's ever a synchronization problem, you might find that one of these old applications appears on your device, apparently from nowhere.

FIGURE 4.20

You use the Delete screen to remove applications and application data files from the phone memory or a memory card.

To make sure an application is removed permanently from your device, you might want to go in and manually remove it from the Backup folder on your desktop computer. Following are the default locations of the Backup folder on Windows and Macintosh computers:

- Windows—`C:\Program Files\palmOne\UserName`
- Macintosh—`/Mac HD/Applications/Palm/Users/UserName`

In both paths, the *UserName* part at the end should be replaced with the user name you entered for synchronization. If you browse to the Backup folder on your computer, look for files with extensions of `.prc` and `.pdb` for the application you want permanently removed. Delete these files and you never have to worry about the application reappearing on your device as a ghost.

View Application Information

At some point, you might need to get a handle on what applications are installed on your device and, more important, how much memory each one takes up. You might also need to check on the version of an application to see whether an upgrade is in order. Regardless of your motives, it can be helpful to view the applications on your device and relevant information about them. To view application information, follow these steps:

1. Press the Application button to open the main application screen.

2. Press the Menu button, navigate down the App menu to the item called Info, and press the Center button to issue the menu command and view the Info screen. The Info screen shows the amount of memory each application on your device takes up (see Figure 4.21). It's especially important to take note of the memory gauge near the top of the screen that shows how much of the main memory is currently occupied by applications.

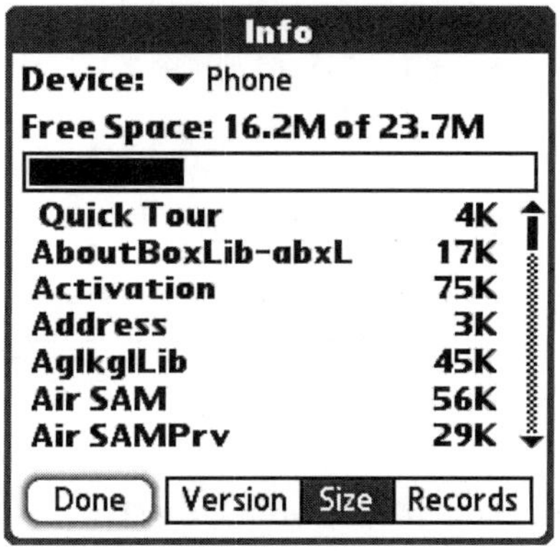

FIGURE 4.21

The Info screen lists all the applications installed on your device, along with how much memory each of them occupies.

3. Near the top of the Info screen is the Device pick list, which enables you to change the application list to show applications stored on a memory card (Memory Card) as opposed to the main device memory (Phone). If you have a memory card installed in your device, you can tap this pick list and select Memory Card to see the applications installed on it.

4. The Info screen also displays the version of every application on your device as well as the version of the Palm OS that your Treo uses. To access this information, just tap the Version box near the bottom of the screen. Figure 4.22 shows the same application list as Figure 4.21, except the application versions are now being displayed.

> **NOTE**
> The Info screen provides an easy way to assess how much memory you have available and see which applications take the biggest toll on precious device memory. Should you ever have to make hard decisions about trimming down the applications on your device, the Info screen can help you determine which applications to target for removal.

5. As you probably realize by now, many applications keep up with their data by storing records in memory. For example, each contact in the Contacts application takes up one record in memory. If you want to get a feel for how much data the applications on your device are managing, tap the Records box in the Info screen. The application list changes to show how many records are being used for each application. As an example,

Figure 4.23 reveals that the Contacts application on my device has 157 records. This means I have 157 contacts in the application.

FIGURE 4.22

In the Info screen, you can determine the version of any application as well as the version of the Palm OS on your device.

FIGURE 4.23

The Info screen also shows you how many data records each application is currently storing.

6. When you're finished analyzing the applications on your device, tap the Done button to close the Info screen and return to the main application screen.

Now that you have a feel for determining how much memory an application occupies and what version it is, it's time to revisit the application screen and learn how to tweak the application categories.

Categorize Applications

Applications on your Treo are organized into categories, and you can filter the main application screen to show only applications in a certain category. By default, the application screen shows all applications, as is indicated by the All category at the top of the screen in the category pick list; All isn't truly a category, it just represents all the categories combined. To select a specific category and filter the applications to only those in that category, tap the category pick list at the top of the screen and select a new category. You can also press the Application button repeatedly to cycle through categories that have applications assigned to them; empty categories are not shown when you press the Application button.

To make application categories even more useful, you can reorganize applications into different categories. Not only can you change the category for an application, but you can also create and delete categories. Follow these steps to change the category for an application:

1. Press the Application button to open the main application screen.
2. Press the Menu button, navigate down the App menu to the item called Category, and press the Center button to issue the menu command and view the Category screen. The Category screen shows the category for each application in a pick list next to the application name (see Figure 4.24).
3. To change the category for an application, tap the pick list next to the application name and select a new category from the list.
4. The last category in the application category pick list is Edit Categories, which is actually a command, not a category. This command allows you to create, delete, and rename categories. Select Edit Categories from the pick list to open the Edit Categories screen, shown in Figure 4.25.
5. To create a new application category, tap the New button in the Edit Categories screen. You are prompted to enter the new category name. You can also rename a category by selecting it in the category list and tapping the Rename button.

TIP

One way to reduce the toll that applications take on device memory is to install some applications on a memory card instead of the main device memory. Some core applications can't be moved from main memory, but many applications can be moved. You learn how to copy an application from the main memory to a memory card in "Add a Memory Card" later in this chapter.

NOTE

Although the number of records an application uses can certainly provide a clue about an application's memory usage, don't get too carried away when interpreting the record count. A single record in one application might be equivalent to 50 records in another application, so simply counting records isn't enough to determine whether an application is hogging too much memory. (That's what the Size box in the Info screen is for.) More than likely, if you have a bunch of records in an application, it means you use the application quite a bit, so parting with it would probably be difficult anyway.

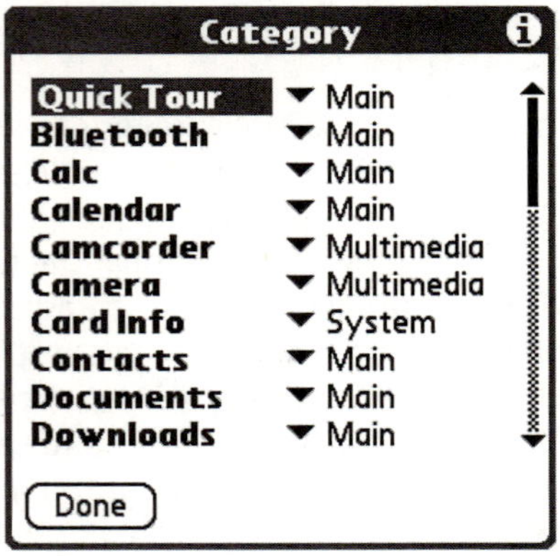

FIGURE 4.24

The Category screen shows the category for each application on your device.

FIGURE 4.25

You use the Edit Categories screen to create, delete, and rename application categories.

> **NOTE** The Unfiled category is an automatic category designation that applies to applications that have not been explicitly categorized.

6. To delete an application category, tap the Delete button. Keep in mind that any applications assigned to the deleted category are automatically moved to the Unfiled category.

7. Tap the **OK** button to finish editing categories. When you're finished tweaking application categories, tap the **Done** button to close the Category screen and return to the main application screen.

In addition to altering the organization of applications by category, you can change the view of applications on the main application screen. More specifically, you can choose a more compact list view as opposed to the default icon view. To change the application view, follow these steps:

1. Press the Application button to open the main application screen.
2. Press the Menu button, navigate over to the Options menu, and press the Center button to issue the initially selected menu command, Preferences. The Preferences screen appears, showing a couple of options for changing the manner in which applications are displayed (see Figure 4.26).

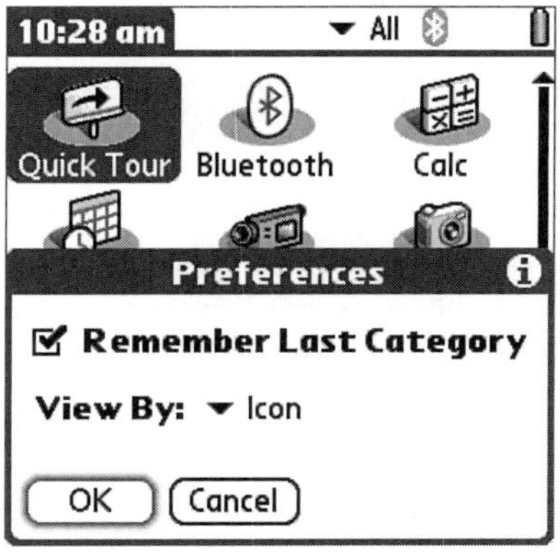

FIGURE 4.26

The Preferences screen allows you to remember the last category viewed and change the appearance of applications in the application screen.

3. The Remember Last Category setting determines whether the application screen remembers the last category viewed. If it's not selected, the application screen always starts with the All category selected when you press the Application button. When this check box is selected, the option remembers the last category you were viewing. Feel free to set this option to suit your personal preference.
4. The View By setting dictates how applications are displayed in the application screen. The default option, Icon, results in applications being displayed with large icons arranged in horizontal rows. If you want a more compact look, change the setting to List, which displays applications with small icons arranged in vertical columns (lists). Figure 4.27 shows the main application screen with the List view setting.

FIGURE 4.27

In List view, applications are displayed with small icons arranged vertically on the screen.

5. When you're finished changing application view preferences, tap the OK button to close the Preferences screen and return to the main application screen.

You might be perfectly happy with the default settings for the application view, but it's nice to know that you can change them if you want to customize the application screen's appearance.

Add a Memory Card

Next to processor speed, the most significant factor in the performance of any computer is memory. Given that every design decision on Treo devices must be carefully weighed against size, cost, weight, and ruggedness, it stands to reason that memory is the biggest Treo bottleneck. As pointed out in "Understanding the Treo 650 Memory System" in Chapter 1, "Meet Your Treo," the Treo 650 has an even more pronounced memory bottleneck than the Treo 600 because of its shift to the Non-Volatile File System (NVFS) memory system, which is considerably less efficient than its predecessor.

If you use desktop computers as a comparison for smartphones such as the Treo, it might seem strange that the Treo has such a memory issue. The problem has to do with the cost of compact memory, which is higher than the cost of desktop or even notebook memory and incredibly higher than the cost of hard drives. The comparison to hard drives is important because handheld devices, especially mobile phones, typically don't have hard drives, so they must rely on some form of memory as residual storage. When you look at trying to replace the storage space of a hard drive with memory, cost suddenly becomes a big problem.

Because compact RAM for handheld devices is relatively expensive, Palm decided to design the Treo with enough RAM to handle average usage, but not enough to handle extreme applications, such as storing a lot of photographs, MP3 music, or videos. For these types of applications, you must turn to memory cards for a solution. Treo devices support memory cards via an expansion card slot located along the top edge of the device. The expansion card slot on Treo devices supports the following types of memory and expansion cards:

- *SD*—Secure Digital, memory
- *MMC*—Multi Media Card, memory
- *SDIO*—Secure Digital I/O, peripherals

Secure Digital (SD) memory cards are small Flash memory storage devices based on Multi Media Card (MMC) memory cards. SD memory cards are slightly thicker than MMC cards, although both can be used in the Treo expansion card slot. SD cards are faster and have more memory storage capacity than MMC cards; the high end of SD cards is currently 2GB in storage, but this number will likely continue to rise. SD cards also have built-in security features for distributing licensed content, such as digital music and eBooks. If you have a fairly new digital camera, there's a good chance it uses an SD memory card, in which case you can probably share the card with your Treo.

Secure Digital I/O (SDIO) is a different animal altogether than SD and MMC. The SD in the name has to do with SDIO cards being the same size as SD cards and designed for use in the same expansion slots. However, SDIO cards are designed to add functionality, not memory, to handheld devices. For example, SDIO cards are currently available for adding Wi-Fi (802.11b) network connectivity, GPS (Global Positioning System) tracking, bar code scanning, and video graphics adapter (VGA) output for interfacing with a digital projector, to name a few applications. SDIO cards are incredibly powerful for extending your Treo's functionality, but they don't help in terms of extending your device's memory.

NOTE The latest innovation in SD memory cards is a built-in USB port, which means you can plug in your SD card directly to the USB port on your computer to access the data on the card.

Getting back to memory cards, in all likelihood you'll end up using an SD memory card to expand the memory of your Treo. The expansion card slot on your device initially includes a dummy card used to seal and protect the slot. If you later opt to not use an expansion card, placing the dummy card back in the slot is a good idea. However, you'll probably grow so dependent on the additional memory of a memory card that you'll never want to remove it!

When you first purchase a memory card, you might need to format it for use with your device. If you're reusing a memory card from another device, formatting it to clear off old data is not a bad idea. To format a memory card on your Treo, follow these steps:

> **NOTE** Treo 600 and 650 devices support memory cards up to 2GB in size. Larger memory cards can be used but you will only be able to access 2GB of their available memory.

1. Press the Application button to open the main application screen.
2. Press the C key to jump near the Card Info application, and then navigate with the five-way navigator to select the Card Info application.
3. Press the Center button to launch the Card Info application. The Card Info screen appears and displays information about the expansion card currently installed in your device (see Figure 4.28).

FIGURE 4.28

The Card Info screen displays information about the currently installed expansion card.

> **NOTE** The information shown on the Card Info screen is divided into directories of known data types. For example, Figure 4.28 reveals two directories that contain images and audio. If a third directory existed containing data in a format unknown to the Treo, it wouldn't be displayed.

4. To format the memory card, press the Menu button, navigate down the Card menu to the Format Card item, and press the Center button to issue the menu command and view the Format Card screen. The Format Card screen prompts you to confirm the formatting of the card. Keep in mind that any data currently stored on the card is wiped out when the card is formatted. Tap the OK button to continue with the card formatting.
5. Before the card formatting begins, you're prompted to enter the new name of the card. This name can be any text you want—if you use multiple memory cards, this is a great time to assign the card a name that uniquely identifies it. For example, you might use the name Music for a card that holds all your music; a card that holds other application data could be called Data. Tap the Format button to proceed with the formatting process.

You can transfer information to and from a memory card in several ways. The simplest approach is to use the Palm Desktop software, as was explained earlier in the "Install and Remove Applications" section. Although that section focused on installing applications to your device, the same approach applies to installing files to a memory card. In other words, you use a desktop application to specify which files to install, and they are installed on the memory card when you synchronize your device. As an example, Figure 4.29 shows the palmOne Quick Install application on a Windows PC. In the figure, you can see that three MP3 music files are scheduled for copying to the memory card on the next device synchronization.

> **TIP** If the formatting of the memory card fails, check to make sure the write-protect switch isn't turned on. Every SD card has a small write-protect switch that prevents the card from being written to or erased (formatted). Check the documentation for your specific memory card for details on its write-protect switch.

Copying files back and forth between the main memory and a memory card is also possible. For example, you can actually off-load applications from your device's main memory to a memory card, which can be useful for preserving precious main memory. Not every application is capable of being moved to a memory card, but it's a good idea to move applications that can be moved, especially if you don't swap expansion cards often. If you're constantly changing cards, you might get annoyed with losing access to the application when you remove the card.

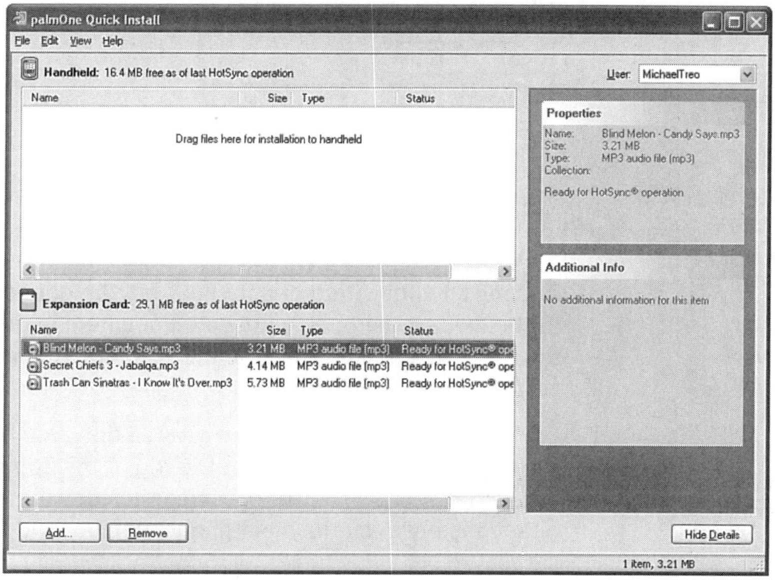

FIGURE 4.29

You can use the palmOne Quick Install desktop application to copy files from your desktop computer to a memory card in your Treo.

> **TIP** If you need to rename a memory card, as opposed to formatting it and erasing its contents, the Card menu for the Card Info application contains a Rename Card command that allows you to rename the memory card.

To copy an application or a data file from your device's main memory to the currently installed memory card, follow these steps:

1. Press the Application button to open the main application screen.
2. Press the Menu button, navigate down to the Copy menu item, and press the Center button to issue the menu command. The Copy screen appears, showing a list of applications and data files that can be copied from the phone to the memory card (see Figure 4.30).

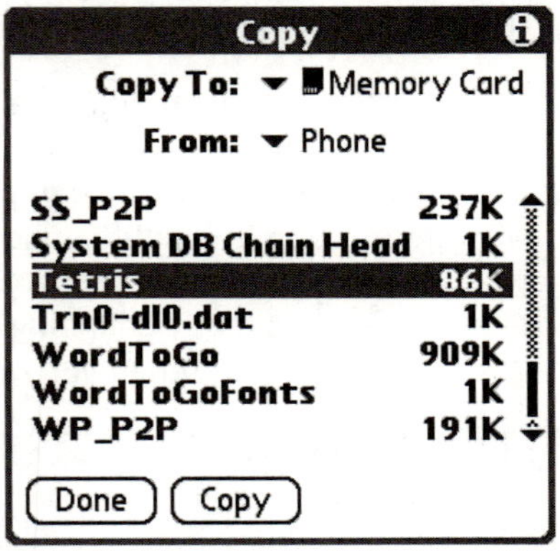

FIGURE 4.30

The Copy screen enables you to copy applications and application data files from the phone memory to the memory card, and vice versa.

> **TIP** To confirm that an application has been copied to the memory card, tap the Done button and then select the memory card from the category pick list near the top of the application screen. You should see the application icon, which means the application is indeed stored on the memory card.

3. To copy an application or data file from the phone's memory to the memory card, scroll to select the item in the list, and then tap the Copy button. The file is copied to the memory card.
4. You can easily copy files in the reverse direction by changing the Copy To and From fields at the top of the Copy screen. In other words, you can use this screen to copy files in both directions between the main phone memory and the memory card.

The only problem with the Copy screen is that it only copies files, which means the original file is not removed after the copy is made.

In most cases, what you're really looking for is a move, not a copy. This becomes a two-step process, in that you first copy a file to the memory card and then delete it from the device's main memory. You just learned how to carry out the first step, and you explored the second step earlier in the chapter when you found out how to remove applications; see "Remove an Application" if it's already a fuzzy memory.

Back Up Your Treo to a Memory Card

There is no doubting the importance of backing up your Treo regularly, and there are a few options to consider for performing backups. If you synchronize your device regularly, it's automatically backed up. You can use the Palm Desktop software to completely restore applications and data to your device in the event of an accidental hard reset or some other device problem that erases the memory. However, there are third-party backup options worth considering.

With third-party backup solutions, you have two primary options: Back up to your desktop computer using a desktop backup application, or back up to a memory card using a Treo application. The first approach is similar to synchronizing with the Palm Desktop software, except that third-party backup applications typically offer more advanced features, such as restore points that enable you to restore your device to its state on a particular date and time. A good desktop backup application to check out is BackupBuddy by Blue Nomad (http://www.bluenomad.com/).

The other third-party backup option involves backing up your device directly to a memory card without using your desktop computer at all. In this case, the backup software is either installed on your device or already resident on a memory storage card. Either way, the application runs and backs up your device to the memory card, which can then be removed and stored in a safe place. This backup option is helpful because you can use it while traveling—you don't need access to a desktop computer.

As I explained, the backup software for performing a memory card backup can be located in your Treo's main memory or on the memory card itself. In fact, several manufacturers offer backup cards that are essentially memory cards with preinstalled backup software. If you buy a backup card, you don't need to install anything special on your device. Palm makes a 64MB backup card that's available from the palmOne Store at http://store.palmone.com/.

If you already have a memory card that you want to use for performing backups, you should look into backup software for your device. The same software I mentioned earlier for performing backups to your desktop, BackupBuddy (http://www.bluenomad.com/), is also a good option for performing memory card backups. Figure 4.31 shows the BackupBuddy application, which offers two options via buttons: Backup and Restore.

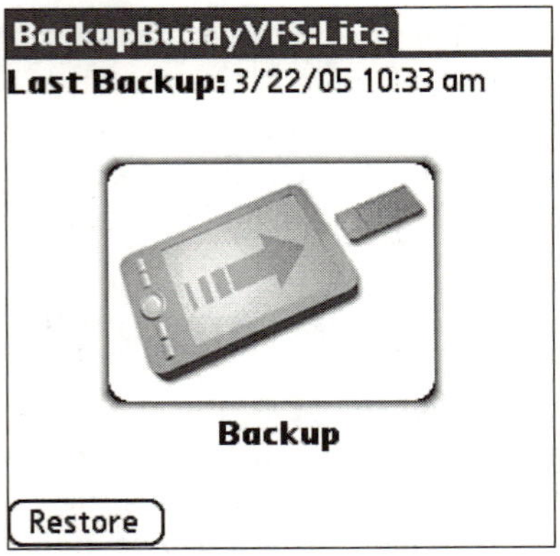

FIGURE 4.31

With the Backup Buddy application, you can back up and restore your device to and from a memory card.

To initiate a backup to the memory card using BackupBuddy, just tap the Backup button. The backup proceeds with a gauge showing the progress.

After you've backed up your device to the memory card, you can remove the card and store it away in case you need to restore from it. If you ever need to restore a backup from the memory card, just reinsert the memory card, launch the BackupBuddy application, and tap the Restore button.

Manage Files

One software limitation of Treo devices that has always bothered me is the lack of a built-in file manager. I realize that the goal is to keep the devices extremely end-user friendly, but there are always situations in which you want to see exactly what files are stored on your device and where. Unfortunately, there is no built-in file manager in Treo devices, so you have to look to third-party applications for managing files.

> **TIP** Updating the memory card regularly with fresh backups is a good idea. Even if you use a different memory card on a regular basis for day-to-day storage needs, try to get in the habit of inserting and updating the backup card at least once a week.

One of the best file management applications I've found is FileZ by nosleep software. FileZ is not only simple and easy to use, but also free. You can download a free copy of FileZ by linking from the nosleep software website at http://nosleepsoftware.sourceforge.net/. Even if you decide to spend money on a different file management application for your Treo, FileZ is a good example of how all file managers work. Figure 4.32 shows the main screen in FileZ when you first launch the application.

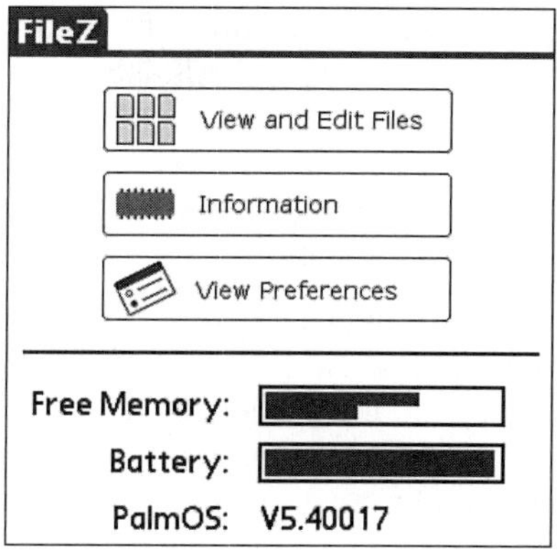

FIGURE 4.32

The main screen in FileZ includes a few buttons along with a couple of gauges with memory and battery information.

The FileZ application is handy for taking a quick look at the free memory and available battery charge. You can tap the memory and battery gauges to get more exact data. The real value of the FileZ application is in its role as a file manager. To access the file management features of FileZ, tap the View and Edit Files button to open the file screen shown in Figure 4.33.

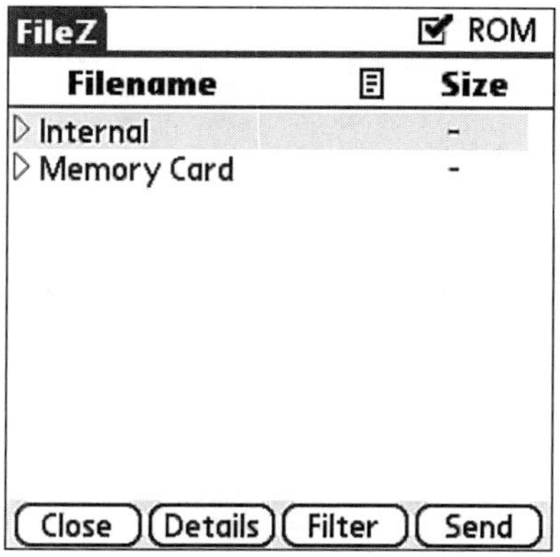

FIGURE 4.33

The file screen in FileZ shows the two primary storage areas on your Treo, the internal memory and the memory card.

If you're accustomed to using a hierarchical file manager such as Windows Explorer, you'll feel right at home with FileZ. The two items in the list in Figure 4.33 represent the

NOTE Another good file manager worth considering is ZLauncher by ZZTECHS, which includes a sophisticated application launcher that's much more powerful than the standard application screen. To learn more about ZLauncher, check out the ZZTECHS website at http://www.zztechs.com/.

TIP You can also access the details of a folder by tapping to select the folder and then tapping the Details button.

two highest level storage areas on your device, which are the internal memory and the memory card. Things don't get interesting until you begin drilling down into the memory areas to see what's stored in them. To do so, you simply tap the little arrow icon to the left of the item in the list. Figure 4.34 shows the memory card open to reveal several folders and files.

In Figure 4.34, you can see that I've opened the AUDIO folder on the memory card to reveal several MP3 songs stored on the card. I've even tapped to select one of the songs, as shown by the small check mark next to it. To find out more about a file, select the file and tap the Details button to open the file details screen shown in Figure 4.35.

The file details screen includes three different tabs for accessing different pieces of file information. The default tab, General, displays the filename and size. The other two tabs, Attrs and Dates, include information such as file attributes and modification times and dates. You can modify the file attributes and date/time information for a file, and then tap the Save button to save the changes.

The FileZ application does more than just help you access and manage files. If you return to the main FileZ screen by closing the file screen, you can access memory, synchronization, and battery information and explore very detailed device preferences.

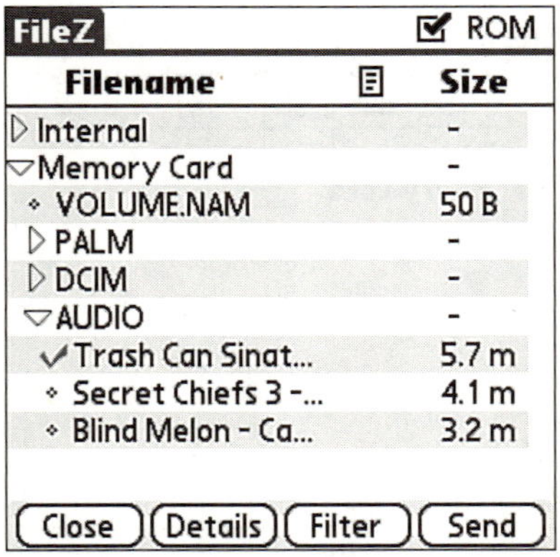

FIGURE 4.34

FileZ enables you to drill down into folders to see the files stored in them.

FIGURE 4.35

The file details screen in FileZ displays information about a file and allows you to delete or send the file.

Summary

This chapter has covered quite a bit of territory, including some critical Treo concepts such as synchronization, application installation and categorization, memory cards, and file management. I hope this chapter has hammered home the significance of the Treo-to-PC connection in terms of how important it is to share data between your Treo and desktop computer on a regular basis. This information sharing isn't a necessity for using your Treo, but it can certainly improve the usability of your device. The next chapter tackles a topic somewhat related to synchronization—exploring the ins and outs of managing Treo contacts.

5

Managing Treo Contacts

One of my early frustrations with mobile phones was entering contact information. I had already been using a contact manager on my desktop computer for years, so I had my contacts in electronic form, but I had no way to move them to my mobile phone. One of the obvious but sometimes overlooked features of Treo devices is its contact management capability, which allows you to take your electronic Rolodex with you on the go.

The Contacts application on your Treo serves as a contact manager that keeps track of all your contacts, including their email addresses, phone numbers, snail mail addresses, photos, birthdays, and any other information you'd like to associate with them. Although you can populate the contact list solely through creating contacts on your device, it's a good idea to synchronize contacts from a desktop contact manager, such as Palm Desktop or Microsoft Outlook. Regardless of how you build your contact list, the Contacts application gives you lots of flexibility in managing contacts.

IN THIS CHAPTER

- Contact Essentials
- Create a New Contact
- Customize Contact Data
- Duplicate and Delete Contacts
- Categorize, Filter, and Sort the Contact List
- Assign a Caller ID Ring Tone
- Send and Receive Contacts Wirelessly

Contact Essentials

Most information stored on your Treo device is stored as a *record*, which is a discrete chunk of data that represents one logical piece of information. The Contacts application stores each individual contact on your device as a record. In this way, you can think of the Contacts application as a simple database. Because your Treo device is a mobile communicator, which implies communication with other people, contact records in many ways represent some of the most important information on your device. Therefore, understanding how to manage and manipulate them efficiently is important.

To launch the Contacts application, tap its icon on the main application screen or press the Option button followed by the Calendar button, assuming you haven't changed the default application button settings. The main screen in the Contacts application consists of a master list of all contacts stored on your device. Later in this chapter in "Categorize, Filter, and Sort the Contact List," you find out how to filter and sort this list to help make it easier to access certain contacts. For now, it's important to just get comfortable moving around within the list by using the Up and Down buttons on the five-way navigator.

Scrolling through the contacts with the Up and Down buttons moves you through the contacts a line at a time. To move through the list a page at a time, hold down the Option key while pressing the Up and Down buttons. The phone numbers for each contact are listed immediately below the contact, which helps you quickly access and dial a contact without having to open the entire contact. You can also select the contact itself instead of its number, which opens the contact—just press the Center button on the five-way navigator or tap the contact name. After a contact is open, you can view all its details, such as snail and email addresses, a photo of the person, his or her birthday, and so forth.

> **TIP** To quickly place a call to a contact from the Contacts application, just scroll to select the contact's phone number in the contact list, and then press the Center button on the five-way navigator. If you press the Center button with the contact name selected, the contact is opened instead of dialed.

While viewing a contact, you can still use the Up and Down buttons to step through the contacts one at a time. In other words, if you're viewing a contact and you press the Down button until you reach the bottom of the contact, pressing Down again opens the next contact in the list. This method is a great way to step through a list of contacts to find a piece of detailed information, such as an email address or a ZIP code. When used with filtering, this technique gives you the ability to step through a related series of contacts. You can also use the Up button in a similar fashion to scroll to the top of a contact and then on to the previous contact in the list.

Similar to most other data on your Treo, contacts can be categorized to help keep them organized. You can even create your own categories to logically divide contacts. For example, I have several different categories of business contacts along with categories for family and friends. This helps me quickly access a certain group of contacts rather than sift through the entire contact list.

The remainder of this chapter focuses on managing and organizing contacts and generally squeezing the most functionality out of the Contacts application as possible.

Create a New Contact

One of the most useful features of any mobile communicator is contact management. Treo devices are no different, and you'll no doubt find yourself using the Contacts application extensively to enter new contacts. Fortunately, entering a new contact in the Contacts application is easy. To create a new contact, follow these steps:

1. Press the **Option** key followed by the **Calendar** button to launch the Contacts application. You can also navigate to the Contacts application on the application

screen and launch it if you've changed the Option + Calendar application button combination.

2. Tap the **New Contact** button in the lower-left corner of the screen to begin creating a new contact. The Contact Edit screen opens, as shown in Figure 5.1.

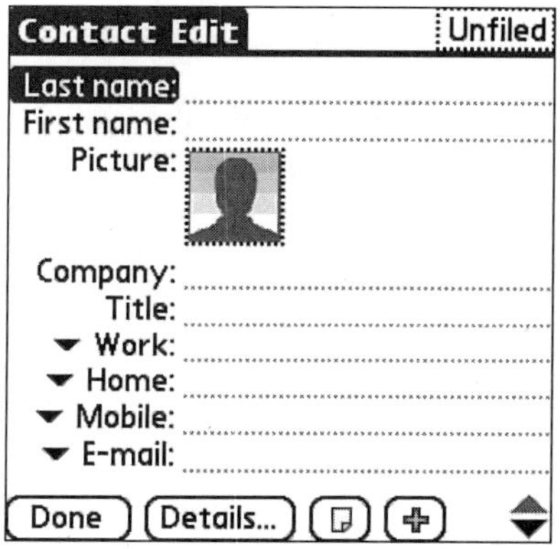

FIGURE 5.1

The Contact Edit screen is where you enter all the details associated with a contact.

3. You can enter lots of fields of data for a contact, but you can also enter as few fields as you want. Of course, you want to enter the name of every contact. However, beyond that, you're free to supply as much or as little detail as you'd like. I mention this because often it's useful to enter a new contact's name and phone number (or email address) first, and then go back and fill in more details later. The Contact Edit fields are larger than a single screen, so you have to use the five-way navigator or tap the scroll buttons in the lower-right corner to navigate through the fields.

4. You can use the Picture field to specify a picture for the contact, which is displayed on the screen as a photo caller ID when that person calls you. To set the picture, tap the outline of the head. A menu appears that prompts you to select Camera or Photos. Choose **Camera** if you are with the person and want to take his or her picture, or go with **Photos** if you already have the person's picture stored as an image on your device.

NOTE If you synchronize with Microsoft Outlook on your desktop computer, note that the Picture field on your Treo is synchronized by storing the photo caller ID image as an attachment in the Outlook contact.

5. As you continue entering contact details, pay close attention to the fields that have a small down arrow next to them. They are similar fields in a group that can be mixed and matched. For example, you can tap the AIM field and change it to MSN if the contact uses MSN

Messenger instead of AOL Instant Messenger (AIM). The phone number and email fields work in a similar fashion.

6. Near the bottom of the contact information you'll see the Birthday field for specifying the contact's birthday. To set the birthday, tap where it says **-Tap to Add-**. The Select Birthday screen shown in Figure 5.2 opens. Tap the month and day of the birthday to set it; if the person's birthday is today, just tap the **Today** button.

FIGURE 5.2

Use the Select Birthday screen to set a contact's birthday by selecting a date on the calendar.

NOTE When a contact's birthday rolls around, the Calendar application shows the person's name in Day view with a little birthday cake icon next to it.

TIP You can delete the birthday for a contact by tapping the Delete button in the Birthday screen. The birthday is then removed from the contact, including the reminder if it was set.

7. After selecting the birthday, you're prompted to set a reminder for it. A reminder is optional, but it's a great idea if you find yourself forgetting birthdays of close friends, family members, and co-workers. Figure 5.3 shows the Birthday screen, which displays the selected birthday along with a Reminder check box and the number of days in advance that you'd like to be reminded. Tap the number **7** if you'd like to change the time frame for the reminder. When you're finished, tap the **OK** button to complete the birthday setting.

8. If you have additional text information you'd like to associate with a contact, you might want to include it as an attached note. Tap the **Note** button (small paper icon) at the bottom of the Contact Edit screen to add a text note as a contact attachment. A note entry screen appears where you can enter text for the contact (see Figure 5.4). After entering the note text, tap the **Done** button to save the note as an attachment for the contact.

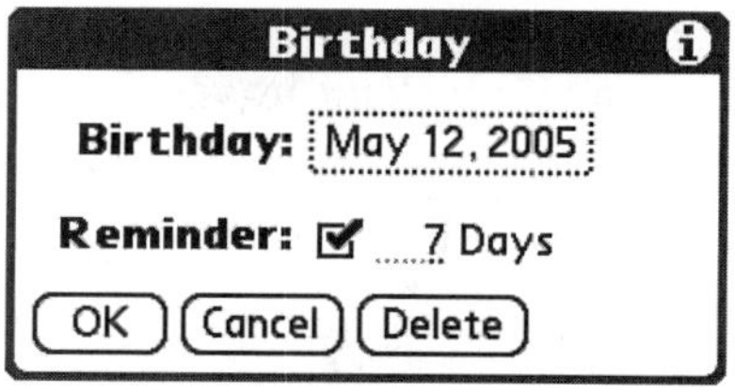

FIGURE 5.3

The Birthday screen gives you an opportunity to set a reminder for the birthday, including the number of days in advance for the reminder.

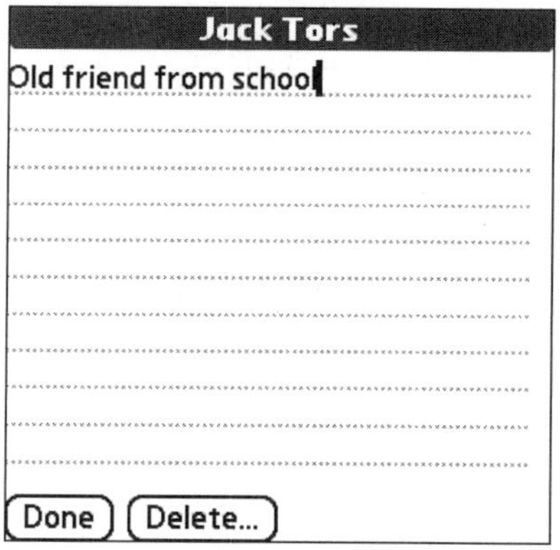

FIGURE 5.4

The note entry screen consists of a large text edit field where you enter a text attachment for a contact.

NOTE Just below the Birthday field you'll notice several custom fields. You can use these fields to enter any custom information you'd like to add to your contacts. I say "contacts" because any changes you make to custom fields apply to all your contacts. You learn how to rename custom fields later in this chapter in the "Customize Contact Data" section.

9. The last piece of business associated with creating a new contact is filing the contact. By default, all new contacts are automatically considered unfiled, so it's a good idea to file your contacts. Filing a contact simply involves assigning a category to it. To select the category for a contact, tap the **Details** button to open the Contact Details screen (see Figure 5.5).

10. In addition to specifying the category for the contact, the Contact Details screen also allows you to flag the contact as private. If you recall, private records on your Treo have limited access based on your security settings. For example, you can limit private records so that a password is required to view or edit the data. You can also configure the security settings to completely hide private data until the password is entered or just mask the data. For details on how to configure security settings

for private records, see "Secure Your Treo with a Password" in Chapter 3, "Customizing and Personalizing Your Treo."

Figure 5.5

The Contact Details screen enables you to specify the category for a contact and designate the contact as private.

> **Tip** You can delete the note for a contact by tapping the Delete button in the note entry screen. The note is then removed from the contact.

> **Tip** To add a field to a contact, tap the button with the plus icon at the bottom of the Contact Edit screen, and then choose the field you'd like to add.

11. When you're finished entering the new contact, tap the **Done** button to close the Contact Edit screen and save the contact. It's immediately added to the main contact list.

You can create as many contacts as your device's memory allows. Some Treo users have several hundred contacts stored on their devices, so it's unlikely that you'll run into serious problems when it comes to overloading the Contacts application. Also, it's worth pointing out that if you're synchronizing your device with your desktop computer, any new contacts you create on your device carry over to the desktop the next time you synchronize.

Customize Contact Data

The Contacts application includes numerous data fields for providing lots of specific information for a contact. Even so, you will likely want to include additional information at some point that isn't reflected in the default fields. Although you could enter the information as an attached note, which might not be a bad idea depending on the information, you should consider creating a custom field. Custom fields are simple text fields that you can rename to anything you choose. For example, you could create a custom field called Spouse Name for entering the name of each contact's spouse.

It's important to understand that custom fields apply to all your contacts. So if you create a custom field while editing a particular contact, the field changes in all of your contacts. This means you should be careful about changing custom fields that you have already created. For example, if you've been using a custom field called Spouse Name and you later change it to Pet Name, you run the risk of mistaking a contact's spouse with his or her pet—not good! If you've already begun using a custom field, you're generally better off creating a new one instead of changing the old one.

NOTE The Unfiled category is an automatic category designation that applies to contacts that have not been explicitly categorized.

When I talk about "creating" a custom field, what I'm really talking about is renaming a custom field. Your Treo supports nine custom fields that are initially named Custom 1, Custom 2, and so on. To "create" a custom field of your own, you simply rename one of these fields to suit your needs. Following are the steps required to rename a custom field:

TIP Other possibilities for custom fields include fields for a contact's anniversary, children's names, and hobbies, to name a few. If you manage a sales force, you might consider creating a custom sales quota field.

1. Press the **Option** key followed by the **Calendar** button to launch the Contacts application. You can also navigate to the Contacts application on the application screen and launch it if you've changed the Option + Calendar application button combination.

2. Press the **Menu** button and navigate over to the Options menu. Then scroll down to the Rename Custom Fields menu item and press the **Center** button on the five-way navigator (or simply tap **Rename Custom Fields**). The Rename Custom Fields screen opens (see Figure 5.6).

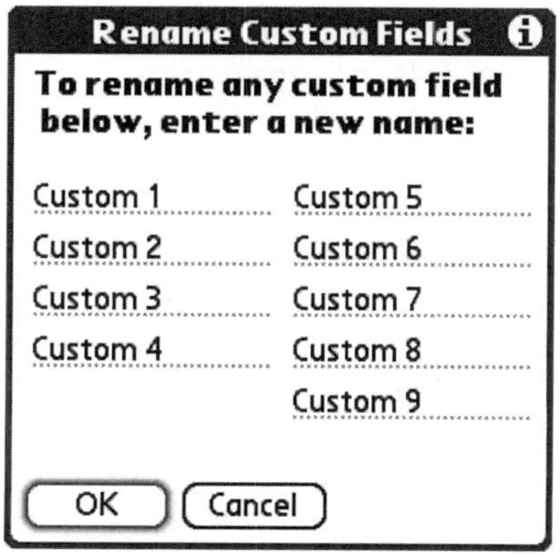

FIGURE 5.6

The Rename Custom Fields screen displays all the custom contact fields so that you can rename them.

3. As Figure 5.6 shows, there are nine custom contact fields that you can rename and use however you want. To rename a field, just navigate to it and change the text. Tap the **OK** button when you're finished to commit the changes opens (see Figure 5.6) .

4. To see the custom field changes, create a new contact and scroll down to the bottom of the information fields. Figure 5.7 shows where I renamed two custom fields to allow me to enter a contact's spouse name and pet name.

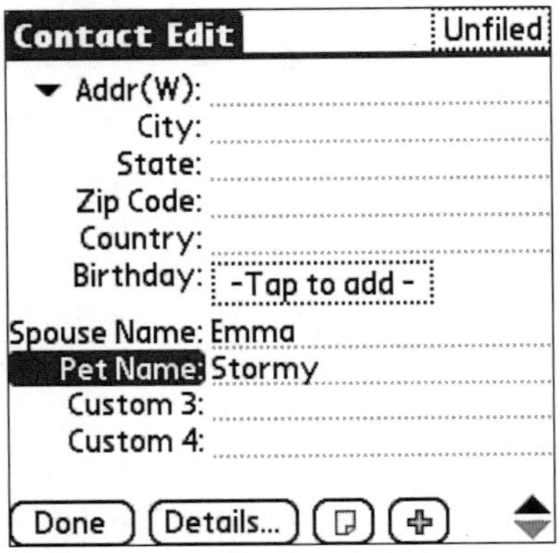

FIGURE 5.7

By renaming two custom fields, I can now specify the name of a contact's spouse and pet.

You can rename all nine custom contact fields if you want. The real trick to using custom fields is getting them to synchronize with your desktop computer. If you're using the Palm Desktop software, there's no problem because custom fields synchronize automatically. However, if you're synchronizing with a desktop PIM, such as Microsoft Outlook, you need to manually map each custom field on your device to a field in Outlook.

Follow these steps to map a custom contact field for synchronization with Outlook on a Windows computer:

1. If HotSync Manager isn't already running, launch it.

2. Right-click the **HotSync Manager** icon in the taskbar, and click **Custom** on the menu that appears. The Custom dialog box opens to display a list of synchronization data types (conduits), as shown in Figure 5.8.

3. Make sure your user name is selected in the pick list at the top of the window, and then click to select **Contacts (Outlook)** in the Conduit list. Click the **Change** button to edit the synchronization settings for contacts.

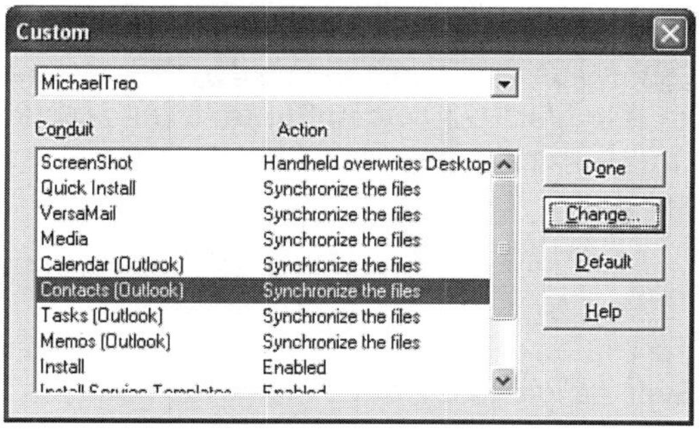

FIGURE 5.8

The Custom dialog box for HotSync Manager provides access to the different data types available for synchronization.

4. In the Change HotSync Action dialog box that opens, click the **Settings** button to edit the Outlook synchronization settings for contacts.
5. In the Outlook Contacts Settings dialog box that opens, click the **Advanced** button to access advanced contact settings. The Contact Advanced Settings dialog box opens, which is where you change the mapping of contact fields during synchronization (see Figure 5.9).

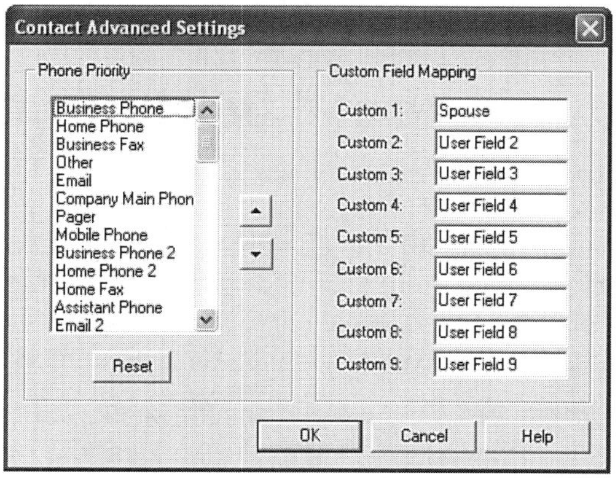

FIGURE 5.9

The Contact Advanced Settings dialog box for HotSync Manager provides access to custom field mappings for contact synchronization.

6. The right side of the Contact Advanced Settings dialog box lists the custom fields on your device. The list is admittedly a little confusing because it doesn't show

the correct names of the fields if you've changed them. For example, the first custom field shows up as Custom 1 even if you've renamed it to Spouse Name. To map a custom Treo field to a field in Outlook, just enter the name of the Outlook field next to the custom contact field. It just so happens that Outlook has a field called Spouse, so you can map the Spouse Name field (Custom 1) to Outlook's Spouse field by entering **Spouse** next to Custom 1. Click **OK** when you're finished mapping fields.

7. Click **OK** in the Outlook Contacts Settings dialog box, followed by **OK** in the Change HotSync Action dialog box. Finally, click **Done** in the Custom dialog box to wrap up the mapping process.
8. Now go into Outlook on your desktop computer and set the spouse name for a contact. Look under the Details tab for a field labeled Spouse's name. (The field labels don't always match the actual field names exactly.) Enter the name and save the contact.
9. Synchronize your device with the desktop computer, and the custom field Spouse Name then takes on the name you entered in Outlook, meaning that the name from Outlook overwrites the name on your device.

NOTE The procedure for mapping custom contact fields for synchronization on a Macintosh computer are similar to the steps outlined here for Outlook on a Windows computer.

Custom contact fields give you a lot of flexibility in tweaking the Contacts application to work exactly the way you want it to. Being able to map those custom fields to your desktop PIM is the icing on the cake in terms of taking maximum control of your contact management.

Duplicate and Delete Contacts

Now that you've entered some contacts and learned how to customize them to your heart's content, it's time to explore the general management of contacts. The Contacts application allows you to duplicate and delete contacts, which can be quite useful for creating new contacts that are similar to old ones or when you need to prune old contacts from your contact list. The commands for managing contacts are found on the menus for the Contacts application.

Duplicating a contact can be useful when many are similar for contacts. For example, a good candidate for duplication is someone who works at the same company as an existing contact and shares similar phone numbers and email. To duplicate a contact in the Contacts application, follow these steps:

1. Scroll down the contact list to select the contact you'd like to copy.
2. Press the **Menu** button and scroll down to the Duplicate Contact menu item. Press the five-way navigator (or simply tap **Duplicate Contact**) to duplicate the contact. Figure 5.10 shows a contact selected while the Duplicate Contact command is being issued.

Figure 5.10

To duplicate a contact, you must select it and then issue the Duplicate Contact command from the Record menu.

3. The new duplicate contact immediately opens after you create it, as shown in Figure 5.11. You can then edit the contact to reflect the differences between the new contact and the original. If nothing else, make sure you change the name of the new contact to clarify exactly who the new contact is, especially because it's initially created with the word "Copy" as part of the name.

Figure 5.11

After duplicating a contact, you get an opportunity to edit the new contact and change any of its details.

4. When you're finished editing the new contact, tap the **Done** button to close the Contact Edit screen and save the contact. It's immediately added to the main contact list.

Sooner or later, creating and duplicating contacts leaves you in a situation where you need to do some pruning. To delete a contact in the Contacts application, follow these steps:

1. Scroll down the contact list to select the contact you'd like to delete. Press the five-way navigator to open the contact, and then tap the **Edit** button to edit the contact. The contact is opened for editing and displayed in the Contact Edit screen.
2. Press the **Menu** button and then press the five-way navigator to issue the initially selected menu command, Delete Contact. The Delete Contact screen prompts you to confirm the contact deletion (see Figure 5.12).

FIGURE 5.12

The Delete Contact screen prompts you to confirm the deletion of a contact.

> **TIP** In the Palm Desktop application on Windows computers, you access archived data by selecting the appropriate data type on the left side of the screen, and then selecting Open Archive from the File menu. On the Macintosh side of things, navigate to the user folder for your device and double-click the User Data Archive file.

3. You'll notice the Save Archive Copy on PC check box in the Delete Contact screen. If you select this option, a copy of the contact is saved in an archive file on your desktop computer when the contact is deleted. Archive files are managed differently for each desktop PIM application, so you need to refer to your specific PIM documentation to find out how to view and restore archive data.
4. To follow through with the deletion of the contact, tap the **OK** button. The contact is then deleted and removed from the contact list.

While duplicating and deleting contacts, you probably noticed some menu commands for sending and beaming contacts. These commands are extremely handy for sharing contacts with other people wirelessly, and you learn about them later in this chapter in the "Send and Receive Contacts Wirelessly" section.

Categorize, Filter, and Sort the Contact List

If you've built up a hefty list of contacts, you'll likely find yourself tiring of scrolling through the list to find a contact. Although you can certainly use the helpful technique of typing the first few letters of a contact's name to filter the contact list, there are some other options.

Earlier in the chapter, you learned how to categorize contacts when creating them by selecting a category from a list. Although categorizing contacts is helpful purely for organizational purposes, it plays a vital role in accessing contacts, too. At the top of the Contacts application you'll see a pick list containing a list of categories. To filter contacts according to a particular category, just tap the Category pick list and select a category other than All. Figure 5.13 shows the Category pick list on my device, which reveals several different categories.

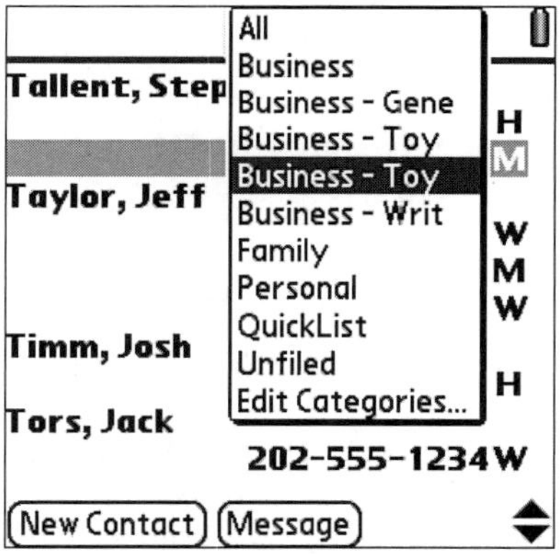

FIGURE 5.13

You can use the Category pick list in the Contacts application to filter contacts based on a single category.

Your ability to filter contacts on a particular category depends entirely on how well you've categorized the contacts to begin with. You've already learned how to assign a category to a contact, but you haven't learned how to create and manage categories.

To edit the categories for your contacts, follow these steps in the Contacts application:

1. Tap the pick list at the top of the main Category list, and take special note of the last item in the list, Edit Categories. Tap **Edit Categories** in the pick list to open the Edit Categories screen, which is shown in Figure 5.14.
2. To create a new contact category, tap the **New** button in the Edit Categories screen. You are prompted to enter the new category name. You can also rename a category by selecting it in the category list and pressing the **Rename** button.

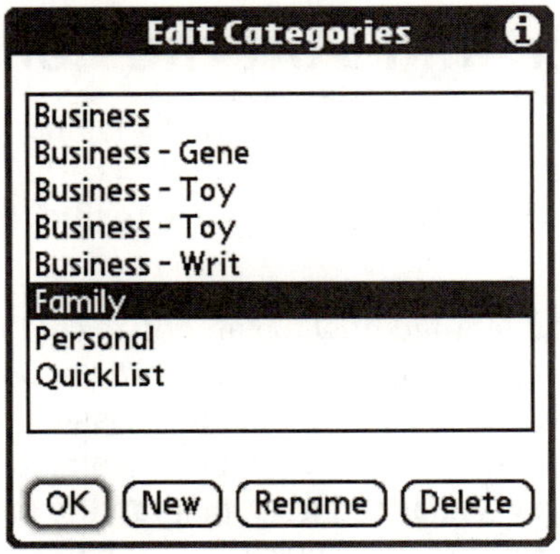

FIGURE 5.14

The Edit Categories screen enables you to create, delete, and rename categories for contacts.

3. To delete a contact category, tap the **Delete** button. Keep in mind that any contacts assigned to the deleted category are automatically moved to the Unfiled category.
4. Tap the **OK** button to finish editing categories. The modified categories take effect immediately and are ready to be used in categorizing your contacts.

If you recall from Chapter 4, "Synchronizing with Your Desktop Computer," applications are categorized similarly to contacts. In fact, most of the data on your Treo can be categorized using categories. However, each type of data has its own unique set of categories that can be edited and managed independently of the categories for other data types. Each application has a limit of 16 total categories, including the built-in Unfiled category.

Getting back to the contact list, you might find yourself needing to sort the list based on company name instead of contact name. For example, if you regularly deal with several contacts from different companies, scrolling through the contact list on a company by company basis might be more helpful. There is a simple setting that allows you to easily switch between sorting the contact list by contact name or company name.

To change the sorting of the contact list in the Contacts application, follow these steps:

1. Press the **Menu** button and navigate over to the Options menu. Then scroll down to the Preferences menu item and press the five-way navigator (or simply tap **Preferences**). The Preferences screen opens, as shown in Figure 5.15.
2. The Preferences screen shows two different options for sorting the contact list: Last Name, First Name and Company, Last Name. Select the first option if you want to sort the contact list by contact name, or go with the second option if you want to sort by company name.

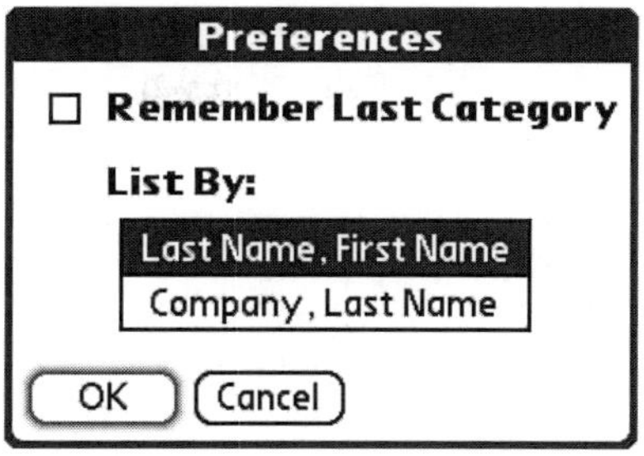

FIGURE 5.15

The Preferences screen for the Contacts application enables you to change the sorting of contacts in the contact list.

3. The other setting in the Preferences screen, Remember Last Category, is surprisingly handy if you regularly filter the contact list using a category other than All. By selecting this option, you tell the Contacts application to remember the filter category in the Category pick list and never reset it back to All. Normally, the application reverts to All when you leave it and return.
4. When you're finished with the Contacts application preferences, tap the **OK** button to commit the changes and return to the main contact list.

Filtering and sorting contacts are tasks that are highly dependent on how many contacts you have and how well organized (categorized) they are. You might use only 20 or 30 contacts, in which case filtering and sorting might be overkill. On the other hand, if you push much past 50 with your contact count, I highly recommend taking the time to do some basic categorization so that you can filter and sort contacts for more efficient access.

Assign a Caller ID Ring Tone

Earlier in this chapter, you found out how to assign a picture to a contact so that it appears as a picture caller ID when the contact calls you. Although this feature is cool, an even more practical takeoff on the same feature involves caller ID ring tones. In other words, you assign a unique ring tone to a contact so that you quickly know who is calling just by recognizing the ring tone. Unfortunately, there isn't a contact field for setting a caller ID ring tone. Although this might seem like an oversight by the Treo designers, it is in all likelihood a deliberate design move.

To understand why there is no contact field for setting a unique ring tone, consider that you are unlikely to set a unique ring tone for every contact in the contact list. It's just not feasible to think that you'd remember that many different tones. Caller ID ring tones make more sense when applied to a handful of contacts who call you most often. Typically, they are the same contacts you call regularly. You can think of these contacts as your "favorites." As it turns out, caller ID ring tones are assigned to favorites in the Phone application of your device.

A *favorite* is a piece of information you'd like to be readily accessible via a special link in the Phone application. A favorite can be a speed dial number, an email address, or a Web address, to name a few options. In the case of caller ID ring tones, you're dealing with a speed dial number as a favorite. It works like this: You create a favorite based on a certain phone number. In the process of creating this favorite, you specify a ring tone for the phone number. Then when that number is detected on an incoming call, the ring tone is played. In this way, caller ID ring tones actually operate independently of contacts, but the two topics are still closely related.

To set a caller ID ring tone for a phone number (contact), follow these steps:

1. Press the **Phone/Send** button to launch the Phone application.
2. Along the bottom of the main Phone screen are several favorites arranged as cells in a grid. There are actually many more favorites than the few shown on the main screen. You need to navigate past the built-in favorites so that you can add some favorites of your own. So press the **Down** button on the five-way navigator repeatedly until the favorites list expands to reveal more favorites. Figure 5.16 shows the expanded favorites list.

FIGURE 5.16

The expanded favorites list shows numerous favorites along with a navigation bar along the bottom to view additional favorites pages.

3. Along the bottom of the current favorites page, you'll see a navigation bar with numbers on it. This bar indicates that there are additional favorites pages you can access. Tap **2** on the navigation bar to move to the second favorites page. You then see a list of empty (undefined) favorites, as shown in Figure 5.17.

FIGURE 5.17

Page two of the Phone favorites consists solely of empty (undefined) favorites.

4. To customize one of the favorites in the empty list, just tap it; feel free to tap any of them. The Add Favorite screen opens (see Figure 5.18).

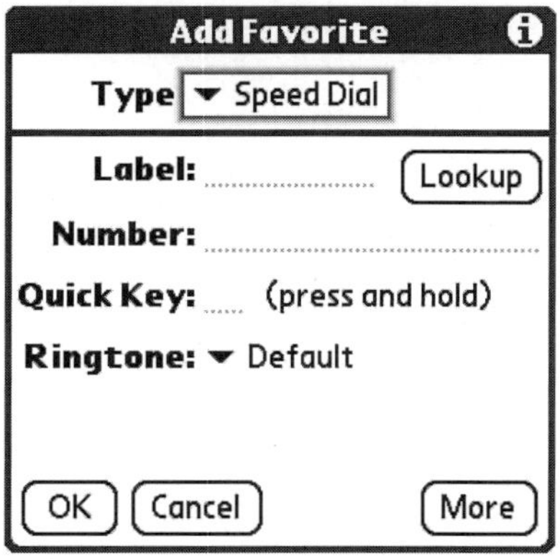

FIGURE 5.18

In the Add Favorite screen, you can add a Speed Dial favorite that establishes a caller ID ring tone.

5. It is possible to create several different kinds of favorites—you learn more about favorites in Chapter 7, "Using Your Treo as a Mobile Phone." For now, you're going to focus on creating a Speed Dial favorite, so make sure that **Speed Dial** is selected in the Type pick list.
6. To choose a contact and phone number for the favorite, tap the **Lookup** button. Then select a phone number for a contact, and tap the **Add** button to add the

person to the favorite. You also have the option of establishing a Quick Key for the phone number, which is a way to dial the number quickly by using a short key combination. You can skip the Quick Key for now, as it's covered in more detail in Chapter 7, "Using Your Treo as a Mobile Phone."

7. The last step is selecting the actual ring tone. Tap the **Ringtone** pick list and explore the different ring tones that are available. Keep in mind that your goal is to choose a unique and recognizable ring tone that immediately identifies the caller to you.

8. After settling on a ring tone, tap the **OK** button to finish editing the favorite. The favorite is then added to the favorite list, as shown in Figure 5.19. From now on, any time the contact calls you using the specified phone number, the ring tone you selected is played.

FIGURE 5.19

After creating a Speed Dial favorite for a contact, you see the contact listed on the favorites page.

As I mentioned a moment ago, you learn a great deal more about favorites in Chapter 7. I gave you a sneak peek here because you have to use favorites to establish a caller ID ring tone for a contact.

Send and Receive Contacts Wirelessly

One of the most common transactions in business is exchanging business cards. Business cards represent one of the most basic forms of communication in the business world. When you think about it, each contact on your Treo acts somewhat like a virtual business card. With your Treo device, you can even create and identify a single contact that serves as your own virtual business card. This is important because your device is capable of sending and receiving contacts with little effort on your part. In other words, it offers a high-tech way to share virtual business cards.

A few different options are available for sending and receiving contacts with your Treo. One approach involves using one of two messaging options to send a contact to another device, which can be a Treo device or any other computer, for that matter. The messaging options involve using email or Bluetooth. The other approach is Palm specific and involves sending a contact via infrared to another Palm device—referred to as *beaming* a contact.

To send a contact via email or Bluetooth, follow these steps:

1. Press the **Option** key followed by the **Calendar** button to launch the Contacts application. You can also navigate to the Contacts application on the application screen and launch it if you've changed the Option + Calendar application button combination.
2. Scroll through the contact list to select the contact you'd like to send.
3. Press the **Menu** button. Scroll down to the Send Contact menu item, and then press the five-way navigator (or simply tap **Send Contact**). The Send With screen opens (see Figure 5.20). Tap the messaging transport approach you'd like to use, and then tap the **OK** button.
4. If you selected Bluetooth, your device immediately starts looking for discoverable Bluetooth devices. After a few seconds of searching, a list of devices is displayed from which you can choose (see Figure 5.21). Tap to select the device to which you want to send the contact, and then tap **OK**.
5. Depending on whether you have established a Bluetooth connection with the device in the past and flagged it as a trusted device, you might have to enter a passkey for the device. The device's owner supplies this information. Other than that, sending the contact is mostly automatic.

Keep in mind that you can also send a contact via more traditional channels, such as email and SMS. If you select these options, you're prompted to specify to "To" address for the contact.

TIP

If you want to take your ring tones to another level entirely, you might want to look into a third-party application called LightWav by Toysoft. LightWav enables you to customize contacts with caller ID ring tones and to assign ring tones to alarms using MIDI, Wave, and MP3 songs. To learn more about LightWav, check it out on the Web at http://www.toysoft.ca/lightwav.html.

TIP

Another command on the Record menu of the Contacts application is Send Category, which is much more powerful than Send Contact. The Send Category command sends the entire category of contacts currently displayed on the screen. So if you want to send all your contacts to another computer, just select All as the category and issue the Send Category command.

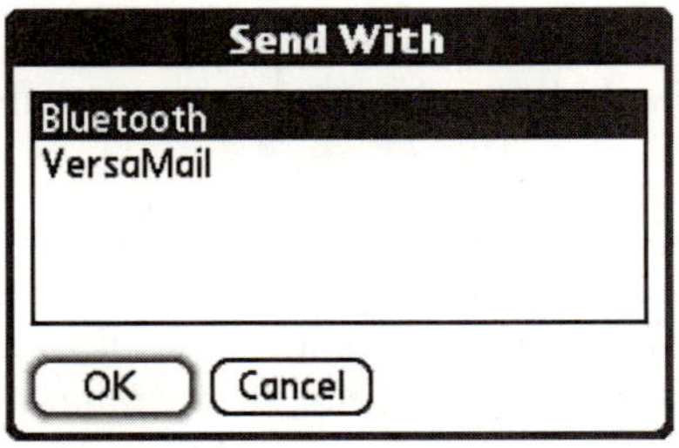

FIGURE 5.20

In the Send With screen, you choose how you'd like to send a contact.

FIGURE 5.21

The Discovery Results screen displays a list of devices that you can send the contact to via Bluetooth.

> **TIP** Similar to Send Category, a Beam Category command beams the entire category of contacts currently displayed on the screen. So if you want to beam all your contacts to another device, just select All as the category and issue the Beam Category command.

Perhaps even more interesting than sending a contact via Bluetooth or email is the capability of beaming contacts via infrared. Most Palm devices support transferring contacts via infrared, so you shouldn't have any trouble sharing contacts with other Treo devices and other devices in the Palm/palmOne family, not to mention numerous other mobile handheld devices that also support infrared. To beam a contact via infrared, follow these steps:

1. Press the **Option** key followed by the **Calendar** button to launch the Contacts application. You can also navigate to the Contacts application on the application screen and launch it if you've changed the Option + Calendar application button combination.

2. Scroll through the contact list to select the contact you'd like to send.
3. Press the **Menu** button. Scroll down to the Beam Contact menu item, and then press the five-way navigator (or simply tap **Beam Contact**). The Beam screen opens, as shown in Figure 5.22, and your device begins looking for another Palm device to beam the contact to.

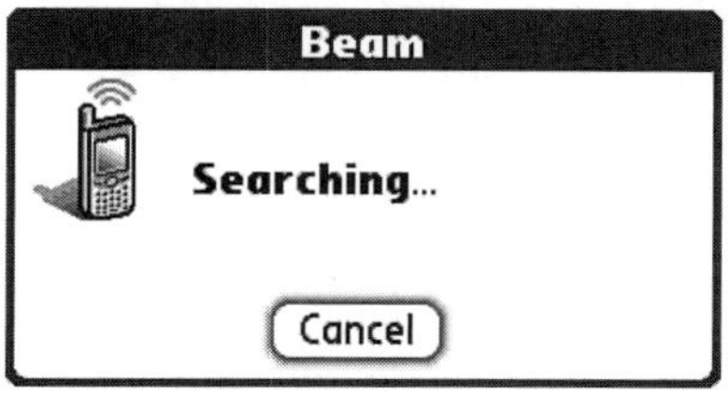

FIGURE 5.22

The Beam screen displays the status of the beam operation as the contact is sent.

4. When the Beam screen appears, lining up the infrared port on your Treo with the infrared port on the other device is essential. This involves aiming the top edges of the devices at each other. For example, you can set two Treo devices on a flat surface with their antennas aimed at each other. Keep in mind that infrared ports on Palm devices are designed to work within a range of about three feet, so you must keep the devices fairly close to each other.
5. The person on the other end of the beaming needs to accept the contact and specify a category for it. Otherwise, the contact is sent with no additional effort on your part.

> **NOTE** When attempting to beam contacts between a Treo 650 and a Treo 600, some users have reported problems with the devices not seeing each other if the Treo 650 has a username longer than 10 characters. You can change your username by selecting Users from the Tools menu in the Palm Desktop application on your desktop computer. Just make sure you update the new username in any applications that required you to enter the name.

If you're on the receiving end of an infrared contact transfer, first make sure you have your device's infrared port turned on. Then when the beamed contact notification arrives, select a category for it and accept it to receive the contact. The contact is then added to your contact list.

One other handy feature associated with beaming contacts is identifying a particular contact as your own virtual business card. This makes it possible to quickly beam your business card contact without having to search through the contact list to find it. To designate a contact as your business card, open the contact to edit it, and press the Menu button. Choose the Select Business Card command on the Record menu to indicate that the current contact should be your business card. When you're prompted to confirm the business card designation, just tap the Yes button. You've now established a business card contact for your device.

> **TIP** An even quicker way to send your business card is to hold down the shortcut key for the Contacts application, which by default is Option + Calendar. In other words, press and hold the Option key and the Calendar button for a couple of seconds to beam your business card.

To quickly send your business card to another Palm device, press the Menu button in the Contacts application and select Beam Business Card from the Record menu. Your business card contact is then beamed to another Palm device exactly as though you had selected it in the contact list and beamed it. You can think of the business card contact as a shortcut for quickly and easily beaming your own contact information.

Summary

If you're a people person, I hope you enjoyed this chapter. People management on Treo devices takes place in the Contacts application, which is quite flexible in allowing you to enter, manage, and share contact data with others. As useful as it is, the Contacts application is but one part of the Treo's PIM puzzle. The next chapter continues discussing PIM features by tackling the calendar, tasks, and memos.

6

Getting Productive with the Calendar, Tasks, and Memos

Chapter 5, "Managing Treo Contacts," showed you how to manage contacts using your Treo. Although contacts are certainly a critical part of the personal information manager (PIM) equation, they don't tell the whole story. Contacts are useful for sending messages and originating phone calls, but they don't help you schedule events, keep track of tasks, and jot down memos. Your Treo is equipped for handling all these tasks by way of the Calendar, Tasks, and Memos applications. This chapter guides you through the details of using these three applications to round out your PIM skills.

IN THIS CHAPTER

- Get Acquainted with the Calendar
- Create an Event
- Purge Events
- Customize the Calendar Views
- Send an Event to Someone
- Publish Your Calendar Online
- Tweak the Calendar Preferences
- View and Create Tasks
- Send a Task to Someone
- Edit Task Preferences
- Manage Memos

Get Acquainted with the Calendar

The Calendar application, which I also refer to simply as "the calendar," provides an electronic equivalent of a paper calendar that you can use to schedule events. Calendar events can be appointments, meetings, or anything else that can be scheduled in a block of time. If you're already familiar with using a similar software calendar in a PIM software client, such as Microsoft Outlook, you'll be right at home with the Treo calendar. An important part of using the calendar is synchronizing calendar data on your device with calendar data on your desktop computer. This process is carried out during the normal device synchronization that the HotSync Manager application handles.

The Treo calendar has some advantages over a traditional desktop calendar that are hard to beat. More specifically, the Calendar application supports several views that allow you to essentially zoom in and out on the calendar. In this way, you can view a single day's worth of events, or back out and view a week, month, or even year on the calendar. Following are the five different views the Calendar application supports:

- *Day*—Shows the hours in a day, including events scheduled for that day
- *Week*—Shows the days in a week, including a glimpse at events for each block of time
- *Month*—Shows the days and weeks in a month, including a glimpse at events for each day
- *Year*—Shows the days, weeks, and months in a year, with no information about events
- *Agenda*—Shows today's events along with upcoming events and other PIM data, such as current tasks and messages

All the calendar formats produce a view based on the currently selected time period. This time period is typically an hour that's set to the current date and time when you first open the calendar. The default calendar view is Day view, which shows a list of hours in the current day in one-hour increments (see Figure 6.1). The default Day view shows hours in the range of 8:00 a.m. to 5:00 p.m.

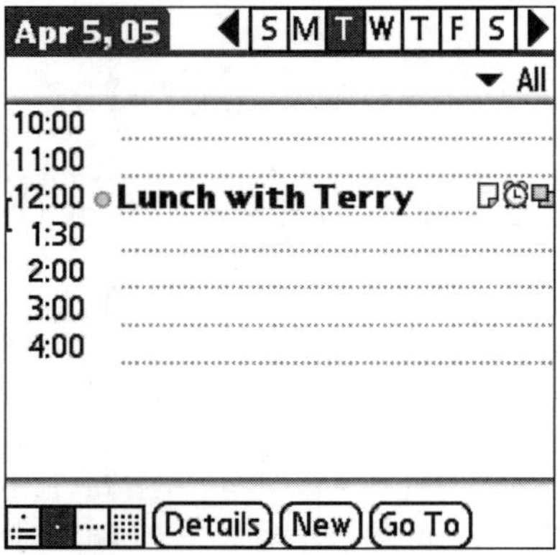

FIGURE 6.1

The Calendar application's Day view shows the hours in a day, including event details.

The calendar's Day view shows a day as a sequence of hours listed vertically down the screen. Events are shown immediately next to the time at which they are scheduled to start. A small bracket extends down from the left of the event's start time to show how long the event is scheduled to last. This gives you a visual cue for how your time is allocated for the day. Speaking of visual cues, along the top-right edge of the Day view is a series of boxes that show the current week as a list of days arranged horizontally. To navigate to a different day, just tap the box for the corresponding day of the week.

If you imagine zooming out of Day view to see the current week as a table of dates and times, you arrive at Week view, which shows the days in a week (see Figure 6.2).

Week view expands on Day view by showing a list of days across the screen to form a complete week. The hours in the day are still shown, but they are very small and, therefore, can contain only small shaded rectangles that indicate events, as opposed to event details. Even with the compressed display of hours in a day, Week view in many ways offers a better glimpse of your scheduled time than Day view. This is primarily because the shaded rectangles (bar graphs) used to show events are a clear indicator of how much time they take up.

TIP To jump to a specific date, tap the Go To button near the bottom of the screen and select the date.

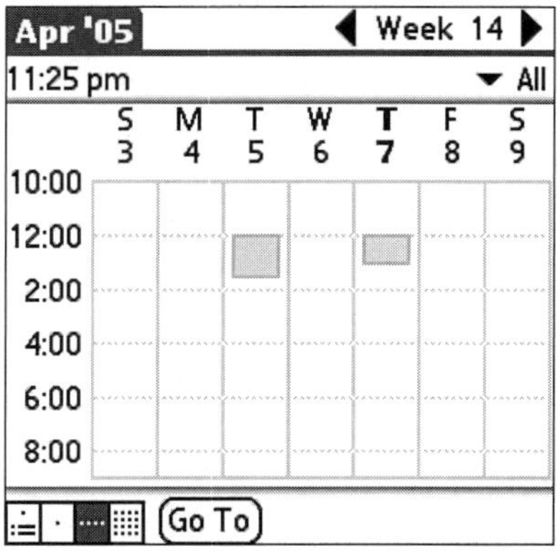

FIGURE 6.2

Week view shows the days in a week, along with a vertical listing of hours in each day and events scheduled for each day.

As you continue to zoom out of the calendar, the next view is Month view, which looks a lot like a traditional month view on a paper calendar (see Figure 6.3).

By now, you've probably caught on to how I'm switching between views. A series of boxes in the lower-left corner of the screen correspond to Agenda, Day, Week, and Month views, from left to right. If you look closely at Figures 6.1, 6.2, and 6.3, you can see a different box highlighted for each view.

The calendar's Month view is more what you expect of a software calendar in terms of being organized as weeks flowing horizontally to show a full month of days. Month view allows even less detail in terms of conveying events, but you can still see tiny bars that do a passable job of showing how much time is scheduled for a particular day.

Before I get to Agenda view, you might recall that I mentioned a Year view earlier, even though there doesn't appear to be a Year box in the navigational controls at the lower left. Presumably because Year view doesn't convey any information about your scheduled events, you access this view from a menu instead of the navigational controls. To see the calendar in Year view, press the Menu button and then scroll down to select

Year view. Figure 6.4 shows the calendar in Year view, where you can see quite a lot of information crammed onto one screen.

FIGURE 6.3

Month view shows the days and weeks in a month, including tiny representations of appointments and meetings.

FIGURE 6.4

Year view shows the months in the year as you might see them on a paper wall calendar.

Even though Year view doesn't display any information for events, it's still handy for looking up a date to see what day it falls on or for generally navigating around the calendar in broad strokes.

The last view in the Calendar application is Agenda view, which departs from the other views by not focusing entirely on a particular period of time. Instead, Agenda view focuses on upcoming events, even if they are spread out across several dates. Agenda view shows any events for the current day first, but it also shows events on the near horizon (see Figure 6.5).

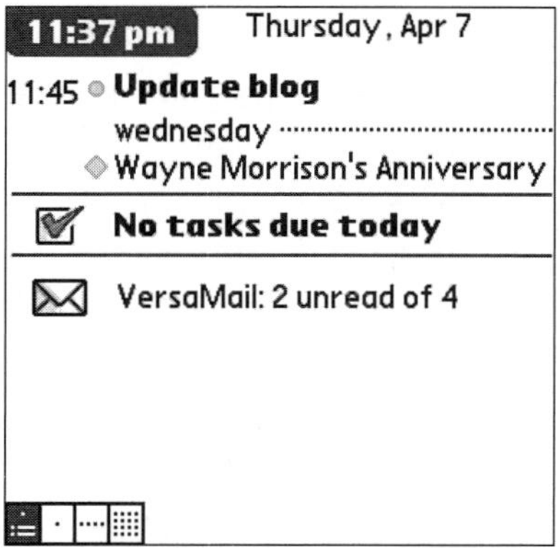

FIGURE 6.5

Agenda view shows events for today as well as upcoming events and current tasks and messages.

Agenda view is handy because it shows you detailed information for the current day along with events that are coming up. The idea is to give you a concise listing of all your upcoming events without having to navigate through all the scheduled dates. Because there is more screen space in Agenda view, it provides detailed information about each event, including the exact start time, a description, and icons indicating whether the event has an attached note, has an alarm set, and is repeating. You learn how to create events with all these properties in the next section.

Notice in Figure 6.5 that the first event shown, Update blog, is scheduled for the current day, and the second event, Wayne Morrison's Anniversary, is an upcoming event for a day in the near future. You can tell the difference because the first event is shown in bold and has a start time next to it, indicating that it occurs today; the second event has only its description shown. Below the two events is a section of screen devoted to tasks; in this case, there aren't any. And finally, a section is available for email messages. In the example in Figure 6.5, I have four messages waiting, with two still unread.

Create an Event

Creating events in the Calendar application is a straightforward process. Think of an event as anything you would want to write on a paper calendar—an appointment, a meeting, or anything else that occurs on a certain date with a start time and an end time. Follow these steps to create an event:

NOTE Events actually don't require a start time and end time. You can create an event with no time at all (just a date), such as a birthday or an anniversary, in which case the event doesn't show up as taking any time out of the day. You can also designate an event as being an all-day event, such as an all-day meeting, in which case it's displayed so that it takes up all the time in the day.

1. Press the **Calendar** button to launch the Calendar application. You can also navigate to the Calendar application on the main application screen and launch it if you've changed the Calendar button to launch a different application.

2. Tap the **New** button near the bottom of the screen to begin creating a new event. The Set Time screen appears, as shown in Figure 6.6.

3. To set the start and end times, just tap the appropriate box (**Start Time** or **End Time**), and then tap the hours and minutes in the corresponding lists to the right. If the event is scheduled to last all day, tap the **All Day** button. On the other hand, if there is no specific time frame for the event, tap the **No Time** button. Finally, if the event is taking place in a certain time zone and you want to make sure the time is correct in case you should travel outside the time zone, tap the **No Time Zone** pick list and select a time zone. When you're finished setting the times for the event, tap **OK**.

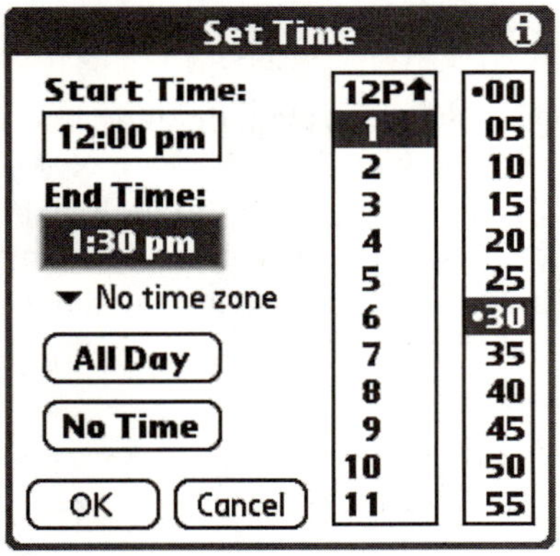

FIGURE 6.6

The Set Time screen is where you enter the time details for an event, including the start and end times.

4. After setting the start and end times for the new event, you are returned to the calendar's Day view, where you get an opportunity to enter a description of the event in its time slot. Figure 6.7 shows how I've described a lunch meeting with a friend.

5. The event is now created, but you might want to flesh out a few more details. With the event selected in Day view, tap the **Details** button near the bottom of the screen. The Event Details screen opens, as shown in Figure 6.8.

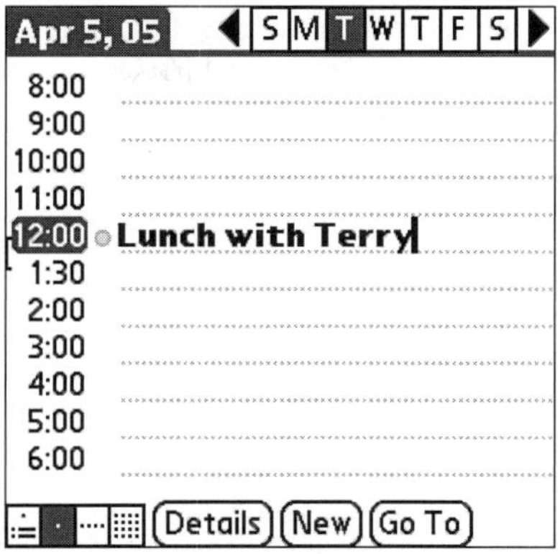

FIGURE 6.7

The new event is completed by entering a description in the calendar's Day view.

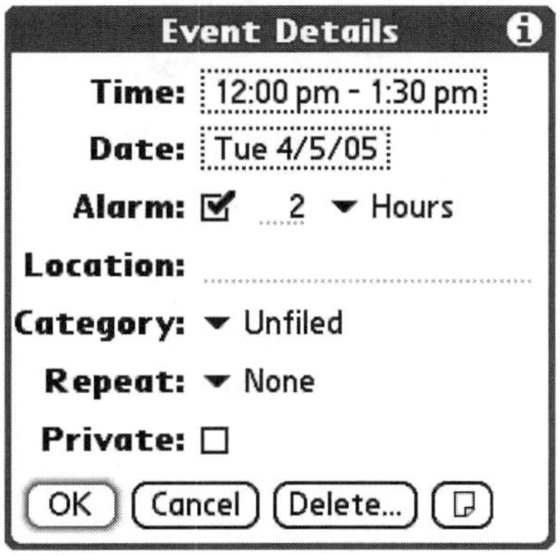

FIGURE 6.8

The Event Details screen enables you to set an alarm for an event and specify a location, a category, and whether the event is repeating.

6. If you'd like to schedule an alarm for the event, tap the **Alarm** check box and then specify the amount of time in advance that the alarm should sound. This amount of time can be expressed in minutes, hours, or days. To keep track of where the event is taking place, enter the location in the Location field. This is simply a text field, so you can enter any descriptive text about the location.
7. Similar to other PIM data on your Treo, events can be categorized. To set a category for the new event, tap the **Category** pick list and choose a category. The event can also be declared private by selecting the **Private** check box. If you recall, private records on your Treo have limited access based on your security settings. For example, you can limit private records so that a password is

> **TIP** There is a quick shortcut you can use for entering contacts into event descriptions. When you get to the part of the description where you need to enter the name of a contact, press the Menu button followed by the L key. This is the keyboard shortcut for the Phone Lookup command, which allows you to look up a contact and insert it into an event description. Of course, you can also navigate the menu via the stylus or five-way navigator.

required to view or edit data. You can also configure the security settings to completely hide private data until the password is entered or to just mask the data. For details on how to configure security settings for private records, see "Secure Your Treo with a Password" in Chapter 3, "Customizing and Personalizing Your Treo."

8. Another important detail worth exploring when creating a new event is the Repeat option. If you tap the **Repeat** pick list, you can choose a time repetition that results in the event occurring more than once. For example, if you want to schedule a weekly sales meeting as an event, you choose Every Week in the Repeat pick list. Examples of other possible values include Every Other Week, Every Month, and Every Year. There is also a Daily Until value for indicating that an event occurs daily but ends at some point in the future. And finally, you can select Other if you'd like to fine-tune your own time repetition. If you choose Other, the Change Repeat screen shown in Figure 6.9 opens.

FIGURE 6.9

The Change Repeat screen is used to create a customized repetition schedule for an event.

9. The Change Repeat screen displays a series of boxes along the top for choosing the unit of measure for the event repetition (by day, week, month, and so on). After selecting the unit of measure, enter how many units are between each repeating event in the Every field. For example, if you select Month as the unit of measure and enter 3 in the Every field, the event repeats every 3 months (quarterly). You can then tap Day or Date to determine the basis for exactly when the event occurs. When you're finished fine-tuning the event repetition, tap the **OK** button.

10. If you have additional text information that you'd like to associate with an event, you might want to include it as an attached note. To add a text note as an event attachment, tap the **Note** button (small paper icon) at the bottom of the Event Details screen. A note entry screen appears where you enter text for the event (see Figure 6.10). After entering the note text, tap the **Done** button to save the note as an attachment for the event.

NOTE The Unfiled category is an automatic category designation that applies to events that haven't been explicitly categorized.

FIGURE 6.10

The note entry screen consists of a large text edit field where you enter a text attachment for an event.

11. When you're finished entering the new event, tap the **OK** button to close the Event Details screen and save the event. Notice in Figure 6.11 that the event now includes additional icons to indicate that it has a note attached, that it has an alarm, and that it's repeating.

Events don't really get interesting until you save yourself the embarrassment of missing one, thanks to an alarm. For example, I tend to be forgetful about appointments and meetings because I don't usually have all that many, given my line of work. Figure 6.12 shows an appointment reminder that kept me from missing a lunch with my brother. You'd think a person wouldn't need reminding to eat, but as I said, I tend to be forgetful about some things.

TIP You can delete the note for an event by tapping the Delete button in the note entry screen. The note is then removed from the event.

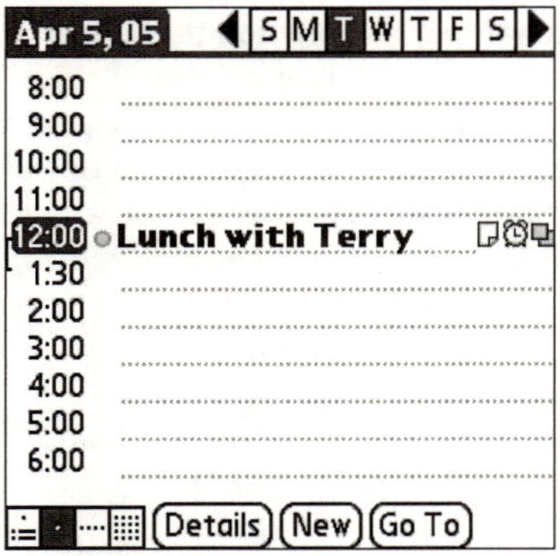

FIGURE 6.11

The event in Day view now includes note, alarm, and repeating icons.

FIGURE 6.12

Event information is displayed in an Alert screen when the alarm for an event is triggered.

Before leaving the topic of creating events, it's worth passing on a little trick that I ran across on a Treo message board. A Treo user explained how he used the event alarm feature of the Calendar application to get out of sticky social situations. For example, if you're desperately in need of a fake phone call to interrupt an uncomfortable situation and give you an excuse to leave, you can schedule an event in advance with an alarm that sounds like a phone's ringer. There is nothing tricky about doing this except specifying an alarm sound that actually sounds like a phone ring.

You learned how to change the sounds for an application in Chapter 3, "Customizing and Personalizing Your Treo," in the "Choose, Create, and Download Ring and Alert

Tones" section. To briefly recap what you learned in Chapter 3, you can access the sound preferences for the Calendar by pressing the Menu button and navigating over to the Options menu. Then scroll down and select the Sound Preferences command. In the Preferences screen that appears, you must select Tones for the Calendar application, and then change the Alarm Sound setting so that it sounds like a phone ring.

All that's left to do is create an event with an alarm that goes off at a suitable exit time, and you should have a perfect exit plan for cutting short an uncomfortable blind date or a dinner with the in-laws!

Purge Events

If you use your Treo to schedule a considerable portion of your life, you will no doubt accumulate quite a few events over time. And unlike contacts and some other PIM data, events probably won't mean nearly as much after they drift into the past. Fortunately, the Calendar application includes a purge feature for deleting all events older than a certain date. For example, you can delete all the events older than a week in the past with a single command. This is a useful way to conserve memory and clear out old events you no longer need.

To purge events in the Calendar application, follow these steps:

1. Press the **Menu** button and scroll down to the Purge menu item. Press the **Center** button on the five-way navigator (or simply tap the **Purge** menu item) to issue the Purge menu command, which displays the Purge screen (see Figure 6.13).

FIGURE 6.13

The Purge screen prompts you to purge events later than a specified amount of time.

2. The Purge screen includes a pick list for specifying how old events must be to be purged. For example, the default value of 1 Week results in all events older than one week being deleted from your device. Purging events periodically is a good idea to help save memory, although you might decide to keep events farther back than a week if you find yourself needing to reference them. You can set the purge period as far back as a month if you want, which means that only events older than a month are purged.

TIP

The Purge screen provides a handy way to blitz all old events at once. Of course, purging events like this can also be dangerous if you aren't careful. Just make sure you want to purge the events in question before going through with the purge operation.

3. To follow through with the event purge process, tap the **OK** button. If you change your mind about purging events, just tap **Cancel**.

Unless you have lots of free memory and are attached to old events, I encourage you to purge events on a regular basis. You can always choose to archive them on your desktop computer as part of the purge process. That way, they aren't completely lost forever if you prefer to keep a history of your meetings and appointments.

Customize the Calendar Views

NOTE

You'll notice a Save Archive Copy on PC check box in the Purge screen. If you select this option, a copy of the purged event is saved in an archive file on your desktop computer when the events are deleted. Archive files are managed differently for each desktop PIM application, so you need to refer to your specific PIM documentation to find out how to view and restore archive data.

Earlier in the chapter you learned about the different calendar views and the unique manner in which they display calendar data. You'll be pleased to know that you have some degree of control over how these views display your data. For example, you can turn off the category pick list near the top of the Day, Week, and Month views if you find that you don't use it and it gets in the way. You can also change the default view that's used each time you launch the Calendar application. (Initially, the default view is Day view.) And finally, several settings can be altered for each specific view.

To customize the different views in the Calendar application, follow these steps:

1. Press the **Menu** button and navigate over to the Options menu. Then scroll down to the **Display Options** menu item and press the **Center** button on the five-way navigator (or just tap **Display Options**). The Display Options screen opens (see Figure 6.14).

2. The first option, Show Category List, determines whether the category pick list is displayed in the Day, Week, and Month views. This pick list enables you to filter events by category, which means that only events in a certain category are shown. If you use categories heavily and would like to be able to filter events, you should consider enabling this option.

3. The Default View option is where you specify the default view shown when the Calendar application is launched. This setting is unique to your work style and boils down to how wide a time frame you want to see when the calendar first opens. For example, if you want to see the events for the day first, set the Default View option to Agenda or Day. If you'd prefer a bigger picture of upcoming events, set it to Week or Month.

4. The Agenda, Day, and Month boxes in the Display Options screen act as tabs that allow you to tweak each view individually. For example, Figure 6.14 shows the

Day view settings, which consist of check boxes for showing time bars and the category column and for compressing the Day view. Time bars are the little brackets next to an event that indicate how long it lasts. (You saw an example of time bars in Figure 6.1.) The category column just to the left of an event's description allows you to quickly view and edit the category for the event. And finally, the Compress Day View option causes the Day view to eliminate unscheduled time slots, if necessary, to help fit scheduled events on the screen.

> **NOTE** The Show Category List option applies only to the Day, Week, and Month views, not the Agenda view.

FIGURE 6.14

You can use the Display Options screen to customize the appearance of different calendar views.

5. Tap the **Month** box in the Display Options screen to customize the Month view (see Figure 6.15). All three Month view settings relate to displaying a particular kind of event. More specifically, you can control whether the Month view shows timed events, untimed events, and daily repeating events.

6. Tap the **Agenda** box in the Display Options screen to customize the Agenda view (see Figure 6.16). This view is probably the most interesting, in that it shows events in the context of other data, such as tasks and email messages. The first two options, Show Due Tasks and Show Messages, enable you to include tasks and email messages in the Agenda view, which can be quite useful.

> **NOTE** When multiple events overlap in time, the time bars turn red to indicate the conflict.

FIGURE 6.15

You can use the Month tab of the Display Options screen to select exactly what kinds of events are displayed in the Month view.

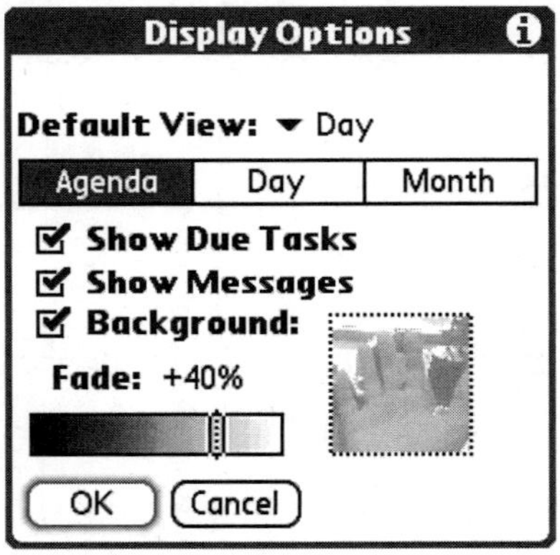

FIGURE 6.16

In the Agenda tab of the Display Options screen, you can fine-tune the display of information in Agenda view as well as specify a background image for the view.

7. The third Agenda view option, Background, allows you to select a background image for the Agenda view. Just tap the box next to the Background label, and select a picture stored on your device or on a memory card. You might need to alter the fade on the picture so that the Agenda view contrasts with the image better. To do so, just tap and drag the **Fade** slider until you get the desired fade effect. When you're finished, tap **OK** to finish tweaking the display options. Figure 6.17 shows the calendar in Agenda view with a background image.

FIGURE 6.17

Adding a background picture to the calendar's Agenda view can make the view more visually appealing.

Now that you have the Calendar application's views dialed in to meet your own needs, it's time to turn your attention to another important topic: how to send events to other people.

Send an Event to Someone

As with most of the PIM data on your Treo, events can be sent to other people (devices) via several different mechanisms. You can use email, SMS, Bluetooth, infrared, and even a Wi-Fi connection (via a Wi-Fi expansion card) to send an event. Sending an event via infrared is a little different from the other approaches, so this section focuses first on sending an event using email, SMS, or Bluetooth.

> **TIP** Another command on the Record menu of the Calendar application is Send Category, which is much more powerful than Send Event. The Send Category command sends the entire category of events currently displayed onscreen. So if you want to send all your events to another computer, just select All as the category and issue the Send Category command.

To send an event via email, SMS, or Bluetooth in the Calendar application, follow these steps:

1. Tap the **Day View** box in the lower-left corner of the screen to switch to Day view; none of the other views supports sending events. Then tap to select the event you'd like to send.
2. Press the **Menu** button, scroll down the Record menu to the Send Event menu item, and press the five-way navigator. (You can also simply tap the **Send Event** menu item.) The Send With screen appears. Tap the messaging transport approach you'd like to use, and then tap the **OK** button.

TIP Similar to Send Category, the Beam Category command beams the entire category of events currently displayed onscreen. So if you want to beam all your events to another device, just select All as the category and issue the Beam Category command.

3. Your device immediately starts looking for discoverable Bluetooth devices. After a few seconds of searching, a list of devices from which you can choose is displayed. Tap to select the device to which you want to send the event, and then tap **OK**.

4. Depending on whether you have established a Bluetooth connection with the device in the past and flagged it as a trusted device, you might have to enter a passkey for the device. The device's owner will supply this information. Other than that, sending the event is mostly automatic.

Keep in mind that you can also send an event via more traditional channels, such as email and SMS. If you select an option such as email or SMS, you are prompted to specify the "To" address for the event.

You also have the option of sending an event via infrared, which is a little different from the other approaches. Most Palm devices support transferring events and other PIM data via infrared because it's the original wireless technology used in PDAs, so you shouldn't have any trouble sharing events with other Treo devices and other devices in the Palm family. To beam an event in the Calendar application via infrared, follow these steps:

NOTE When attempting to beam events between a Treo 650 and a Treo 600, some users have reported problems with the devices not seeing each other if the Treo 650 has a username longer than 10 characters. You can change your username by selecting Users from the Tools menu in the Palm Desktop application on your desktop computer. Just make sure you update the new username in any applications that require you to enter the name.

1. Tap the **Day View** box in the lower-left corner of the screen to switch to Day view; none of the other views supports beaming events. Then tap to select the event you'd like to send.

2. Press the **Menu** button, scroll down to the Beam Event menu item, and press the five-way navigator (or simply tap **Beam Event**). The Beam screen appears, and your device begins looking for another Palm device to beam the event to.

3. When the Beam screen appears, lining up the infrared port on your Treo with the infrared port on the other device is crucial. To do this, aim the top edges of the devices at each other. For example, you can set two Treo devices on a flat surface with their antennas aimed at each other. Keep in mind that infrared ports on Palm devices are designed to work within a range of about three feet, so you must keep the devices fairly close to each other.

4. The person on the other end of the beaming needs to accept the event and specify a category for it. Otherwise, the event is sent with no additional effort on your part.

If you're on the receiving end of an infrared event transfer, first make sure you have the infrared port of your device turned on. (To do this, launch the Prefs application and tap

Power to enable the Beam Receive option.) Then when the beamed event notification arrives, select a category for it and accept it to receive the event. The event is then added to the calendar and appears on the appropriate date.

Publish Your Calendar Online

You might not realize it, but you have the option to take the synchronization of calendar events beyond the obvious approach of synchronizing your device with a desktop computer. I'm talking about the prospect of synchronizing your device with an online calendar so that you can access your schedule from the Web. An online calendar can serve as a useful central repository for calendar events because you can make it accessible to other people.

Several online calendar options are available, but I've found Yahoo! Calendar, a free service of Yahoo!, particularly useful. The Yahoo! Calendar service relies on a software component called Intellisync for Yahoo!, which takes care of the details of synchronizing data with your Treo device. In reality, Intellisync for Yahoo! is just a conduit that integrates with the HotSync Manager application.

> **NOTE** Feel free to do some research and explore other online calendar options. I don't have any affiliation with Yahoo!, by the way. I just found its online calendar to be relatively easy to set up and use with Treo devices.

Before you can use the Yahoo! Calendar, you need to register a free Yahoo! account, assuming you don't already have one. You can register a new account directly from the Yahoo! Calendar Web site at http://calendar.yahoo.com/. If you don't already have a Yahoo! ID, click Sign Up on the Yahoo! Calendar page and follow the steps to create an account.

You can start using the Yahoo! Calendar as soon as you register and log on with your Yahoo! ID. In fact, Yahoo! Calendar is a useful application to use as a PIM client if you don't use Microsoft Outlook or some other similar application. Yahoo! also offers free email, address book, and notepad applications that you can use with the Yahoo! Calendar and also synchronize with your device.

> **NOTE** The Yahoo! Calendar can also be synchronized with desktop PIM applications. Currently, the only desktop applications supported are Microsoft Outlook, ACT!, and Lotus Organizer on Windows computers. Outlook Express is also supported, although it allows you to synchronize only the address book.

To synchronize the Yahoo! Calendar with your Treo device, you must download and install the Intellisync for Yahoo! application on your desktop computer. Although Intellisync for Yahoo! is a desktop application, its primarily role is providing a conduit that serves as a synchronization mechanism between the calendar on your device and the online Yahoo! Calendar application. Click Sync in the upper-right corner of the Yahoo! Calendar Web page to download and install the Intellisync for Yahoo! application.

After installing Intellisync for Yahoo!, launch the application to begin synchronizing your Treo device with your online Yahoo! calendar. Before actually initiating the synchronization process, setting up the Intellisync for Yahoo! application for synchronization is important. Click the Setup button to get started. The Settings & Configuration dialog box shown in Figure 6.18 opens, which requires you to log on with your Yahoo! ID and password.

FIGURE 6.18

Before you can set up Intellisync for Yahoo!, you must log on to your Yahoo! account.

After logging on to the Intellisync for Yahoo! application with your Yahoo! ID and password, the Intellisync for Yahoo! Configuration dialog box opens (see Figure 6.19). In this dialog box, you specify which types of PIM data you'd like to synchronize between your device and Yahoo!. Click the check box next to the Calendar application to enable the synchronization of calendar data.

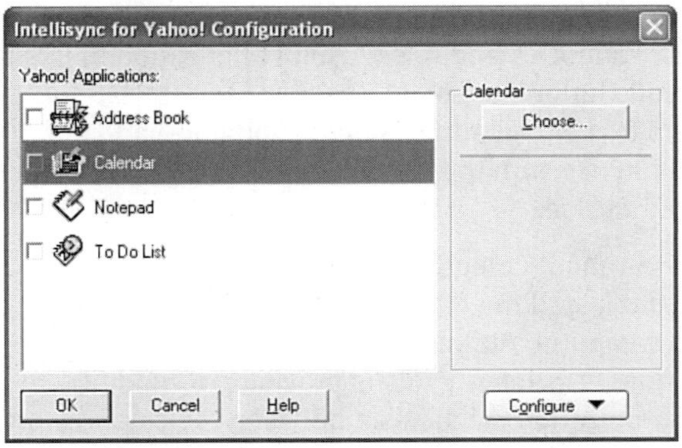

FIGURE 6.19

To enable the synchronization of calendar data, you must select the Calendar check box in the Intellisync for Yahoo! Configuration dialog box.

The Choose Application dialog box opens immediately after you select the Calendar application. This dialog box contains a list of applications for use in synchronizing with Yahoo! Calendar. Make sure Synchronize is selected near the bottom of the dialog box, click to select Palm Handheld in the list, and then click OK to commit the setting.

> **NOTE** The only downside to the Yahoo! Calendar is that it's designed for a one-to-one synchronization with your device. In other words, you can't simultaneously synchronize your Treo device directly with a desktop PIM application and an online calendar. However, you could instead synchronize your Treo with a desktop PIM application, and then synchronize the desktop PIM with an online calendar. This sounds messy, but it's not a bad option if you want to use both a desktop PIM application and an online calendar. Otherwise you'll have to choose between using Microsoft Outlook, for example, and Yahoo! Calendar because you can't synchronize your device directly with both at once.

Click OK again to close the Intellisync for Yahoo! Configuration dialog box and accept the new settings. You are returned to the main Intellisync for Yahoo! application window, where you can then click the Sync button to synchronize your device calendar with Yahoo! Calendar. Keep in mind that the actual synchronization doesn't take place until you synchronize your device via the HotSync Manager application.

To finally synchronize your Treo calendar with the online Yahoo! Calendar, all you must do is connect your device to your desktop computer and press the HotSync button on the Multi-connector cable. The synchronization should proceed and synchronize events between your device and the online Yahoo! Calendar. Figure 6.20 shows my Yahoo! Calendar after synchronizing events from my device.

The online Yahoo! Calendar application has all kinds of cool features that are outside the scope of this book. For example, you can create a group calendar for a specific group of people and then share events. With Yahoo! Calendar, you can also go beyond the online calendar to use an online address book, task manager, and notepad application and synchronize them all with your device. Just keep in mind that you can use a desktop PIM application or the online approach, but not both simultaneously. To synchronize a desktop PIM application and an online PIM manager with your device, you must first synchronize your device to the desktop application, and then synchronize the desktop application with the online manager.

Tweak the Calendar Preferences

Getting back to the Calendar application on your device, you can customize several preferences to get the calendar running exactly as you want. For example, you can control the time frames shown in Day view and Month view. So if your work day is from 7:00 to 4:00 instead of 9:00 to 6:00, for example, you can customize the start and end times to show only those hours.

To change the calendar preferences in the Calendar application, follow these steps:

1. Press the **Menu** button and navigate over to the Options menu. Then scroll down to the Preferences menu item and press the **Center** button on the five-way navigator (or tap **Preferences**). The Preferences screen opens, as shown in Figure 6.21.

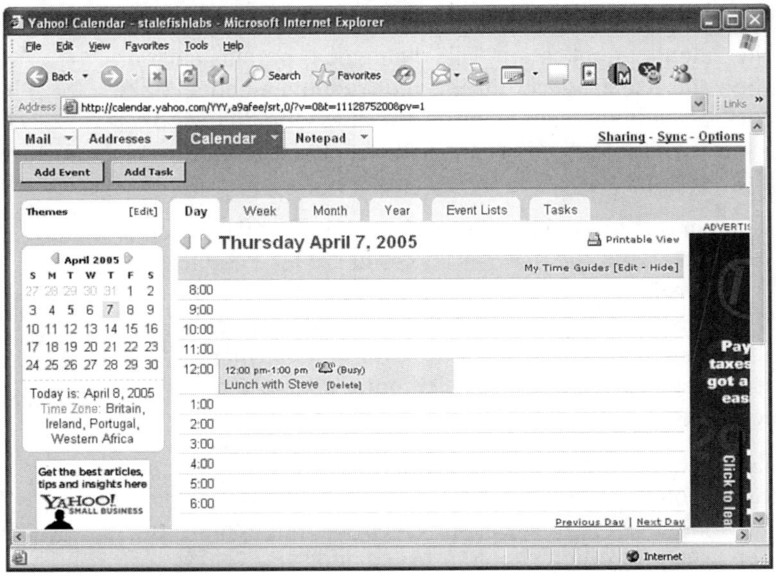

FIGURE 6.20

An event entered on my Treo device appears in the online calendar after synchronizing.

TIP If a conflict is encountered while synchronizing your device with the Yahoo! Calendar, the Palm Conflict Notifier window appears. This conflict likely stems from trying to directly synchronize your device with a desktop PIM client and the Yahoo! Calendar at the same time, which isn't allowed. To correct the conflict, you must disable one of the synchronization applications from HotSync Manager.

2. The first two options, Start Time and End Time, determine the time frames shown in Day view and Month view. Unless events are created that carry over beyond the start and end times, the Day view is limited to showing the time frame established by the start and end times. The Month view is a little less exact and tends to begin with the start time but ignore the end time.

3. The second option in the calendar's Preferences screen is New Events Use Time Zones, which determines whether new events are dependent on the current time zone. If this option is enabled, all new events must have a time zone set, and their times are automatically adjusted to reflect the device's current time zone.

4. When you're finished setting the calendar preferences, tap **OK** to accept the changes and return to the main Calendar application.

Now that you've successfully dissected the Calendar application and how to customize its behavior, you can move on to tasks.

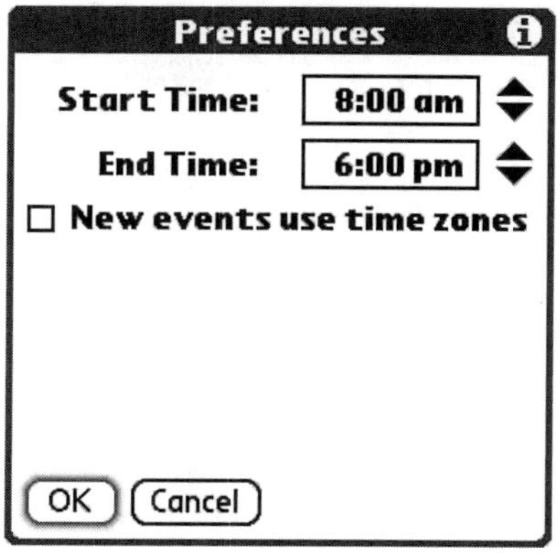

FIGURE 6.21

In the Preferences screen, you can customize the times shown on the calendar and specify whether all new events use time zones.

View and Create Tasks

The Tasks application on your device handles the management of tasks. Some users struggle to know when to use a task as opposed to an event. Unlike events, tasks aren't as exacting in terms of timing. For example, most tasks have due dates, but the due date is literally just a date without a time associated with it. Contrast this with events, which usually have a specific start time and end time. Additionally, because tasks are typically reserved for projects or actions that have a completion, you designate a task as being completed or not. So tasks are handy for processes or actions that have a due date associated with completing the task.

To manage tasks using the Tasks application, follow these steps:

1. Press the **Application** button to open the main application screen.
2. Press the **T** key to jump near the Tasks application, and then navigate with the five-way navigator to select the **Tasks** application if it isn't already selected.
3. Press the **Center** button to launch the Tasks application. The Tasks screen appears, revealing a single task that reminds you to register your device with Palm (see Figure 6.22).
4. Notice in Figure 6.22 that the register task has a small note icon next to it, which indicates that a note is attached to the task. To view the note, just tap the note icon next to the task in the list. When you're finished viewing the task, tap the **Done** button to close it.

FIGURE 6.22

The Tasks screen displays a list of tasks, which serves as an electronic to-do list.

5. Creating a task simply involves tapping the New button and entering the task description and due date (if desired). Tap the **New** button to get started. After entering a short task description, tap the due date column just to the right of the description. In the pick list that appears, you specify a due date for the task (see Figure 6.23).

FIGURE 6.23

Use the due date pick list for a task to specify a due date, which is optional.

6. When specifying the due date for a task, you can select **No Date** if the task is open-ended and doesn't have an exact due date. Or select **Choose Date** if you'd like to select a specific date that's not represented in the pick list. The Due Date screen shown in Figure 6.24 enables you to navigate quickly to a specific year, month, and day.

FIGURE 6.24

The Due Date screen is used to select an exact due date for a task.

7. You can specify several details when creating a task. With the task selected in the task list, tap the **Details** button. The Task Details screen appears, as shown in Figure 6.25.

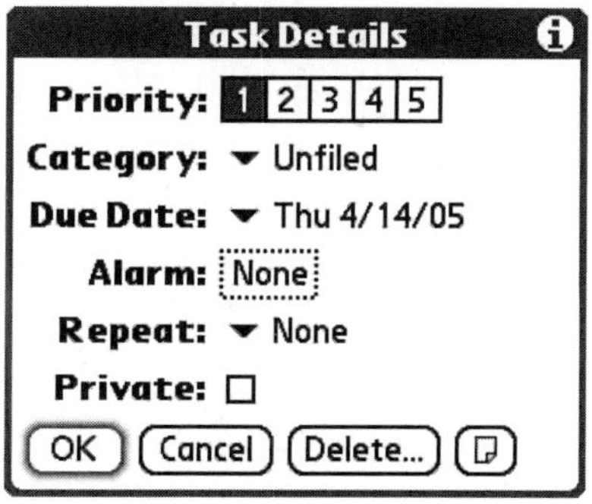

FIGURE 6.25

The Task Details screen is used to enter details for a task, such as its priority and category, and to indicate whether it is repeating.

8. Enter the task details, including a description, the priority level (1 is the most urgent and 5 is the least urgent), the category, the due date, whether you want an alarm to notify you of the task's due date, and whether the task is repeating. You can also flag the task as private by selecting the **Private** check box.

> **TIP** To delete a task, select the task and press the Menu button. Press the Center button on the five-way navigator to issue the Delete Task command (or tap it) on the Record menu. Or edit the task and tap the Delete button in the Task Details screen.

9. You can add a note to the task in the Task Details screen by tapping the **Note** button and entering a text note that you'd like to associate with the task.
10. When you're finished editing the task details, tap the **OK** button to accept the changes.

Even if you aren't a taskmaster in terms of documenting every little thing you do in your life, you might still find the Tasks application useful. My Treo goes almost everywhere I go, so with important tasks stored on my device, I find it handy to have access to them from anywhere.

Send a Task to Someone

You're probably starting to get the idea that just about any record on your Treo can be sent to another device with little effort. Chapter 5, "Managing Treo Contacts," showed you how to send contacts using any of several delivery mechanisms, and "Send an Event to Someone" earlier in this chapter explained how to send events. You might have caught on at the time that the process of sending an event is identical to that of sending a contact. The same process applies to sending tasks. For this reason, I'll spare you the details of a play-by-play description of sending tasks.

> **TIP** You can easily purge old tasks by using the Purge command on the Record menu. Purging tasks is identical to purging events, which you learned how to do earlier in the chapter. If you elect to purge any tasks, make certain you want to purge the tasks in question before going through with the purge operation.

All you need to know about sending tasks is that sending is carried out via the Send Task and Beam Task commands available on the Record menu. There are also Send Category and Beam Category commands for sending an entire category of tasks at once. If you don't quite remember how these commands work for other PIM data types, check out the "Send an Event to Someone" section earlier in this chapter or "Send and Receive Contacts Wirelessly" in Chapter 5.

Edit Task Preferences

The Tasks application includes several preferences that can be tweaked to alter the sorting and display of tasks in the main task list. To change the preferences for the Tasks application, follow these steps:

1. Press the **Menu** button and navigate over to the Options menu. Then scroll down to the Preferences menu item and press the **Center** button on the five-way navigator (or tap the **Preferences** menu item). The Preferences screen appears, as shown in Figure 6.26.

FIGURE 6.26

The Preferences screen includes several settings for customizing the look and feel of the task list.

2. The Sort By option presents a pick list of settings that control the order of tasks in the task list. You can sort the task list by priority, due date, category, and various combinations of these task properties.
3. Other options in the Preferences screen include check boxes for hiding or showing completed tasks, due dates, priorities, and categories. One option that doesn't directly affect the appearance of the task list is Record Completion Date, which records the completion date of finished tasks as the due date for the tasks. In other words, the due date of the task is automatically altered to match the actual completion date.
4. The last option in the Preferences screen is Alarm Sound, which enables you to customize the alarm sound played for a task alarm. Tap the **Alarm Sound** pick list to select a different alarm sound.
5. When you're finished setting the task preferences, tap **OK** to accept the changes and return to the main Tasks application.

The task preferences might not dramatically change the way you use the Tasks application, but they do allow you to carefully configure the main task list so that it shows exactly the task information you want to see. Besides, you might find it worth the effort to simply change the alarm sound for tasks.

Manage Memos

The Memos application is simply a list of text notes that you can edit and organize. You can think of a memo as an electronic Post-It note, where you can quickly jot down any information worth remembering for later. I've used memos for construction parts lists, grocery lists, project notes, and even driving directions. You'll likely find your own unique uses for memos.

To create a new memo, follow these steps:

1. Press the **Application** button to open the main application screen.
2. Press the **M** key to jump near the Memos application, and then navigate with the five-way navigator to select the Memos application, if it isn't already selected.
3. Press the **Center** button to launch the Memos application. The Memos screen appears, revealing a list of memos currently stored on your device; this list is likely empty if you haven't already created any memos. Figure 6.27 shows a memo list that consists of a single memo.

FIGURE 6.27

The Memos screen displays a list of memos, which are roughly akin to electronic Post-It notes.

4. To create a new memo, simply tap the **New** button in the lower-left corner of the screen. The memo entry screen appears, which is simply a big text edit field. To enter the memo text, just start typing.
5. You can customize a couple of details for a memo by tapping the **Details** button near the bottom of the screen. The Memo Details screen allows you to edit the category for the memo and specify whether the memo is private (see Figure 6.28). To categorize the memo, simply tap the **Category** pick list and select a category. To flag the memo as private, tap the **Private** check box. Tap the **OK** button to finish entering memo details.

> **TIP** The name of a memo that appears in the memo list is the first line of text in the memo. So you can name a memo by entering the text you want on the memo's first line.

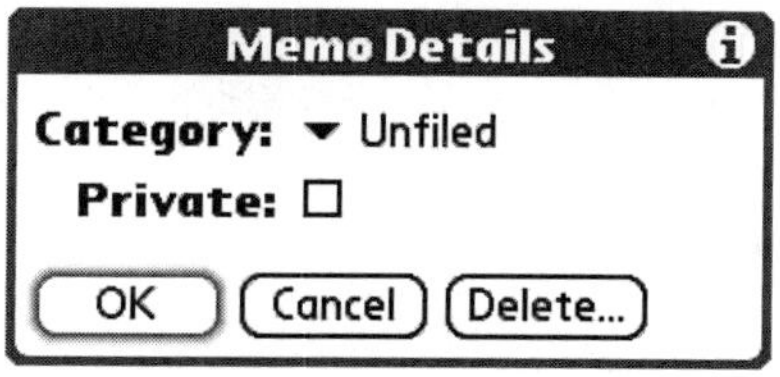

FIGURE 6.28

You can use the Memo Details screen to specify the category for a memo and flag it as private.

6. When you're finished entering the new memo, tap the **Done** button to save and close it.

The new memo is added to the memo list, where you can tap it to view its text. Keep in mind that because memos can be categorized like other types of PIM data, you can easily filter the memo list by using the pick list at the upper-right corner of the Memos screen. Beyond that, the Memos application is quite simple.

Summary

I suspect you probably already had a good idea about how your Treo device manages PIM data, such as events, tasks, and memos. Even so, this chapter has provided an important piece of the PIM puzzle by guiding you through the ins and outs of the applications that give you access to events, tasks, and memos. In many ways, these applications work in concert with each other as well as the Contacts, Messaging, and Phone applications. You've already learned how to use the Contacts application, but Part III, "Staying Connected with Your Treo," focuses on how to carry out communications by using your Treo as a phone, an email, and a text-messaging tool, not to mention how to browse the Web and connect with other devices via Bluetooth.

Staying Connected with Your Treo

Part III

7

Using Your Treo as a Mobile Phone

With all that the Treo is capable of doing as a handheld computer, it's almost possible to overlook that it's a mobile phone at heart. The Treo is such a powerful mobile phone, however, that overlooking its mobile phone capabilities is impossible. With numerous options when it comes to dialing, managing multiple calls, and identifying callers by both aural (unique ring tones) and visual (photo caller ID) cues, the Treo is one of the most advanced mobile phones you can get. Perhaps the most interesting aspect of the Treo as a mobile phone is how you can multitask while on a call. For example, you can leave the Phone application to carry out other tasks during a conversation. This chapter explores the Treo 650's mobile phone features inside and out.

IN THIS CHAPTER

- Treo Phone Essentials
- Manage Phone Calls with Ease
- Create and Manage Favorites
- Secure Your Treo Phone
- Access the Call Log
- Call via Voice Activation
- Revisiting Ring Tones
- Tweak the Phone Preferences

Treo Phone Essentials

The first thing to get straight for the mobile phone capabilities of Treo devices is the *mobile radio*, which is a hardware component in your device that's responsible for connecting the device to a wireless phone network. Unlike most mobile phones, which are "on" at all times if powered up, the mobile radio on your Treo can be turned on and off independently of the device. This allows you to work with your Treo "offline" without any regard for incoming calls or, more important, without any worries of interfering with a sensitive electrical environment, such as on an airplane. Using your Treo with the radio turned off also offers the added benefit of saving battery life.

To turn the mobile radio on your Treo on and off, follow these steps:

> **NOTE** The radio used for mobile telephony is not the only radio built into your Treo. There's also a Bluetooth radio for establishing wireless Bluetooth connections. When I refer to the "mobile radio," I'm talking about the primary radio in your device that's used for phone/data communications. I will always be specific when referring to any other radios, as in "Bluetooth radio."

> **NOTE** Step 1 assumes that the mobile radio on your Treo isn't already turned on. You can easily tell whether the radio is on by looking for a small signal strength indicator in the upper-right corner of the screen—it appears as a small antenna icon just to the left of the battery icon.

1. Make sure your device is on, and then hold down the **Power/End** button until a screen appears notifying you that the radio is turned on. An indicator appears in the upper-right corner of the screen (next to the battery icon) that shows the signal strength of the network connection.
2. Hold down the **Power/End** button again until a screen appears indicating that the radio is turned off. You won't be able to make or receive phone calls or connect for data services (messaging, Web browsing, and so forth.).

It bears repeating that if you're in a situation in which you don't want to or can't receive calls (an airplane, for example), you should turn the mobile radio off. Not only does the mobile radio eat up battery power while it's on, but it also eats up even more power attempting to find a network when you're out of range. So if you know you're going to be out of range for a while, save your battery and turn the mobile radio off.

Speaking of the mobile radio, it holds the key to some important device information that you might want to access at some point. This information includes your mobile phone number, data services username, software version number, and several other tidbits of information that you may or may not ever need. Follow these steps to take a look at your device information:

1. Press the **Phone/Send** button to launch the Phone application. The main Phone screen appears.
2. Press the **Menu** button, navigate over to the **Options** menu, and then scroll down and select **Phone Info**. The Phone Info screen appears, as shown in Figure 7.1.
3. The Phone Info screen contains several pieces of information about your Treo phone, most of which is admittedly a bit cryptic. The first piece of information is your phone number, which you probably already know. The second field depends entirely on your wireless carrier and contains the username for accessing wireless data services. The Electronic Serial Number (ESN) is next; this hexadecimal number uniquely identifies your device. You can request this number when you initially set up data services or otherwise need to identify your device to a service provider. The last field of interest is Software, which contains the version number of your device. In Figure 7.1, the version number is sandwiched between the text Treo650- and -SPCS, which in this case is 1.03. The remaining information in the Phone Info screen is advanced device information that you're unlikely to ever need.

FIGURE 7.1

The Phone Info screen displays information about your device, such as the phone number, data services username, and software version number.

4. When you're finished viewing the Phone Info screen, tap **OK** to exit back to the main Phone screen.

NOTE Your Treo's version number might be formatted slightly differently based on your wireless carrier. However, you should still be able to pick out a number in the form *x.xx* without too much trouble.

Now that you know how to turn the mobile radio on and off and access phone information, you're ready to actually start using your Treo as a mobile phone.

Several Ways to Dial

One of the most common tasks associated with any phone is dialing a number to originate a call. There are numerous ways to dial a number with the Treo phone. The most obvious ways are to simply tap numbers on the Dial Pad in the Phone application or press the numeric keys on the keyboard. The keyboard automatically changes to numeric entry mode when you're in the Phone application, so you don't have to press the Option key to dial numbers. Figure 7.2 shows the Phone application with the Dial Pad visible and a number being dialed.

NOTE If you've changed the Phone application to show wallpaper instead of the Dial Pad (see "Select Wallpaper for the Phone" in Chapter 3, "Customizing and Personalizing Your Treo"), you can still dial a number by typing number keys on the keyboard. The Dial Pad automatically appears as soon as you begin typing.

Although dialing a phone number by manually entering the numbers is probably the most familiar way to initiate a call on your Treo, it certainly isn't the most efficient. Following are the primary ways you can make a call with your Treo:

1. Tap the numbers on the Dial Pad or press the number keys on the keyboard. Optionally, if the Typing Starts Contacts Search setting is enabled (see the "Tweak the Phone Preferences" section later in this chapter),

pressing keys on the keyboard allows you to spell a contact's name instead of dialing a number—enter the contact's first initial followed by his or her last name. Usually you'll get a match within three or four characters.

FIGURE 7.2

The Dial Pad in the Phone application is a simple approach to dialing a phone number to initiate a call.

> **TIP** To quickly dial a plus sign for an international call, hold down the zero key until the 0 turns into a +.

> **NOTE** A *favorite* is a piece of information you'd like to be readily accessible via a special link in the Phone application. You learn about favorites later in the chapter in "Create and Manage Favorites."

2. Dial a number from the call history—press the **Phone/Send** button once to view the call history, and then scroll to select the number/contact to dial.
3. Tap a speed dial favorite or hold down the quick key for a favorite.
4. Tap the number of a contact in the Contacts application; you can quickly jump to the Contacts application from the phone via the Contacts favorite.
5. Tap a phone number in a message or web page.
6. Reply to a message via a phone call—tap the **Respond** button with the message selected, and then select **Call Sender** from the pick list that appears.
7. Paste a phone number into the Phone application.

As you can see, there are quite a few ways to initiate a phone call through various applications on your Treo. Of course, all these methods require the mobile radio to be turned on. I find that the call history and favorites are the quickest and most efficient ways to make calls. More than likely, you can isolate the majority of your calls to a few numbers. These numbers make great candidates for favorites, which allow you to establish a speed dial shortcut for dialing the numbers. With a speed dial favorite, you can navigate the list of favorites and tap the number (contact) to dial it. You can also go a step further and assign a quick key for a favorite; with this method, you simply hold down a key on the keyboard to dial the number.

Adjust the Call Volume and Control the Speakerphone

The call volume is something you'll likely need to adjust from call to call based on a variety of factors, such as the quality of the connection, the loudness of the person's voice, and so on. To adjust the volume of a call, just press the top and bottom of the Volume button on the left side of your device, and then press the Side button just below the Volume button to confirm the setting change. Normally, the Volume button controls the volume of rings, but during a call, it changes to control the call volume. Even so, there's only one true volume setting, meaning that the ring volume changes when you change the call volume.

> **TIP** You can turn the speakerphone on and off quickly by pressing the Space key on the keyboard.

A feature closely related to the call volume is the speakerphone, which is controlled by tapping the Spkr-phone button on the Phone screen during a call. When speakerphone is enabled, the Spkr-phone button changes to Cancel Spkr so that you can turn off the speakerphone if you want to return to the traditional phone earpiece. The call volume is important for the speakerphone feature because you'll likely need to turn up the volume to hear the person on the other end of the line.

While I'm on the subject of the speakerphone, you might be wondering about wireless headsets and hands-free car kits. You can use these devices with your Treo, thanks to the Bluetooth wireless networking support built into your device. Check out Chapter 11, "Communicating Wirelessly with Bluetooth," for details on how to connect your Treo to a Bluetooth headset or hands-free car kit for wireless hands-free phone calls.

> **NOTE** You're probably already aware that some states, such as New York, now require mobile phone users to use hands-free headsets or car kits if they plan to use a mobile phone while driving. In these states, Bluetooth headsets and car kits aren't just luxuries; they are necessities if you want to drive and use your Treo as a mobile phone.

Prevent Accidental Screen Taps

If you don't use a headset of some kind when talking on your Treo phone, you might realize that sooner or later your face will accidentally brush against the screen and be interpreted as a tap. This can potentially result in putting the caller on hold or even hanging up the call, depending on where the tap registers on the screen. Fortunately, you can prevent accidental screen taps easily by disabling screen taps entirely during calls. This feature is called Keyguard and was first mentioned back in Chapter 3, "Customizing and Personalizing Your Treo." Two aspects of the Keyguard feature are specific to the Treo phone.

Follow these steps to configure Keyguard and disable the touchscreen during phone calls:

1. Press the **Application** button to open the main application screen.
2. Press the **P** key to jump near the Prefs application, and then navigate with the five-way navigator to select the Prefs application.
3. Press the **Center** button to launch the Prefs application. The Preferences screen appears and displays several options for tweaking device settings.
4. Navigate to **Keyguard** on the Preferences screen under the General heading, and press the **Center** button to open Keyguard preferences. Figure 7.3 shows the Keyguard Preferences screen.

FIGURE 7.3

You can use the Keyguard Preferences screen to disable the touchscreen when using the Treo phone.

5. The two check boxes near the bottom of the Keyguard Preferences screen are for disabling the touchscreen during phone calls. More specifically, the first setting disables the touchscreen when an incoming call arrives, which prevents you from accidentally answering a call by touching the screen. The second option applies to calls in progress and disables the touchscreen during all calls. If you're concerned about accidental screen taps, it's a good idea to select both check boxes.
6. Tap the **Done** button when you're finished tweaking the Keyguard settings.

Generally speaking, I find that disabling the touchscreen during phone calls is a good idea. However, if you like to use the stylus, you might want to experiment and see whether you really do accidentally bump the screen with your face. This setting is ultimately a personal preference.

Manage Phone Calls with Ease

The Phone application on your Treo provides a great deal of flexibility in managing calls you make and receive. You can easily put calls on hold, make additional calls, and conference people together into a single call. The buttons on the main Phone screen change to reflect the current state of the phone and the available options.

When an incoming call arrives, you have the option of answering or ignoring the call, as shown in Figure 7.4.

If you don't want to bother using the buttons on the screen, you can answer or ignore a call by using the familiar Phone/Send (green) and Power/End (red) hardware buttons to answer and ignore the call, respectively. You can also press the bottom part of the Volume button to mute the ringer on an incoming call. If you want to get a little more aggressive in muting all calls from a particular person, you can create a favorite for that person and set the ring tone to No Sound. You learn how to do this later in the chapter in "Create and Manage Favorites."

NOTE Keep in mind that the Keyguard settings mentioned here apply only to the touchscreen, not the keyboard. So you can still answer a phone call by pressing the Phone/Send button as well as hanging up and putting calls on hold by navigating through the onscreen buttons with the five-way navigator.

FIGURE 7.4

Answer and Ignore buttons appear on the main Phone screen when an incoming call arrives.

After you're connected on a phone call, there are a few options at your disposal. You can hang up the call, turn on the speakerphone, put the caller on hold, return to the Dial Pad, and mute the microphone. These options are clearly visible as buttons in Figure 7.5.

TIP Use the Ringer switch on the top of your device to quickly mute all device sounds (except the speakerphone), such as the ringer on incoming calls.

FIGURE 7.5

There are several things you can do after you're connected on a phone call.

> **TIP** You might notice that Figure 7.4 shows a picture of the caller. You enable picture caller ID by assigning a picture to the Picture field of a contact. Check out the section "Create a New Contact" in Chapter 5, "Managing Treo Contacts," to find out how to set this field for a new contact.

The Dial Pad button visible at the far right is used to access the Dial Pad during a call. This is important if you need to enter a PIN code for accessing an online account or maybe to dial the name of a person into a phone directory. Below the Dial Pad button is the Mute button, which mutes the microphone on your device.

The Hold button is probably the most interesting feature on the main call screen. By tapping the Hold button, you place the caller on hold. You might want to put someone on hold while you perform some other task on your device or so that you can initiate another phone call to establish a three-way conference call. Figure 7.6 shows the Phone screen with a caller on hold.

Although the Dial Pad and Mute buttons disappear when a caller is placed on hold, a new Add Call button appears. This button is used to make another phone call so that you can maintain two calls at once or conference two calls into a single three-way call. If you tap the Add Call button and make another call, the two calls appear together on the Phone screen with the original call on hold and the new call active. The Add Call button is now gone, but another new button has been added: Conf. You can use the Conf button to conference the two calls to form a single three-way call. Figure 7.7 shows the Conf button available for conferencing two calls.

The Treo is fairly rigid in terms of how it allows you to manage conference calls. For example, you can join calls only if you initiate the second call yourself. In other words, you can't establish a conference call if someone calls while you're on a call. However, you can initiate a three-way call if you received the first call and dial the second one. Additionally, you're limited to creating only a three-way call: that is, you plus two other calls. And finally, you aren't allowed to separate out a conference call after you've joined callers. I mention these limitations because other handheld communicators, such as BlackBerry 7100 devices, are more flexible in terms of allowing you to join more than two callers and breaking out individual callers from a conference call. Even with these limitations, however, you'll likely find your Treo to be capable for most of your calling needs.

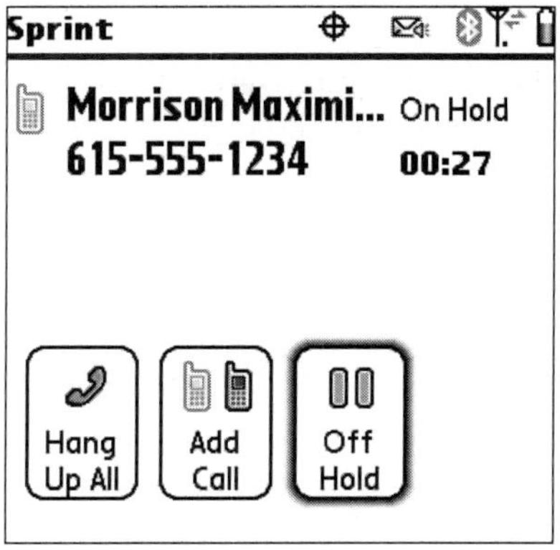

FIGURE 7.6

The Phone screen changes to show fewer options when a caller is placed on hold.

FIGURE 7.7

The Conf button appears when you initiate two calls, and it enables you to join them in a single conference call.

I mentioned that you can't conference in a call you receive if you're already on a call. In this case, the Treo phone uses call waiting to put the current call on hold and activate the new call. Although you can't conference the two calls, you can swap between them at will. Figure 7.8 shows two calls, along with the Swap button that enables you to switch between them.

FIGURE 7.8

Use the Swap button to switch between calls when you receive the second call via call waiting.

> **NOTE** You might be wondering what happens when a call arrives and you're listening to music in the RealPlayer application. If someone calls you while a song is playing, the song continues to play during the ring but pauses if you answer the call. Similarly, if you place an outgoing call, the currently playing song is paused. In either case, you must return to RealPlayer to continue playing the song. To find out more about playing music with RealPlayer, check out Chapter 13, "Listening to Digital Music."

The Swap button is certainly handy for managing two calls. You can also tap directly on the calls to swap between them.

Create and Manage Favorites

Favorites, one of the most important features in the Phone application, serve to tie the phone together with several other applications on your Treo. A favorite is a piece of information you'd like to be readily accessible via a special link in the Phone application. It can be a speed dial number, an email address, or a web address, to name a few possibilities. By default, several favorites are displayed at the bottom of the main Phone screen, as shown in Figure 7.9.

The favorites visible in Figure 7.9 are just the tip of the iceberg. To open the full favorites screen, press the Down button on the five-way navigator to scroll through the list of favorites until the list expands to fill the screen. Figure 7.10 shows the full favorites screen with several buttons in view.

You can tap any favorites button to activate that particular favorite, or you can navigate through the favorites with the five-way navigator.

For example, tap the Camera favorites button to immediate launch the digital camera. The list of favorites gives you an idea of how flexible favorites can be. You might notice page numbers at the bottom of the screen for accessing additional pages of favorites. Just tap one of the numbers to jump to another whole page of favorites.

FIGURE 7.9

Several favorites are accessible near the bottom of the main Phone screen.

FIGURE 7.10

You can access numerous favorites buttons by expanding the favorites list.

You can edit individual favorites buttons as well as the placement and ordering of buttons on the favorites pages. However, the best way to understand how favorites work is to create a new one. You can create the following types of favorites:

> **NOTE** If you're wondering how to forward calls to another number, this topic is covered later in the chapter in "Tweak the Phone Preferences."

- *Call Log*—Open the phone's call log
- *Dial Pad*—Display the Dial Pad
- *Contacts*—Open a contact in the Contacts application
- *Application*—Launch an application
- *Speed Dial*—Dial a number by using the phone
- *Message*—Send an SMS/MMS message by using the Messages application
- *Email*—Send an email message by using the VersaMail application
- *Web Link*—Open a web link by using the Blazer web browser

As you can see, there's quite a bit of flexibility in how you can create and use favorites. However, you'll likely find yourself creating favorites primarily for phone numbers (speed dial). To create a new speed dial favorite in the Phone application, follow these steps:

1. Press the **Down** button on the five-way navigator until the favorites list opens to fill the entire screen.
2. Tap a number at the bottom of the screen until you arrive at a page with empty favorites buttons.
3. Tap a blank favorites button to begin editing it. The Add Favorite screen appears, as shown in Figure 7.11.

FIGURE 7.11

Use the Add Favorite screen to create a new favorite.

4. The first field in the Add Favorite screen identifies the type of favorite, which in this case is Speed Dial. The type of favorite affects the remaining fields in the Add Favorite screen. For a speed dial favorite, you must enter the label and phone number for the favorite. Optionally, you can also specify a quick key that you can press and hold down at any time to quickly dial the number. Finally, you can change a favorite's ring tone so that you can easily identify the person when he or she calls. You used this field back in Chapter 5, "Managing Treo Contacts," when you first learned how to create a caller ID ring tone.
5. When you're finished entering the information for the new favorite, tap **OK** to finish creating it. The favorites button changes to show the label for the favorite.

> **TIP** If you're creating a favorite based on an existing contact, tap the Lookup button, and then scroll to select the contact by using the Phone Number Lookup screen.

> **NOTE** It might seem a little strange that you can enter the ring tone for a speed dial favorite because you hear a ring tone only on an incoming call. The ring tone for a speed dial favorite has nothing to do with initiating a call and is used only to help identify a particular caller (number) when the person calls you.

To use a favorite, just tap the favorites button for it. Optionally, if you established a quick key for the favorite, hold down that key to use the favorite.

As you've seen, favorites buttons are arranged on pages in the Phone application. You can rearrange the buttons on the pages in any order you want by editing the pages. To edit the favorites pages, follow these steps:

1. Press the **Down** button on the five-way navigator until the favorites list opens to fill the entire screen.
2. Press the **Menu** button, and then scroll to select the **Edit Favorites Pages** command from the **Record** menu. The Edit Favorites Pages screen appears, as shown in Figure 7.12.
3. To reorder a favorites button on the page, tap and drag the button to its new position. What makes this technique so powerful is that you can actually drag a favorites button down to a completely different page, in which case the new page appears immediately. If you drag a favorites button to a spot occupied by an existing favorite, the two buttons are swapped.
4. To edit a favorite, just tap it in the Edit Favorites Pages screen. The Edit Favorite screen appears, which is almost identical to the Add Favorite screen you saw in Figure 7.11.
5. To delete a favorite while editing it, tap the **Delete** button. After deleting a favorite, the button on the page where it existed is cleared.

> **TIP** To always mute a particular caller's ring tone, just create a favorite for the person and set his or her ring tone to No Sound.

> **TIP** If you need to enter additional digits that must be dialed after the number, such as a phone extension, tap the More button and enter the digits in the More Options screen.

FIGURE 7.12

The Edit Favorites Pages screen allows you to reorder and edit favorites buttons.

6. When you're finished editing favorites, tap the **Done** button to exit the Edit Favorites Pages screen.

Favorites are an incredibly powerful part of the Treo user interface, and when used wisely, can dramatically improve the speed and efficiency of how you work with your device.

Secure Your Treo Phone

As with any mobile device, security is an important issue with Treo devices. More specifically, phone security is important in that you might want to prevent your phone from being used to make expensive calls if it falls into the wrong hands. Or maybe you need to let someone borrow your Treo to make an emergency call, and you want to make sure the person doesn't abuse the situation. Regardless of your motives, a feature known as Phone Lock makes it possible to limit calls made with your device. When Phone Lock is enabled, your phone can be used only to make emergency calls, such as 911, unless a special lock code is entered. You can also add up to three more emergency numbers that can be dialed when the phone is locked. This makes Phone Lock an ideal feature for allowing a friend or family member to dial only a few preset numbers and nothing more.

To turn on the Phone Lock feature in the Phone application, follow these steps:

1. Press the **Menu** button, navigate over to the **Options** menu, and then scroll down and select the **Phone Lock** command. The Phone Lock screen appears, as shown in Figure 7.13.

FIGURE 7.13

The Phone Lock screen allows you to enable the Phone Lock feature.

2. The two check boxes in the Phone Lock screen determine how and when Phone Lock is activated. The first option locks the phone each time the mobile radio powers off, and the second option locks the phone immediately. Although these two options appear as check boxes, they are mutually exclusive, meaning you can select only one at a time. When you initially select one of the check boxes, you're prompted to enter your device's lock code. By default, this code is the last four digits of your mobile phone number. It's a good idea to change the code by tapping the **Change Lock Code** button; this button appears only when one of the Phone Lock options is set.
3. You're allowed to specify up to three emergency numbers that can be dialed while the phone is locked. To do this, tap the **Advanced** button, which appears only when neither Phone Lock option has been set.
4. When you're finished setting the Phone Lock feature, tap **OK** to accept the changes and close the Phone Lock screen.

The Phone Lock feature gives you a degree of security in terms of controlling how your Treo is used to make calls. Although you might find it somewhat of an inconvenience on a day-to-day basis, it's a great option to have when other people have access to your device.

Access the Call Log

You might not realize it, but the Treo phone keeps a history of every call that's made and received. You can access this listing of calls, known as the *call log*, easily to review and return calls. To access and use the call log, follow these steps:

NOTE The call log is a comprehensive listing of calls made and received. This list is different from the call history, which is a brief listing of recent calls that you can access quickly by pressing the Phone/Send button.

1. Tap the **Call Log** favorite near the bottom of the Phone screen, or press the **Phone/Send** button and select **Call Log** from the top of the call history. The Call Log screen appears (see Figure 7.14).

2. The calls listed in the call log have small icons to the left that indicate whether the call was made (left arrow), received (right arrow), or missed (dim right arrow). You can tap any call in the call log to dial the number. Or select a call in the log and press the **Details** button, which shows information about the call, including the name and number of the caller, the date, the time, and whether your phone was roaming for the call.

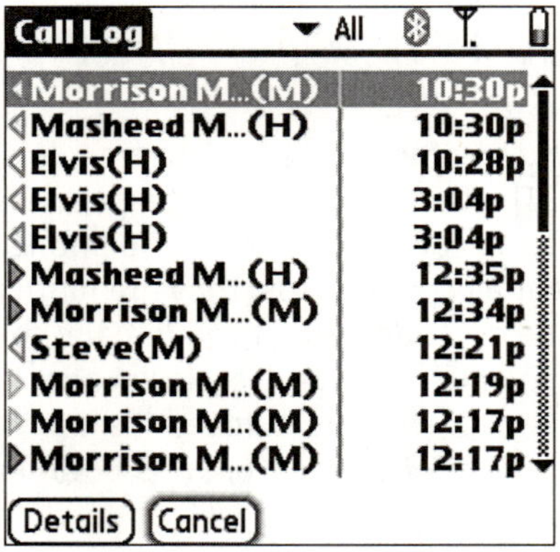

FIGURE 7.14

The Call Log screen displays a detailed history of calls made and received on your Treo.

TIP You can change the font for the call log by pressing the Menu button, navigating over to the Options menu, and then scrolling and selecting the Font command.

3. You can delete individual entries from the call log by selecting a call, pressing the **Menu** button, and then scrolling to select the **Delete Item** command from the **Record** menu. If you'd like to clear out the entire call log at once, select the **Purge** command from the same menu.

4. When you're finished with the call log, tap the **Cancel** button to return to the main Phone screen.

You might want to purge the call log from time to time to conserve memory, not to mention erasing your history of calls for security purposes. Unless you have a reason for wanting to keep track of every call on your phone, it's generally safer to clear the log every so often just in case your device ever falls into the wrong hands. Of course, your contact list might already give them everything they want, but there's no sense aiding them by keeping a fat call log. Even if you don't run in the same celebrity circles as Paris Hilton, you might still prefer to keep your history of calls to yourself.

Call via Voice Activation

Unfortunately, there's no built-in support for voice dialing in Treo devices. However, several applications make it possible to initiate calls with your voice, which is important if you plan to use your Treo with a Bluetooth hands-free car kit. One of these applications, Voice Dial, is endorsed by Palm and is available as a trial version directly from the palmOne website. Voice Dial is actually developed by VoiceSignal and must be purchased after the trial period of 14 days if you want to continue using it.

> **NOTE** The Voice Dial application is available from the palmOne website at http://www.palmone.com/us/support/downloads/treo/treovoicedialing.html.

The Voice Dial application has numerous settings for fine-tuning how accurately it recognizes what you're trying to say. Instead of going through these settings in detail, I'd rather just focus on the basics of how the application works. When you first launch the application, you're prompted to say a command, as shown in Figure 7.15. This command can be in the form "Call *Number*" or "Call *Contact Name*." You can also specify the location of the contact if you use the latter option, as in "Call Frank Rizzo Home."

FIGURE 7.15

The main Voice Dial screen prompts you to say a command to dial a phone number by voice.

When you say a command, Voice Dial immediately begins trying to determine how you want it to dial the phone. If you've spoken a number, the number is repeated to you to confirm that it's correct before initiating the call. You can simply say "Yes" or "No" to confirm the number or reject it and try again. If you've spoken a contact, Voice Dial attempts to find the correct match in your contact list. Again, you say "Yes" or "No" to indicate whether the correct contact was found. If you didn't specify a location and the contact has multiple phone numbers, Voice Dial prompts you to say the location, as in "Home," "Office," and so forth. Figure 7.16 shows a call being connected after correctly matching a contact I spoke aloud.

FIGURE 7.16

The Voice Dial application finishes by connecting to the Treo phone and dialing the specified contact.

There are lots of little nuances to the Voice Dial application that are worth exploring, but unfortunately, these topics are beyond the scope of this chapter. If voice dialing is an important feature for you, I encourage you to explore the Voice Dial application and experiment with the various settings.

Revisiting Ring Tones

Back in Chapter 3, "Customizing and Personalizing Your Treo," you learned a fair amount about ring tones and how to download and assign them on the Treo. Earlier in this chapter, you found out how to assign a ring tone to a favorite so that you can easily identify callers via a unique ring tone as well as mute undesired callers, if necessary. Along the lines of a unique ring tone for favorites, there are some additional ring tone settings that you haven't learned about yet. To access and modify these settings in the Phone application, follow these steps:

1. Press the **Menu** button, navigate over to the **Options** menu, and then scroll down and select the **Sound Preferences** command.

2. Tap the **Tones** box in the upper-middle part of the screen to view the ring tone options for the Phone application. The tone preferences appear on the screen, as shown in Figure 7.17.

FIGURE 7.17

The tone preferences consist of ring tones for phone events, such as a known caller, an unknown caller, and a call that arrives while you're roaming.

3. You can set five different tones in the tone preferences: known caller, unknown caller, roaming, voicemail, and service. The known caller tone is played when an incoming call arrives from a number that matches a contact in your contact list. Conversely, the unknown caller tone is played when a number doesn't match any contacts. With these two tones alone, you can immediately know whether a call is from a stranger or not without having to look at your phone. The remaining ring tones apply to calls received while you're roaming, voicemail notifications, and service notifications, such as when you move in and out of wireless network coverage. To change any of the tones, just scroll to select a different tone from the correspon- ding pick list.

> **TIP** You can record a new tone of your own by tapping the New button and recording the tone.

> **NOTE** The Manage button in the lower-right corner of the tone preferences screen is used to manage tones. Tone management is covered in Chapter 3 in the section "Choose, Create, and Download Ring and Alert Tones."

4. When you're finished configuring the phone ring tones, tap the **Done** button to return to the main Phone screen.

Seeing that you'll probably end up using your Treo in a hands-free setting at some point, getting audible cues for who is calling you is helpful. By setting the ring tones for the Treo phone, you can determine quickly whether a caller is familiar. Couple this feature with a unique caller ID ring tone for important callers, and you can often know whether to answer your phone without even looking at it.

Tweak the Phone Preferences

There are a few phone preferences I haven't touched on yet, and they are worth addressing before wrapping up this chapter. Some of these preferences are accessible from the phone's General Preferences screen, which you open via the General Preferences command on the Options menu. Options that you can set in this screen include the following:

- Toggle viewing wallpaper or the Dial Pad on the main Phone screen
- Toggle typing mode on the main Phone screen between dialing a number or searching for a contact
- Enable/disable the display of calendar events on the main Phone screen
- Enable/disable the display of favorites buttons on the main Phone screen, along with how many rows of buttons are shown

Other phone preferences include call forwarding, roaming, and several advanced settings accessible via the Phone Preferences screen. You open this window by selecting the Phone Preferences command on the Options menu of the phone. Of these preferences, it's particularly important to take note of the call forwarding setting. By default, the setting is disabled so that no calls are forwarded. However, you can easily forward calls from your Treo by enabling this option and entering the phone number you want calls forwarded to. Calls are forwarded to this number regardless of whether your Treo or its mobile radio is turned on or off. This setting depends on your wireless carrier and is accessible only when the mobile radio is turned on; the specifics of how it works might vary for your particular service.

> **TIP** If you find that the voicemail notification icon on your device is hanging around even after you've listened to your messages, you can clear the icon manually by tapping the Clear Voicemail icon in the Phone Preferences screen.

The final screen of phone preferences relates solely to how your device dials phone numbers. I'm referring to the Dial Preferences screen, which is accessed by selecting the Dial Preferences command on the Options menu of the Phone application. If you live in North America and your wireless carrier requires full 10-digit phone numbers when dialing, you might want to select the North American Dialing check box as well as the first check box below it. This setting applies only to seven-digit phone numbers, which are numbers where the area code isn't specified. A related setting involves automatically dialing a +1 in front of the area code, which you can also set in the Dial Preferences screen. Both settings apply only to North American users and only when you're dealing with seven-digit phone numbers or your wireless carrier requires a +1 in front of the area code.

> **TIP** Generally speaking, it's a good idea to always enter full 10-digit numbers for all your contacts.

I hope this quick tour of the Treo phone preferences has helped give you a more complete picture of what the Treo phone has to offer and, more important, how you can configure it to better suit your needs.

Summary

Seeing that you likely got rid of your mobile phone when you made the switch to a Treo, it's safe to say that the Phone application is one of the most important applications on your device. Therefore, learning how to use it effectively and efficiently to make, receive, and manage phone calls is important. This chapter has explored just about every nook and cranny of the Treo phone and, I hope, revealed some useful tips and techniques you can use to maximize the mobile phone features of your device.

8

Staying In Touch with Email

My name is Michael Morrison, and I'm an email junkie. I can't help it; it's just too efficient and convenient not to use it as much as possible. My friends joke with me that it's much easier to get in touch with me via email than by phone. Given my love of email, it should come as no surprise that I wasted no time embracing wireless email on my Treo. In fact, you could say that now I'm eating my cake and having it too! The problem with traditional email has been accessibility. Having access to wireless email just about anywhere at any time is truly an amazing leap forward for modern communications. Maybe you aren't as big a nerd as me, and you don't see wireless email on your Treo as having such a big impact on your mobile lifestyle. Just wait until you get that first eBay outbid notice, and then you'll understand where I'm coming from!

IN THIS CHAPTER

- The Scoop on Treo Email
- Create an Email Account in VersaMail
- Receive and Read Email Messages
- Create an Email Signature
- Managing Email Folders and Messages
- Take Control of Your Email with Filters
- Tweak Advanced VersaMail Settings

The Scoop on Treo Email

Unlike some other mobile devices such as the BlackBerry 7100 series, the Treo 600/650 separates text messaging from email messaging. Apparently, Palm's logic is that email communication is different enough from Short Message Service/Multimedia Messaging System (SMS/MMS) communication that they shouldn't be combined. I don't necessarily disagree—if nothing else, the Treo's separation of text and email messaging makes it a little easier to understand how each form of communication works as well as how they differ from one another. The end result is that you use two different applications for email and text messaging: VersaMail (email) and Messaging (text messaging).

To use the VersaMail account on your Treo to manage email effectively, knowing how many email accounts you want to use and how they are set up is important. Maybe you already have an account or two on a desktop or notebook computer, or maybe you're starting fresh with an entirely new account. Either way, it's worth covering some email basics before jumping into the specifics of the VersaMail application.

Examine Email Protocols

The first email concept you need to get straight is email protocols, which are important because they govern the structure of email messages and how they are delivered. Although a single protocol is used for sending email messages, there are a couple of options for receiving email messages from a mail server. Following are the email protocols VersaMail supports:

- *Simple Mail Transfer Protocol (SMTP)*—For sending email messages
- *Post Office Protocol (POP)*—For receiving email messages
- *Internet Message Access Protocol (IMAP)*—For receiving email messages

> **NOTE** If you choose to synchronize the VersaMail application with a Microsoft Exchange Server email server, you won't use any of the email protocols mentioned here. Instead, your messages are sent back and forth directly with the Exchange email server. This approach typically applies only to corporate email accounts, as opposed to individual accounts on services such as Hotmail and AOL.

SMTP is used to send email messages from the VersaMail application and is the only protocol available for this purpose. In other words, learn to love SMTP because it's your only option. Fortunately, SMTP is a capable protocol and serves your email sending needs just fine.

Both POP and IMAP are used to retrieve email messages from a mail server (not an Exchange mail server). These protocols handle the details of downloading email messages from a mail server and making them available to the Inbox. There are some differences between the protocols that will likely influence your choice of which protocol to use. However, the ultimate decision as to which protocol you use might come down to which one your mail server supports. Most Internet service providers (ISPs) support POP, so it's probably the protocol you will be forced to use unless you're connecting to a corporate mail server that supports IMAP.

IMAP is more powerful than POP, in that it provides a finer level of control over how email messages are retrieved from a server and stored on your device. IMAP allows you to synchronize the VersaMail application directly with a mail server, which alleviates the issue of deciding whether to leave copies of messages on the server or remove them after they've been retrieved. IMAP also supports multiple mail folders for organizing incoming email automatically.

Before you get the idea that IMAP is the ultimate email protocol, let me back up and say that POP is a perfectly good protocol for retrieving email with your Treo. POP is popular and is quite likely the email protocol you'll find yourself using because it's the only option for retrieving email from many mail servers. The point to take from this discussion is that, should you have the option, IMAP is a more powerful protocol, and you should consider using it. However, in the absence of IMAP, POP will serve your needs just fine. If you have a dial-up Internet service, a broadband cable modem, or DSL service, you will likely use POP; IMAP is typically available only in corporate environments with dedicated mail servers.

You might forgo SMTP, POP, and IMAP if you're using either of the following:

- Microsoft Exchange Server email
- Web-based email

If your email is running on Microsoft Exchange Server, likely through work, you use a special feature of VersaMail called ActiveSync to synchronize email directly with the Exchange server. Alternatively, you might be using one of several Web-based email accounts, such as Google Gmail. In this case, you'll probably just forgo VersaMail entirely and access your email through the Blazer Web browser—just open the Gmail web page and log on to access your email, just as though you were on a desktop or notebook computer. Check out Chapter 10, "Browsing the Wireless Web," to learn more about using the Blazer Web browser that comes with your Treo.

Email Synchronization Uncovered

Email synchronization is the process of reconciling email messages on two computers so that they match each other. More specifically, when you synchronize email between two computers, their email folders end up looking exactly alike. Unfortunately, Palm uses the term "synchronization" quite loosely when describing the email capabilities of VersaMail and HotSync. The Palm documentation gives the impression that the Treo 650 email synchronization features are much more powerful than they truly are.

But first the good news: If you're using an email account on Microsoft Exchange Server, you're in luck because VersaMail and HotSync support true email synchronization for Exchange through a built-in software component called Microsoft Exchange ActiveSync. This software takes care of wirelessly synchronizing your email, contacts, and calendar with an Exchange server. Wireless synchronization is a powerful and handy feature, but it has a nagging limitation in that you can synchronize only the main Inbox folder, not subfolders. So if you move messages around and organize them into folders on your PC, the changes aren't synchronized to your Treo. However, possibly this limitation will be lifted in a future version of Exchange ActiveSync.

The bad news for email synchronization is that you can't truly synchronize email on your Treo 650 via a POP email account. I know, the Palm documentation says that synchronization via POP is possible, but the word *synchronization* should be enclosed in quotes. Palm is simply talking about using your Treo-to-desktop connection to send and receive email messages directly with a POP mail server. In other words, there's no actual connection between VersaMail on your device and Outlook on your PC. What makes matters worse is that Palm has been less than forthcoming in admitting to this limitation, opting instead to allow VersaMail users to flounder and try in vain to get synchronization to work when it really doesn't.

> **NOTE** It's worth pointing out that some Treo users have reported success in synchronizing POP email with Outlook, but I've never seen it work in person. Numerous other users, myself included, who have been unable to get it working can attest to it being a tricky feat at best and potentially impossible in many situations. I'm left to conclude that the feature either isn't present or is extremely buggy at best. In either case, the net effect is that true POP email synchronization between VersaMail and Outlook isn't really an option with the Treo 650, at least not with the software available as of this writing.

The real problem with the lack of true POP synchronization is that there's no good way to keep your Treo and your desktop computer on the same page if you use a POP email account. Remember that POP email is not a server-side email solution, meaning that email only passes through the mail server instead of residing there. Typically, a POP email client downloads messages from the server and then instructs the server to delete the messages. In other words, the email messages ultimately live on the client; Outlook Express is a good example of an email client that works in this manner. This approach to storing messages on the client presents a huge problem for synchronization because it means that clients must communicate with each other. Compare this setup to IMAP, in which mail always stays on the server. Synchronization across multiple clients is no big deal because all they have to do is connect to the server and grab everything; clients don't have to know about each other to stay synchronized.

I have some hope that a future version of HotSync or, more specifically, the Outlook conduits for HotSync will allow true POP synchronization. In the meantime, you're better off not trying to share a POP email account between your Treo and another computer unless you don't mind keeping them in sync manually. There are some workarounds involving blind-copying messages to yourself and then filtering them according to the sender, but I'm not sure if these methods are worth the trouble. Probably your best bet for now is to turn off email synchronization entirely for POP accounts, set VersaMail so that it leaves messages on the server, and then manually delete messages on both your Treo and your desktop computer to keep them in sync. Sent messages still aren't synchronized, but you can at least keep your two Inbox folders more or less on the same page with each other.

Create an Email Account in VersaMail

> **NOTE** VersaMail is set up by default to leave messages on the server for POP accounts. See the "Tweak Advanced VersaMail Settings" section later in this chapter to find out how to change this setting.

The first step in using VersaMail to access email wirelessly on your Treo is to create an email account. Although I use the word "create," in reality you're just setting up VersaMail to access an existing email account. In other words, an email account doesn't truly exist on your Treo; you're using your Treo to access an email account hosted by an email server somewhere. Semantics aside, from the perspective of VersaMail, you have to "create" an account so that VersaMail knows how to access it. For the purposes of this chapter, "creating an account" refers to the process of informing VersaMail about an email account.

You have two options for creating an email account for use in VersaMail:

- Create the account on your desktop/notebook computer, and then synchronize it with VersaMail.
- Create the account directly in VersaMail on your device.

The approach you use primarily has to do with whether you already have an email account set up on your desktop computer. There's also the issue of what kind of desktop computer you are using—the first approach is an option only on Windows computers. If you have a Windows computer and you'd like to go with the first option, you have some added flexibility because the VersaMail Account Setup Wizard on your PC is usually capable of finding existing email accounts set up on your computer and transferring them automatically to VersaMail. Then the account creation boils down to simply synchronizing the account with your device.

If you're creating a new email account, as opposed to finding and setting up an existing account, you need to gather a few pieces of information about your account:

- Your email address, username, and password
- The email protocol used for incoming mail, such as POP or IMAP
- The name of the incoming mail server
- The name of the outgoing mail server (SMTP is assumed as the protocol)
- Any security features for the account, such as Secure Sockets Layer (SSL), Authenticated Post Office Protocol (APOP), or Extended Simple Mail Transfer Protocol (ESMTP)

> **NOTE** Although they don't necessarily solve the POP synchronization problems of VersaMail, you might consider some third-party email applications if you're itching to try something different. SnapperMail, the most popular VersaMail replacement, is available online at http://www.snappermail.com/wireless/email/. Another promising third-party Treo email client is ChatterMail, which you can find out about at http://www.chatteremail.com/.

> **NOTE** In keeping with VersaMail's tenuous connection to Microsoft Outlook, I have to report that I struggled when trying to get VersaMail to detect existing email accounts I had set up in Outlook. Again, it appears that the whole VersaMail-Outlook relationship is better suited to Exchange-based email accounts rather than POP and IMAP accounts.

With this information in hand, you're ready to get down to the business of telling VersaMail about your email account.

Create the Account from Your Desktop Computer

Palm provides a desktop application for Windows called VersaMail Setup that makes it possible to set up VersaMail email accounts on your PC. Follow these steps to use the VersaMail Setup application to create a new account:

1. Launch the VersaMail Setup application on your PC. The first step of the Account Setup Wizard appears, as shown in Figure 8.1.

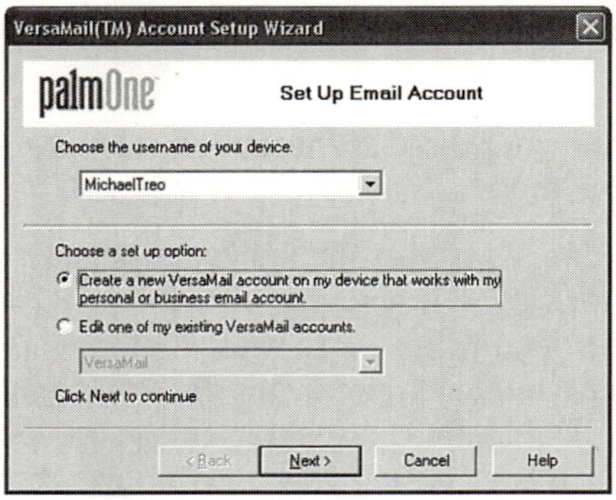

FIGURE 8.1

The first step in setting up a new email account in VersaMail involves selecting your device username and choosing a setup option.

2. First, select the username you use to synchronize your device with your desktop computer. After that, you're ready to choose a setup option. The first option, creating a new VersaMail account, is what you use to create a new email account. However, before going with that option, check to make sure an account isn't already set up by clicking the second option (for editing an existing account) and taking a look at the drop-down list. If you see an account in addition to VersaMail, you already have an account on your device, and you can select and edit it instead of creating a new account. Otherwise, go with the first option to create a new account, and then click the **Next** button.

3. Figure 8.2 shows the next step in the wizard, which prompts you about the new email account. Keep in mind that the email account in question is new only to VersaMail—it must already exist outside VersaMail. If you're lucky, VersaMail finds an existing account on your PC, and you can select An Email Account Detected on This PC to use the existing account settings. This option keeps you from having to enter the email account settings manually. Unfortunately, this process doesn't always work reliably, so you might have to select the A Mail Service from This List option, which isn't quite as automatic. If you don't see your mail service in the list, scroll to the bottom and select **Other**. Then click the **Next** button to continue with the email setup process.

> **NOTE** Editing an existing email account is virtually identical to creating a new account, except that the account details are already entered for you. So the remaining steps generally apply in either case.

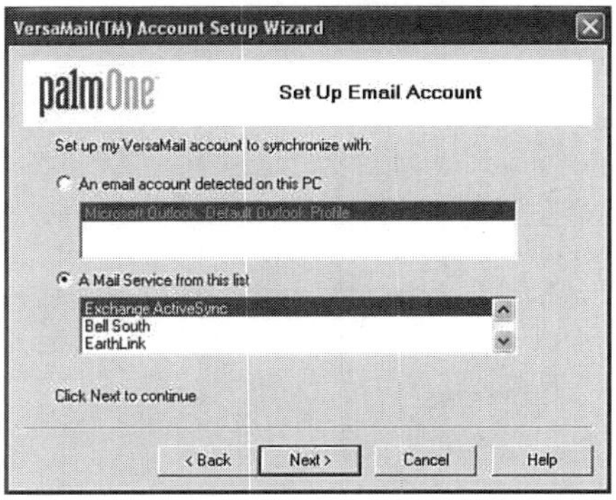

FIGURE 8.2

You can choose an account that VersaMail Setup finds on your PC, or you can create one from a list of mail services.

4. If you found your mail service in step 3, you need to just follow the service-specific setup from here on. Rather than go through the details of each service, I want to show how to set up an email account through the Other option, which applies to any POP or IMAP email account. So if you selected Other in step 3, the next choice you have to make is simply between IMAP and POP. After making this choice, click the **Next** button to continue.

> **NOTE**
> If you selected Exchange ActiveSync as your email service, you need to make sure you get the appropriate email settings from your network administrator to enter in the VersaMail Setup application.

5. Figure 8.3 shows the next setup step, Enter Account Settings, which gets into the details of your account settings. Specify the name you'd like to use for the email account, which is simply a descriptive name of your choosing. Then enter your username, password, and email address, which you should already have for the account. After entering these account settings, click the **Next** button to continue.

6. Figure 8.4 shows another page of account settings that prompts you to enter the mail servers for the account. The mail servers are the most important information on this page. After entering the incoming and outgoing mail servers, you have the option of enabling server authentication, which depends entirely on your specific email account. If your account requires additional settings, such as SSL security for outgoing email, you need to click the **Advanced Settings** button to access and enter advanced email settings.

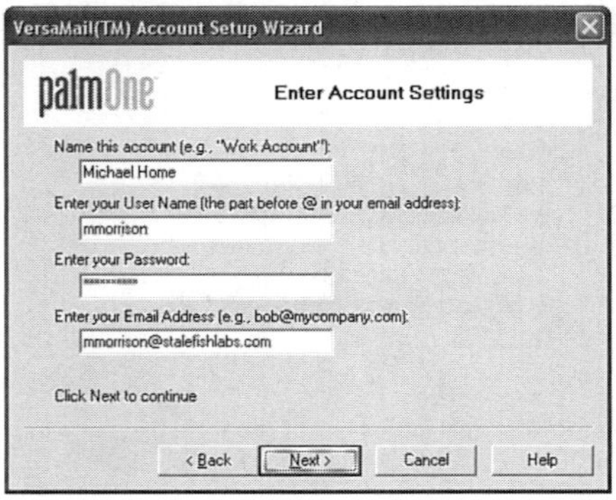

FIGURE 8.3

Entering the first page of email account settings is a critical part of the email account creation process.

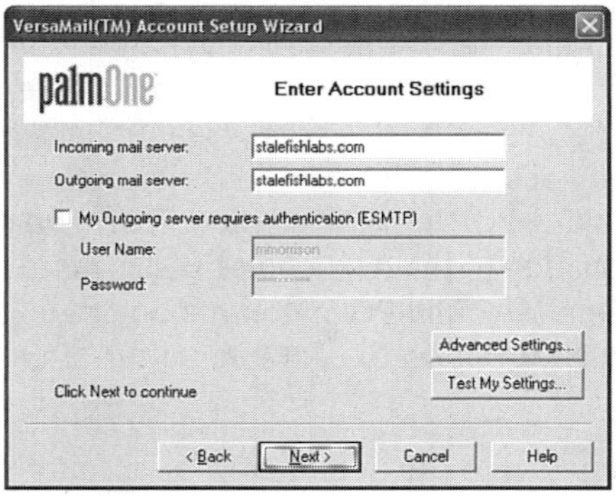

FIGURE 8.4

The second page of account settings primarily prompts you for the mail servers.

7. It's important to test your new email account to make sure the settings are correct. To do so, just click the **Test My Settings** button in the page shown in Figure 8.4. A dialog box similar to the one in Figure 8.5 should open and confirm a test of the account. If you get an error while testing the account, step back through the wizard and double-check the settings. If you're satisfied with the email test, click the **Next** button to continue.

8. You're almost finished. The next to last step in the email setup process is to declare that you're finished or elect to create another account. If you opt to create another account, just follow these steps again for the new account. Otherwise, select the **I'm Finished** option, and click the **Next** button.

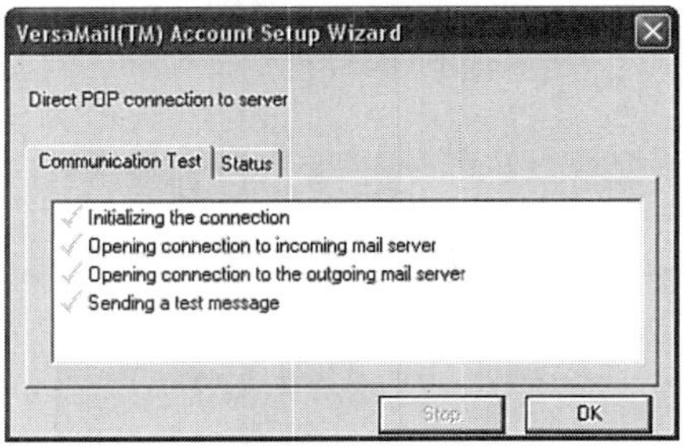

FIGURE 8.5

Testing the new email account is a good way to ensure that you've entered the account settings correctly.

9. The last page in the setup wizard reminds you that a HotSync is necessary for the new account information to get transferred to your device. The actual transfer of account information is technically part of the synchronization process. Click the **Finish** button to close the wizard, and then press the **HotSync** button on the Multi-connector cable to perform a HotSync and transfer the account to your device.

The email account is now created and ready to use in VersaMail. In fact, you might find it has already connected and pulled down email messages. Just to clarify from the earlier discussion on synchronization, if you're using an Exchange or IMAP email account, the Inbox on your Treo will match the Inbox on your PC. However, if you're using a POP account, "synchronizing" the account simply involves retrieving messages from the POP mail server. Regardless of synchronization issues, you now have the capability of accessing email wirelessly from your Treo, which is incredibly cool.

Create the Account on Your Treo

You don't have to use your desktop computer to establish an email account with VersaMail; you can create a new account directly on your Treo. The steps are very similar to those for creating a new account with the VersaMail Account Setup Wizard, except you enter the information directly on your device. Follow these steps to create a new email account directly in the VersaMail application on your Treo 650:

1. Press the **Option** key followed by the **Messaging** button to launch the VersaMail application. You can also navigate to VersaMail on the main application screen and launch it if you've changed the Option + Messaging application button combination. The VersaMail application opens, and if no accounts have been set up in VersaMail, the account setup process should automatically start. If not, press the **Menu** button, navigate over to the **Accounts** menu, and scroll down and

select the **Account Setup** command. The Account Setup screen appears, as shown in Figure 8.6.

FIGURE 8.6

The Account Setup screen displays the accounts currently set up in VersaMail.

2. Tap the **New** button to begin creating a new email account, or tap **Edit** to edit an existing account. Another Account Setup screen for entering an account name and mail service appears (see Figure 8.7).

FIGURE 8.7

The initial step in the account setup process prompts you to enter an account name and select a mail service.

3. First enter the account name, which is just a descriptive name, and then select the mail service, just as you saw earlier in the desktop email account creation process. If you select **Other**, you're also prompted to specify the protocol, which can be POP, IMAP, or Exchange ActiveSync. Tap the **Next** button to continue setting up the account.

4. The next few screens in the account creation follow the same general information-gathering approach as the desktop email setup. You specify the username, password, email address, and mail servers. You then have the option of tweaking advanced email settings, such as the port number for the mail servers, and specifying whether SSL is required for security. When you're finished entering account information, tap the **Done** button to finish creating the new account.

When you're finished creating the new account, it immediately attempts to synchronize or otherwise connect to a mail server and retrieve any available messages.

Receive and Read Email Messages

Although VersaMail automatically attempts to get any available messages when you first create a new account, you're probably curious about how to retrieve messages after the initial setup. There are two approaches for doing this:

- Manually instruct VersaMail to synchronize messages whenever you want.
- Set an automatic synchronize schedule so that mail is retrieved at a regular interval, such as every 15 minutes.

You can use the first approach at any time to force a mail retrieval—just tap the Get button on the main VersaMail screen. Speaking of the main VersaMail screen, you might notice that only one email account is shown at any given time. The account is identified in the upper-left corner of the screen (see Figure 8.8). To switch between accounts, press the Menu button and scroll down to select a different account.

Getting back to email retrieval, the second option involves setting regularly scheduled synchronizations, which is important if you want email to arrive without having to request it manually. To set VersaMail for automatic email retrieval, follow these steps:

NOTE I'm admittedly using the word "synchronize" a bit freely here to stay in keeping with the terminology used in VersaMail. For POP email accounts, email is sent and received directly through the mail server as opposed to synchronizing with the Outlook Inbox on your desktop computer.

TIP An even quicker method of switching between email accounts is holding down the Option key and pressing the Messaging button, just as you would to launch the VersaMail application. You can use this key combination repeatedly to cycle through email accounts.

1. Press the **Menu** button, navigate over to the **Options** menu, and then scroll down and select **Preferences**. The main VersaMail Preferences screen appears, as shown in Figure 8.9.

FIGURE 8.8

The main VersaMail screen shows the email messages associated with a specific email account, which in this case is named Michael.

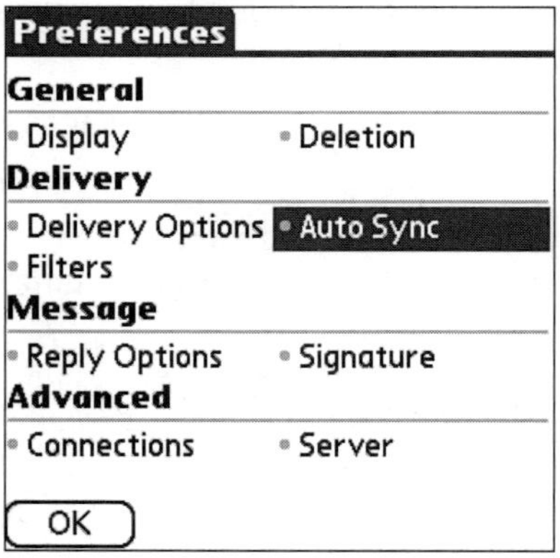

FIGURE 8.9

VersaMail has quite a few preferences available for fine-tuning the mobile email experience.

2. In the Preferences screen, tap **Auto Sync** to open the Auto Sync screen and enable automatic email synchronization—just tap to enable the **Sync Automatically** check box. After you select the check box, the Auto Sync screen shows the actual options available for scheduling email synchronization, as you can see in Figure 8.10.

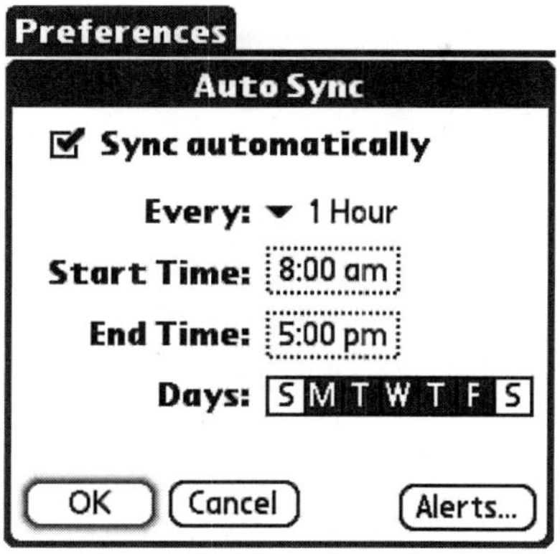

Figure 8.10

To set up VersaMail to synchronize automatically, you must specify the interval, time range, and days for synchronization.

3. The Every field in the Auto Sync screen is probably the most important field because it determines how often synchronization takes place. The start and end times determine a range of time during which the synchronization takes place, with the idea being that you probably don't need synchronization to happen at night while you're asleep. Similarly, the Days field shows on what days email is synchronized. Because my work and personal email are often the same, I set the Days field so that my device synchronizes every day of the week.
4. Aside from the auto-synchronization settings, you can tap the **Alerts** button in the Auto Sync screen to tweak the alerts associated with automatic email synchronization. By default, you are alerted when a new email message arrives as well as when synchronization fails. You also have the option of specifying what alert sound is played for these events.
5. Tap the **OK** button to finish configuring the auto-sync option and return to the VersaMail Preferences screen. Tap **OK** again to return to the main VersaMail screen.

I didn't mention in the previous steps that all the VersaMail settings accessed via the Preferences screen apply only to the currently active email account. To change the preferences for

Tip

If you're accessing a corporate email account that requires a virtual private network (VPN) connection, make sure to install a suitable VPN client on your device. After the client is installed successfully, you can establish a VPN connection by pressing the Menu button in VersaMail, navigating over to the Options menu, and then scrolling down and selecting Connect VPN.

Tip

Even though your device warns you about battery drain if you set the email synchronization interval to any value less than one hour, I find it more useful to go with a fairly short time period, such as every 15 minutes. Then again, if you don't receive a lot of emails and don't need up-to-the-minute email retrieval, by all means stick with a longer interval.

> **TIP** If you see a flashing asterisk in the upper-left corner of the screen, it means a reminder awaits your action. New email messages can trigger a reminder, in which case you simply tap the flashing asterisk to view the reminder and access the new messages. Reminders can also be generated by other applications, such as the Calendar application generating a reminder for appointments.

another account, you must first select the account so that it's in view on the main VersaMail screen.

Regardless of whether you retrieve email manually or set it up to arrive via auto-synchronization, new email messages appear in the main VersaMail screen when they arrive. This screen displays a list that shows the sender of unread emails in bold as well as the time the message was sent and the subject of the message (take a look back at Figure 8.8). To read a message shown in the main VersaMail message list, just tap the message. Figure 8.11 shows an email message open in VersaMail.

Reading a message in VersaMail is much like reading a message in any other email client. You might notice a few buttons along the bottom of the screen for replying to, forwarding, and deleting the current message. If you tap the Reply To button, you're prompted to reply to just the sender or to all the people referenced in the message header (To, Cc, and Bcc). Figure 8.12 shows a message being replied to. If you tap the Fwd button to forward a message, you're given the opportunity to specify a recipient for the message.

FIGURE 8.11

When you open a message in VersaMail, the body of the message is displayed onscreen along with a series of buttons for managing the message.

After entering the body of the message reply, just tap the Send button to send the message. You can also tap the Outbox button to move the message to the Outbox folder without actually sending it yet—it's sent as part of the next synchronization. Or you can tap the Drafts button to save the message to the Drafts folder, which indicates that you aren't quite ready to send it yet. And finally, if you change your mind entirely, just tap Cancel.

One thing I neglected to mention about receiving email messages is that messages aren't always received in their entirety. In fact, by default any message larger than 5KB is only partially retrieved from the mail server. You can tell whether a message hasn't been downloaded fully because an additional button is visible when you're viewing the open message. Figure 8.13 shows this extra button just to the right of the Delete button. To download the complete message, tap this button and then confirm that you want to download the message by tapping Yes. This feature prevents you from having to wait for long messages to download to find out what they are; you can quickly isolate junk and unwanted email and clear them out before downloading them in their entirety.

> **TIP** To open the first message in the message list quickly, press the Space key. You can continue pressing the Space key to step through open messages as you're reading them.

FIGURE 8.12

Replying to a message simply involves entering the message text and tapping the Send button.

Download

The entire message is then downloaded and appears in VersaMail. If the message has any attachments, which is often the case when messages aren't initially received in full, you'll see them near the bottom of the message, as shown in Figure 8.14. In this example, the attachment is a Microsoft Excel spreadsheet called Construction2005.xls.

Attachment

To open an attachment in an email message, just tap the attachment. Assuming the attachment type is supported, the attachment is then opened in the appropriate application. Table 8.1 lists the attachment types supported by default in the Treo 650, along with the application used to open each type.

Figure 8.13

A special download button appears if a message is too large to be received in its entirety.

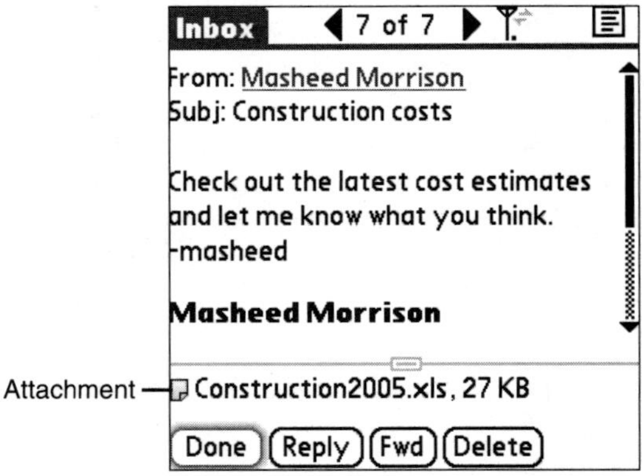

Figure 8.14

Email attachments appear at the bottom of a message with a little paper icon next to them.

Table 8.1 Email Attachment Types Supported by the Treo 650

Type	Treo Application
Contact (vCard)	Contacts
Appointment (vCal)	Calendar
Memo	Memos

Type	Treo Application (continues)
Text document	Memos
Palm application (PRC)	Applications launcher
Office document (Word, Excel, PowerPoint)	Documents to Go
Image (JPEG, GIF, TIFF, BMP)	Pics&Videos
Video (MPEG)	Pics&Videos
Ringtone (MIDI)	Ringtone Manager
MP3 music	RealPlayer

If you aren't satisfied with the standard attachment support in the Treo, you can install third-party applications to handle additional data types. Examples include eReader for reading eBook attachments, Adobe Reader for viewing PDF files, and Macromedia Flash Lite for viewing Flash animations.

NOTE Compressed ZIP files are also supported as attachments, in which case VersaMail extracts the files from the archive to device memory.

Compose and Send an Email Message

I covered the sending of email messages in the previous section only briefly when mentioning replying to and forwarding messages. It's worth examining the sending side of the email equation a bit more closely to understand exactly how to create and send emails. To compose a new email message in VersaMail, follow these steps:

1. Make sure you have the email account selected in VersaMail.
2. Tap the **New** button on the main VersaMail screen to open the New Message screen (see Figure 8.15).
3. Tap the **To** field in the New Message screen to enter the message recipients. In the Recipient List screen that appears, enter the recipients or select them from your contact list—tap the **Lookup** button to select recipients from the contact list. When you're finished entering or selecting recipients, tap the **Done** button.
4. Back on the New Message screen, it's important to enter a subject for the message. After the subject comes the body of the message, which is the actual message text.
5. You might notice a few icons in the upper-right corner of the New Message screen. You use the page icon on the far right to access additional recipient fields, including Cc and Bcc recipients. Recipients placed in the Cc field receive a copy of the message and are visible to other people who receive the message; Bcc recipients receive a copy of the message but are hidden from view.

FIGURE 8.15

Use the New Message screen to enter the message recipient (To), the message subject, and the body of the new message.

6. The paper clip icon allows you to add an attachment to the message. (Please refer back to Table 8.1 for a list of supported attachment types.) You can actually attach any file you want, but other Treo devices can open only the supported types unless the recipient has installed third-party software for handling additional attachment types. Figure 8.16 shows the Attachments screen, where you select attachments on your device by type.

> **NOTE**
> The page icon in the upper-right corner of the VersaMail screen that appears when viewing an email is actually a header control. More specifically, the control determines whether an email message's full header or short header (the default) is displayed.

7. To add an attachment to the message, first select the attachment type in the Type pick list. The available attachments of that type are then displayed in the list immediately below the type. Tap to select an attachment in this list, and then tap the **Add** button. You can add multiple attachments of different types if you'd like. Tap the **Done** button when you're finished adding attachments.

8. One last setting you might want to consider when creating a new email message is the priority of the message, which can be normal or high. By default, all new messages have a priority of normal. To change the priority to high, press the **Menu** button, navigate over to the **Options** menu, and scroll down and select **Set Priority to High**.

9. When you're ready to send the message, tap the **Send** button to send it. You also have the option of tapping the **Outbox** button to move the message to the Outbox folder without actually sending it yet—it's sent as part of the next

synchronization. Or you can tap the **Drafts** button to save the message to the Drafts folder, which keeps it from being sent until you indicate that you're ready to send it.

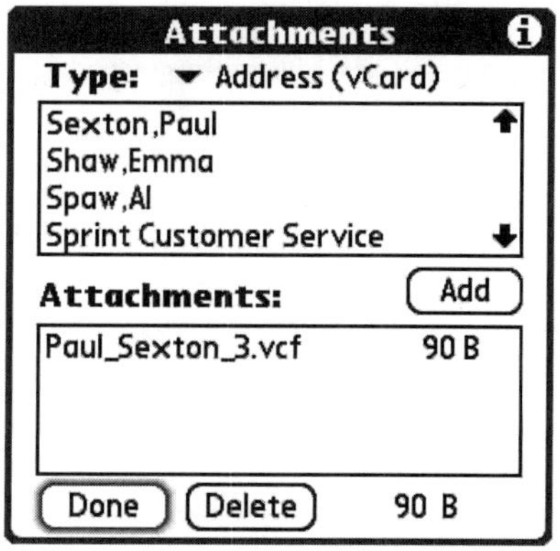

FIGURE 8.16

The Attachments screen is where you select attachments for an email message to be sent.

Depending on whether you opted to send the message now or place it in the Outbox, the new message is delivered immediately or queued for sending the next time you synchronize email. If you saved the message as a draft, you have to open and send it for it to actually get sent.

Create an Email Signature

Email signatures are a common part of the email experience, and you can use them to automatically place contact information at the bottom of every message you send. Follow these steps to create an email signature in VersaMail:

1. Press the **Menu** button, navigate over to the **Options** menu, and scroll down to select the **Preferences** command. The Preferences screen appears, as shown earlier in Figure 8.9.
2. Tap **Signature** in the Preferences screen to open the Signature screen (see Figure 8.17).
3. You must first enable the signature feature by tapping the **Attach Signature** check box. After doing so, an edit box appears where you can enter text that you'd like to appear as your email signature. You'll likely enter your name, company name, and possibly an email address, phone number, and/or Web address. When you're finished entering the signature, tap the **OK** button to save it.

4. Tap **OK** again in the Preferences screen to return to the main VersaMail screen.

Your email signature is now ready to go. You can send an email to yourself if you want to check that the signature works properly.

FIGURE 8.17

The Signature screen allows you to enable and specify a signature that's added to the end of each email message you send from your device.

Managing Email Folders and Messages

The VersaMail application includes a folder structure for storing messages within each email account you have set up. The following folders are created by default any time you create a new email account and cannot be changed:

- *Inbox*—Stores received messages
- *Outbox*—Stores messages waiting to be sent
- *Drafts*—Stores messages you aren't ready to send yet
- *Sent*—Stores messages that have already been sent
- *Trash*—Stores deleted messages until you empty the trash and permanently delete them

These folders follow the same general structure of email folders in a desktop email client, such as Microsoft Outlook. To access the different folders on your Treo, just tap the folder pick list in the upper-right corner of the main VersaMail screen. The message list changes to show only the messages stored in the currently selected folder.

You can perform several operations on email messages from within the message list. To do so, you must first select a message (or messages) by tapping the small bullet to the left of the envelope icon for the message. When a message is selected, the small bullet changes to a small checkmark. You can also select and deselect all messages in the current folder by issuing the Select All and Deselect All commands from the Message menu.

> **TIP** Deleted messages are automatically stored in the Trash folder. To empty messages from the Trash folder and permanently delete them, press the Menu button and scroll down to select the Empty Trash command. Tap Yes in the confirmation screen to follow through and empty the trash. The Deletion section of the VersaMail preferences includes a setting for automatically emptying messages in the Trash folder that are older than a certain time frame; the default setting automatically empties the trash of messages that are older than one day.

With one or more messages selected, you can issue commands, and they will apply only to the selected messages. For example, to delete selected messages, press the Menu button and scroll down to select the Delete command. To quickly delete older messages without having to select them, press the Menu button and scroll down to select the Delete Old command. The Delete Old Messages screen appears and enables you to specify the folder and a time frame for deleting old messages; all messages older than the specified time frame are deleted from the specified folder. This is a powerful technique to delete a lot of messages at once, so be careful when you use it.

You might be wondering whether you can create your own message folders for organizing email messages. You can certainly create folders that co-exist with the default VersaMail email folders. Probably the best way to create a new folder is to do it as part of moving an existing message to it. Follow these steps to create a new folder while moving a message to it from the Inbox:

> **NOTE** When you delete a message from the message list, you're prompted to confirm the deletion and asked whether you want to delete the message from the server. If you're sharing an email account with a desktop computer, you might want to leave the message on the server so that the desktop email client can retrieve it. Otherwise, you could end up deleting the message before it makes it to the desktop email client. Of course, for junk mail, this might not be a bad idea.

1. Select the message by tapping the small bullet just to the left of the envelope icon.
2. Select the **Move To** command from the **Message** menu. The Move Message(s) To screen appears, as shown in Figure 8.18. The message folders shown in the figure are target folders for moving messages. Folders with an asterisk next to them contain unread messages.
3. Tap the **Edit Folders** button to open the Edit Folders screen, which displays a list of custom folders along with buttons for editing them (see Figure 8.19) .
4. Tap the **New** button to begin creating a new folder. Folders in VersaMail are also referred to as categories, which is why the screen that appears next is called Edit Categories. Enter the name of the new folder, and then tap the **OK** button. The folder is added to the folder list you saw in Figure 8.19. Tap **OK** again to return to the Move Message(s) To screen.

5. Scroll to select the newly created folder, and then tap the **OK** button. The selected messages are moved to the new folder. Perhaps more important, the new folder is now accessible via the folder pick list in the upper-right corner of the main VersaMail screen.

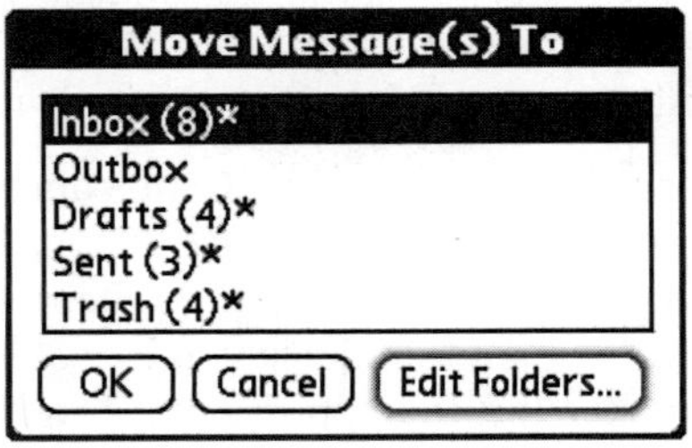

FIGURE 8.18

The Move Message(s) To screen is used to move email messages between folders and to access the folders for editing.

FIGURE 8.19

The Edit Folders screen is where you create and edit custom email folders.

> **TIP** You can mark selected messages as read (normal font) or unread (bold font) by selecting Mark Read and Mark Unread in the Message menu.

You now have a good feel for how messages are displayed as well as how folders are used to store and organize them. What you haven't learned is how to alter the default sorting of messages in the message list for a given folder. The Display section of the VersaMail preferences includes a setting for controlling message sorting. In fact, several interesting settings are available in the Display preferences. Follow these steps to access and change them:

1. Tap the **Display** button at the bottom of the main VersaMail screen to open the Display Options screen (see Figure 8.20). The Display button is a shortcut for opening the Display Options within the VersaMail preferences.

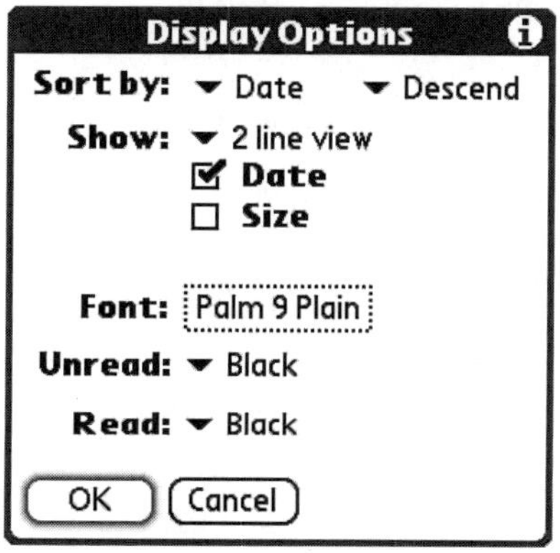

FIGURE 8.20

The Display Options screen includes several preferences related to how email messages are displayed.

2. The Sort By setting determines how messages are sorted. Tap the first pick list to change the sorting to be based on email subject, sender, date, or size. The second pick list enables you to reverse the sorting by switching from descending order to ascending order.
3. The Show setting determines how many lines are displayed for an email message (one or two), along with whether the message date and size are displayed. Although the one-line view is more efficient (only the sender is visible), being able to see the subject of each message in the default two-line view can be helpful.
4. You can use the Font setting to change the font family, size, and style used throughout the VersaMail application. This is entirely a personal preference, but it's worth pointing out that if you can handle reading a smaller font, you'll be able to see more messages on the screen; you might have to experiment with different fonts to change the size.
5. The last two display settings, Unread and Read, relate solely to the color of read and unread messages displayed in the message list. By default, messages are distinguished only by unread messages being in a bold font. If you want to make this distinction a bit more obvious, try changing the color of one or both of them. I find that changing unread messages to a bright color helps make them more obvious, but changing the color of both messages is too much for me.

6. Tap the **OK** button when you're finished tweaking the email display preferences.

I'd say you now have a good handle on email message management, but there are still a few more interesting topics you have yet to uncover.

Take Control of Your Email with Filters

If you receive any volume of email at all, you might want to consider creating a few filters to help you organize mail as it comes in. You can also use filters as a way to screen out junk mail and save yourself some time deleting it by hand. There is an important caveat for creating filters, however—only messages that meet filter criteria are downloaded to your device. This means you'll probably want to create a generic filter that passes all unfiltered email to the Inbox folder. If you don't do this, messages that don't match a filter are ignored and never make it to your device.

To create an email filter in VersaMail, follow these steps:

1. Press the **Menu** button, navigate over to the **Options** menu, and scroll down to select the **Preferences** command. The Preferences screen appears, as shown earlier in Figure 8.9.
2. Tap **Filters** (under the Delivery heading) to open the Filters screen (see Figure 8.21).

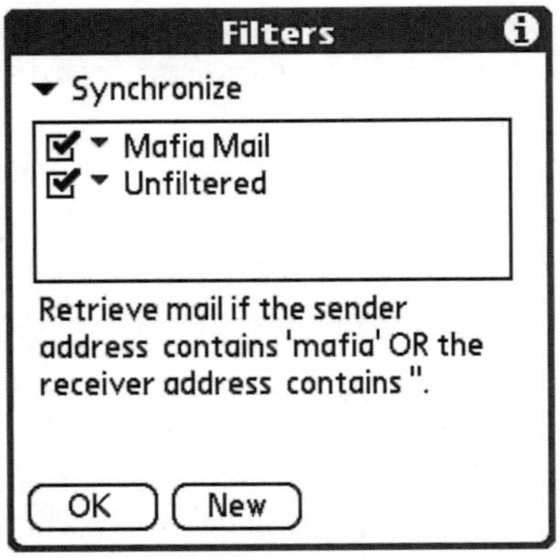

FIGURE 8.21

The Filters screen contains a list of all the filters you've created and allows you to create and edit filters.

3. The Filters screen contains a list of the filters you've created, along with a pick list just above the filters for selectively applying filters to synchronized email

messages and messages retrieved through a direct email server connection. You enable and disable filters by checking and unchecking them in the list; you can enable and disable filters uniquely for synchronized versus connected messages. You can also change the order in which filters are applied by tapping the small down arrow next to a filter and selecting **Move Up** or **Move Down** to move it up or down in the list. Filters are processed in order from top to bottom in the list. To create a new filter, tap the **New** button to open the Filter Editor screen (see Figure 8.22).

FIGURE 8.22

The Filter Editor screen is where you enter the specifics of how a filter actually filters email messages.

4. The name of the filter is just a descriptive name that helps you identify the filter in the filter list. The "if" part is what defines the filter mechanics—you can set the first pick list to **To**, **From**, **Subject**, **Cc**, or **Size**. This selection serves as the control field for the filter. You then specify how the field affects the filter by selecting **Contains**, **Starts With**, or **Does NOT Contain** in the second pick list. The match text for the filter, which can be a word or phrase, is entered next. Finally, you tell the filter what folder to store messages in that match the criteria. The example in Figure 8.22 is used to filter email from my hockey friends so that it goes into the custom Hockey folder. My recreational hockey team is called Music City Mafia, so I set up the filter to check for the word "mafia" in the Subject field of any email message. If there's a match, the message is moved to the Hockey folder. Tap the **OK** button when you're finished creating a new filter.

TIP To create an "Unfiltered" filter that catches all unfiltered messages so that they aren't overlooked, just select To in the first filter pick list and Contains in the second pick list. Don't enter anything as the match text, and select Inbox as the destination folder. Also, make sure this filter is moved to the bottom of the filter list so that it attempts to filter only messages that other filters miss.

5. Tap **OK** to exit the Filters screen, and then tap **OK** again to return to the main VersaMail screen.

With a few email filters in place, VersaMail is now running on autopilot in terms of automatically matching certain messages and routing them to appropriate folders. You will certainly want to experiment with filters as you get more comfortable using them. If you run across a common word or phrase in junk mail messages, by all means create your own junk mail filter that routes them straight to the Trash folder.

Tweak Advanced VersaMail Settings

The VersaMail application has a few additional settings that haven't been touched on yet. The first of these settings relates to how email messages are delivered to your device. Follow these steps to modify the VersaMail delivery options:

1. Press the **Menu** button, navigate over to the **Options** menu, and scroll down to select the **Preferences** command. The Preferences screen appears, as shown earlier in Figure 8.9.
2. Tap **Delivery Options** to open the Delivery Options screen (see Figure 8.23).

FIGURE 8.23

The Delivery Options screen includes a variety of options for controlling exactly how email messages are delivered to your device.

3. The Get option is somewhat of an optimization to minimize the amount of data transferred when delivering messages. You can choose to get entire messages or just message subjects. The Ask Every Time check box is a manual override for the Get option; if selected, it causes a screen to be displayed each time you get mail that prompts you to get entire messages or subjects.

4. The Get Only settings apply only to IMAP email accounts and allow you to indicate that you want to get only unread messages, as opposed to all messages on the server. You can also specify that you want to get mail only within a certain time frame, from as small as a day to as large as a month.

5. The Download Attachments setting causes attachments to be downloaded automatically. However, the total message size (including attachments) must still fall below the maximum message size for the attachment to download automatically. Otherwise, you have to explicitly get the entire message. The maximum message size defaults to 5KB, but you can raise it up to nearly 5MB (5,000KB, to be exact). This size limits only the amount of email data that's retrieved automatically; you can always perform a "get" on a specific message to download it in its entirety, even if it's larger than the maximum size.

6. The last setting in the Delivery Options screen relates to the format of email messages. More specifically, you can specify whether messages are retrieved as plain text or with HTML formatting supported. The default setting preserves HTML formatting for the display of messages in VersaMail. However, regardless of this setting, VersaMail always sends messages as plain text even if they were received with HTML formatting; the HTML formatting is stripped out of sent messages.

> **NOTE** Although an entire message with attachments can be as large as 5,000KB, the actual text of a message can't be larger than 60KB.

7. When you're satisfied with any email delivery changes, tap the **OK** button to return to the VersaMail Preferences screen.

Before you return to the main VersaMail screen, there's another batch of preferences worth exploring. I'm referring to the server preferences, which are accessed by following these steps:

1. Tap **Server** in the Preferences screen (under the Advanced heading) to open the Servers screen (see Figure 8.24) .

2. The Servers screen is important in that it controls how email messages are treated upon being delivered from a mail server to your device. The first check box in Figure 8.24 applies only to POP accounts and, by default, leaves mail on the server after downloading it to your device. This setting is recommended if you're using a POP account on your device as well as a desktop computer because it allows your desktop computer to access the messages.

3. The second check box determines whether deleting a message on your device also deletes it from the server. How you set this option depends entirely on how you use the email account. If the account is used solely by your device, you'll definitely want to enable the option. On the other hand, for shared accounts you might want to perform all deletions from the server via your desktop computer, in which case you might want to leave the option disabled.

FIGURE 8.24

Use the Servers screen to determine what happens to mail on the server after it has been delivered to your device.

4. Tap the **OK** button to finish up with the email server preferences, and then tap **OK** again to exit the Preferences screen.

NOTE There are a few IMAP-specific settings that you'll see for IMAP accounts. For example, you can set the IMAP root folder, deleted mail folder, and sent mail folder.

At this point, you've exhausted just about every setting possible for fine-tuning the VersaMail application so that it functions exactly as you want it to. One other group of preferences is associated with email connections, but it's unlikely that you'll need to change it. The connection preferences deal primarily with the timeout period for establishing an email connection and whether VersaMail should automatically disconnect after sending and receiving messages. If you'd like to take a look at these settings, they are located in the Connections section of the VersaMail Preferences screen.

Summary

I've said many times that I think wireless mobile email is the killer app for mobile devices, and I'm not entirely alone in that thought. Whether I'm ever proved correct in my thinking, there's no doubt that accessing email wirelessly from the convenience of your Treo can be extremely handy. And for people who travel a lot, wireless Treo email can be downright life altering! Okay, maybe I'm exaggerating a bit, but I'm hoping that this chapter has shed some light on the email capabilities of your Treo. I'll be the first to say that VersaMail has some limitations, but overall it's a capable mobile email client.

9

Communicating with Text and Multimedia Messages

Although it has been a little slower to catch on in the United States, text messaging has been quite the rage in Europe and Japan for some time. A subset of U.S. business users have realized the impact of text messaging, thanks to the surprising popularity of BlackBerry text-messaging devices. As with newer BlackBerry devices, the Treo 600 and 650 represent a new generation of devices that combine a mobile phone with a true text-messaging device, including a full QWERTY keyboard. If you aren't already a text-messaging junkie, be prepared. It can certainly be addictive!

Text Messaging Basics

Text messaging is a highly efficient means of mobile communication and in many ways is competing with voice telephony communication. It's often easier to receive a text message and reply to it at your own convenience than answer a live voice call and deal with an issue in real time. This is the primary reason that so many business users have adopted the BlackBerry platform as their mobile communication devices of choice. With the Treo, Palm aims to take the success of the BlackBerry platform to a broader range of users. Traditionally, most BlackBerry devices have been pure text-messaging pagers. So with the exception of a few newer BlackBerry phones, there's the added benefit of Treo devices combining the features of a mobile phone and a text-messaging pager.

One potential source of confusion with respect to Treo devices and text messages has to do with exactly what constitutes a text message. Obviously, you know it must contain text, but so do Word documents and web pages, and they aren't considered text messages. A *text message* is a message consisting purely of text (and possibly attached files) that's sent electronically over a network from one place to another. Treo devices support the following primary types of text messages:

IN THIS CHAPTER

- Text Messaging Basics
- Compose and Send an SMS Text Message
- Compose and Send a Multimedia Message
- Chat via SMS Text Messages
- Manage Text Messages
- Customize QuickText for Speedy Chatting
- Create a Message Signature
- Fine-Tune Messaging Preferences

- *Email message*—A text message addressed to an email address and sent through a wireless service provider or an email server. Can accept attachments.
- *Short Message Service (SMS) message*—A text message addressed to a phone number or special code and sent through a wireless service provider. Cannot accept attachments.
- *Multimedia message*•A text message addressed to a phone number or special code and sent through a wireless service provider with attached media objects, such as voice memos, pictures, and video clips.
- *Instant message*—A text message sent in the context of a live conversation between two connected parties; instant messages are sent and received through a client instant-messaging application (AOL Instant Messenger, for example). Can accept attachments based on the client application.

The most important point to remember from this list of text message types is the distinction between the first three (email, SMS, and multimedia messages) and the last one (instant message). The distinction is that an instant message involves the notion of a live connection between two parties; the other types of messages are delivered regardless of whether anyone is on the other end to receive them when they are sent. This distinction might seem minor, but it makes a huge difference in terms of how instant messages are handled compared to email, SMS, and multimedia messages. More specifically, the standard Treo Messaging application handles email, SMS, and multimedia messages together in a seamless manner, but it doesn't handle instant messages at all. However, you can use the Messaging application to carry on chat threads that resemble true instant messaging; you can also download and install a true instant-messaging client as a third-party application.

NOTE All wireless service providers are free to use their own solutions for supporting multimedia messaging. Most providers use the popular Multimedia Messaging System (MMS); others, such as Sprint, use their own system. The Sprint system, called PictureMail, involves using a web page for accessing attached media objects online as opposed to actually attaching objects to an MMS message.

Now that you understand the distinction between instant messages and the other three main types of text messages, it's worth taking just a moment to cover the differences between email, SMS, and multimedia messages. As you might already know, email messages are routed through email servers and often traverse a variety of network and computer configurations along the way. Email messages are addressed to email addresses by using the familiar `name@domainname` format, which most people are familiar with. SMS and multimedia messages are different from email messages both in terms of how they are delivered and how they are addressed.

SMS and multimedia messages are *peer-to-peer messages*, which means they don't go through a server in the same way that email does. Instead, they are sent directly from one device to another one, much like a phone call is made directly from one mobile phone to another one. Moreover, SMS and multimedia messages are sent solely through your wireless service provider. The only significant differences, at least from the user's perspective, between these two message types is the support for attached media objects and the maximum message size (160 characters) imposed on SMS messages—there's no standard maximum size for MMS messages.

> **NOTE** You must have a mobile phone number (SMS address) associated with a contact for the contact to be used as an SMS message recipient.

SMS is a text-messaging protocol that allows you to send messages to people by simply specifying the phone number of their handheld device. SMS messages can be sent to anyone with a mobile device that supports SMS, and your mobile phone number serves as your unique ID for SMS messaging. So if a mobile phone or handheld is capable of SMS messaging, you send the owner a message by simply addressing the message to his or her mobile phone number. The same thing applies to multimedia messaging—a mobile phone number serves as the target address for messages.

> **NOTE** With a few exceptions, such as SMS services that use short codes, SMS addresses are typically just mobile phone numbers. A short code is a special SMS address that's typically a four-, five-, or six-digit number. Short codes are usually assigned to special wireless services, such as Google SMS, and are sometimes used for special promotions. For example, the television show American Idol uses a short code that viewers can use to vote on show participants via SMS.

What makes SMS particularly useful for Treo devices is that it provides a way to communicate with people who use traditional mobile phones that don't have full-blown email access. Although SMS is somewhat new to American mobile phone users, its widespread success in other parts of the world give it a stable and interesting base of applications that are available to all SMS users.

The success of SMS has spawned some neat applications and services that you might not have realized existed. For example, one of my favorite SMS applications is Google SMS, which enables you to carry out a Google search purely through SMS messages. You send an SMS message with your search keywords, and Google returns several messages to you with the search results. Google SMS is a simple and elegant application of SMS and a great example of how to make a popular service available to mobile devices.

Compose and Send an SMS Text Message

If a mobile phone or handheld is capable of SMS messaging, you send the owner a message by simply addressing the message to his or her mobile phone number. Follow these steps to compose and send an SMS message using your Treo device:

1. Press the **Messaging** button (just to the lower right of the five-way navigator) to launch the Messaging application. You can also navigate to the Messages application on the main application screen and launch it if you've changed the Messaging application button.
2. Tap the **New** button to open the Compose screen (see Figure 9.1) and begin creating a new message.

FIGURE 9.1

Use the Compose screen in the Messaging application to compose a new text message.

3. The To field is where you specify the recipient of the text message. It's important to point out that the text message could be an email or SMS message—the distinction isn't made until you indicate whether the message is being sent to an email address or a mobile phone number. Press the number keys on the keyboard to enter the message recipient's phone number in the To field. If the recipient of the SMS message is already listed in your contact list with his or her mobile phone number, you can tap the pick list next to the To label to look up the contact. Just select **Lookup in Contacts** from the pick list, and then select the contact. To address the message to multiple recipients, separate their addresses by commas.

4. Press the **Down** button on the five-way navigator to move to the message body (or just tap the message body with the stylus), and begin entering the message text (see Figure 9.2).

5. You can speed up the entry of text messages by using a handy feature of the Messaging application called QuickText. QuickText is a list of commonly used sentences and phrases that you can quickly select and insert into text messages. To insert some QuickText, tap the **QuickText** button near the bottom of the screen; this button is just to the right of the Cancel button and has a graphic of a quote on it. A list of commonly used phrases is then displayed (see Figure 9.3) .

> **TIP**
> Google SMS is a useful service that enables you to perform Google searches quickly via SMS messages. To initiate a Google SMS search, send an SMS message with the form g search terms to the Google SMS address 46645 (GOOGL). As an example, if you want to search for CDs by Tom Waits, you would send a message containing g tom waits discography to the SMS address 46645. Google SMS returns the top three search results to you as SMS messages. There are a few special searches you can perform via Google SMS: Send an area code as the search term to find the area it covers, send a phone number to get a phone book listing, and send a business type and ZIP code to get a listing of businesses. For more information, visit the Google SMS website at http://www.google.com/sms/.

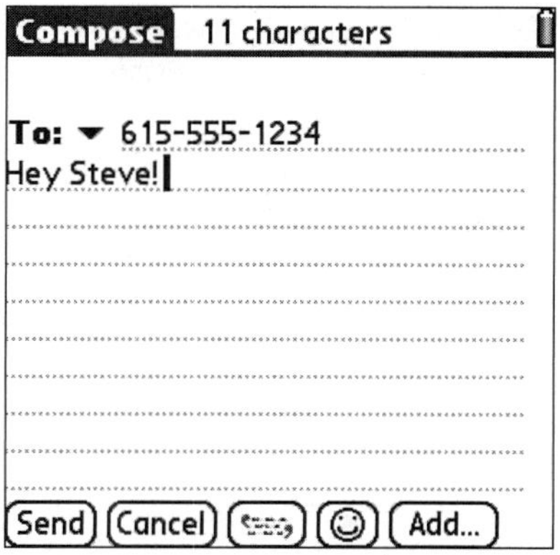

FIGURE 9.2

Entering a text message simply involves typing in the body of the message on the Compose screen.

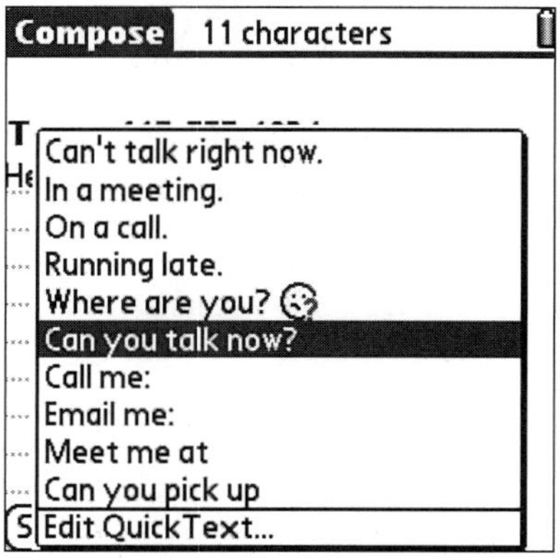

FIGURE 9.3

You can use the QuickText feature to quickly enter common sentences and phrases into text messages.

6. Although text messaging is inherently limited in terms of conveying emotion, emoticons are commonly used to add a touch of emotion here and there. Also known as smileys, *emoticons* are small icons that hint at a particular emotion, often humor or sarcasm. To insert an emoticon into a text message, just tap the **Emoticon** button, located to the right of the QuickText button. Figure 9.4 shows an emoticon being selected after tapping the Emoticon button.

NOTE Later in this chapter in "Customize QuickText for Speedy Chatting," you learn how to edit and add your own sentences and phrases to QuickText.

FIGURE 9.4

Emoticons are a quick and easy way to inject a little emotion into text messages.

> **TIP** If you want to send a text message to an email address instead of a mobile phone number, you can enter the address in the To field. Keep in mind that this approach to email involves using your device's wireless carrier, not a POP or IMAP email service. If you want to use a traditional POP/IMAP email account, you must use the VersaMail application on your device instead of the Messaging application or a third-party equivalent, such as SnapperMail. Chapter 8, "Staying in Touch with Email," explores the VersaMail application in detail.

7. By default, all text messages have a priority level of normal. You can change the priority level to high if you want the recipient to realize that this message is of greater than normal importance. To change the priority level, press the **Menu** button, and then scroll down to and select **High Priority**.

8. If you can't finish entering a message, you can save a draft of the message for later. Just press the **Menu** button, and then scroll down to and select **Save as Draft**. The message is saved in the Draft folder, where you can access it later, finish typing it, and send it. Later in this chapter in "Manage Text Messages," you find out how to navigate the message folders and access saved messages.

9. When you're ready to send the message, tap the **Send** button near the bottom of the screen. After a few seconds, the message is sent to the recipient.

The message is delivered and appears in the recipient's Inbox of his or her device. Keep in mind that text messages are sent and received even if you're on a phone call. You receive SMS text messages to the Inbox folder of the Messaging application, which is the default screen that appears when you first launch the application.

Compose and Send a Multimedia Message

You can take text messaging to another level by embedding media objects, such as voice memos, pictures, and video clips. In doing so, you effectively turn a simple text message into a multimedia message. To compose and send a multimedia message by using the Messaging application, follow these steps:

1. Compose a new text message as you learned how to do in the previous section. Specify the recipient in the To field, enter the message body, use any QuickText you'd like, and insert any desired emoticons.
2. Tap the **Add** button in the lower-right corner of the screen to begin turning the text message into a multimedia message. The Compose screen changes to give you options for adding a voice memo or a picture and/or video clip (see Figure 9.5).
3. To add a voice memo to the message, tap the **Add Voice Memo** button. The Recorder screen appears, as shown in Figure 9.6, and allows you to record a voice memo. Tap the big **Record** button to begin recording the memo with the normal microphone used when talking on the phone; press the same button to stop recording. If you're satisfied with the recording, tap the **Done** button. If not, tap **Re-record** and try again.

TIP An even quicker way to enter an emoticon while composing a text message is to hold down the Center button on the five-way navigator. You can then select an emoticon from the list that's displayed to be inserted into the message.

NOTE Keep in mind that emoticons are actually inserted into messages as text symbols, not graphical images. So when you insert an emoticon, you see its text representation in the message. If the person on the receiving end is using a device that can interpret emoticons, he or she sees the emoticon text as an icon. Otherwise, the text representation is shown, which is understood by most people who are familiar with text messaging.

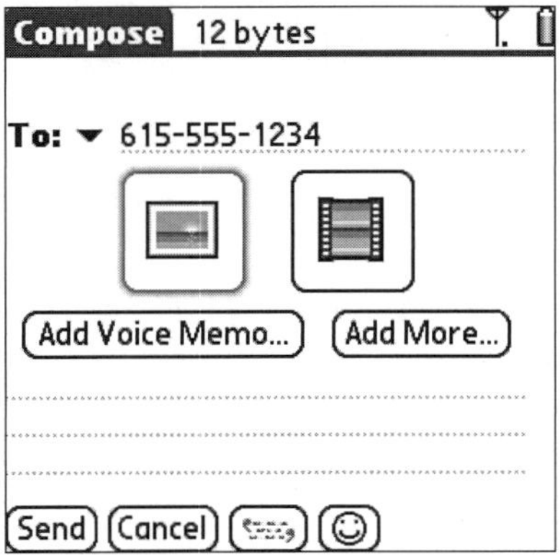

FIGURE 9.5

You can use the Compose screen to add a voice memo, picture, or video clip to a multimedia message.

FIGURE 9.6

The Recorder screen is used to record voice memos for multimedia messages.

> **TIP**
> To include a mobile phone number as the callback number for an SMS message, press the Menu button, and then scroll down to and select Callback Number. You can then opt to select your own mobile phone number, some other number, or no callback number at all from a pick list.

4. In addition to adding a voice memo to a multimedia message, you can add pictures and video clips by tapping the **Add More** button. A pick list appears that prompts you to select a picture (Add Picture) or a video clip (Add Video). Figure 9.7 shows the Select Picture screen, where you select a picture to be added to a multimedia message. If you want to take a new picture for the message, select **Take New Picture**. Otherwise, scroll and select the picture you'd like to add to the message.

5. You can continue adding pictures and video clips. Just keep in mind that you shouldn't go crazy and bloat the message with too many attached media objects. Tap the **Send** button near the bottom of the screen to send the message. After a few seconds, the message is sent to the recipient.

FIGURE 9.7

The Select Picture screen gives you the option of taking a new picture or selecting an existing picture to add to a multimedia message.

When recipients receive the multimedia message, they use a player or viewer in their device to play or view the attached media objects. For example, if you send a multimedia message to another Treo device, pictures and videos can be viewed in the Pics&Videos application, and voice memos are played by using the built-in audio player.

> **TIP** Text messages aren't sent if the mobile radio isn't turned on. You can still compose messages offline, and they are sent when you next turn the radio on. To turn on the mobile radio, hold down the Power/End button until you hear a tone and a screen appears that indicates you're being connected to the wireless network.

Chat via SMS Text Messages

When most people think of chatting on a computer, they think in terms of *instant messaging*. Instant messaging involves a live connection with another user, during which you type and share text messages in real time. Although instant messaging is incredibly useful, it requires a special client application and, perhaps more important, a live connection that remains constant throughout the conversation. You can certainly download and install an instant messaging application on your Treo, but you might find it isn't necessary because you can use SMS and multimedia messages to closely simulate an instant-messaging conversation.

> **NOTE** SMS text messages are limited to only 160 characters, so the idea is to keep them short and sweet. However, if you find yourself rambling past the 160-character limit, don't fret because the message is simply broken into 160-character chunks sent as separate messages.

Treo devices simulate instant messaging by automatically grouping text message replies into a conversation that looks much like an instant-messaging conversation. For example, if you send a text message to a friend and he or she replies, the two messages appear together in a threaded format that looks as though you two are chatting. Given that SMS messages are typically sent rapidly, it is indeed possible to carry on a chat that seems much like a true instant-messaging conversation. Figure 9.8 shows a conversation being carried out via SMS by using the Messaging application.

> **NOTE** Adding a video clip to a multimedia message is almost identical to adding a picture. You can choose to take a new video clip or select from the videos already stored on your device.

Message grouping in the Messaging application is automatic and helps tie an ongoing discussion into a single thread. Contrast this feature with a typical email application that lists messages and their replies individually or at best as a sequence of messages with headers, footers, and other distractions littered between messages. Also, given the limited screen real estate on Treo devices, the compact nature of text message conversations is useful.

FIGURE 9.8

The Messaging application automatically groups message replies so that they flow like an instant-messaging conversation.

> **TIP** While carrying on a conversation as a sequence of message replies, don't forget to take advantage of QuickText whenever possible. This feature can dramatically increase your speed at composing replies.

Manage Text Messages

Just like all other information stored on your Treo device, text messages can be managed carefully to make sure they are organized properly and aren't wasting precious storage space. Because text messages can accumulate rapidly, you want to be vigilant at managing them and keeping only the truly important messages.

The first thing to understand about text messages is their storage structure in the Messaging application. Similar to a desktop mail client, the Messaging application includes several folders in which text messages are stored. Following are the folders used in the Messaging application to organize text messages:

- *Inbox*—Stores newly arrived messages
- *Outbox*—Stores newly created messages until they are sent
- *Sent*—Stores messages that have been sent
- *Drafts*—Stores messages-in-progress that have yet to be sent
- *Templates*—Stores message templates used to create new messages
- *Saved*—Stores messages that were saved for later viewing

You can access these message folders from the pick list at the top of the Messaging screen. Regardless of which folder you're viewing, the messages are displayed with special status icons to the left of their headings that indicate the status of each message. In addition to the status icons, unread messages are displayed in a bold font, and read messages are shown in plain text. Following are some examples of how messages are distinguished via status icons:

- Text message
- Chat session
- Multimedia message with a picture and/or video
- Multimedia message with a voice memo
- Voicemail page

> **NOTE** The VersaMail email application on your Treo uses a similar folder structure as the Messaging application. However, the folders in the Messaging application are static and can't be modified, whereas in VersaMail, you can edit, create, and delete folders. This limitation in the Messaging application has to do with text messaging being intended more for quick messages that don't necessarily require as much organization as email correspondence.

Now that you have a feel for where text messages are stored and how they are displayed according to their status, take a look at how to manage them. To get started with managing text messages in the Messaging application, follow these steps:

1. The first management task to learn is sorting messages according to a different criterion. To change the sorting of messages, press the **Menu** button and navigate over to the View menu. Scroll down to and select the **Sort by Name** menu item. The messages are then sorted by the name of the sender/recipient instead of the date. To return to sorting messages by date, which is the default setting, select the **Sort by Date** item.

> **NOTE** High-priority messages are indicated by a red exclamation point.

2. To mark a message as unread so that it appears in bold again, select the message in the message list, and press the **Menu** button. Scroll down to and select the **Mark as Unread** menu command. The message is marked as unread and displayed in bold in the message list.

> **TIP** If your list of text messages gets unwieldy, you can quickly navigate to the top and bottom of the list by pressing the Menu button, navigating over to the View menu, and selecting the Top of List and Bottom of List menu commands.

3. To call the sender of a message, select the message in the message list and press the **Menu** button. Scroll down to and select the **Call Sender** menu command. A screen opens that prompts you to confirm the phone call (see Figure 9.9). To make the call, tap the **Dial** button; tap the **Message** button to respond via a text message if you change your mind about making the call.
4. Deleting messages is another common management task and is simple to do. To delete a message, select it in the message list, and tap the **Delete** button at the bottom of the screen; you can also press the **Menu** button and scroll down to select the **Delete Message** menu command. You are prompted to confirm the deletion. Tap the **Yes** button to proceed with the deletion or **No** to cancel.

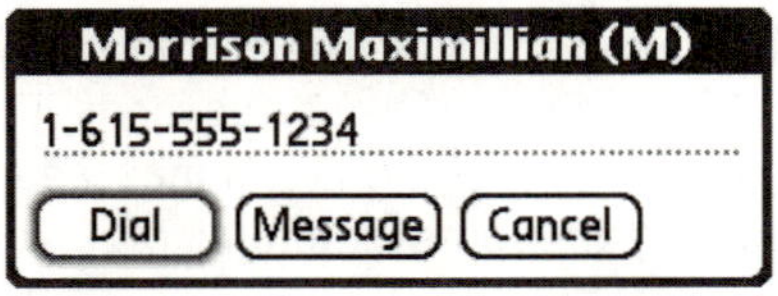

FIGURE 9.9

You can quickly make a phone call to the sender of a text message by selecting the Call Sender command from the Message menu.

> **NOTE**
> You can send and receive text messages while on a phone call. Just press the Menu button and navigate to launch the Messaging application.

5. There's a more powerful option than deleting individual messages. I'm referring to the purge feature, which enables you to delete all messages in a certain folder that are older than a certain date. To purge messages, press the **Menu** button, scroll down to the Purge menu item, and press the **Center** button on the five-way navigator (or simply tap the **Purge** menu item) to issue the Purge menu command, which displays the Purge screen (see Figure 9.10).

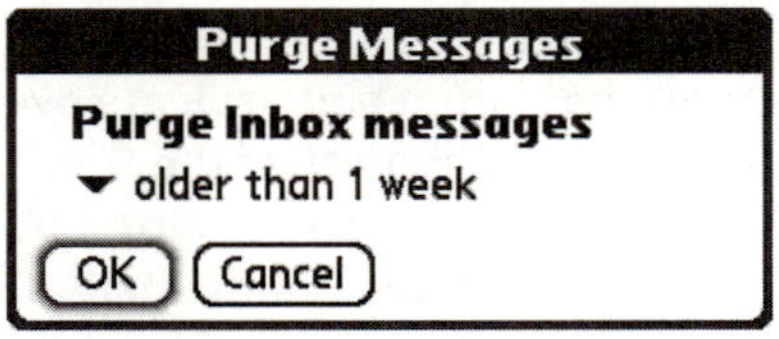

FIGURE 9.10

The Purge screen prompts you to purge messages older than a specified amount of time.

> **TIP**
> The Purge screen provides a handy way to kill all old messages at once. Of course, purging messages like this can be dangerous if you aren't careful. Just make sure you want to purge the messages in question before going through with the purge operation. Also, keep in mind that the purge operation applies only to the currently selected message folder.

6. The Purge screen includes a pick list for specifying how old messages must be to be purged. For example, the default value of 1 Week results in all messages older than one week being deleted from your device. You can set the purge period as far back as a month if you want, which means that only events older than a month are purged. Tap the **OK** button to follow through with the purge, or tap **Cancel** if you change your mind.

Whether you're sorting or deleting text messages, the Messaging application makes it straightforward to manipulate your messages and keep them organized.

Customize QuickText for Speedy Chatting

You might recall from earlier in the chapter that the QuickText feature is used to quickly enter commonly used phrases and sentences when composing a text message. QuickText is simply a list of commonly used phrases and sentences that you don't want to have to type over and over. Although the default QuickText entries are certainly helpful, you can take the usefulness of QuickText to a new level by adding your own entries.

To customize the QuickText entries with your own phrases and sentences, follow these steps in the Messaging application:

1. Press the **Menu** button and navigate over to the Options menu. Scroll down to and select the **Edit QuickText** menu command. The Edit QuickText screen opens, as shown in Figure 9.11.

FIGURE 9.11

The Edit QuickText screen displays a list of the current QuickText entries along with buttons for managing them.

2. To create a new QuickText entry, tap the **New** button. Another screen opens, where you enter the text for the new QuickText entry (see Figure 9.12). Just enter the phrase or sentence, and then tap the **OK** button to accept it. The new entry is added to the QuickText list.
3. To edit a QuickText entry, select the entry in the list and tap the **Edit** button. To delete an entry, select it and tap the **Delete** button.

NOTE In case you've forgotten, you insert a QuickText entry into a text message while composing the message by simply tapping the QuickText button and selecting the phrase or sentence.

4. When you're finished working with QuickText entries, tap the **OK** button to return to the main Messaging screen.

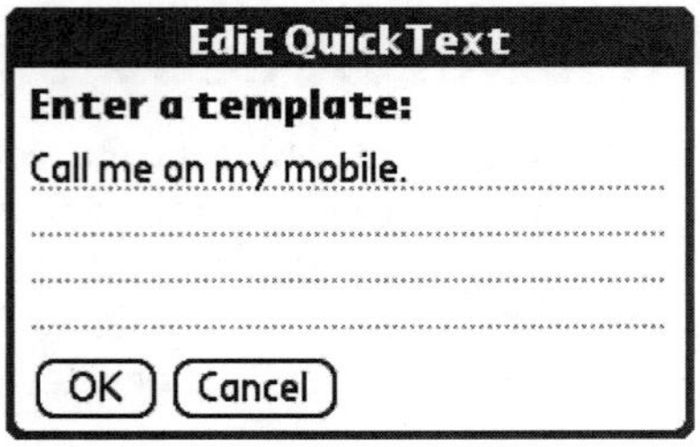

FIGURE 9.12

Creating a new QuickText entry is as easy as typing a commonly used phrase or sentence.

> **TIP** You can include emoticons in QuickText entries but you have to enter them in symbolic form. In other words, to make a traditional smiley face emoticon, you have to enter it as :).

QuickText is a handy feature that you can use to your advantage if you take the time to enter phrases and sentences that you use regularly while text messaging. I encourage you to make an attempt at tracking such phrases and sentences as you create text messages, and then add them as QuickText entries.

Create a Message Signature

You're no doubt familiar with message signatures used to include standard contact information at the end of email messages. Text messages can also include signatures. You may or may not decide that it's necessary to use a signature for text messages, but it's nice to know the option exists.

To establish a text-messaging signature, follow these steps:

> **NOTE** The signature you create for use in the Messaging application is completely different from the signature for VersaMail. To learn more about VersaMail, check out Chapter 8, "Staying in Touch with Email."

1. Press the **Menu** button and navigate over to the Options menu. Scroll down to and select the **Edit Signature** menu command to open the Signature screen (see Figure 9.13).
2. Enter the signature you'd like to use in the Signature Text field. Keep in mind that message signatures typically include your name, your company name, and often a phone number and/or website address. For the signature to appear in new messages you create, tap the **Enable Signature** check box to turn on the signature feature.
3. To finalize the text message signature settings, tap the **OK** button.

If you enter a new signature and enable the signature feature, all text messages from that point on automatically include the signature at the end of the message. A text message signature is a quick and easy way to eliminate extra text entry and automatically include boilerplate contact information in every text message you send.

FIGURE 9.13

You can use the Signature screen to enable and enter a signature that's displayed at the end of every text message you send.

Fine-Tune Messaging Preferences

Like most Treo applications, the Messaging application can be tailored to match your specific-text messaging needs. More specifically, there are preferences you can alter for the Messaging application that affect creating and deleting new messages and options for chat threads associated with text-messaging conversations. To modify the preferences for the Messaging application, follow these steps:

1. Press the **Menu** button and navigate over to the Options menu. Scroll down to and select the **Preferences** menu command. The Preferences screen opens, as shown in Figure 9.14.

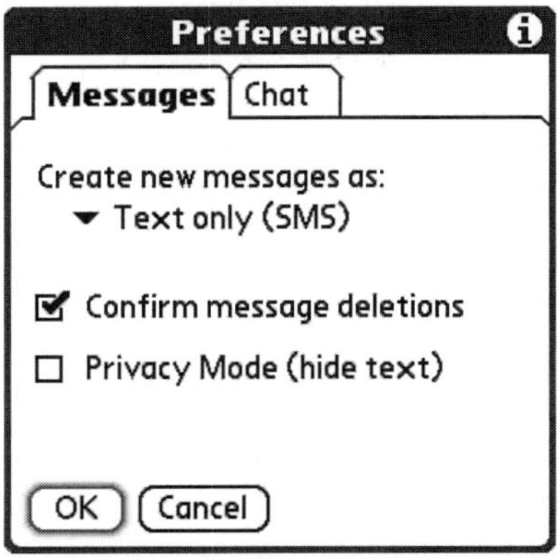

FIGURE 9.14

Use the Messages tab in the Preferences screen to tweak preferences for general text messages.

2. By default, the Preferences screen opens to the Messages tab where you access general text-messaging settings. For example, to alter the default type of new message created, tap **Text Only (SMS)** from the pick list and select **Text and Media** instead. This change simply results in having quicker access to adding voice memos, pictures, and video clips to a new message. If you tend to create more pure text messages without media objects, leave the default setting alone.

3. The two other settings in the Messages tab relate to message deletion confirmations and message privacy. Leave the Confirm Message Deletions check box selected if you want to be prompted to confirm every message deletion; this setting is safer. If you don't want the content of a new message displayed in the incoming message alert screen, select the **Privacy Mode** check box. On the other hand, if you like having a sneak peek at the contents of an incoming message, leave the check box at its default setting of deselected.

4. Tap **Chat** to view the other tab in the Preferences screen. Figure 9.15 shows the Chat tab, which includes several preferences for fine-tuning the handling of chat threads.

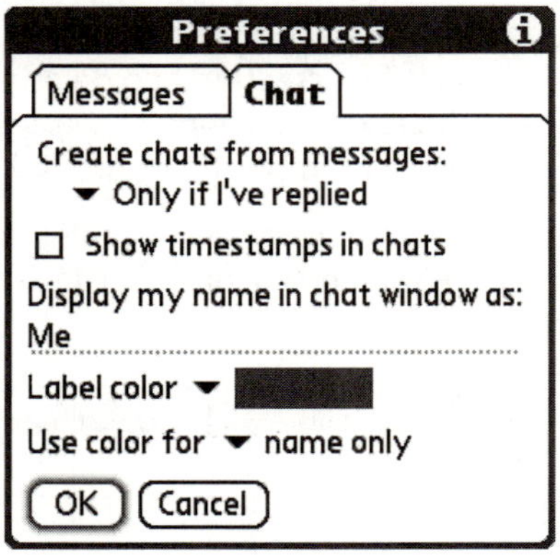

FIGURE 9.15

The Chat tab in the Preferences screen enables you to tweak preferences that apply specifically to chat threads.

5. The first setting determines how a text message gets turned into a chat thread that resembles an instant-messaging conversation. The default setting creates a chat thread only when you reply to a message. Other options result in a chat thread being created never or always, regardless of whether you reply to the message.

6. The Show Timestamps in Chats option instructs the Messaging application to show the date and time of each message in a chat thread. This setting can be

handy if you have a chat thread that continues over long periods. Otherwise, it could be more of an annoyance for brief chats. Below the timestamp setting is a setting for changing how your name appears in the chat window. Keep in mind that this name affects only your end of the chat, so it isn't terribly important other than distinguishing your messages from the person with whom you're chatting.

7. The last two preferences in the Chat tab specify how color is used in the display of chat messages. The first option, Label Color, determines the color of the label for identifying your messages in a chat thread. The second option, Use Color For, determines whether the label color applies just to the name label or to the name and message text. These settings are both personal preferences, so I can't recommend specific settings; the default setting has worked fine for me.
8. When you're finished tweaking the Messaging preferences, tap the **OK** button to commit the changes and return to the main Messaging screen.

The preferences for the Messaging application give you enough flexibility to alter the application so that it's customized to how you work. The good news is that the default settings will likely serve you well, even if you decide not to make any sweeping customizations.

Summary

Whether or not the text-messaging bug has bitten you yet, you will no doubt find text messaging to be a vital feature of your Treo device. Although it's unlikely that text messaging will replace traditional email, it fills an important gap somewhere between the immediacy of a phone call and the delay that often accompanies an email exchange. You can think of text messaging as the text equivalent of Nextel's popular Walkie-Talkie mobile phone feature. The Messaging application on your device is the key to Treo text messaging and provides a seamless interface for carrying out text-messaging conversations.

10

Browsing the Wireless Web

IN THIS CHAPTER

- The Blazer Web Browser and the Wireless Web
- Navigate and Share a Web Page
- Access the Browser History
- Create and Use Bookmarks
- Tweak the Browser Settings
- Save a Web Page for Offline Viewing

Mobile phones and handheld devices have been able to access the Internet for several years now, so the concept of the wireless Web isn't all that new. What is fairly new, however, is the notion of truly being able to wirelessly access and view web pages that aren't specifically designed for a mobile device. Thanks to its relatively high-resolution screen, the Treo 650 makes it possible to view a wide range of web pages without too much scrolling around. Of course, you can also view pages designed for mobile devices via Wireless Application Protocol (WAP), which is also useful. However, using the Blazer Web browser on your Treo device to view a full-size website without wires while away from your desktop PC is an exciting proposition.

The Blazer Web Browser and the Wireless Web

Before getting into the specifics of the Blazer Web browser application, it's important to cover a few important concepts related to mobile browsing. First off, you've probably heard the expression "wireless Web." If so, you were quite likely hearing someone talk about WAP, even if he or she didn't realize it. WAP (pronounced so that it rhymes with "map") is a technology that enables wireless devices to receive data from the Internet and display it on their constrained displays. You can think of WAP as essentially a technology that supports a minimal Web browser on wireless devices. However, as its name clearly states, WAP is not an application but a protocol.

WAP must be supported on both the client (device) and the Web server, and there must also be a WAP Gateway, which is an intermediary between the Internet and the device's mobile network. The WAP Gateway is responsible for converting WAP requests into traditional Web requests and vice versa. Web pages for WAP are somewhat different from traditional web

> **NOTE**
> WAP is an important part of Treo Web browsing because many mobile websites are designed to be viewed by WAP Web browsers. The Web browser in your Treo device actually supports both WAP and HTTP.

pages in that they are written in a special markup language called Wireless Markup Language (WML) instead of the familiar HTML. WML also supports WMLScript, a scripting language that is a simplified version of JavaScript. Web pages designed for WAP tend to be minimal in design as well as content. The number of WAP/WML sites is limited, at least in comparison to normal HTTP/HTML sites.

The Blazer Web browser application is designed to maximize the content area where web pages are actually displayed, which is important for WAP and critical for HTTP. Along the top of the browser screen is a small title area that includes navigational components and information about the current browser session. More specifically, the following information is included in the Blazer browser's title area:

- Toolbar
- Network signal strength icon
- Web page address (URL)
- Go button

All this information is conveyed via text and small icons in the title area, as you can see in Figure 10.1.

FIGURE 10.1

The title area in the Blazer Web browser includes a toolbar, a network signal strength icon, the current web page URL, and a Go button.

The Blazer toolbar provides access to common browser commands and features. Following are the toolbar buttons as they appear from left to right along the top of the Blazer screen:

- *Back*—Navigate back to the previously viewed page.
- *Forward*—Navigate forward to the previously viewed page.
- *Refresh*—Refresh (reload) the current page.
- *Optimized/Wide Page View*—Change the view in the browser between Optimized and Wide Page view.
- *Go to Web Page*—Navigate to a specific web page URL.
- *Home*—Navigate to the default home page.
- *Bookmarks*—Access web page bookmarks.

NOTE Although it's the standard browser provided with Treo devices, the Blazer Web browser isn't the only Treo browser. Other popular third-party browsers include Xiino and WebViewer, both of which boast some features beyond what Blazer has to offer, such as faster page loading and better forms support. Even if you're tempted to go with one of these third-party browsers, make sure you give Blazer a try and check to see whether it meets your needs.

These commands are standard ones found in just about any Web browser. The Blazer Web browser functions just like a desktop Web browser in terms of maintaining a history of visited websites and keeping track of opened pages as a sequence that can be moved through forward or backward. In addition to offering a glimpse of the currently viewed web page, the address bar near the top of the Blazer screen enables you to enter a URL directly and navigate to a specific page by address. Just tap the address bar, enter the URL, and then tap the Go button to the right of the address.

Navigate and Share a Web Page

Through the standard Web browsing features in your Treo device, you have the capability of viewing pages delivered through the WAP or HTTP protocol. WAP pages are specifically designed for viewing on mobile devices; HTTP web pages are designed for a full desktop Web browser but can often be viewed fine on your device. As with a desktop Web browser, you can navigate to any web page you want by simply entering its address. You can also make future visits to a favorite site or page easier by saving a bookmark for the address.

TIP To jump straight to the address bar without using the stylus, press the Space key on the keyboard.

Follow these steps to navigate and share a web page using the Blazer Web browser:

1. Press the **Option** key followed by the green **Phone/Send** button to launch the Blazer Web browser application. You can also navigate to the Web application (Blazer) on the main application screen and launch it if you've changed the Option + Phone/Send application button combination. The Blazer browser automatically opens the default home page, shown in Figure 10.2.
2. The first thing you'll likely want to try out in the Blazer browser is navigating by using links on a web page. You'll notice that hyperlinks appear as underlined text, just as they do in most desktop Web browsers. To follow a link on a page,

just tap the underlined text; you can also tap an image if it serves as a link. As an example, tap the word **Sports** in the page shown in Figure 10.2 to open a sports page in the browser.

FIGURE 10.2

The default home page is displayed when first launching the Blazer Web browser application.

> **TIP** If you plan to use the Blazer browser to access a virtual private network (VPN), you need to install a third-party VPN client on your device; Palm doesn't offer a VPN client of its own. The selection of this client depends on the type of VPN connection you're going to use. After a VPN client is installed, you can establish a VPN connection via the Blazer browser by selecting Connect VPN from the Options menu. To learn more about VPN clients and find one for your Treo, visit this Palm VPN web page: http://www.palmone.com/us/wireless/vpn/.

3. Another common browser navigational task is browsing to a specific web page by using its URL. The quickest way to do this in the Blazer browser is to tap the address field near the top of the screen, enter the URL, and then tap the **Go** button. You can also tap the **Go to Web Page** icon (Earth icon) on the toolbar to open the Go to Web Page screen, where you enter a URL. This screen includes some helper boxes for entering common parts of a URL, such as domain name suffixes (.com, .net, and so forth)—just tap the appropriate box to insert the suffix. Figure 10.3 shows a URL being entered in the Go to Web Page screen.
4. The toolbar provides familiar browser navigation buttons, such as Back (left arrow), Forward (right arrow), Refresh (circular arrows), and Home (house icon). With the View button, you can switch between Optimized view and Wide Page view. Optimized view results in Blazer attempting to resize a web page so that it fits onto the Treo screen. This option works better on some sites than others, so you'll likely find yourself turning it on and off, depending on the site. Just tap the **Optimized/Wide Page View** icon (folder icon next to the Earth icon) on the toolbar to switch between views.

Figure 10.3

In the Go to Web Page screen, enter the URL of a web page so that you can navigate to it in the browser.

5. You can easily send the address (URL) of a web page to someone else via a text message. To do so, navigate to the page in Blazer and press the **Menu** button. Scroll down to and select the **Send Page Address** menu command. A new text message is created with the web page URL inserted into the message body. All you must do is specify the recipient and send the message.

> **Tip**
> Because Sprint is my wireless service provider, my Treo is used on the Sprint PCS Vision system. So the default home page for my browser is the Sprint Vision mobile site.

A couple of other features in the Blazer Web browser are worth pointing out before moving on to bigger things. First, you can search for text on a web page by pressing the Menu button, and then scrolling down to select the Find Text on Page command (or press Menu+D as a shortcut for the command). Issuing this command allows you to find a piece of text on a page quickly. Another command that you probably won't find quite as useful is the Page Info command, which is also located on the Page menu. With the Page Info command, you can view information about the current web page, including its name, URL, and size. If nothing else, the Page Info command is useful for copying a web page's URL so that you can share it with others.

> **Tip**
> An even quicker way to navigate by using links on a page is to use the numbers displayed next to a list of links. For example, instead of tapping the word "Sports" in Figure 10.2, you could also press the 5 key on the keyboard.

Access the Browser History

A common part of the Web experience is navigating forward and backward among pages you've visited. This list of visited pages is stored in a special place in the browser known as the *browser history*. From this list, you can revisit any page. To access the browser history in the Blazer application, follow these steps:

NOTE As in a desktop browser, you can tap a file link to download a file to your Treo device. If you have a memory card installed, you are prompted to choose whether to download the file to the memory card or the main device memory. It's worth pointing out that the Blazer browser has a 2MB limit on the size of files that can be downloaded. If you find this limit to be a serious problem, you might want to consider using a third-party browser, such as Xiino or WebViewer.

1. Press the **Menu** button, and then scroll down to and select the **History** menu command. (The History screen is also available from the Go to Web Page screen.) The History screen opens, as shown in Figure 10.4.
2. The History screen lists all recently viewed web pages. Use the scrollbar or the Up and Down buttons on the five-way navigator to scroll through the pages in the list. You can tap any page in the list to immediately navigate to that page in the browser; the History screen automatically closes if you navigate to a page in the history list.
3. If you'd like to clear the history list, just tap the **Clear All** button in the History screen. You can also save a page in the history list as a bookmark by tapping the **Bookmark** button. You are then prompted to add the page as a new bookmark; more on bookmarks in the next section.
4. When you're finished with the history list, tap the **Cancel** button to return to the main browser screen.

FIGURE 10.4

The History screen in the Blazer browser contains a list of all recently visited web pages.

The browser history is a great way to get a recap of pages you've visited recently. Because you might want to keep the history of pages you've visited private, clearing the browser history regularly isn't a bad idea, especially if you allow other people to access your device. Maybe you have nothing to hide, but privacy is an important part of mobile computing, and the browser history is one area in particular where your privacy can be compromised.

Create and Use Bookmarks

Bookmarks play an important role in Web browsing by allowing you to easily organize and revisit memorable web pages. Your Treo ships with a few bookmarks to get you started, and you might have already stumbled across them. Bookmarks are similar in many ways to Favorites, which are also used to organize memorable information, but bookmarks are limited solely to Web addresses. Additionally, bookmarks are accessed only in the Blazer application. The Blazer application actually consists of two main views: Page view and Bookmarks view. You access the bookmarks on your device by switching from Page view (the default) to Bookmarks view.

> **TIP** Here's a sneaky little tip for downloading an image from a web page. Tap and hold on any image with the stylus for a second or two. A Save Image screen opens, which you use to save the image on your device. Just select where you'd like to save the image (Pics&Videos application or storage card), and it's downloaded and stored on your device.

To access the bookmarks stored on your device, follow these steps:

1. Press the **Menu** button, and then scroll down to and select the **Bookmarks View** menu command (or Menu+V). The Bookmarks screen opens, as shown in Figure 10.5.

FIGURE 10.5

The Bookmarks View of the Blazer browser shows a list of the bookmarks stored on your device.

2. You'll notice in Figure 10.5 that three bookmarks are stored on my device, and there is room on the screen for a total of 10 bookmarks. If you look down in the lower-right corner of the screen, you'll see a series of boxes for accessing additional banks of bookmarks—10 total—thus allowing you to store up to 100 bookmarks on your device. Try tapping these boxes to navigate through the bookmark storage areas.

TIP The Backspace key on the keyboard serves as a handy shortcut for the Back command.

3. There are two ways to add a new bookmark to the list of bookmarks. The first approach is to use the **Add Bookmark** command from the Page menu while viewing the page you'd like to bookmark. This approach is the most efficient, as it automatically grabs the page's URL and name without requiring you to type anything. The other approach is tapping a blank entry in the bookmark list. If you tap a blank entry, the New Bookmark screen opens, as shown in Figure 10.6.

FIGURE 10.6

The New Bookmark screen prompts you to enter the name, description, and URL of a new bookmark.

NOTE You might not be able to delete some of the default bookmarks that are initially set on your device. These built-in bookmarks are fixed and cannot be modified or deleted.

4. To enter a new bookmark in the New Bookmark screen, simply enter the name, description, and URL. When you tap the URL field, the Set URL screen opens and assists you in entering the URL with a default URL prefix and the familiar suffix helper boxes. When you're finished entering the bookmark information, tap the **OK** button to finalize its creation. The bookmark is then added to the bookmark list, as shown in Figure 10.7.

5. You can edit a bookmark in the list by selecting the bookmark and tapping the **Edit** button. To delete a bookmark, you must tap the **Edit** button first, and then tap the **Delete** button in the Edit Bookmark screen.

Bookmarks are a great way to remember websites and help organize your favorites for frequent access. You'll find that your bookmark list changes over time as you explore new sites and tire of older ones.

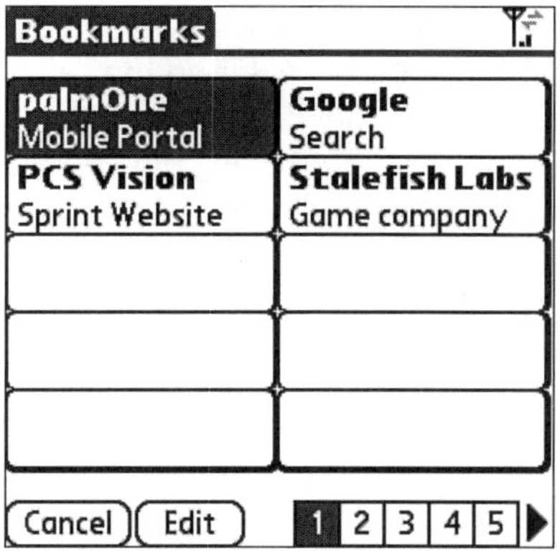

FIGURE 10.7

The bookmark list changes to reflect the newly created bookmark, although the first bookmark in the list is initially selected.

Tweak the Browser Settings

The Blazer Web browser includes several options you can alter to control how web pages are displayed and stored. In addition to changing familiar settings such as the default home page, you can also disable images for faster page loading as well as modify numerous other settings that affect the browser operation. To fine-tune preferences for the Blazer browser, follow these steps:

> **TIP**
> To beam a bookmark to another Palm device, select the bookmark in the bookmark list and press the Menu button. Scroll down to and select the Beam Bookmark menu command to begin beaming the bookmark. Make sure you align the infrared ports of the two devices.

1. Press the **Menu** button and navigate over to the Options menu. Scroll down the Options menu to select the **Preferences** command. The Preferences screen opens and provides access to three tabs of browser options (see Figure 10.8) .
2. The first tab of preferences is the Page tab, which includes settings for the start page, the home page, and whether the address bar is visible on the browser screen. The start page is controlled by the Start With pick list and determines what page the browser displays when it's first launched. You can set this option to the last page viewed, the bookmark list, the home page, or a blank page. I find the Last Page Viewed setting to be the most useful, as it allows you to leave the Blazer browser and return without the page changing.
3. To set the home page, tap the **Home Page** field. The default value of this setting is likely a mobile website for your wireless service provider, which you may or may not find useful. Feel free to change the home page to any page of your

choosing. If you ever want to restore the default home page, just tap the **Restore Default** button. The Show Address Bar option causes the browser's address bar to be displayed. You should turn off this option only if you want to maximize screen space and don't mind not having direct access to the address bar.

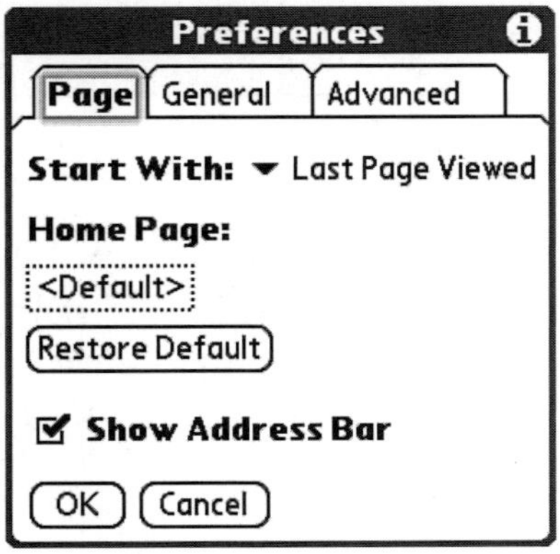

FIGURE 10.8

The Preferences screen in the Blazer application provides access to three different tabs of browser options.

4. When you're finished with the Page tab preferences, tap the **General** tab to access general browser preferences (see Figure 10.9).

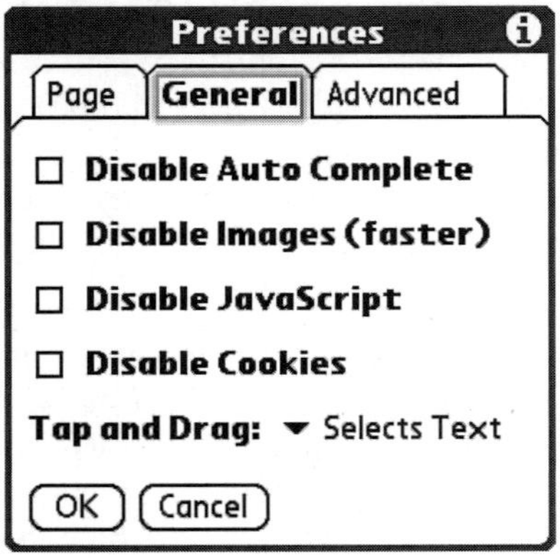

FIGURE 10.9

In the General tab, you can disable several important browser features as well as alter the behavior of the stylus when browsing.

5. Most of the preferences in the General tab are used to disable browser features that you might want to eliminate for optimization or security purposes. More specifically, you can disable Auto Complete for text entry, images, JavaScript, and cookies. Disabling Auto Complete doesn't really have a performance or security implication; it's primarily a personal setting if you find auto-completion of text entry to be an annoyance. Disabling images is entirely an optimization issue, as pages load much faster without images. JavaScript and cookies are primarily security related, although JavaScript can cause somewhat of a performance issue in causing some pages to load slowly. You might want to check the settings of your desktop browser to decide about disabling these features. The last setting in the General tab allows you to change the action that occurs when you tap and drag the stylus. The default action is to select text on the page, although you might consider changing the setting so that you can use the stylus to scroll the page; this setting is a good idea only if you don't need to select text for copying and pasting.

> **TIP** If you've accumulated a library of web page bookmarks on your desktop computer and would like to move them over to your Treo, you'll be glad to know that an application called Pocket Favorites by Chapura makes this task possible. With Pocket Favorites, you can synchronize Internet Explorer browser favorites with bookmarks on your Treo. To learn more, visit the Chapura website at http://www.chapura.com/.

6. When you're finished with the General tab preferences, tap the **Advanced** tab to access advanced browser preferences (see Figure 10.10).

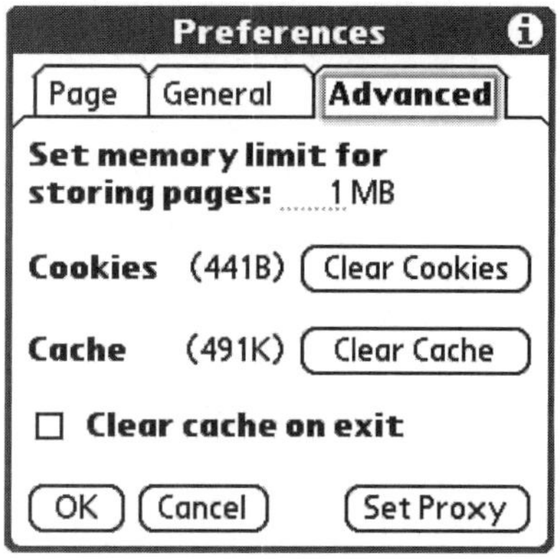

FIGURE 10.10

The Advanced tab provides access to browser cache and cookie settings.

7. The preferences in the Advanced tab primarily relate to memory as it applies to the browser cache and cookies. The first preference is the most important because it establishes how much memory is set aside for the cache. Unless you have a good reason for tinkering with this setting, I recommend sticking with the

> **NOTE** In addition to JavaScript, the Blazer Web browser supports the Java runtime environment, thanks to an add-on made available by Palm. For more information, visit http://www.palmone.com/us/support/jvm/.

> **TIP** One exception to my suggestion of not tinkering with the size of the browser cache is if you happen to have plenty of free memory. In this case, feel free to increase the browser cache some. For example, you might try doubling the cache and seeing whether it helps the browser's performance noticeably. If so, the memory loss might be worth it; if not, change the size back to the default and consider it a lesson learned!

> **TIP** If your data service provider requires a proxy for connecting to the Internet, tap the Set Proxy button in the Advanced tab. After enabling the proxy, you're prompted to specify the port number for the proxy. Your data service provider should supply this information.

default value. Next up are two buttons for clearing cookies and the cache. Similar to a desktop Web browser, if you need to clear cookies or the cache for the Blazer browser, this is the place to do it. To automatically clear the cache each time you exit the browser, disconnect from the Internet, or turn off your device, you can select the Clear Cache on Exit option at the bottom.

8. When you're finished with the Blazer browser preferences, tap the **OK** button to accept the changes and return to the main browser screen.

You might want to use the Blazer Web browser for a while before going too crazy changing its preferences. Some preferences have a dramatic effect on how web pages are displayed, so it's important to make sure you understand the impact of any changes you make. Of course, it's easy to undo changes, so experimenting with different browser preferences isn't wrong either.

Save a Web Page for Offline Viewing

Seeing that mobile devices are often used in areas without Internet access, such as airplanes, it can be helpful to download and save a web page so that you can view it offline. The Blazer browser makes it incredibly easy to save a page for offline viewing. To do so, follow these steps:

1. Navigate to a page in the Blazer browser.
2. Press the **Menu** button and then scroll down to and select the **Save Page** command. The New Saved Page Bookmark screen opens and looks surprisingly similar to the window you saw earlier for creating a new bookmark. In fact, saving a page for offline viewing involves creating a bookmark for the page.
3. The name and description of the page to be saved are shown in the New Saved Page Bookmark screen. Feel free to edit this information if you'd like. Otherwise, tap the **OK** button to accept the new bookmark and save the page for offline viewing. A confirmation screen appears and lets you know that the page was successfully saved. Tap the **OK** button to continue.

Figure 10.11

You can use the New Saved Page Bookmark screen to specify the details of a page to be saved for offline viewing.

4. After saving the page for offline viewing, you are taken to the bookmark list. Figure 10.12 shows the bookmark list with the saved page bookmark clearly in view. Notice a small orange (trust me, it's orange) triangle in the upper-right corner of the bookmark—this icon indicates that the page is saved for offline viewing.

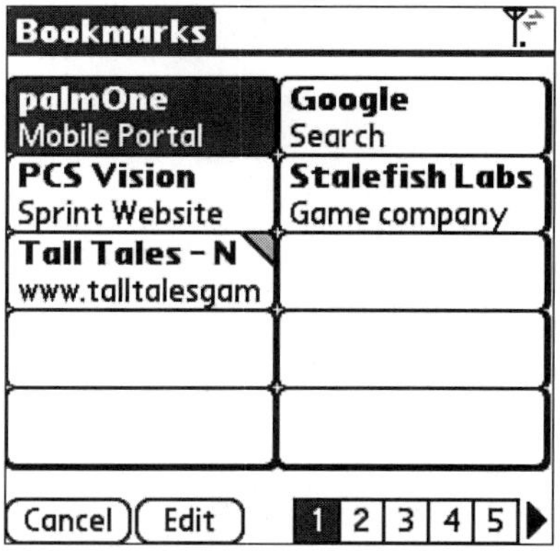

Figure 10.12

Saved pages that can be viewed offline appear in the bookmark list with a small orange triangle in the upper-right corner of the bookmark.

After a page has been saved for offline viewing, it appears in the bookmark list almost like any other bookmark you've created. There are two differences, however. The first difference is the visual cue of the small orange triangle in the upper-right corner of the bookmark. The second difference is that when you edit a saved page bookmark, there's no URL for you to edit. This is because the page has been downloaded to your device and, therefore, has no need to reference a URL on the Internet. In this way, you can't think of offline web pages as updating themselves in any way. If you want to read a new version of an offline web page, you need to delete the previous bookmark and save the page again.

Summary

Web browsing on the go is one of the killer features of handheld devices such as the Treo. Although the limited screen real estate makes some websites a bit more challenging to view as compared to a desktop Web browser, the Treo is far beyond most mobile phones and handheld devices, thanks to its relatively high-resolution screen. Additionally, I hope you've found that the Blazer Web browser is plenty capable when it comes to performing basic browser functions and rendering the vast majority of web pages reliably. Although there are some third-party options that you might consider eventually if you find yourself stretching the limits of Blazer, more than likely you'll find that Blazer suits your browsing needs just fine.

11

Communicating Wirelessly with Bluetooth

IN THIS CHAPTER

- What Is Bluetooth?
- Enable and Disable Bluetooth
- Pair Up with a Bluetooth Headset or Car Kit
- Synchronize Without Wires
- Transfer Files and Data Wirelessly with Bluetooth
- Use Your Treo as a Wireless Modem
- Assessing Bluetooth Security Issues

If you've ever heard the term PAN and thought someone was confusing a networking acronym, this chapter might surprise you. PAN stands for *personal area network*, which describes a network with a much smaller "footprint" than a local area network (LAN) and is measured in feet instead of yards. The leading PAN technology is Bluetooth, which is a wireless networking standard that allows devices to communicate with each other within in a range of about 30 feet. The idea behind Bluetooth and PANs in general is to make it possible to establish a small wireless network around yourself to help eliminate wires between devices. Your Treo has full support for Bluetooth networking and can use Bluetooth to communicate with devices ranging from wireless headsets to hands-free car kits to global positioning system (GPS) receivers. And don't forget that you can use Bluetooth to wirelessly synchronize your Treo with your desktop computer.

What Is Bluetooth?

Bluetooth is a wireless communication standard geared toward removing the wires between computers and their peripherals. For example, you can purchase a Bluetooth keyboard, mouse, and printer to eliminate the wires that typically connect these peripherals to your desktop or notebook PC. Similarly, Bluetooth has become popular in the mobile realm for using a mobile headset or hands-free car kit to communicate with a mobile phone. This is the most common application of Bluetooth to Treo devices.

Bluetooth effectively enables you to operate a wireless network limited to a very small area (usually up to 10 meters, or 32 feet). For a Treo device using Bluetooth, the "network" consists of your Treo and a Bluetooth headset, hands-free car kit, or GPS receiver, to name a few examples. Bluetooth devices communicate over a 2.45 gigahertz (GHz) radio connection, similar to the one used by baby monitors, garage door openers, and cordless phones. For this reason, interference is technically possible if you operate a Bluetooth headset with your Treo in the same area as other wireless equipment. However, the specific design of the Bluetooth communication protocol helps alleviate the problem.

The Bluetooth specification defines three different classes of devices, each of which offers a varying level of wireless signal strength and, therefore, a different operating distance (see Table 11.1).

Table 11.1 Classes of Bluetooth Devices

Device Class	Signal Strength	Range
Class 1	100 milliwatts	Up to 100 meters (328 feet)
Class 2	2.5 milliwatts	Up to 10 meters (32 feet)
Class 3	1 milliwatt	Well under 10 meters (32 feet)

Your Treo device is a Class 2 Bluetooth device, so you can expect a Bluetooth headset to give you a range of around 10 meters, or 32 feet. This is assuming, of course, that the headset is also a Class 2 device. If it's a Class 3 device, you can expect a reduced range. Keep in mind that I'm talking about the distance between your Treo and the Bluetooth headset—generally speaking, you'll likely keep the two devices in close proximity to one another, so the 10-meter limit is unlikely to present a serious problem.

NOTE The name Bluetooth is derived from Harald Bluetooth, who was king of Denmark in the late 900s (that's correct, the tenth century). Along with simply serving as an unusual and unique name, Bluetooth is named after the Danish king because King Bluetooth is known for unifying the previously warring tribes of Denmark, Norway, and Sweden. Bluetooth is considered somewhat of a unifying technology between devices that otherwise have no means of communicating with each other wirelessly.

Every Bluetooth device is responsible for supporting one or more *profiles*, which describe the Bluetooth applications available for use with the device. Following are some examples of Bluetooth profiles:

- Headset Profile
- Hands-Free Profile
- Serial Port Profile
- General Object Exchange Profile
- Fax Profile
- LAN Access Profile
- File Transfer Profile
- Human Interface Device Profile
- Audio Video Remote Control Profile
- Basic Printing Profile

The Treo 650 supports the first four profiles, which together allow you to connect your device to headsets (Headset Profile), hands-free car kits (Hands-Free Profile), other devices via a wireless serial connection (Serial Port Profile), and other devices for sharing discrete pieces of data, such as contacts (General Object Exchange Profile).

Another other important topic worth covering is the version of Bluetooth supported in Treo devices. As you shop for Bluetooth headsets and hands-free car kits, you might run across a version number for their Bluetooth support. Although Bluetooth is currently up to version 2.0, the majority of Bluetooth accessories currently available are designed for Bluetooth version 1.1. Treo devices are designed around Bluetooth 1.1, so you have a wide range of Bluetooth headsets and hands-free devices from which to choose. Newer versions of Bluetooth include version 1.2 and version 2.0, both of which are backward-compatible with version 1.1. So you shouldn't encounter any compatibility problems when it comes to buying headsets and hands-free devices for your Treo.

I want to close this Bluetooth primer by tackling a common source of confusion associated with Bluetooth: how it differs from the popular Wi-Fi (802.11a/b/g) wireless networking technologies. First, Bluetooth and Wi-Fi are not competing technologies; they are designed to solve uniquely different problems. The fundamental goal of both technologies is to eliminate wires between devices, but the scope of the wires they are intended to eliminate differs. Bluetooth focuses on low-power short-range connections between devices, such as the connection between a mouse and a PC. Wi-Fi addresses network connections between computer systems, such as the Ethernet cable between a computer and a router. To some degree, each technology overlaps the other from time to time. As an example, both Wi-Fi and Bluetooth adapters are available for wireless printing and can both be used for wireless synchronization. To help understand the relationship between Bluetooth and Wi-Fi, think of Bluetooth as the wireless equivalent of USB and Wi-Fi as the wireless equivalent of Ethernet. This is not an exact analogy, but from a general perspective, it's reasonably accurate.

NOTE

You might have seen the Universal Wireless Keyboard that Palm offers for use with many of its devices. Although wireless Bluetooth keyboards exist, Palm's Universal Wireless Keyboard uses an infrared connection to Palm devices, not a Bluetooth connection. A popular Bluetooth wireless keyboard for Treo devices is the Stowaway Bluetooth Keyboard by Think Outside. This keyboard is available from the palmOne online store at http://web.palmone.com/products/Category.jhtml?ID=20022.

NOTE

Several Bluetooth printers are on the market that you can use with your Treo, such as the Canon i80. With a Bluetooth printer, you can wirelessly print pictures, tasks, memos, business cards, and schedules from your Treo. Even if your printer doesn't include built-in Bluetooth support, you can easily turn it into a Bluetooth printer by using a Bluetooth printer adapter, such as the HP BT1300 or Bluetake BT210; these adapters plug into the printer's USB or parallel port.

NOTE The only immediate competitor to Bluetooth is Infrared Data Association (IrDA), which is the infrared technology often found on notebook and handheld computers that enables you to communicate wirelessly with another computer or printer. Although IrDA currently enjoys a much larger install base than Bluetooth, the tide is rapidly turning. The major drawback to IrDA is that it requires a clear line of sight and a distance of no more than about a meter between the two devices that are communicating. Compare this to Bluetooth, which requires no line of sight and a communication distance typically in the 10-meter range.

Enable and Disable Bluetooth

Similar to the mobile radio that sends and receives wireless voice and data on your Treo, there's a Bluetooth radio that is responsible for wireless communication via Bluetooth. Also like the mobile radio, you can turn the Bluetooth radio on and off whenever you want. The Bluetooth radio has an impact on your device's battery charge, so that's one reason you might consider not leaving the Bluetooth radio on all the time. Another reason has to do with security, which you learn about later in the chapter in the section "Assessing Bluetooth Security Issues."

Regardless of your motives for turning the Bluetooth radio on and off, fortunately it's easy to do. Just follow these steps:

1. Press the **Application** button to open the main application screen (if you aren't already there).
2. Press the **B** key to jump near the Bluetooth application, and then navigate with the five-way navigator to select the Bluetooth application.
3. Press the **Center** button to launch the Bluetooth application. The **Bluetooth** screen displays the Bluetooth status along with a couple of options (see Figure 11.1).

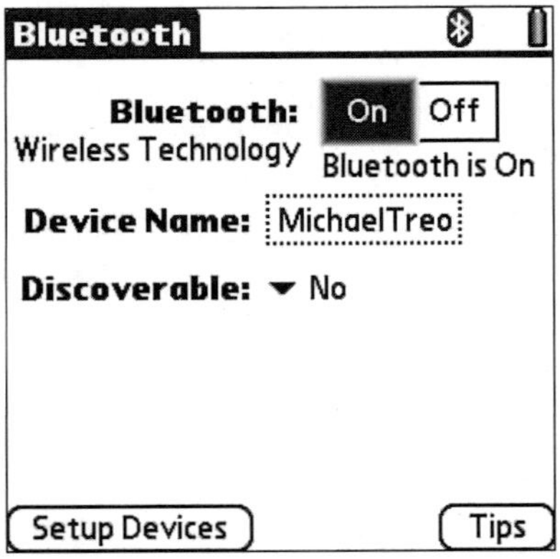

FIGURE 11.1

You use the Bluetooth screen to turn the Bluetooth radio on and off as well as change the Bluetooth device name and make it discoverable.

4. The On and Off boxes on the Bluetooth screen are used to turn the Bluetooth radio on and off. Just below the boxes you can see the current status of the Bluetooth radio; the appropriate box (On or Off) is also highlighted to show the status. Another option on the Bluetooth screen is the device name, which applies solely to Bluetooth communications. By default, the name you use for device synchronization is used as the Bluetooth device name, but you can change it to any name you want. Just keep in mind that this is the name other Bluetooth devices see when you attempt to connect to them. The final option appears only when the Bluetooth radio is turned on and allows your Treo to be discoverable by other Bluetooth devices, which means that other Bluetooth devices can "see" your device and potentially connect to it.

5. If you plan to connect to a Bluetooth device, go ahead and make sure the Bluetooth radio is turned on. You might also want to leave the Bluetooth application open as you continue reading because you use it again to establish Bluetooth connections.

With the Bluetooth radio on, you're ready to connect to a Bluetooth device and communicate over a personal area network.

> **NOTE**
> On the near horizon is a competitor to Bluetooth that could ultimately render Bluetooth obsolete: Wireless USB (WUSB). WUSB is a wireless technology based on the popular USB communication standard. Similar to Bluetooth, WUSB is a short-range wireless technology geared toward connecting devices in close proximity. However, WUSB is much faster than Bluetooth, which could be its killer feature. WUSB is slated to have transfer speeds in the neighborhood of 60MB/sec; Bluetooth supports much slower speeds of 1.5MB/sec. Intel is putting a lot of marketing muscle behind WUSB, but it will be tough to shun the wave of new devices that support Bluetooth, including your Treo. It should be interesting to see how WUSB unfolds and whether Bluetooth can survive against it.

Pair Up with a Bluetooth Headset or Car Kit

Bluetooth can dramatically change the manner in which you use your Treo. For example, a Bluetooth hands-free car kit allows you to leave your device in a briefcase, purse, console, or glove box while carrying on a conversation wirelessly. You can receive a call through a hands-free car kit or make a call by speaking the name or number of the person you want to dial. Similarly, with a Bluetooth headset, you can use a separate wireless earpiece to carry on a conversation while your Treo is tucked safely away in a pocket. Thanks to the simplicity of Bluetooth technology, you can easily connect a Bluetooth headset or hands-free car kit to your device with minimal effort, and then repeatedly connect it from then on with no effort at all. This effectively makes a Bluetooth headset or hands-free car kit even easier to use than their wired counterparts. Just keep in mind that you'll need to charge a Bluetooth headset periodically, as it isn't capable of drawing power from your Treo, as a normal wired headset can.

Follow these steps to establish a connection between your Treo and a Bluetooth headset:

NOTE

In 2004, Bluetooth started appearing as standard equipment in some automobiles, which means you can operate your Bluetooth-enabled mobile phone hands-free while the phone is still tucked away in your pocket or briefcase. Instead of using your phone's speaker, microphone, and controls, you use a set of built-in controls in the automobile. A few vehicle makes and models that were early adopters of Bluetooth include the BMW 3 Series and 5 Series, Lexus LS 430, Acura TL, and Toyota Prius. Numerous other vehicles are rapidly being added to the ranks of the Bluetooth compatible.

1. Before adding the headset to your Treo, you must first turn on the headset and enable it for being discovered by your device. This enabling process is unique to your particular headset. I use a Motorola HS820 headset, which requires me to hold down its multifunction (power) button for five seconds to be discoverable. When your headset is powered on and ready for discovery, you can proceed with adding the headset to your device.

2. In the Bluetooth application, tap the **Setup Devices** button to set up the headset as a trusted Bluetooth device. Every Bluetooth device has a passkey, which is a short password similar to a PIN code used to gain access to the device; most headsets, however, are configured from the factory with a fixed passkey that you can't change. A trusted Bluetooth device is a device you set up so that you enter its passkey only once, and from then on you can quickly connect to it without having to enter the passkey. After tapping the **Setup Devices** button, the Setup Devices screen appears, as shown in Figure 11.2.

3. Tap the **Hands-free Setup** button to set up the headset. You then see a welcome window before your device begins looking for the headset. Just tap the **Next** button to continue. The Discovery Results screen appears, and your Treo begins looking for the headset (see Figure 11.3) .

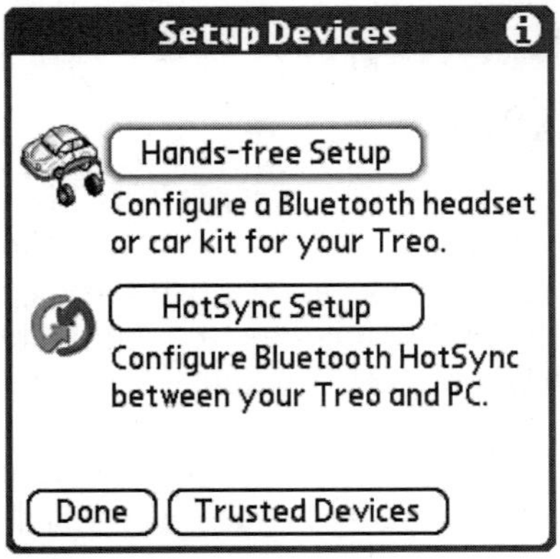

FIGURE 11.2

The Setup Devices screen is where you begin setting up any Bluetooth device for use with your Treo.

FIGURE 11.3

The Discovery Results screen searches your immediate vicinity for any discoverable Bluetooth devices.

4. It's important that the Show pick list near the top of the Discovery Results screen be set to Nearby Devices. Other options in the list include All Known Devices and Trusted Devices; All Known Devices lists all known Bluetooth devices, and Trusted Devices shows only those devices you've already set up as trusted. If your headset isn't found at first, tap the **Find More** button to try again. When the headset is found, it appears in the device list, as shown in Figure 11.3. Select the headset in the list and tap the **OK** button to connect to the headset. Before the connection can be established, you must enter the passkey for the headset in the Bluetooth Security screen (see Figure 11.4).

> **NOTE**
> Bluetooth 1.0 had several design flaws that made it difficult to implement reliably across a variety of devices and accessories. Consequently, Bluetooth 1.1 is generally considered the first stable version of Bluetooth in widespread use.

5. Every Bluetooth device has an associated passkey, which serves as a PIN code that's required to pair up with the device. For peripheral devices such as headsets that don't really have security implications, the passkey is typically just 0000. Enter the passkey for your headset in the Bluetooth Security screen and tap the **OK** button. You then see a confirmation that the connection between your Treo and headset has been established successfully. The headset is ready to use with your Treo.

FIGURE 11.4

The Bluetooth Security screen prompts you to enter the passkey for the Bluetooth headset, which is likely 0000.

To try out the newly connected headset, launch the Phone application and call someone. Make sure to put the headset on so that you can hear the conversation. If a trusted Bluetooth headset is on and in range, it's automatically used when you make a call. You can immediately tell whether a Bluetooth headset is in use because a Cancel button appears on the main Phone screen that enables you to bypass the Bluetooth headset and use the standard Treo speaker/microphone instead (see Figure 11.5).

FIGURE 11.5

If a Bluetooth headset is activated for a phone call, a Cancel button appears that enables you to cancel using the headset on the call.

Figure 11.5 reveals how the Spkr-phone button that normally appears is replaced by a Cancel button for disabling the Bluetooth headset. If you tap the Cancel button, the headset is ignored for that call, and your device reverts to using the standard built-in earpiece and microphone. The Spkr-phone button also reappears, allowing you to use the speakerphone feature if you want.

> **NOTE** Making your device discoverable can be both good and bad. On the good side, it makes it much easier to establish connections with other Bluetooth devices because your device is immediately "seen" when it gets in Bluetooth range and can be connected to. However, some security risks are associated with Bluetooth that might make you think twice about leaving the Bluetooth radio on all the time, especially in crowded areas where numerous other devices could be on the prowl. The "Assessing Bluetooth Security Issues" section later in this chapter explores Bluetooth security in detail.

Synchronize Without Wires

Using a Bluetooth headset or hands-free car kit to talk on the phone without wires (and hands) is certainly nifty, but you can do a lot more with Bluetooth. If you don't already have Bluetooth functionality built into your notebook or desktop computer, you might want to consider buying a Bluetooth adapter. They are compact USB devices similar in size to small USB flash memory "drives," and they give your computer full support for Bluetooth communications.

One of the most useful types of Bluetooth communications you can perform with your Treo and a desktop computer is wireless synchronization. All you have to do is get within wireless range (usually within 32 feet), launch the HotSync application on your Treo, and press the synchronization button in the HotSync application. Before you can use this feature, however, you must set it up. Follow these steps to do so:

> **TIP** If you plan to use Bluetooth only to connect to a wireless headset or hands-free car kit, you'll probably want to set the Discoverable option to No. The reason is that your Treo initiates the connection with a headset or car kit, so there's no need for the Treo to be discoverable by those devices. Discoverability typically enters the picture when you want to connect your Treo with another computer, such as your PC, or another handheld device.

1. Make sure Bluetooth is enabled on both your Treo and your desktop/notebook computer.
2. Launch the Bluetooth application on your Treo.
3. In the Bluetooth application on your Treo, tap the **Setup Devices** button to begin setting up the wireless synchronization pairing. A welcome window appears explaining that you are now setting up the wireless HotSync feature—tap the **Next** button to continue. The Discovery Results screen appears, and your Treo begins looking for the desktop computer (see Figure 11.6).
4. Make sure the Show pick list near the top of the Discovery Results screen is set to Nearby Devices. If your computer isn't found at first, tap the **Find More** button to try again. When the computer is found, it appears in the device list, as shown in Figure 11.6. Select the computer in the list and tap the **OK** button to connect to it. Step 1 of the Bluetooth HotSync Setup appears (see Figure 11.7).

FIGURE 11.6

The Discovery Results screen searches the immediate vicinity for your desktop computer.

FIGURE 11.7

The first step of the Bluetooth HotSync Setup reminds you that a virtual serial port is required on your desktop computer.

5. The first step in the Bluetooth HotSync Setup clarifies that you must have a virtual serial port created on your desktop computer for Bluetooth communication. Although this is a standard part of using Bluetooth on a desktop computer, you might want to double-check that your computer has this virtual serial port enabled; use the Bluetooth software on your desktop computer to do so. After you're satisfied that the virtual serial port is up and running on your computer, tap the **Next** button on your Treo to continue. Step 2 of the Bluetooth HotSync Setup appears next (see Figure 11.8).

FIGURE 11.8

The second step of the Bluetooth HotSync Setup instructs you on enabling the virtual serial port from within the HotSync Manager application on your desktop computer.

6. Follow the directions in Step 2 of the Bluetooth HotSync Setup by selecting the virtual serial port as the local connection port in the HotSync Manager application on your desktop computer. Figure 11.9 shows the COM port selected that matches the Bluetooth virtual serial port. If you aren't sure what COM port your computer is using for the virtual serial port, use the Bluetooth software on your desktop computer to access and find the virtual serial port settings.

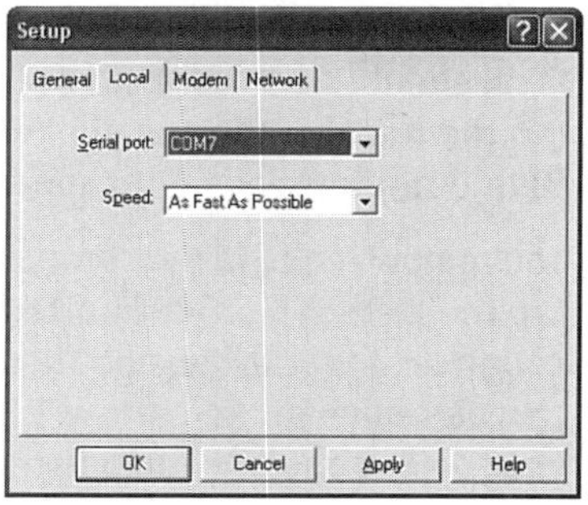

FIGURE 11.9

You must set the local connection in the HotSync application on your desktop computer to the COM port of the Bluetooth virtual serial port.

7. After setting the COM port on your desktop computer, tap the **Next** button on your Treo. Step 3 of the Bluetooth HotSync Setup appears next, as shown in Figure 11.10.

FIGURE 11.10

The third step of the Bluetooth HotSync Setup instructs you to enable the local serial connection type for HotSync Manager on your desktop computer.

8. This step is basically asking you to enable the local serial connection type for synchronization. If you've been synchronizing via the Treo Multi-connector, the HotSync application on your computer probably has only local USB enabled as a connection type. It's perfectly fine to have both types of connections enabled, which still allows you to synchronize via the USB cable if you're charging your Treo. After enabling the local serial (Bluetooth) connection type for synchronization, tap the **Next** button on your Treo. The final step of the Bluetooth HotSync Setup appears, as shown in Figure 11.11.

9. You're now ready to synchronize wirelessly via Bluetooth. Just tap the **Launch HotSync** button to launch the HotSync application on your device, and then tap the HotSync button (circular blue and red arrows) in the middle of the screen if your device doesn't immediately start synchronizing.

10. At this point, your desktop computer prompts you to establish a connection with your Treo and asks you to enter a passkey for the Bluetooth connection. This passkey is something you make up so that the two machines can verify each other. Keep in mind that the Bluetooth connection doesn't know you are controlling both machines, so it requires authentication in the form of the same passkey on both machines. Just make up a short passkey and enter it on your

TIP

Palm offers a software update for the Treo 650 that's important to install if you plan to use a Bluetooth hands-free car kit. This update dramatically improves the Treo's support for hands-free car kits. To download the Carkit Update for Treo 650, follow this link: http://www.palmone.com/us/support/downloads/treo650carkitupdate/index.html.

NOTE

Although I refer to a hands-free car kit several times throughout this chapter, you might certainly run across other kinds of hands-free Bluetooth devices, such as a portable hands-free device that doesn't necessarily have to be used in an automobile. However, for the sake of keeping the distinction obvious, I refer to a hands-free car kit as the hands-free alternative to a headset.

desktop computer. You are then prompted to enter it on your Treo;
you probably also want to select the check box for declaring your desktop computer as a trusted device on your Treo. You might then be prompted one additional time to allow the connection on your desktop computer. Just click **OK** to allow the connection, and if you don't want to have to okay the connection in the future, click to enable the check box that automatically allows a serial connection to your device.

NOTE The idea behind trusted Bluetooth devices is to eliminate the passkey entry step when it's a secure device that you connect to regularly, such as a headset, car kit, or even your desktop computer. Generally, setting up other people's computers as trusted devices isn't a good idea.

Wireless Bluetooth synchronization is now set up and ready to go between your Treo and desktop computer. To synchronize in the future, just launch the HotSync application on your Treo and tap the HotSync button.

FIGURE 11.11

Step 4 of the Bluetooth HotSync Setup allows you to initiate your first wireless Bluetooth synchronization.

Transfer Files and Data Wirelessly with Bluetooth

Synchronization is an excellent option for transferring files from your desktop computer to your Treo via Bluetooth. However, there isn't all that much flexibility when sending files back to the desktop computer from your Treo. And besides, sometimes it's a hassle to go through the entire synchronization process just to send a file or two back and forth between machines. The good news is that it's possible to transfer files and data wirelessly between your Treo and desktop computer via Bluetooth without having to synchronize.

> **TIP** If your Treo doesn't find the headset, first check to make sure the Bluetooth radio on the Treo is turned on. If Bluetooth is already turned on, double-check that you have turned on the headset and set it correctly so that it can be discovered. On my Motorola headset, it took a few tries before I realized how long the multifunction button had to be held down to enter "discovery" mode.

The technique used to send files and data differs depending on which direction you're sending them. The following steps show you how to send a file from a Windows desktop computer to your Treo:

1. Double-click the Bluetooth icon in your taskbar to open the My Bluetooth Places window. The main area of this window is initially empty, but you can use it to find your Treo by clicking **Search for Devices in Range** in the column on the left. The main area changes to reveal your Treo as a found Bluetooth device (see Figure 11.12).

2. Pay close attention to the icon representing your Treo in the My Bluetooth Places window. If it has a small red checkmark in the lower-left corner of the icon (as shown in Figure 11.12), you have already paired the device to your desktop computer and can transfer files to your Treo without having to do anything special. If there's no checkmark, your Treo isn't paired with the desktop computer, and you have to enter passkeys for both machines.

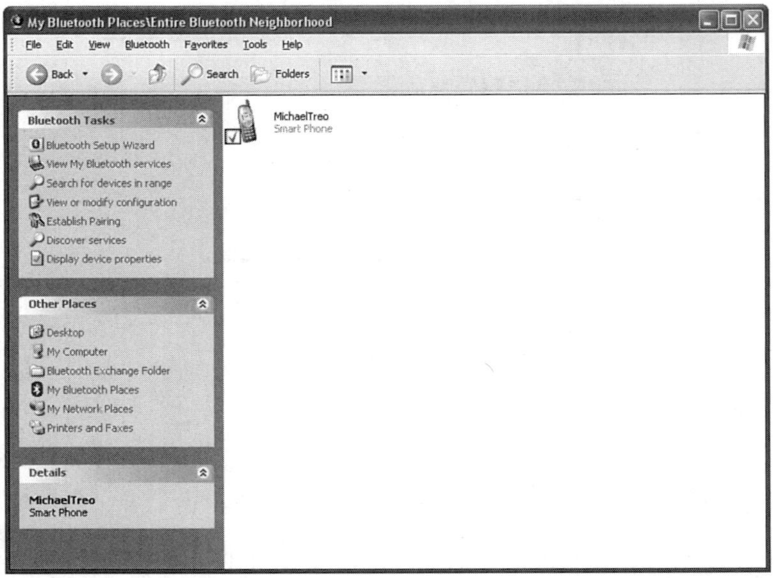

FIGURE 11.12

Use the My Bluetooth Places window on your desktop computer to access your Treo via Bluetooth.

3. To transfer a file from your desktop computer to your Treo, launch Windows Explorer and browse to select the file. Then drag the file from Windows Explorer and drop it onto the Treo icon in the My Bluetooth Places window. You're prompted on your Treo to accept the file, and then it's transferred. The file type is taken into consideration during the transfer, which determines where it is stored. For example, images are stored as pictures alongside other pictures on your device.

NOTE If you're unsure of the passkey for your headset, refer to the manual for it. If you're the kind of person who avoids reading manuals at all costs, give 0000 a try first because it's typically the passkey used for most Bluetooth headsets and hands-free car kits.

It's a little hard to believe that transferring a file from your desktop computer to your Treo can be done wirelessly with a simple drag and drop, but it's true. And that's not all—you can also send files from your Treo back to your desktop computer with little effort. In fact, your Treo makes it easy to send both files and PIM data via Bluetooth. When I say "files and PIM data," I'm referring to files such as images and documents as well as PIM data, such as contacts, tasks, and calendar events. The only real distinction between sending files and sending data is that PIM data is automatically incorporated into Microsoft Outlook or Palm Desktop on your computer; files are stored in a special Bluetooth exchange folder.

TIP To get the most out of a hands-free headset or car kit, you need to be able to dial without touching your Treo. Although the Treo doesn't come standard with a voice-dialing application, you can buy one as an add-on application. Check out the "Call via Voice Activation" section in Chapter 7 to find out more.

To transfer a file or piece of PIM data from your Treo to your desktop computer, follow these steps:

1. On your Treo, launch the application used to access the file or data you want to send to your desktop computer. For example, if you want to send a picture, launch the Pics&Videos application.
2. Within the application, navigate to select the file or data you want to send.
3. Press the **Menu** button and scroll down the main menu to select the command that sends the file or data. This command varies from application to application. In the Pics&Videos application, the command is just **Send**, but in the Contacts application, it is **Send Contact**. Issue the command to begin sending the file or data.
4. In the Send With screen, you're prompted to specify how you want to send the file or data (see Figure 11.13). Tap **Bluetooth** in the list of options, and then tap the **OK** button.

NOTE Your Treo is capable of managing only one Bluetooth connection at a time. As an example, this means you can't use a Bluetooth hands-free car kit and a Bluetooth GPS receiver at the same time. This is an unfortunate limitation because those two Bluetooth devices are handy when driving.

FIGURE 11.13

The Send With screen prompts you to select how you want to send the file, which in this case is a picture.

5. The Discovery Results screen is displayed so that you can select the device or devices where you want to send the file or data. Figure 11.14 shows where I've selected only my desktop computer. Also note in Figure 11.14 that the little key icons next to my desktop computer and Motorola headset indicate that they're trusted devices.

FIGURE 11.14

In the familiar Discovery Results screen, you select one or more devices to receive the file or data.

6. The file or data is then sent. Depending on whether your Treo is already paired to your desktop computer, you might have to enter passkeys to establish a serial connection.

7. The file or data has been sent, but where exactly did it go? To access a newly transferred file on your desktop computer, click Bluetooth Exchange Folder under Other Places in the column on the left. If you don't already have this window open, double-click the Bluetooth icon in the taskbar to open it. This folder contains all the files sent to your desktop computer from your Treo. If you sent PIM data and Outlook is your PIM client on your desktop computer, the data was sent straight into Outlook, and there's no file stored in the Bluetooth Exchange folder. Just go to Outlook and check for the new data.

> **TIP** If you're using an external Bluetooth adapter for your desktop/notebook computer, it's important to install the software for it before trying to set up Bluetooth HotSync synchronization.

> **TIP** If your Treo doesn't find your desktop computer, first check to make sure the Bluetooth radio on the Treo is turned on. If Bluetooth is already turned on, double-check that you have enabled Bluetooth on your computer and set it correctly so that it can be discovered; usually, desktop computers are set with discovery enabled by default.

I hope these examples have demonstrated how much convenience Bluetooth offers in terms of sharing information between your Treo and desktop computer wirelessly. After you get used to Bluetooth, you'll start to wonder how you survived so long on cumbersome wired connections.

Use Your Treo as a Wireless Modem

One Bluetooth feature that caused quite a stir among Treo users when the Treo 650 was first released is dial-up networking, which involves using your Treo as a wireless modem to access the Internet on a notebook computer. In other words, you use the data portion of your mobile phone service to establish a data connection with your Treo; you already do this any time you access the Blazer Web browser. However, when using dial-up networking, your Treo passes along the wireless network connection to your notebook computer, effectively turning your Treo into a wireless modem. This feature caused a stir because wireless carriers disabled it in the Treo 650s they sold.

> **NOTE** Figure 11.9 and these Bluetooth HotSync synchronization steps apply to a Windows computer, but you should be able to follow along and carry out the same general process on a Macintosh computer.

You can easily tell whether your device has Bluetooth dial-up networking enabled because a Dial-up Networking option appears in the main Bluetooth application screen of your device (just below the Discoverable option) if the feature is available. If you don't see this option, check with your wireless carrier to see whether a Bluetooth dial-up networking update is available for your device. Some wireless carriers, such as Sprint, deliberately disabled Bluetooth dial-up networking, but after receiving considerable pressure from users, they opted to offer an update to enable it.

The specific steps for enabling Bluetooth dial-up networking vary considerably from one wireless carrier to another, so it's better to share with you the general steps required to use it. Following are the general steps for establishing and using a Bluetooth dial-up networking connection between your Treo and a notebook (or desktop) computer:

> **TIP** If your desktop computer isn't finding your Treo, make sure you have the Treo set so that it's discoverable. The Discoverable setting is accessible from the main screen of the Bluetooth application on your device.

> **TIP** To pair your Treo with your desktop computer, right-click the Treo icon in the My Bluetooth Places window on your desktop computer, and click Pair Device on the shortcut menu. You're then prompted to enter passkeys on both devices to establish the pairing. Don't forget that this passkey can be anything of your choosing; all that matters is that it matches on each machine.

1. Pair your Treo with the notebook computer.
2. Set up your notebook computer for a dial-up networking connection. Typically, this task involves using special software provided by your wireless carrier for entering the username and password associated with your wireless data services account. For example, on Sprint networks, this information is your PCS Vision username and password. You can access this information on your Treo from the Network section of the Prefs application. When setting up dial-up networking on your notebook computer, you must also enter the access point name (APN) for your wireless carrier's Internet access point. Your wireless carrier should supply the APN for its network.
3. Enable the dial-up networking feature on your Treo by enabling the Dial-Up Networking option on the main Bluetooth screen.
4. Access your Treo device from your notebook computer, and initiate the dial-up networking service.
5. Enter the appropriate dialing information (provided by your wireless carrier), and dial to connect to the wireless Internet.
6. When you're finished using the wireless Internet connection, disconnect from the dial-up networking service on your notebook computer, and then disable dial-up networking on your device.

Regardless of who your wireless carrier is, you should be able to follow these general steps to establish a Bluetooth dial-up network connection between your Treo and a notebook computer. I apologize for the lack of details for this task, but there's just too much variation between carriers to go down a more specific path here. At any rate, you'll likely find that Bluetooth dial-up networking is a decent alternative when you aren't able to connect to a traditional wired or Wi-Fi network with your notebook. Just make sure to double-check how your data plan is structured so that you know how much you're being charged (if anything) when using your Treo as a wireless modem.

Assessing Bluetooth Security Issues

There have been some concerns in the mobile community about Bluetooth security as more devices ship with support for Bluetooth. The concerns primarily have to do with Bluetooth being capable of opening a notebook PC, handheld, or mobile phone to wireless attacks. Part of the problem is that some users don't realize that, by enabling Bluetooth on their devices, they might be opening a gateway for unwanted communications, much like accessing the Internet without a firewall. Another part of the problem concerns a few faulty Bluetooth implementations that exposed several models of mobile phones to attack.

> **NOTE** Files are sent back and forth with your Treo using the Bluetooth General Object Exchange Profile, which is based on the Object Exchange (OBEX) communications protocol. OBEX is designed to allow the exchange of binary objects between devices and is supported in Palm devices as far back as the Palm III for sharing PIM data. OBEX is typically associated with infrared communication but is also used regularly now for transferring files and data via Bluetooth.

In reality, Bluetooth is a sophisticated technology that addresses security seriously. Bluetooth connections require acceptance by the user and are capable of using 128-bit encryption with other security protocols. The real concern with Bluetooth security isn't so much the technology itself as it is the manner in which people use it. As an example, your front door doesn't pose a security risk unless you leave it unlocked. The door offers security by virtue of the lock, but you must take some responsibility in shutting and securing the lock after you pass through the door. Similarly, Bluetooth requires some responsibility on the user's part if it is to offer maximum security.

> **NOTE** The actual location of the Bluetooth Exchange folder on your desktop computer is My Documents\Bluetooth Exchange Folder.

To better understand your responsibility in keeping your Treo secure from Bluetooth attackers, it's important to understand the types of attacks that can be launched against a Bluetooth device. The simplest and least dangerous form of Bluetooth attack is known as *Bluejacking*, which is more of an annoyance than a true security attack. In Bluejacking, another Bluetooth user sends an unsolicited message (usually as an electronic business card) through a Bluetooth connection to your device. You certainly have the option of rejecting the message, but just the fact that you're prompted by it, unsolicited, is a hassle. To send you a Bluejack message, of course, the other person has to be within 10 meters (32 feet) of your device, but this can be accomplished easily with anonymity in a crowded area.

> **NOTE** The unlocked GSM Treo 650 available directly from Palm was the first device to offer Bluetooth dial-up networking support. Wireless carriers have promised updates to enable the feature on their phones—some have delivered, some not.

It's important to understand that Bluejacking doesn't put your device at risk in any way. Both parties in a Bluejack communication are in complete control of their devices, and the Bluejacker has no way of extracting any information from your device. That's why I refer to Bluejacking as more of an annoyance than a true security attack. Even so, some people are shocked to receive an unsolicited message or, with some phones, an image or a sound. They wrongly assume that someone has attacked their phone or given

> **NOTE** You can enter the Bluetooth dial-up networking settings on a Windows computer entirely through the Phone and Modem applet in Control Panel. Even so, your wireless carrier should provide you with information about how to enter these settings.

them a virus. Quite the contrary; some people have turned Bluejacking into a more positive experience by using it as a way to meet new people. To learn more about Bluejacking and view the official Bluejack Code of Ethics, visit http://www.bluejackq.com/.

A much more serious Bluetooth security attack is known as *Bluesnarfing*, which involves another Bluetooth user gaining access to your device data and literally stealing information from your device. The at-risk data can include your contact list, text messages, memos, and anything else stored on your Treo. Although Bluesnarfing has certainly taken place in the past, it relied on a hole in Bluetooth implementations on specific mobile phones, not on a weakness with Bluetooth itself. In other words, the Bluetooth technology is secure enough to prevent Bluesnarfing, assuming that device manufacturers implement Bluetooth properly on their devices. Fortunately, there are no reported security problems with the Bluetooth implementation on Treo devices.

Another topic closely related to Bluetooth security is *Bluetooth sniping*, which involves using specially modified equipment to send and receive Bluetooth signals over a long range, currently up to 1 mile. When combined with Bluesnarfing, Bluetooth sniping presents an extremely dangerous opportunity for hackers to breach Bluetooth devices from a long distance. So far, Bluetooth sniping has been used primarily as a way of simply exploring the limits of the Bluetooth technology. It does open up the prospect of attackers operating from afar, assuming that they've figured out a way to access your device.

> **NOTE** The term "Bluejacking" doesn't refer to hijacking; instead, it originated with a person named Jack who anonymously sent the Bluetooth message "Buy Ericsson" to a Nokia phone user while waiting in line at a bank.

Now that you understand what's at risk with Bluetooth from a technological level, it's important to explain your side of the security equation. As with many technologies, it turns out that the Bluetooth technology is surprisingly secure; the real weak link is us humans. Bluetooth is obviously a communication technology that allows you to connect devices wirelessly. The key to keeping your Treo secure is ensuring that only devices you want connected to it are indeed connected to it. This involves some vigilance on your part to ensure that you don't inadvertently allow someone else to connect to your device. How can this happen?

First, start with the biggest Bluetooth issue of all—making your device discoverable. Your Treo can be set as discoverable or invisible, with the former option allowing any other Bluetooth device to see your device. Although seeing is different from connecting, by making your device discoverable, you significantly increase the chances of someone attempting a security attack against you. It's just too easy for hackers to fish for devices in a crowded area and take a stab at breaching one of them. As I've already said, Bluetooth is pretty solid in terms of its security, but remaining invisible is much safer than being discoverable—at least if you're a Bluetooth device. So keeping your device invisible (undiscoverable) is the best defense against Bluejacking.

TIP: I recommend initially pairing your Treo with your headset or hands-free car kit in a private area (a safe distance away from other potential Bluetooth users) and then being cautious about allowing others to tinker with your device.

On the other hand, the discoverable feature is built into Bluetooth devices for a reason. For example, your desktop PC probably requires your Treo to be discoverable to connect and synchronize wirelessly. In this example, it might be advantageous to keep your device discoverable when you're at home or in your office. You might find a reasonable tradeoff in keeping your device discoverable some of the time and then setting it to invisible when you're in crowded areas where an anonymous attacker might be more apt to strike.

Another area in which many Treo devices are potentially at risk is pairing. When you pair your device with another device, each device is added to the other's device list and given the capability of connecting to each other. In most cases, this arrangement is fine because you *want* to initiate a connection with a device. If someone is able to secretly pair her device with yours, however, she could feasibly connect to your device without your knowledge. For this reason, most Bluetooth device users have to be careful about allowing other people to borrow their devices.

To summarize, here are a few tips to help maximize Bluetooth security with your Treo:

- Make your device discoverable only when absolutely necessary.
- Pair up with new devices only in private, out of range of other potential Bluetooth users.
- Don't allow anyone else to tinker with your Treo.
- Don't respond to unsolicited messages you receive.

If you follow these guidelines, you should be able to safely enjoy Bluetooth's benefits with minimal worries about your device's security.

Summary

Whether or not you embrace personal area networking as part of your mobile computing experience, your Treo is one of the most powerful PAN devices available today. Through its support of numerous Bluetooth profiles, your Treo makes it possible to use a wide range of Bluetooth devices, including wireless headsets, hands-free car kits, GPS receivers, and printers, not to mention the capability to connect to your desktop or notebook computer via Bluetooth. In some ways, Bluetooth can still be considered an emerging technology, but it's an emerging technology that you can do some cool things with today.

Your Treo as a Portable Entertainment Device

Part IV

Taking and Sharing Digital Pictures and Videos

I have a confession to make. I once told my friend Stephen how dumb I thought it was to include digital cameras on mobile phones. At the time, it seemed to me to be just another gadget I would never use, with the sole purpose of making phones more expensive. Then Stephen explained how he had his website set up so that he could take pictures with his mobile phone and send them to his blog for immediate publishing. Although Stephen's setup still sounded gadgety, he made me rethink my initial conclusions about cameras and mobile phones. Of course, now it's official that the only dumb thing was me jumping to conclusions about the usefulness of having a digital camera embedded in a phone. I use the digital camera on my mobile phone regularly, even though I have a fairly small camera as well.

This chapter is about the digital camera embedded in your Treo device. You learn what the camera is capable of and how to use it to take pictures and video clips. You even learn how to create an online picture blog similar to the one my friend created that allows you to publish pictures to the Web directly from your Treo device.

IN THIS CHAPTER

- Digital Picture Essentials
- Take a Digital Picture
- Shoot a Digital Video
- Edit, Organize, and Beam Pictures and Video Clips
- View Your Pictures as a Slide Show
- Create an Online Picture Blog

Digital Picture Essentials

Your Treo device is equipped with a digital camera located on the back in the upper-left corner. Unlike the digital camera on the Treo 600, the camera on the Treo 650 supports both digital pictures and digital video. You can take as many digital pictures or shoot as much digital video as your device's memory allows. In reality, you'll find that a memory card is essential for using the digital camera.

The Treo's digital camera can take pictures in one of two resolutions: 640×480 or 320×240. If you have any experience with standalone digital cameras, you realize that the Treo's camera is considerably lower-resolution than "pure" cameras. On the other hand, 640×480 is better than many other mobile phones with cameras and is good enough for taking casual pictures when all you have on hand is your Treo.

> **NOTE** Some Treo users were disappointed that Palm didn't increase the maximum resolution of the Treo camera in the 650, but you have to remember that a higher-resolution camera requires more memory for storing pictures. Seeing that the 650 already had some memory issues because of the different file system, increasing the camera's memory requirements probably didn't seem like a good idea. Perhaps even more important, wireless service providers wouldn't be too happy about people sending large pictures over relatively limited wireless data connections. You probably won't see significantly higher-resolution cameras on phones until wireless network speeds increase considerably.

The real benefit of including a digital camera on a mobile phone is not so much the quality of the pictures but the flexibility you have in sharing them. It's unlikely that handheld communication devices will ever catch up with standalone digital cameras, but they aren't supposed to. Then again, I don't know of a standalone digital camera that enables you to send pictures wirelessly to friends and family and even publish them directly to a website.

Keep in mind that digital cameras embedded in mobile phones aren't good news to everyone. If you work at a company that is fairly guarded about trade secrets, and most are, you might run into the problem of not being allowed to bring a camera phone into the office. Although camera phones could certainly be misused in a corporate environment, so could numerous other items that are not banned. Besides, if you really want to carry out corporate espionage, you can use plenty of cool spy gadgets that are less conspicuous than a camera phone. Having said all that, however, you might still run into a problem with corporate heavies who think you're going to reenact *The Falcon and the Snowman* with your Treo and their trade secrets. If you encounter this situation, just buy one of the non-camera Treo devices that are now available. And then promptly jump ahead to the next chapter because you won't be taking any pictures with your non-camera Treo!

> **NOTE** Even though the camera in the Treo 650 is the same resolution as the camera in the 600, the 650 camera generally takes higher-quality pictures in terms of clarity, color, and so on.

Take a Digital Picture

The digital camera on your Treo device is extremely easy to use. Follow these steps to take a picture and share it with someone:

1. Press the **Application** button to open the main application screen.
2. Press the **C** key to jump near the Camera application, and then navigate with the five-way navigator to select the Camera application.
3. Press the **Center** button to launch the Camera application. The digital camera immediately turns on, and the screen becomes a viewfinder for the camera (see Figure 12.1). Aim the camera lens (on the back of the device in the upper-left corner) at the target you want to photograph.

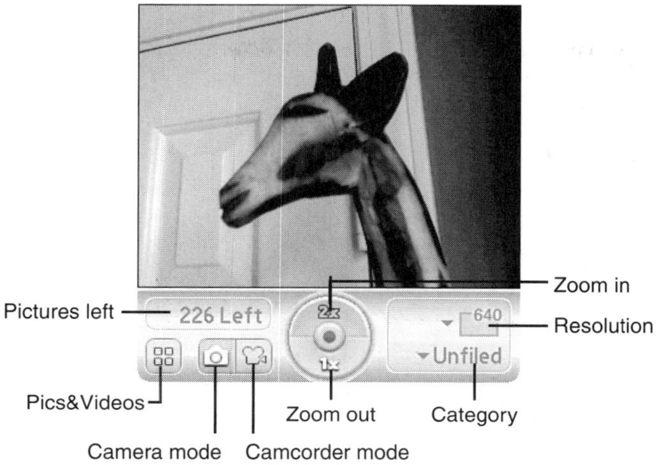

FIGURE 12.1

Most of the screen in the Camera application serves as a viewfinder for the digital camera.

4. To change the camera resolution, tap the resolution pick list in the lower-right area of the screen, and select **320 x 240** instead of 640 x 480.
5. Zoom in and out with the camera by pressing the **Up** and **Down** buttons on the five-way navigator. (There are only two zoom levels.)
6. When you're ready to take a picture, just press the **Center** button. You hear a shutter sound and the picture is displayed along with a series of buttons along the bottom of the screen for deciding what to do with the picture (see Figure 12.2).
7. To save the picture, tap the **Save** button on the toolbar, which is the first button that has a floppy disk icon. If you want to delete the picture and try again, tap the **Delete** button with the trashcan icon.
8. If you'd like to share the picture with someone else, you can send it by using one of several approaches, depending on your wireless service provider. You can send the picture as an attachment along with an email or

TIP You might notice a little round mirror adjacent to the camera lens on the back of your device. With this mirror, you can aim the camera at yourself for taking self-portraits or pictures of yourself with friends and family. Just make sure you can see yourself in the mirror when you snap the picture!

NOTE You use the other pick list in the lower-right corner of the Camera screen to select an album for organizing new pictures and videos. You learn how to create and manage albums later in this chapter in "Edit, Organize, and Beam Pictures and Video Clips."

multimedia message, or you can use your provider's proprietary picture service. For example, Sprint offers Picture Mail, which stores all pictures on a website. When you send a picture via Picture Mail, you're really sending a thumbnail and a link to the Web page where the picture is stored. To send a picture directly from the Camera application, tap the **Send** button (with the envelope icon) and specify the recipient (see Figure 12.3).

FIGURE 12.2

The picture preview screen in the Camera application gives you an opportunity to decide what to do with a freshly taken picture.

> **TIP** To turn off the shutter sound that's played when you take a picture, press the Menu button and set the Shutter Sound option to Off. Of course, you can also slide the Ringer Switch on the top of your device to Silent, which mutes all sound.

> **TIP** You can use effects on pictures you take by pressing the Menu button, and then changing the Effects option to Black & White or Sepia.

You'll find that most of the time you'll take pictures and save them on your device for later. To view a picture after you've saved it, tap the Pics&Videos button in the lower left of the Camera screen (refer to Figure 12.1), which has four small squares to indicate several pictures. Figure 12.4 shows the Pics&Videos screen, which provides access to all the pictures and videos stored on your device.

You can do lots of neat things with a picture after you've taken it, such as adding audio, drawing on it, setting it as your wallpaper, viewing it as part of a slide show, organizing it into a photo album, and beaming it to someone. You learn how to perform most of these tasks a bit later in the chapter. Before you get into that, however, continue to the next section to find out how to shoot digital video clips.

FIGURE 12.3

All you have to do to send a picture as part of a message is to specify the recipient.

FIGURE 12.4

The Pics&Videos application acts as a file viewer for pictures and videos and allows you to organize, edit, and send them to others.

> **TIP** To turn on the date stamp feature for your pictures, press the Menu button and set the Date Stamp option to On. Future pictures will have a visible date stamp in the image's upper-right corner.

Shoot a Digital Video

Shooting a digital video is surprisingly similar to taking a digital picture. In fact, you use the same application, even though it has a different name on the main application screen. I'm referring to the Camcorder application, which can be launched separately from the Camera application. In reality, Camera

NOTE

Treo devices on the Sprint network use the Picture Mail service instead of multimedia messages. So if you want to send a picture directly without using Picture Mail, save the picture and then attach it to an email message in the VersaMail application.

TIP

To change the automatic naming of pictures, press the Menu button and create your own custom naming convention by using the Auto Naming field.

To shoot a digital video, launch the Camcorder application from the main application screen or tap the Camcorder button in the lower-left area of the Camera application. Two buttons next to each other enable you to toggle quickly between Camera and Camcorder. When you switch to Camcorder, the zoom control in the lower middle of the screen changes to a Record/Pause/Stop control for the camcorder. Press the Center button on the five-way navigator to begin recording a video clip. Figure 12.5 shows a video being recorded. To stop recording, press the Center button again. To pause recording so that you can continue without creating a new clip, press the Up button. Then press the Center button again to continue filming.

As you shoot a video, the length of the video counts up in seconds just above the Camera/Camcorder buttons near the bottom of the screen. At the same time, the amount of available time counts down. This time reflects how much memory you have available for shooting video. It's probably not a good idea to blow all your available memory on video, but it's still helpful to know how much room you have left if you wanted to do so.

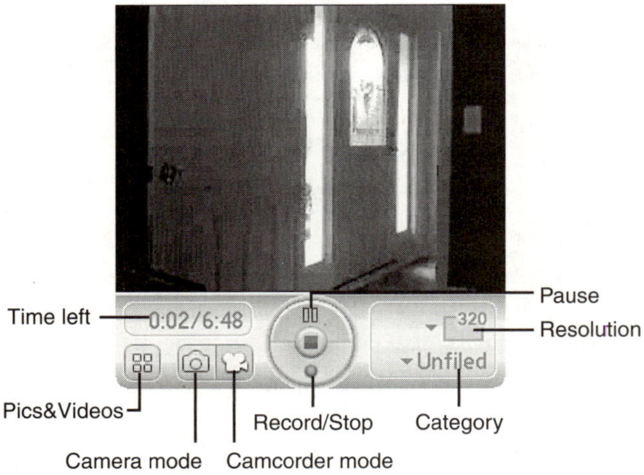

FIGURE 12.5

The Camcorder application makes it easy to shoot digital videos with your Treo.

Similar to the Camera application, you can choose from two video resolutions when shooting video in the Camcorder application: 176×144 and 320×240. You make this selection in the lower-right corner of the screen in the resolution pick list. Selecting the lower resolution (176×144) gives you about double the available time for video because it's roughly half the resolution of the higher setting, 320×240. The decision of which resolution to use comes down to how much quality (resolution) you need versus how much memory you have available.

> **NOTE** You can also access the Pics&Videos screen by launching the Pics&Videos application directly from the main application screen.

After you finish shooting a video clip, you're presented with options for what to do with the new clip. Figure 12.6 shows how you can play, save, delete, send, upload, and even adjust the volume of the newly recorded video clip.

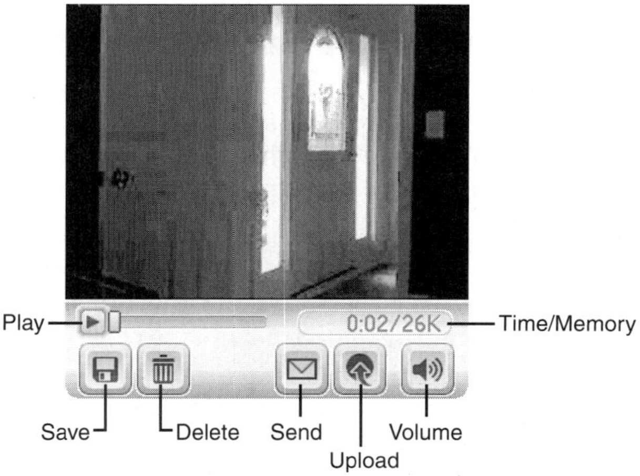

FIGURE 12.6

The Camcorder application gives you a chance to view a newly recorded video clip before saving, deleting, or sharing it with others.

To play a new video clip, just tap the Play button (small arrow) on the left just below the clip. To save the clip, tap the Save button (disk icon) just below the Play button. To the right of the Save button is the Delete button (trashcan icon). The familiar Send and Upload buttons appear to the right of the Save and Play buttons. And finally, the last button on the right is the Volume button (speaker icon) for adjusting the volume of the video clip.

> **NOTE** If you synchronize your device with your desktop PC and would like to access the pictures on your PC, just browse to the `My Pictures\palmOne Photos\` folder.

Edit, Organize, and Beam Pictures and Video Clips

Taking digital pictures and filming digital video clips are only half the fun. The Pics&Videos application makes it possible to edit, organize, and beam pictures and

> **NOTE** The Pics&Videos application is closely related to the Camera/Camcorder application, but it is, in fact, its own separate application. However, you can quickly switch between the two applications by tapping the button in the lower-left corner of each one.

> **TIP** To turn off the microphone while filming a video clip, press the Menu button and set the Microphone option to Off.

video clips with ease. Perhaps the most important task in regard to pictures and video clips is storing them on a memory card and deleting them to make space for new pictures and clips. Follow these steps to copy and delete *media objects* (pictures and video clips) in the Pics&Videos application:

1. Press the **Menu** button, and then scroll down to and select the **Copy to Card** menu command. The Copy to Card screen opens, as shown in Figure 12.7.
2. Tap the media objects that you want to copy to a memory card. A plus sign appears next to each selected object, as you can see in Figure 12.7.
3. Tap the **Copy** button to carry out copying the media objects. Keep in mind that this is a copy, not a move, so the pictures still reside in main memory until you delete them.
4. Speaking of deleting media objects, to delete an object, just select it in the Pics&Video screen, press the **Menu** button, and then scroll down and select **Delete** in the Media menu. Then tap the **Delete** button to confirm the deletion.

FIGURE 12.7

Use the Copy to Card screen to copy media objects to a memory card.

While I'm on the subject of storing media objects, it's worth tackling the issue of photo albums. I'm using the term "photo album" a bit loosely because a Treo photo album can contain video clips in addition to pictures, but you get the idea. To access the photo albums on your device in the Pics&Videos application, follow these steps:

1. Press the **Menu** button, navigate over to the Album menu, and then scroll down to and select the **Manage Albums** menu command. The Manage Albums screen opens, as shown in Figure 12.8.
2. The Manage Albums screen reveals how media objects are stored separately in main memory (Device) and on a memory card (Card). You create photo albums in each area of memory separately to organize media objects stored in each area. To create a new photo album, tap the **New** button and enter the name of the photo album (see Figure 12.9).

TIP If you're interested in taking video to the next level by watching movies and other video formats on your Treo, you might want to check out The Core Pocket Media Player (TCPMP). TCPMP is an open-source application that you can download free at http://tcpmp.corecodec.org/.

FIGURE 12.8

In the Manage Albums screen, you can create, rename, and delete photo albums in main memory and on a memory card.

3. Tap the **OK** button to continue and select the media objects to be stored in the photo album. Figure 12.10 shows the Organize Pond album, where I can tap and select the pictures to be placed in the newly created Pond photo album; notice the plus signs beside the selected pictures.
4. When you're finished selecting pictures for the album, tap the **Done** button. Back in the main Pics&Videos screen, you can easily view just the pictures in the new photo album by tapping the pick list at the top of the Pics&Videos screen and selecting the album.

TIP To switch between viewing media objects in main memory and the current memory card in the Pics&Videos application, tap the first or second box in the upper-right corner of the screen; you use the third box to access pictures that have been uploaded to the Web.

FIGURE 12.9

The New Album screen prompts you to enter the name of the new photo album.

FIGURE 12.10

The Organize Pond screen enables me to tap and select pictures for my newly created Pond photo album.

> **TIP** To select and deselect multiple media objects, tap the Space key as you scroll through the objects.

5. Within a given photo album, you can sort the media objects in it by selecting one of several sort criteria from the Album menu—sorting an album by date, name, or size as well as manual sorting. To sort a photo album manually, tap and drag the media object in the list to change its order. This order is important if you choose to view the album as a slide show; see "View Your Pictures as a Slide Show" later in the chapter.

Similar to individual media objects, you can beam, upload, send, and copy photo albums with little effort. You can find commands for these tasks on the Album menu.

In addition to organizing pictures in photo albums, you can edit and manipulate the pictures. Follow these steps to edit your pictures in the Pics&Videos application:

1. The first way to edit a picture is to establish its position for viewing. Many pictures you take will be larger than the Treo's screen and, therefore, aren't entirely visible at once. If you tap a picture in the main list to view it full screen, you can then tap and drag the picture to determine which part is displayed. This new picture position is remembered for future viewings; this feature is especially important for slide shows.
2. You might find that you need to rotate a picture. If so, select the picture, press the **Menu** button, and then scroll down to and select the **Rotate Picture** command. The Rotate Picture screen opens with options for selecting rotated versions of the picture in 90-degree increments (see Figure 12.11).
3. Perhaps more interesting than rotating a picture is being able to draw directly on a picture. To draw on a picture, select the picture, press the **Menu** button, and then scroll down to and select the **Draw on Picture** command. The Draw on Picture screen opens, as shown in Figure 12.12, and you can draw on the picture using several different pen strokes and colors as well as add text.

TIP You can also delete media objects by pressing the Backspace key while in the Pics&Videos screen without having any objects selected. The Delete screen opens, where you can tap and select pictures and video clips for deletion.

NOTE The pick list at the top of the Pics&Videos application actually contains both categories and photo albums. All and Unfiled are default categories; all photo albums are custom created. By default, all new pictures and video clips are stored in the Unfiled category until you move them into a photo album.

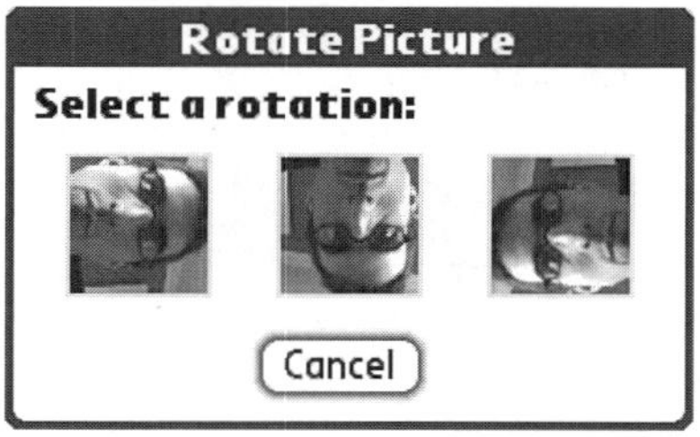

FIGURE 12.11

You can use the Rotate Picture screen to rotate a picture in 90-degree increments.

4. In the lower-right corner of the screen are buttons for changing the color and pen stroke width and for adding text to a picture. I hope you find a more important use for this feature than drawing a beard on yourself!
5. You can also edit each media object on your device to add text notes, if you like. To edit the details for a media object, select **Edit Details** from the Media menu.

In the Media Details screen that opens, you can view information about the media object, change its photo album, and add notes (see Figure 12.13). Tap **Done** when you're finished with the media details.

FIGURE 12.12

You can use the Draw on Picture screen to draw on and add text to a picture.

FIGURE 12.13

The Media Details screen displays information about a media object along with options for changing its album, entering a text note, and even deleting the object.

6. One last tweak you can make to a picture involves adding an audio clip. Maybe you want to record a brief story to explain a picture. If so, select **Add Audio** from the Media menu. The familiar Recorder screen opens and allows you to record an audio clip that's attached to the picture.

As you've seen, you can do quite a lot with pictures and video clips on your Treo, but you're still not finished. Read on to find out how to assemble media objects to create a mobile handheld slide show.

> **TIP** You can easily organize a photo album at any time by selecting the album from the pick list near the top of the Pics&Videos screen and then tapping the Organize Album button (second from right) near the bottom of the screen.

View Your Pictures as a Slide Show

The Pics&Videos application supports a slide show feature that's surprisingly easy to use. All you must do to launch a slide show is to tap the Slide Show button in the lower-right corner of the Pics&Videos screen. Whatever category or album is currently selected is used as the basis for a slide show—the pictures in the list are displayed consecutively with a brief pause for viewing each one. If you'd like to build a custom slide show, just create a photo album for it and organize pictures into it. To change the order of pictures in the slide show, just tap and drag them around within the photo album.

The main preferences for the Pics&Videos application relate to the slide show feature. If you select Preferences from the Options menu, the Preferences screen opens, as shown in Figure 12.14.

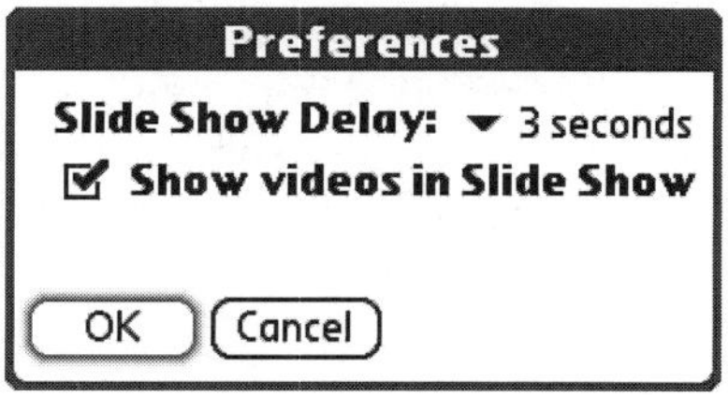

FIGURE 12.14

The Preferences screen enables you to fine-tune how slide shows are displayed.

There are only two options you can change in the Preferences screen. The first option determines how long each slide is displayed during a slide show. The other option determines whether videos are included in slide shows. If enabled, this option causes video clips to be played when they appear in a slide show, effectively allowing you to mix still pictures with video clips for a truly multimedia presentation.

Given that you can draw on and add text to pictures, the slide show feature is a compelling option for creating handheld demonstrations and presentations, much as you might create in a more full-featured desktop application such as PowerPoint. All you need is an expansion card, such as Presenter-To-Go by Margi Systems (http://www.margi.com), and you can even display Treo slide shows on large screens via digital projection.

Create an Online Picture Blog

The last stop in this little tour of the picture and video options available to you doesn't have anything directly to do with your Treo device. I'm referring to online picture blogs, which you can use to automatically upload pictures you have taken with your mobile device and share them with others. There are several different online picture blogs, also known as *photo blogs*, such as SplashBlog (http://www.splashblog.com) and TypePad (http://www.typepad.com). For the purposes of demonstrating how to set up a photo blog for your Treo, I opted to use SplashBlog.

As you might have guessed, SplashBlog consists of two components: a website and a Treo application. The Treo application enables you to specify what pictures you want to publish, and the website is where they end up getting published. To get started with SplashBlog, you must first visit the SplashBlog website and download the Treo application. Here's the link: http://www.splashblog.com/. SplashBlog offers a 30-day trial that you can use to create an account and experiment with the service. You can create a new account using your desktop PC on the SplashBlog website or directly in the SplashBlog application on your Treo.

After you've installed the SplashBlog application on your device and created a SplashBlog account, you can launch the SplashBlog application and begin publishing pictures. The application starts off with a sample blog and an empty blog based on your user name. Go ahead and tap the blog with your name on it. Then tap the Add Photo button to add a photo to the blog. Tap to select a photo from the list shown in the SplashBlog Photo Picker screen. If you don't know the name of the picture to add, you can switch to Preview mode by tapping one of the little buttons along the bottom of the screen. After selecting a photo, you're prompted to enter information about it, including the title and a caption (see Figure 12.15).

FIGURE 12.15

The SplashBlog Edit screen prompts you to enter the title and caption for the new blog photo.

When you're finished editing the photo information, tap the OK button to add the photo to the blog on your device. Keep in mind that at this point the photo has not actually been published to the online blog. Add another picture or two if you want, and when you're ready to publish them to the Web, just tap the Sync button. Depending on how many photos you've added, the SplashBlog application churns away for a few moments. When it finishes, the pictures are ready and available for viewing in your online photo blog. Just visit the SplashBlog website, log on to your account, and view your blog. Figure 12.16 shows one of my pictures as it's viewed in the online blog.

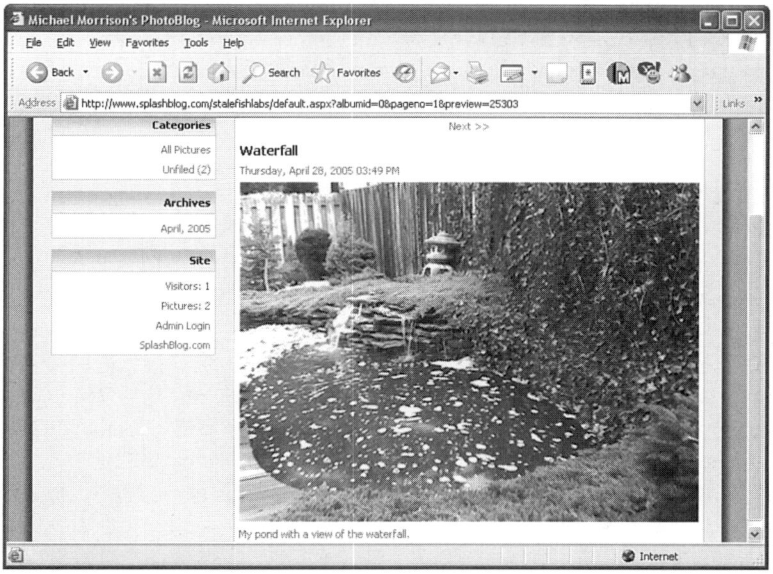

FIGURE 12.16

After syncing your device with the SplashBlog website, the new photos immediately become available for online viewing.

Figure 12.16 reveals how convenient it can be to publish photos from your Treo from any location where you have wireless data access. With an online picture blog, you can document a vacation or other adventure in nearly real time as you take pictures and publish them immediately to the Web for others to see and share.

Summary

Although you might not usually think of a handheld device such as a Treo being all that powerful in terms of multimedia capabilities, this chapter has demonstrated that it serves as a highly capable digital camera and video camcorder. To be fair, the Treo imaging capabilities aren't on par with a standalone digital camera or camcorder, but then, they aren't intended to be. If you want to be able to take reasonable quality digital pictures and shoot short video clips while on the go, the Treo is more than capable. Where it truly shines is in its capability to share and publish pictures and video clips wirelessly. Whether you use email, multimedia messages, or an online picture blog, you'll find no shortage of ways to share your digital pictures and video clips with friends, family, and co-workers.

Listening to Digital Music

Few technology topics have consistently permeated the news as much as digital music the past few years. First Metallica made headlines by being one of the first major artists to literally go after their fans over illegal digital copying of their music. Then it was Napster getting destroyed by the Recording Industry Association of America (RIAA), only to be rebuilt with the same name as an entirely different service. New headlines on this front will continue to appear as the technical and legal issues surrounding digital music continue to change and ultimately lead us toward a new method of entertainment distribution.

The good news for the Treo user is that you can store digital music on your device and play it whenever you want. Granted, there are still a few technical snags to contend with, but overall the digital music scene for Treo devices is quite positive. In fact, the device has built-in media player that you can use to play music, providing it's in the correct format. Even if your music is in a different format, however, you still have plenty of options for playing it on your Treo device. This chapter clues you in on how to do it.

IN THIS CHAPTER

- Digital Music Basics
- Transfer and Play Music on Your Treo
- Create a Playlist
- Tweak the RealPlayer Preferences
- Upgrade to a More Powerful Music Player
- Use Digital Music as Tones

Digital Music Basics

You're probably already aware that digital music is just music that has been converted so that it can be played back using a CD player, computer, MP3 player, and so forth. The term *MP3* is commonly used to refer to digital music because MP3 is the original and probably still the most popular format for encoding digital music. However, there are other competing formats you need to know about to successfully play digital music on your Treo.

Currently, there are three major digital music formats:

- *MP3*—MPEG-1 Audio Layer 3; the original digital music format that brought digital music into mainstream culture

- *WMA*—Windows Media Audio; Microsoft's answer to MP3 that offers better compression and support for digital rights management
- *AAC*—Advanced Audio Codec; Apple's answer to Microsoft, and the music format used on the immensely popular iPod players and iTunes service

> **NOTE** The Treo's RealPlayer application also supports audio in the RealAudio format, which is typically used on desktop computers for playing audio streamed in real time over a network connection. Unfortunately, the Treo's RealPlayer application doesn't currently support streaming audio. It can be used only to play RealAudio files (.rm and .rmj file extensions) that you download to your device.

> **NOTE** The network speed of current mobile phone networks makes streaming audio a difficult proposition, at least for now. However, you could use Bluetooth or a Wi-Fi expansion card to tap into a faster network connection and access streaming audio.

These formats determine the specifics of how analog sound waves are encoded digitally as 1s and 0s. The specifics matter little when understanding how to play digital music on your Treo, but the music formats matter a great deal because not all are supported equally. For example, the built-in RealPlayer application supports only the MP3 format, which is a big problem if you've spent hundreds of dollars downloading 99¢ songs from iTunes or MSN Music. If you have a large library of WMA or AAC (iTunes) songs, you'll want to look into a third-party Treo media player, such as Pocket Tunes or Kinoma Player, covered later in this chapter.

Another reason you might consider using a third-party media player is if you'd like anything beyond the most basic control over how music is played. For example, if you'd like to stream music over a network connection or fine-tune the sound with an equalizer, you need to look beyond the built-in RealPlayer application.

Regardless of what media player you use, the primary limitation to listening to digital music on a Treo device is memory. Although some formats do a better job at compressing music than others, digital music is greedy when it comes to memory. Even fairly short songs (under two minutes) can weigh in at 2MB, and longer songs can stretch up to 4MB or 5MB and beyond. The Treo designers realized this problem and decided that a memory card would be required to listen to music on the Treo 600/650. So if you want to listen to music on your device, you need to invest in a memory card. Fortunately, the price of memory cards is dropping constantly, and you can get a fairly large card (512MB+) without breaking the bank. I encourage you to get at least a 256MB card so that you can put enough songs on it to make things interesting. Also keep in mind that you'll likely be using the memory card for other Treo applications, which is more reason to go as large as you can afford. Of course, you can buy multiple memory cards and swap them out if you have lots of music and other data you want to have readily available.

When playing music on your Treo, you have the option of playing the music through the standard internal speaker or plugging headphones into the headset jack, which is on the bottom of the device just left of the Multi-connector. The internal speaker works better than you might think for listening to digital music, but you should invest in a Treo stereo audio headset if you plan to listen to much music on your device. You can also buy a stereo headphone adapter that allows you to use any set of stereo headphones with your device. Visit the Palm store to find more information about these products: http://web.palmone.com/.

I need to go back to digital music formats for just a moment before moving on to transferring and playing music on your device. Earlier I mentioned the iTunes and MSN Music online services for purchasing individual digital songs. Although these services are great for downloading individual songs quickly and playing them on your computer, they present some challenges to playing music on your Treo. This is because most online digital music services rely on *digital rights management* (*DRM*), which is a locking mechanism designed to limit the playback of songs to only the person who purchased them. Unfortunately, even if you have legitimately purchased a song, you might find that you can't play it immediately on your Treo. I say "immediately" because you might need to convert the songs to remove the DRM restrictions.

> **NOTE** The headset jack on the Treo is a 2.5mm jack designed for use with special Treo headphones and headsets. To use it with standard-size (3.5mm) stereo music headphones, you need to purchase a Treo stereo headphone adapter.

Apple, Microsoft, and others might not like the idea of you making copies of songs and removing their DRM restrictions, but you have a right to play purchased music on any device you choose. As long as you don't turn around and share a song's unlocked version with someone else, you are within the law in terms of making a copy of purchased music for yourself. One of these days, I hope, software makers and the recording industry will figure out that all people want is convenient access to digital music. Most people are willing to pay for music if they can access it conveniently and play it whenever and wherever they want. End of rant—time to move on!

Transfer and Play Music on Your Treo

The RealPlayer application is the built-in media player for listening to digital music on your Treo. RealPlayer on the Treo supports only the MP3 and RealAudio formats, so you need to make sure your music files are in one of these two formats (most likely MP3). To transfer an MP3 music file to your Treo for playback in RealPlayer, follow these steps:

> **NOTE** These instructions apply to Windows PCs, but you can just as easily transfer digital music files to your Treo using a Macintosh computer. Just launch the Palm Desktop application on a Mac, click the HotSync menu, followed by Install Handheld Files, and then add the music files. You'll still need to perform a HotSync synchronization to initiate the file transfer.

1. Launch the palmOne Quick Install application on your desktop computer, and drag and drop the `.mp3` music file onto it. Figure 13.1 shows the palmOne Quick Install application with a music file added and ready to be transferred to my Treo 650.
2. Figure 13.1 reveals that the palmOne Quick Install window is divided into two areas: one for the handheld memory and one for the memory card. You'll notice that you're

allowed to drag music files only to the memory card area, which confirms that a memory card is required to listen to digital music on a Treo device.

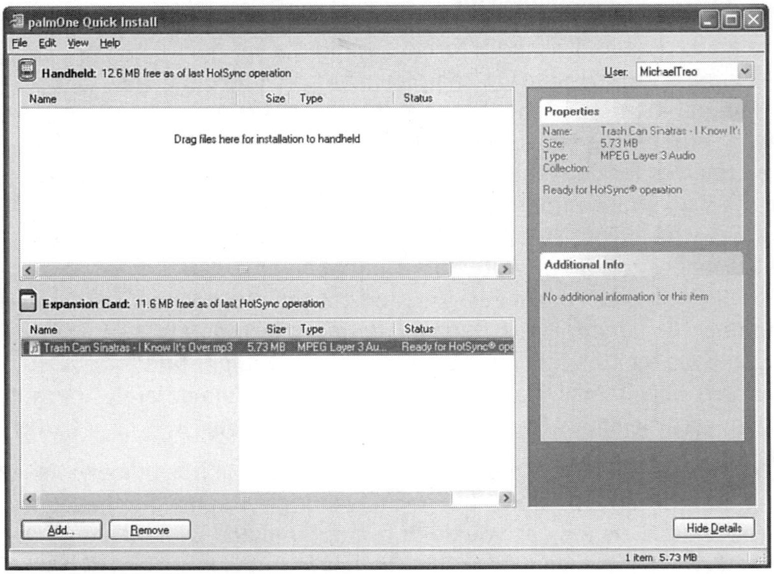

FIGURE 13.1

The palmOne Quick Install window shows the `.mp3` *music file ready to be transferred to my Treo's memory card.*

> **TIP**
> To delete a song from your Treo's memory card, press the Menu button and select the Delete command from the Music menu. You are presented with a list of all songs on the memory card—tap to select the song to be deleted, and then tap Done.

3. Connect your Treo to the desktop computer with the Multi-connector cable, and press the **HotSync** button to synchronize. The music file is installed to the memory card on your device.
4. Hold down the **Side** button (below the Volume button on the left side) on your Treo to launch the RealPlayer application. You can also navigate to the RealPlayer application on the main application screen and launch it if you've changed the Side button to launch a different application.
5. The MP3 song you transferred should be visible in RealPlayer (see Figure 13.2). Of course, if other songs already exist on the memory card, you need to tap the Songs button to select the new song.
6. To begin playing the new song, tap the **Play** button in RealPlayer. You might want to keep RealPlayer open, as you come back to it in a moment when you learn how to control the playback of music.

FIGURE 13.2

The newly transferred song is available in RealPlayer and ready to be played.

Although the palmOne Quick Install approach works fine for transferring music files to your device, you can also use a memory card reader to install files directly to a memory card. Just make sure you copy the music files to one of the following folders on the memory card: `AUDIO`, `SD_AUDIO`, or `RN_AUDIO`. Otherwise, RealPlayer won't be able to find the songs.

> **TIP** If you have the desktop version of RealPlayer installed on your desktop computer, you can also use it to transfer music files to your Treo. Make sure your Treo is on and connected to your computer, and then click the Devices tab in the desktop RealPlayer application. You can then view the music on the device's memory card and add new songs straight from the desktop RealPlayer.

Playing music in RealPlayer is straightforward. To control the playback of music in RealPlayer, follow these steps:

1. Tap the **Songs** button near the bottom of the RealPlayer screen to bring up a list of available songs. A list of songs appears, as shown in Figure 13.3.
2. Tap or use the five-way navigator to select a song for playback. The song begins playing, and information about the song is displayed onscreen.
3. To view additional information about the song, tap the small round information button (lowercase *i*) just below the onscreen song information. Figure 13.4 shows the Song Details screen, which provides additional information about the currently playing song.
4. Several controls in the RealPlayer application affect the playback of music (refer back to Figure 13.2). The top row of control buttons begins with the small Position slider, which is used to move quickly to a specific point in a song. Next

to the Position slider are the Repeat and Shuffle buttons, which determine whether music is played continuously (song after song) and whether songs are played in a random order.

FIGURE 13.3

Use the RealPlayer song list to select a song to be played.

FIGURE 13.4

The Song Details screen provides detailed information about a song, including the format, size, and filename.

5. The bottom row of buttons has the more familiar playback buttons: Play/Pause, Stop, Previous, Next, and Volume. Keep in mind that the hardware Volume button also works just fine for controlling the volume of RealPlayer.

As you've seen, the RealPlayer application is a fairly simple media player, but it does work reasonably well if your primary interest is listening to MP3 music.

Create a Playlist

As you amass songs on your memory card, you will no doubt want to organize them into playlists. The RealPlayer application supports playlists and allows you to create multiple playlists that contain different orderings of available songs. To create a playlist in RealPlayer, follow these steps:

1. Tap the **Playlists** button near the bottom of the screen to bring up the available playlists; if you haven't created any playlists, this list is likely empty.
2. Tap the **New** button in the Playlists screen to create a new playlist. The Edit Playlist screen appears, as shown in Figure 13.5.

FIGURE 13.5

The Edit Playlist screen is used to create new playlists and edit existing ones.

3. Enter the name of the new playlist, making sure it's descriptive enough to distinguish it from other playlists you might create later. Then tap the **Add** button to add songs to the new playlist (see Figure 13.6).
4. To add songs to the new playlist, just tap the ones you want to check them off the list. If you change your mind about a song, just uncheck it. When you're finished, tap the **Done** button.

NOTE The built-in RealPlayer application doesn't support the WMA or AAC (iTunes) music formats, so you won't be able to listen to songs in those formats with RealPlayer. To listen to music with RealPlayer, it must be in the MP3 format. Some online music services that use the MP3 format include Audio Lunchbox, Bleep, eMusic, IUMA, and Magnatune.

NOTE If you switch to a different application while a song is playing in RealPlayer, the song continues to play in the background. Later in this chapter in "Tweak the RealPlayer Preferences," you learn how to turn off this default behavior if you don't want music to play in the background.

FIGURE 13.6

Adding songs to a playlist is as simple as checking them off a list.

> **NOTE** If someone calls you while a song is playing, the song continues to play during the ring but pauses if you answer the call. Similarly, if you place an outgoing call, the currently playing song is paused. In either case, you must return to RealPlayer to continue playing the song. Songs continue to play in the background during other common Treo operations, such as sending and receiving email, browsing the Web, and so forth.

5. Tap the **Done** button in the Edit Playlist screen to finish creating the playlist, and then again to exit viewing the playlist. Finally, one more tap of the **Done** button returns you to the main RealPlayer screen.

6. To play the songs in a playlist, tap the **Playlists** button to view the playlists. Tap the playlist you want, and then tap any song in the list to start playing the playlist beginning with that song.

Playlists provide a handy way to arrange music into meaningful lists that make the listening experience more enjoyable. If you'd like the playlist to loop repeatedly, just tap the Repeat button when listening to a playlist. (Refer to Figure 13.2 to see where the Repeat button is located.)

Tweak the RealPlayer Preferences

There are a handful of preferences you need to know about for digital music and the RealPlayer application. Follow these steps to adjust preferences for RealPlayer:

1. Tap the **Menu** button to open the RealPlayer menu, and then navigate over to the Options menu. Scroll down to and select the **Preferences** command. The RealPlayer Preferences screen appears, as shown in Figure 13.7.

2. The first option in the RealPlayer Preferences screen relates to the auto-power-save feature, which automatically turns off the screen after a specified period of

time. This setting allows you to continue listening to music without the added battery drain of the screen. You can set it to values in the range of 30 seconds to 3 minutes.

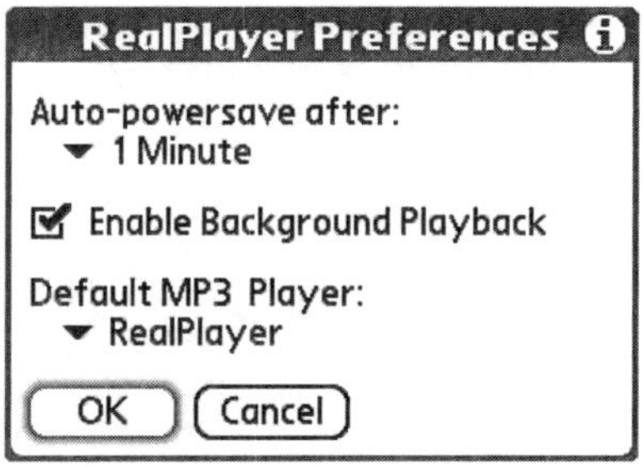

FIGURE 13.7

The RealPlayer Preferences screen has options for determining how the RealPlayer application plays MP3 songs.

3. The Enable Background Playback option determines whether songs continue to play in the background when you leave the RealPlayer application. Unless you find that background song playing is affecting the performance of other applications, you'll probably want to leave this option enabled.
4. The last RealPlayer option simply determines what media player serves as the default player for MP3 music files. If you have another media player installed, you can use this option to decide which player gets called on to play MP3 songs.
5. When you're finished with the RealPlayer preferences, tap the **OK** button to close the screen and commit the changes.

> **TIP** You can use the Side button on the Treo to play and pause music in RealPlayer. Additionally, you can use the Up and Down buttons on the five-way navigator to adjust the volume; use the Left and Right buttons to move to the previous and next songs, respectively.

The RealPlayer preferences are fairly limited in terms of how much they enable you to customize the application, but you might find them useful to revisit on occasion.

Upgrade to a More Powerful Music Player

Throughout the chapter, I've mentioned that you might want to consider a more powerful third-party media player for digital music if you want more features than the built-in RealPlayer application offers. Some of these features might include support for additional music formats, such as WMA and AAC, not to mention streaming audio that you

> **TIP** Use the Select All and Select None buttons to quickly select and deselect all songs for the playlist.

can listen to live over the wireless Web or through another wireless network connection, such as Bluetooth or Wi-Fi.

Several third-party media players are available for Treo devices, but one that stands out is Pocket Tunes by NormSoft. Pocket Tunes supports WAV, MP3, and WMA music files, along with streaming audio, an equalizer, and user interface skins that enable you to change the player's look and feel. Figure 13.8 shows Pocket Tunes busy playing an MP3 song.

FIGURE 13.8

The Pocket Tunes media player takes Treo digital music playback to another level.

It's important to point out that even though Pocket Tunes supports WMA files, it does not support WMA files with DRM restrictions, such as those purchased through MSN Music. However, if you use Windows Media Player to rip songs from CDs in the WMA format, you can play them just fine in Pocket Tunes; when you rip songs yourself, they don't have any DRM restrictions. To download a trial version and check out Pocket Tunes, visit the Pocket Tunes website at http://www.pocket-tunes.com/.

> **TIP** To edit a playlist, tap the Edit button while viewing the songs in the playlist.

Mac users who are more comfortable with the AAC digital music format might want to check into another media player called Kinoma Player. Kinoma Player can play music files in the AAC format, along with video files in the MPEG-4 video format. Similar to Pocket Tunes, Kinoma doesn't support AAC files with DRM restrictions, such as those purchased through Apple's iTunes service. However, you can play unrestricted AAC files (ripped songs) all you want. To download a free trial of Kinoma Player, visit the website at http://www.kinoma.com/.

Use Digital Music as Tones

One final topic worth tackling is a common question I hear from people after they realize how cool it is to listen to digital music on their Treo: Can I use an MP3 song as a ring tone? The short answer is yes, absolutely! The longer answer is that you must rely on a third-party application to do so. In other words, there's no way to do it with built-in Treo applications.

> **TIP** One way to get around the DRM restriction in playing digital music on your Treo is to burn restricted songs to an audio CD and then rip them back down to your computer as MP3 files. Burned audio CDs don't have any DRM restrictions, so you can rip music from them without DRM entering the picture. Admittedly, this process is a hassle, but it's one of the only guaranteed solutions at the moment.

You have a couple of options when it comes to playing digital music as ring tones. The ideal option is to play digital music files as ring tones in the same format you use to listen to them in a media player. This way you don't have to create a special version of each song just for the purpose of using it as a ring tone.
The following third-party applications make it possible to use a digital music file (MP3 or WMA) directly as a ring tone:

- *LightWav*—http://www.toysoft.ca/lightwav.html
- *Treo Guard*—http://www.geakware.com/treoguard/

The other option for playing digital music as a ring tone involves converting from a digital music format to the native ring tone format, which is MIDI. Wav2Tones is a tool by Toysoft, the makers of LightWav (see the preceding bulleted list), that enables you to convert from the WAV audio format to the MIDI format, effectively allowing you to turn sampled digital audio into a MIDI ring tone. To find out more about the Wav2Tones application, visit the Wav2Tones web page at http://www.toysoft.ca/wav2tones.html.

> **NOTE** The WAV format is popular on Windows computers for digital audio in general, so you won't have any problems finding interesting sounds in the WAV format. Of course, you might need to convert digital music from MP3 to WAV before being able to use the Wav2Tones application. Visit http://www.mp3towav.org/ to check out a variety of audio conversion tools, including an MP3-to-WAV converter utility.

Summary

Unless you pump up your Treo with a monster-sized memory card (1GB+), it's unlikely to compete with a dedicated digital music player such as Apple's iPod. However, even a more reasonably sized memory card allows you to store enough music on your device to make it plenty functional as a digital music player. Granted, there are some drawbacks in terms of not being able to play purchased tracks with DRM restrictions, but nothing is stopping you from ripping your own MP3 tracks and listening to them on your Treo. I also have some degree of confidence that Microsoft, Apple, and other interested parties are working toward offering a DRM solution so that legitimately purchased digital music is better supported across all platforms, including the Treo platform. In the meantime, a combination of the built-in RealPlayer and possibly a third-party media player serve as decent Treo digital music options.

14

Using Your Treo for Navigation and Fun

One of the most exciting aspects of a handheld device such as a Treo is the opportunities it creates for fun in often boring situations. For example, how many times have you been in a waiting room with nothing better to do than flip through outdated magazines to kill time? You missed the perfect opportunity to take killing time to a whole new level by playing a game on your Treo. Not only that, but it's also possible to play networked Treo games via infrared, Bluetooth, and even the wireless Internet. This chapter isn't all about games, however. I introduce you to an application that allows you to use your Treo as a television remote control, and then finish up the chapter by introducing you to mobile navigation with a global positioning system (GPS).

IN THIS CHAPTER

- Mobile Gaming Essentials
- Use Your Treo as a Universal Remote Control
- GPS and the Treo

Mobile Gaming Essentials

Mobile games are computer games that you play on a mobile device such as a Treo. Unlike their desktop/notebook counterparts, mobile games have limited resources with which to work. For example, the relatively small screen and limited memory of Treo devices are enough to prevent you from playing a cutting-edge 3D shoot-'em-up on your Treo. Even though Treo devices are fairly constrained compared to desktop computers, they are actually quite powerful when you stack them up against most other mobile phones. If nothing else, the screen size of Treo devices gives them a huge edge over most mobile phones in gaming.

Mobile games aren't exactly new—they date back to 1997 with the original Snake game that appeared on Nokia phones. Although Snake is a simple game, it forever changed the perception of mobile phones: They weren't just communication devices anymore. Many other games followed soon after Snake, and people began to think more about the entertainment capabilities of their phones. Mobile games have steadily improved in the years since Snake, but screen, memory, and processor restrictions on mobile phones have still been a limitation.

NOTE In addition to having an interest in mobile devices from a user's standpoint, I am also a mobile game developer and have written a few books on mobile game programming, the latest of which is Beginning Mobile Phone Game Programming.

Another limitation in mobile games is related to networking. It only makes sense that a wirelessly connected device should allow you to play networked games, but slow network speeds have made it a difficult proposition. Only recently have true networked multiplayer mobile games made an appearance. These games are still tough to develop because of the current bandwidth limitations of most mobile phone networks, but this limitation is on the verge of fading. Newer mobile networks, such as EDGE, CDMA2000, and W-CDMA, are set to widen if not eliminate the bandwidth bottleneck that currently hinders wireless mobile networks.

I mention mobile games and network bandwidth because mobile multiplayer gaming is where the future of mobile entertainment likely lies. Single-player games will always have their place, but the connected social nature of multiplayer games with human opponents is hard to beat. The next couple of sections explore several current single player and multiplayer games that I found interesting for playing on Treo devices.

Play a Single-Player Game

NOTE I'll go ahead and warn you that several of the Treo games I mention in this chapter are published by Handmark. I have no affiliation with Handmark, and I'm not receiving any free games or kickbacks; I just found that the company makes some cool games for Treo devices.

If wearing rented shoes isn't your idea of a fun Saturday night, you might want to consider bowling on your Treo instead of visiting a real bowling alley. On the other hand, maybe you bowl all the time and just want an outlet to gun for a turkey (three strikes in a row) when you're out and about and away from your personalized bowling ball. Either way, I highly recommend Bowling Deluxe by Handmark. It's a great little bowling game with several different input options for controlling the ball.

Figure 14.1 shows the ball en route toward picking up a tough spare. Check out the Handmark website at http://www.handmark.com/ to download a free trial of Bowling Deluxe or to purchase it online.

If bowling, whether real or virtual, isn't your thing, maybe you'll find a simulator of interest. Sort of along the lines of The Sims, Sim City, and so on is a game called Village Sim by LDW Software. Village Sim is a simulator in which you control a tribe of people in an island village and help them thrive and prosper. The game runs in real time, even if your device is turned off, so the village is in a constant state of change whether or not you actually play the game. This feature adds a touch of realism and interest to the game.

Figure 14.2 shows a few villagers wandering around taking care of daily chores. To download a free trial of the game or to purchase it online, visit the LDW Software website at http://www.ldw.com/.

FIGURE 14.1

Bowling Deluxe is a surprisingly fun bowling game that allows you to bowl anywhere you want.

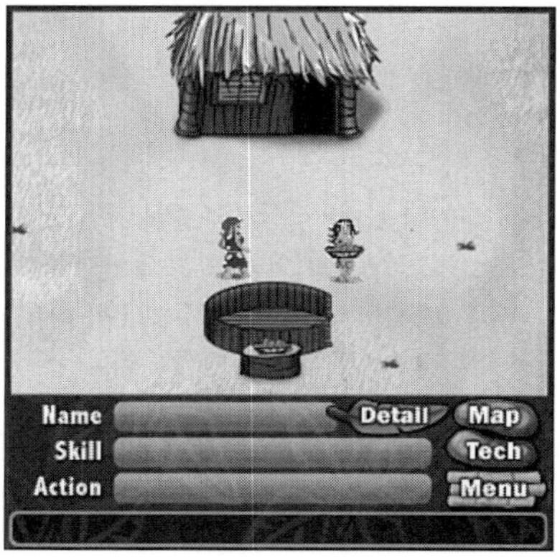

FIGURE 14.2

Village Sim challenges you to oversee an entire island village and its inhabitants in real time.

If you're anything like me, you can't get enough of the classic arcade games that dominated the 1980s. One of the prominent arcade game manufacturers back then was Midway, which created such classics as Joust, Defender, and Robotron. Although it doesn't include Robotron, Midway Arcade Classics for your Treo is a great game pack by Handmark that's worth having. The games are a little unusual in that the control keys don't always align with the five-way navigator on Treo devices. You might need to experiment a bit with the controls, but after you get the hang of it, you'll really have fun with these games: Spy Hunter, Joust, Defender II, Sinistar, and Root Beer Tapper.

Figure 14.3 shows a game of Defender II in progress. Check out the Handmark website at http://www.handmark.com/ to download a free trial of Midway Arcade Classics or to purchase it online.

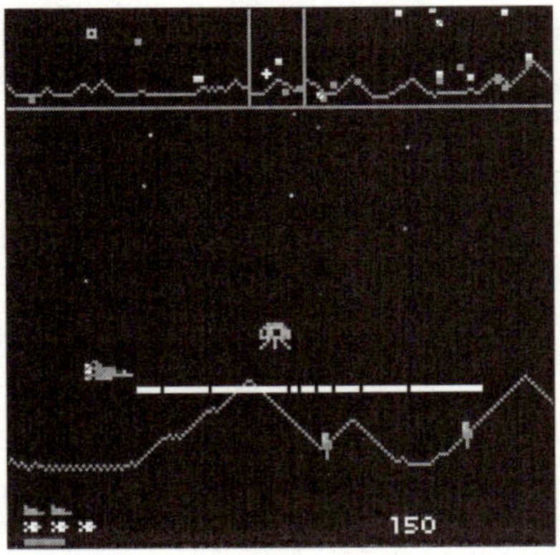

FIGURE 14.3

Defender II still ranks as one of the most challenging of the arcade classics, whether you're playing it on your Treo or at a real arcade.

> **NOTE** Just about every application mentioned in this chapter is available for purchase through online mobile software retailers, such as Handango (www.handango.com) and MobiHand (www.mobihand.com).

There's no doubt that single-player mobile games make great temporary diversions and can even be engaging over a longer period. Even so, the addition of real human players in multiplayer games takes any mobile game to an entirely different level—keeping reading to see how!

Play a Multiplayer Game

In addition to arcade and computer games, I'm a big fan of traditional board games, and who can forget the granddaddy of all board games, Monopoly? It turns out that there's an excellent mobile version of Monopoly available for the Treo, published by none other than Handmark. One feature that makes the mobile version so fun is how fast you can play it—you can literally play an entire game of Monopoly with four players in under 15 minutes. If you're no good at Monopoly, you might even be able to speed up that time!

The Treo version of Monopoly is particularly interesting because it allows for multiple human players via infrared or Bluetooth connections. For infrared, you need to align the devices close to each other, but Bluetooth is more flexible and requires just being within Bluetooth range (approximately 32 feet or less). When playing Monopoly networked, you have the option of hosting or joining a game. If you host a game, a list of devices within range is displayed, in which case you simply select your opponent's Treo from the list. If you elect to join a game that someone else is hosting, the host appears on the join screen, and you can confirm that you want to join the game.

Figure 14.4 shows a game of Monopoly being played, and you can see that the game board is still reasonably detailed, even with the relatively small Treo screen. Check out the Handmark website at http://www.handmark.com/ to download a free trial of Monopoly or to purchase it online.

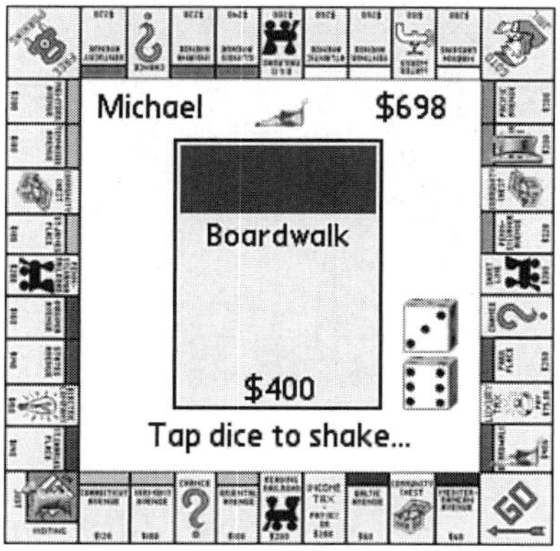

FIGURE 14.4

Monopoly can be played with up to four networked players who are connected via infrared or Bluetooth connections.

While I'm on the subject of classic traditional games, take a look at another one. In Battleship, you attempt to sink your opponent's concealed ships and submarine by firing torpedoes on a grid. Similar to Monopoly, Battleship is published by Handmark and supports multiple networked players. Unlike Monopoly, however, Battleship supports infrared and Internet networking. In other words, you can play Battleship over a wireless network connection without being physically near your opponent.

> **NOTE** Depending on your specific wireless data service plan, you may or may not have a static IP address for your device. If not, your IP address changes each time you close the network connection and start a new one. If you find that you don't have a static IP address, you need to look up your current IP address each time you connect and start a new game.

The main difference between playing a multiplayer network game over the Internet as opposed to using infrared or Bluetooth is that you must specify the host device's IP address to join a game. This address is usually four numbers separated by periods, such as 192.168.0.100. If you elect to host a game, the best thing to do is launch the Blazer Web browser first and visit http://www.whatismyip.com. This website displays your device's IP address, which you can then give to other players so that they can successfully join your game. If you're joining a game, make sure you find out the host's IP address so that you can enter and see the host game.

A heated game of Battleship is shown being played in Figure 14.5. Check out the Handmark website at http://www.handmark.com/ to download a free trial of Battleship or to purchase it online.

FIGURE 14.5

Battleship is a simple but fun game, especially if you play it with a friend over the wireless Internet.

> **NOTE** In case you're wondering, it isn't just a coincidence that most of the current networked multiplayer mobile games are relatively simple turn-based games; that is, you take a turn, another player takes a turn, and so on. Turn-based games are much easier to develop for networks that don't provide high speeds and reliability in terms of data transfer. As mobile bandwidth widens, you'll see more multiplayer games expand beyond turn-based games.

I want to end this round-up of multiplayer games with one more traditional classic. This time I'm talking about a word game—the classic Scrabble game where you attempt to spell words vertically and horizontally using letter tiles. Scrabble is yet another Handmark game and is similar to Monopoly in that it supports networked play via infrared and Bluetooth. The same networking approach used by Monopoly applies to Scrabble for hosting or joining a game.

Figure 14.6 shows a game of Scrabble underway with several words on the board and my tiles visible along the bottom of the screen. Check out the Handmark website at http://www.handmark.com/ to download a free trial of Scrabble or to purchase it online.

I hope you now have a good feel for what's possible in gaming on your Treo. And you can rest assured that games will only improve as developers figure out ways to push the envelope and squeeze more performance out of the Treo hardware.

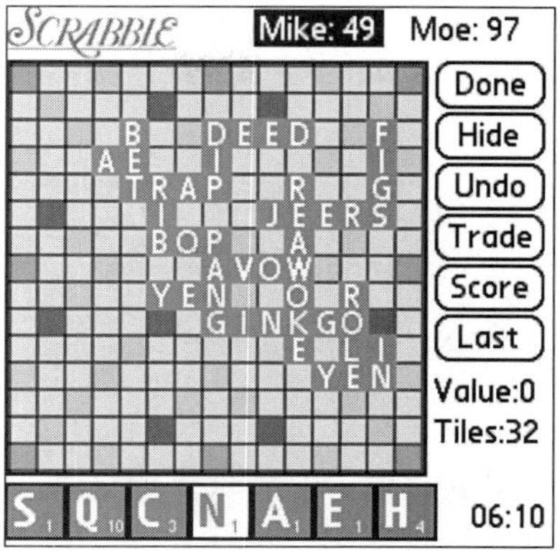

IGURE 14.6

crabble is surprisingly fun on Treo devices, both networked with real people and against omputer players.

Jse Your Treo as a Universal Remote Control

You probably never thought about using your Treo as a universal remote control for media equipment such as your TV, DVD player, cable box, and so forth. It turns out that the infrared port on your device is more than capable of beaming remote control commands to such devices. If you'd like to use your Treo to forgo the many remote controls that crowd the average "media room" these days, you'll want to check out NoviiRemote Deluxe by NoviiMedia.

> **NOTE** NoviiMedia also has a product called NoviiRemote Blaster that includes a high-powered infrared transmitter on an SD card with the NoviiRemote software built in. Unfortunately, as of this writing, NoviiRemote Blaster is not yet available for Treo devices. A version for the Treo is expected at some point and will help solve the problem of relatively weakly powered infrared ports on Treo devices.

NoviiRemote Deluxe ships with numerous "codebases" that you use to find matches for your equipment. For example, I have a Motorola digital cable box and a Sony WEGA television. The Sony TV was easy to match up with a standard codebase in NoviiRemote Deluxe, but I had to experiment a little to find a suitable codebase for the Motorola cable box. An advantage of the application is that it allows you to try different codebases and test them. I just sat in front of my cable box and tried hitting the Power button for different codebases until one of them powered on my cable box. Figure 14.7 shows the virtual remote control screen used to control a cable box via your Treo.

Depending on how popular each piece of your media equipment is, you might have to tinker with NoviiRemote Deluxe to find the right codebase for each piece. However, once you get them dialed in you'll find that controlling your entertainment center via your Treo is quite empowering. Just keep in mind that you'll be limited to a range of

10 to 15 feet, depending on the device you're attempting to control. To download NoviiRemote Deluxe, just visit its website at http://www.novii.tv/.

FIGURE 14.7

The NoviiRemote Deluxe application enables you to use your Treo as a universal remote control.

GPS and the Treo

If you've ever tinkered with a GPS (Global Positioning System) receiver, you already know how handy they can be for marking a geographical location or charting a route from point A to point B. Several GPS receivers are available for use with Treo devices. Although you might stumble across a GPS receiver that you can wire to your Treo, most are Bluetooth devices, which makes sense given that it's much more convenient to forgo a wire from device to device. Following are several popular Bluetooth GPS receivers that you can use with your Treo:

- *TomTom Navigator*—http://www.tomtom.com/
- *Navman Wireless Bluetooth GPS*—http://www.navman.com/
- *Pharos Pocket GPS Navigator*—http://www.pharosgps.com/
- *Holux Bluetooth GPS Receiver*—http://www.holux.com.tw/

A big part of using any GPS receiver with your Treo is the software used to access GPS data. This software can be as simple as a display of GPS coordinates or as advanced as a full-blown graphical map complete with points of interest. Some applications also allow you to enter a destination and then provide exact directions to guide you there. Of course, maps for the more powerful applications have to be downloaded and installed on your device. These maps can get fairly large, so generally you install only a few counties or cities at a time unless you take advantage of a memory card for storing them.

Navigate with a GPS Receiver

Navigating with a GPS receiver can be made easy by selecting the right application. One such application is Mapopolis, which is bundled with some GPS receivers and is also available online at http://www.mapopolis.com/. The Mapopolis website includes maps you can download for areas within the United States, Canada, and western Europe. An even better option, if you don't mind spending more money, is to buy a NavCard, which is a memory card preloaded with maps for the entire United States or a U.S. region.

Figure 14.8 shows the Mapopolis application busy at work guiding me around my hometown of Nashville with the help of a Bluetooth GPS receiver. In this example, I specified a destination, and Mapopolis gave me detailed directions as I traversed the route on the onscreen map.

FIGURE 14.8

By using a powerful mapping application such as Mapopolis, you can max out the effectiveness of a GPS receiver.

Navigating via a GPS receiver is not only cool from a gadget perspective, but can also become an essential tool if you travel a lot to unfamiliar places. I have friends who regularly make business trips to unfamiliar locations, and they find their GPS receivers to be irreplaceable for navigating quickly to their destination without the hassle and distraction of resorting to a paper map.

Find a Geocache

It's one of the oldest games in the world—the treasure hunt! I stumbled across a new hobby a few years ago when I heard about people using GPS receivers to find hidden objects in public places. The activity, known as *geocaching*, has since grown into a fairly large phenomenon. It works like this: Someone hides an object in a public place and records the GPS coordinates. The person then posts these coordinates on the official Geocaching website (http://www.geocaching.com/), along with any pertinent information about the object. Other geocachers then search the Geocaching website by location to learn about hidden objects in their area. The actual objects hidden in a geocache range from small toys to log books where you record your name and date.

Figure 14.9 shows a geocache near where I live that I found with my nephew, Ryan. I have to warn you that even though you have an object's GPS coordinates, it isn't always easy to find.

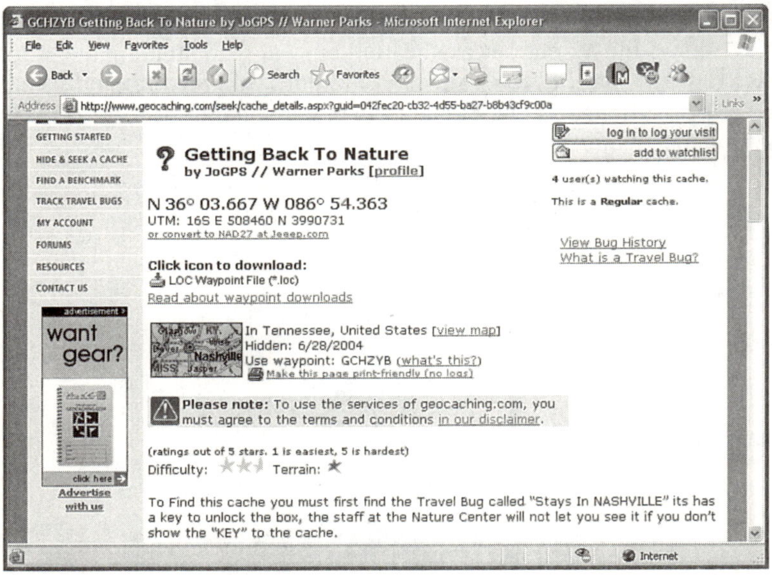

FIGURE 14.9

On the official Geocaching website, you can search for and find geocaches hidden near you.

Geocaching has evolved quite a bit over the past few years. There are now several different kinds of specialty caches, such as "travel bugs," which are objects that are moved from cache to cache. The idea behind a travel bug is that they are tagged with unique identifiers that allow you to track their movement through the Geocaching website. One of the most exciting aspects of geocaching is that you can easily create your own geocache for others to find and enjoy.

Summary

Whether it's playing a mobile game, controlling your television via a virtual universal remote control, or finding an unusual item hidden in the woods, I hope you're leaving this chapter with a new appreciation of what your Treo is capable of. Treo games have come a long way since their humble beginnings and now boast multiplayer network support for infrared, Bluetooth, and Internet gaming. After introducing you to some mobile games, this chapter has explored a surprising use of Treo devices; you've learned that they can serve as universal remote controls to control televisions, DVD players, cable boxes, and other media devices. From there, you found out how useful GPS receivers can be when coupled with a Treo and a good mapping application. You even found out how to use a GPS to go find hidden "treasure."

Improving Your Lifestyle with Your Treo

The majority of this book has focused on using the standard Treo features and applications to enhance your mobile computing and communications experience. What I haven't touched on much is how you can use third-party applications to make your Treo have an impact on your lifestyle. I'm not just talking about your "digital lifestyle"—I'm talking about aspects of your real-world lifestyle that up to now probably haven't involved computers. For example, maybe you've wanted to take control of some personal life goals, such as increasing your income or reshaping your body. Or maybe you'd like to take advantage of your Treo's data storage capabilities to help track medication and store your critical medical information in the event of a medical emergency. All this is possible with a few third-party Treo applications, which you learn about in this chapter.

IN THIS CHAPTER

- Use Handwriting Recognition
- Take Control of a Mobile To-Do List
- Monitor Your Exercise and Count Calories
- Manage Your Medicine and Store 911 Data
- Store Personal Data Securely
- Keep Your Treo Neat and Clean

Use Handwriting Recognition

If you have any history with Palm devices, you're probably familiar with the popular Graffiti input system used on most Palm/palmOne devices other than the Treo. The Graffiti input system is a handwriting-recognition system that translates strokes made with the stylus into characters, effectively allowing you to type via handwriting. Treo devices don't include the Graffiti software, presumably because they have full QWERTY keyboards that are considerably more efficient than writing characters by hand. This feature is great if you've never used a Palm device before, but it could be a serious downer if you're already a Graffiti master from years of Palm usage. For this reason, you might want to consider adding Graffiti as a third-party application.

The third-party application to which I'm referring is Jot, published by Communication Intelligence Corporation (CIC). Jot is actually the same software known as Graffiti 2 in other Palm

> **NOTE**
> The original Graffiti input system was originally replaced on Palm devices because of a lawsuit between Palm and Xerox related to a Xerox patent on handwriting-recognition software. This led to Graffiti 2, which was a licensed version of Jot from Communication Intelligence Corporation (CIC). Although some original Graffiti keystrokes were maintained, Graffiti 2 required Palm users to relearn many commonly used input techniques. However, in 2004 a judge ruled in favor of palmOne, saying that Xerox's patent wasn't valid after all.

devices, such as the Zire and Tungsten series of devices. You can download Jot from MyTreo.net via the following link: http://mytreo.net/downloads/author-CIC.html.

After downloading, installing, and launching Jot on your Treo, a welcome screen offers some options for the Jot experience (see Figure 15.1).

The first option is the most important one: Enable Jot. Make sure this check box is selected if you want handwriting recognition to be enabled on your device. You can quickly turn off handwriting recognition at any time by clearing this option. You use the second option to choose between the Jot and Graffiti 2 input systems. There are subtle differences between the two systems, and if you're coming from an older Palm device, you'll probably want to stick with Graffiti 2. The main differences have to do with how the letters i, k, and t are written—Jot enables you to write them with one stroke, while Graffiti relies on the original Palm two-stroke technique.

The remaining options have to do with how you actually enter handwriting strokes. The Show Mode Mark option determines whether a mode mark is displayed at the top of the screen to show how the screen is divided vertically into two halves. The idea is that you write letters on the left side of the screen and numbers on the right side; the *mode mark* just helps remind you of the two writing areas. The Show Ink option determines whether you can see the strokes onscreen as you draw them. This option is important, and I can't imagine disabling it unless you're a Graffiti wizard and find the ink distracting. You use the final option to choose between thin and thick ink line widths.

FIGURE 15.1

The welcome screen in the Jot application includes options you can set to control handwriting recognition.

When you're finished with the Jot options, you might want to tap Tutorial and run through the tutorial, and then tap Tuner to tune up the recognition system. If you've selected the Graffiti 2 system instead of the Jot system, tap Graffiti2Help for some Graffiti 2 tips. When you're ready to try out Jot, launch an application that requires text entry, such as Memo, and try writing some text. Figure 15.2 shows a memo as I enter it a letter at a time using Jot.

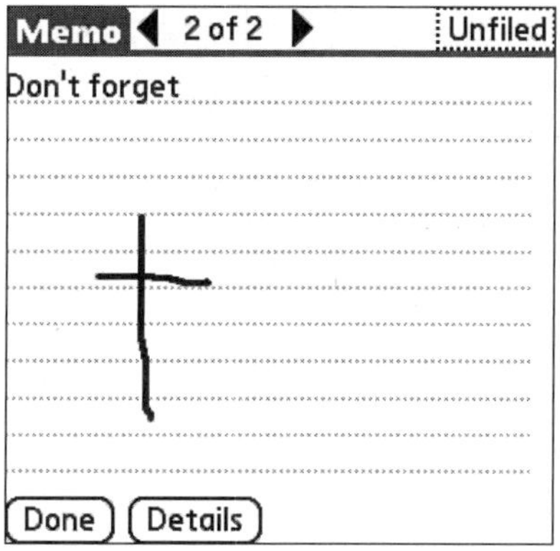

FIGURE 15.2

Entering a memo via Jot requires writing each letter with the stylus, which is admittedly a bit more tedious than using the Treo keyboard.

Although Jot represents a nice throwback to earlier Palm devices, I find the keyboard to be much more efficient at entering text. Even so, I know some Palm purists who still swear by their Graffiti skills and insist on communicating via stylus. To each his own!

Take Control of a Mobile To-Do List

I have to admit to being just a little "old school" when it comes to tasks, to-do lists, and general planning. I do enter tasks into my Treo, but I'm just as apt to quickly write down a note on real paper. Although this works for day-to-day tasks, what about larger life goals? Surely there's a way to take a more planned approach to things such as your overall health and well being, the amount of time you spend with your family, and so on. Fortunately, there is, and it's an application called Life Balance by Llamagraphics. Life Balance is similar to the Treo Tasks application, but it focuses on your overall well being. More important, Life Balance is able to break down your commitment to goals and actually display a pie chart that clearly shows the effectiveness of your planning. You can download Life Balance from the Llamagraphics website at http://www.llamagraphics.com/.

Figure 15.3 shows the main screen in the Life Balance application, which is a hierarchical outline of tasks related to an overall balanced life.

Figure 15.3

Although you will certainly want to tweak it to suit your own lifestyle, Life Balance provides the framework for a balanced life.

The outline shown in Figure 15.3 is just a starting point—by all means, change it to reflect your own lifestyle. You can edit each task in the outline to display specific details, such as how important the task is, the difficulty of achieving it, how much time is required, and so forth. Just select a task and tap the Details button to edit it. As an example, Figure 15.4 shows how to set the importance of a task in the General tab of the Task Details screen.

Figure 15.4

You set the importance of a Life Balance task by dragging a slider bar in the General tab.

Other tabs in the Task Details screen include Time, Effort, and Note. You can use these tabs to specify the amount of time required for the task, the effort needed to complete it, and any notes associated with the task.

After you enter the details for several tasks, you can start to see the balance of your life by viewing the Balance screen. To access it, tap the far-right box in the upper-right corner of the Outline screen (see Figure 15.3). The boxes in the upper-right corner correspond to different views in the Life Balance application; the far-right box takes you to the Balance view, shown in Figure 15.5.

FIGURE 15.5

The Balance view in the Life Balance application shows you the balance of your life as a pie chart based on the tasks you've entered.

Notice in Figure 15.5 that the pie chart on the left is the desired life balance, with the five major Life Balance categories given equal emphasis. The pie chart on the right is your life balance according to the tasks you've entered. Your goal is to reconcile the Actual chart with the Desired chart. In doing so, you can theoretically bring your life into balance with the aid of your Treo.

Monitor Your Exercise and Count Calories

Speaking of a balanced life, one of the most challenging aspects of healthy living for just about anyone who's mobile enough and busy enough to benefit from using a Treo is eating properly and exercising enough. An application called Diet and Exercise Assistant by Keyoe makes it possible to exert some serious control over your diet and exercise needs. Whether your goal is weight loss or just a healthy level of general maintenance, you'll likely find Diet and Exercise Assistant to be a useful application for your Treo. You can download the application from the Keyoe website at http://www.keyoe.com/.

NOTE Diet and Exercise Assistant actually consists of two applications on your Treo: Diet and Foods. The Diet application is the main application where you manage your diet and exercise and chart your progress toward a specific health goal. The Food application is a database of foods that the Diet application uses to help plan a diet.

When you first launch Diet and Exercise Assistant, which is actually called Diet on the main application screen, you're prompted to step through an interview that asks questions about your current health, your goals, what kind of diet plan you're interested in, and so on. The first step includes entering information such as your current age, height, and gender. From there, you enter your current weight along with a goal for a desired weight. You then press on and select a diet plan, such as low calorie, low carb, low fat, or custom. Things start to get interesting toward the end of the interview process, when you're presented with a specific diet plan that lists your target daily caloric intake as well as the number of grams of each food type you need to eat to stay on track (see Figure 15.6) .

FIGURE 15.6

Step 3 of the diet planner summarizes your daily intake of calories and specific amounts of each food type.

Admittedly, it takes a fair amount of discipline to truly benefit from using Diet and Exercise Assistant. However, if you commit to tracking everything you eat, you'll find that you can really take control of your diet and health. Figure 15.7 shows the daily logbook after breakfast, in which case 184 calories were consumed. Basal metabolic rate (BMR) is a measure of how many calories you burn doing normal everyday functions, excluding exercise.

You'll notice several icons along the bottom of the screen. Each icon accesses a different part of the Diet application so that you can chart your diet and exercise in extreme detail. Tracking your food intake and burned calories with such ruthless efficiency might not be your cup of tea, but it's a handy usage of your Treo if you have the desire and commitment to do so.

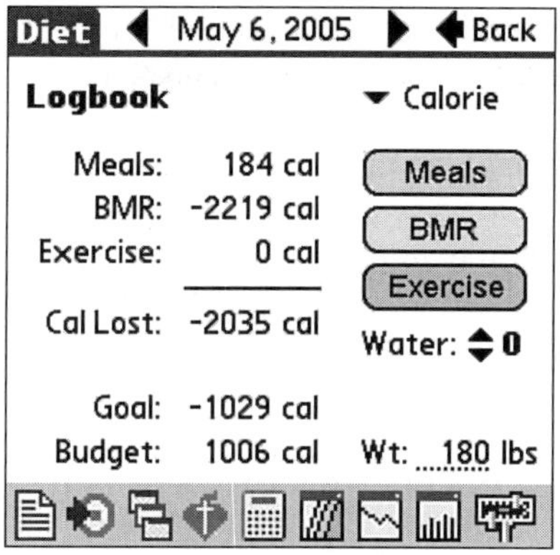

FIGURE 15.7

The daily logbook in Diet and Exercise Assistant is where you see your daily food intake balanced against calories burned through everyday tasks as well as exercise.

NOTE If you want to explore other diet and nutrition applications for your Treo, HealtheTech, Skyscape, and even Weight Watchers offer interesting applications. HealtheTech's application is called BalanceLog, and it's available online at http://www.healthetech.com/balancelog/. Skyscape offers The South Beach Diet OnHand, which is available at http://www.skyscape.com/. And finally, Weight Watchers On-the-Go is available at http://www.weightwatchers.com/pda/.

Manage Your Medicine and Store 911 Data

Before leaving the topic of personal well being, there's one last "lifestyle application" to touch on. I'm referring to OnTimeRx by AmeliaPlex, which is a medication and emergency information management application for your Treo. OnTimeRx not only serves as a central repository for your allergies and important health conditions that need to be revealed in an emergency, but also serves as a reminder system for medicine you take regularly. You can download OnTimeRx from http://www.pillsinyourpalm.com/.

The OnTimeRx application manages your medications by first allowing you to enter the different medications you take regularly, along with the dosage and frequency. Figure 15.8 shows an example of entering a specific medication into OnTimeRx.

After you've entered a medication, OnTimeRx begins tracking it and reminding you when you must take it. A log is then maintained to keep track of when you've taken the medicine along with any dosages you've missed.

NOTE Keep in mind that the specifics of the diet that you chart in Diet and Exercise Assistant are determined by the diet plan you selected when you initially set up the application.

The other important facet of the OnTimeRx application is its management of emergency health information, such as drug allergies and any important health conditions you might have. This information is entered into OnTimeRx as "911" information, with the idea being that someone could access this information in an emergency to find out more about how to treat you. Figure 15.9 shows the resulting 911 screen in OnTimeRx, which shows a couple of health conditions that would be worth knowing in an emergency.

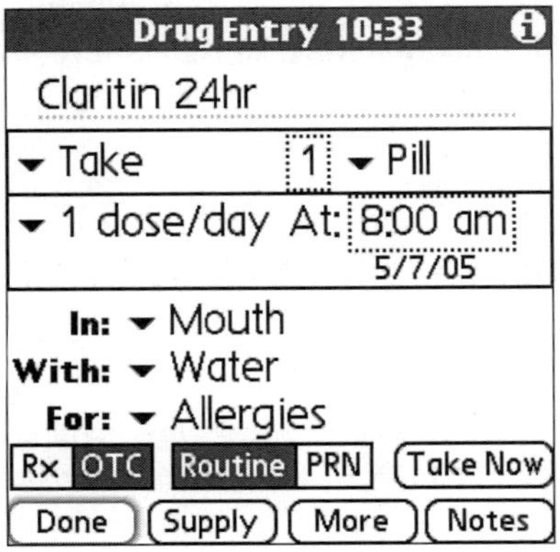

FIGURE 15.8

In this example, a single medication is entered into OnTimeRx, along with its dosage, frequency, and other pertinent information.

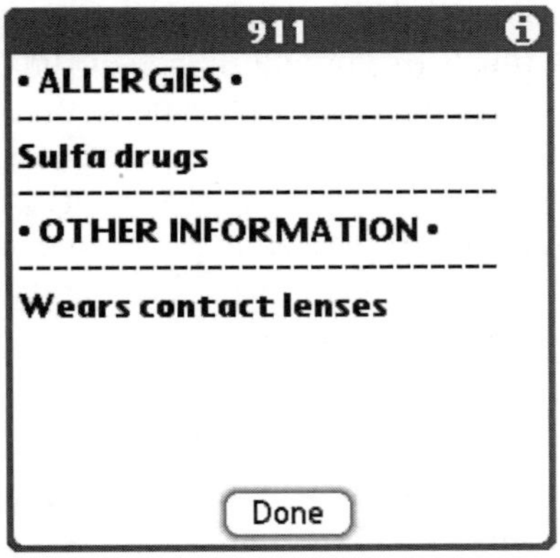

FIGURE 15.9

Although you can enter much more detail, this is an example of a couple of health conditions that would be valuable to know in an emergency.

You can enter as much or as little information into OnTimeRx as you'd like. Of course, this information is valuable only if people know how to access it, so make sure that people close to you know how to launch OnTimeRx and tap the 911 button (located on the main OnTimeRx screen) to access your emergency information.

Store Personal Data Securely

You could argue that medical data is about as personal as data can get. However, there's plenty of sensitive personal data besides medication that you might want to have access to on your Treo. As an example, consider all the different user IDs and passwords you use to access popular Web services, such as Amazon.com and eBay. If you want to access your account on an online service while away from your desktop or notebook computer, you need to know your user ID and password. Additionally, you might decide to log on and access your email from a temporary location, in which case you need to know not only a user ID and password, but also the mail servers involved. All this information can be safely stored away on your Treo.

> **TIP** This probably goes without saying, but be extra cautious about creating a password for DataShield that no one else can figure out. It's great that DataShield combines all your personal data in one place, but it also makes it that much easier for others to get your personal information if your password is compromised and they get their hands on your device.

The application that makes personal data storage possible is Ultrasoft DataShield, which is available for download from the Ultrasoft website at http://www.ultrasoft.com/DataShield/. With DataShield, you can store all kinds of useful data on your Treo that's conveniently protected by a password so that you are the only person who is able to access it.

The first step in using DataShield involves setting up a password, which is critical because you want all your personal data to be secure. After establishing a password, you can begin entering personal data according to each different data type. For example, your eBay user ID and password is entered as the Web Passwords data type, as shown in Figure 15.10. Other data types include Bank Accounts, Clothing Sizes, E-mail Accounts, Frequent Flyer, Insurance Policies, and Serial Numbers, to name a few.

FIGURE 15.10

Entering personal data simply involves specifying the information pertinent to the data type.

Notice in Figure 15.10 that the data entry fields correspond specifically to the data type being entered, which in this case is Web Passwords. After entering several pieces of data, you'll notice that they are readily accessible from a master list in the DataShield screen (see Figure 15.11).

FIGURE 15.11

The main list in the DataShield screen shows all the personal information you've entered.

To access any information in the list, simply tap the item with the stylus. You may be realizing that the DataShield application is fairly simple, in that it just provides access to data you enter. However, the data being broken down conveniently into common data types is a significant advantage compared to just entering the information as raw text. Having a single password that protects all your personal data is another important benefit that makes DataShield a worthwhile Treo add-on.

Keep Your Treo Neat and Clean

The last stop on your little tour of life-altering Treo applications is the NeatFreak Pack, which is actually an application suite by Northglide. NeatFreak Pack consists of two applications, Uninstall Manager and Cleanup, both of which help you keep your device clean of unwanted and unnecessary files that accumulate over time and eat up valuable memory. Uninstall Manager helps you fully uninstall applications that you no longer use, and Cleanup is helpful for tracking down orphan files no longer used by any applications. These two applications work hand in hand to help you keep your Treo streamlined, at least for applications and the memory they occupy. You can download the NeatFreak Pack from the Northglide website at http://www.northglide.com/products.html.

If you have any experience with the Registry Editor on Windows computers, you'll be right at home with the Cleanup application. If not, you'll want to exercise a good dose of caution when it comes to cleaning up files on your Treo. Cleanup gives you a fair amount of flexibility in terms of the files it allows you to clean up, and if you get too aggressive, you can potentially get in trouble by removing a file that an application actually needs. If you make sure to back up files before you delete them, you should be okay. Figure 15.12 shows a screen in the Cleanup application with a list of unused preferences that can potentially be deleted.

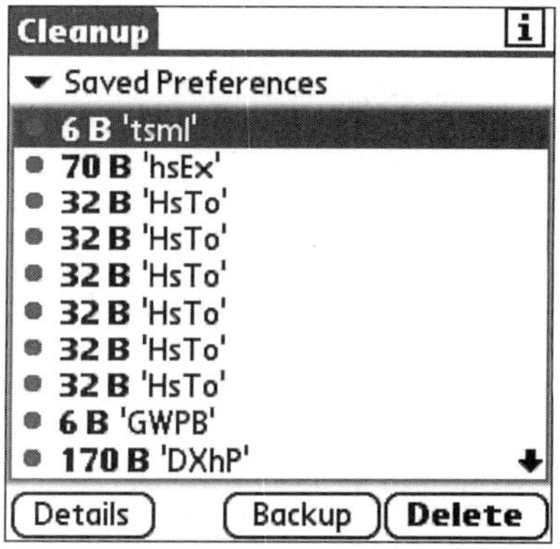

FIGURE 15.12

The Cleanup application enables you to clean up your Treo by eliminating unused files.

I encourage you to read the help information that comes with the Cleanup application—just tap the small *i* icon in the upper-right corner of the screen.

The Uninstall Manager application is similar to Cleanup, except it focuses more on removal of entire applications. Similar to Cleanup, however, Uninstall Manager attempts to go beyond a standard uninstall by tracking down files associated with an application that might not been removed otherwise. Figure 15.13 shows Uninstall Manager as it presents a list of applications that can be uninstalled.

> **TIP**
> See "Back Up Your Treo to a Memory Card" in Chapter 4, "Synchronizing with Your Desktop Computer," for information on how to perform a backup of your device.

It's important to realize that Uninstall Manager is a powerful application that's capable of thoroughly eliminating applications from your device. If you're in doubt about removing an application, be sure to fully back up your device before uninstalling anything.

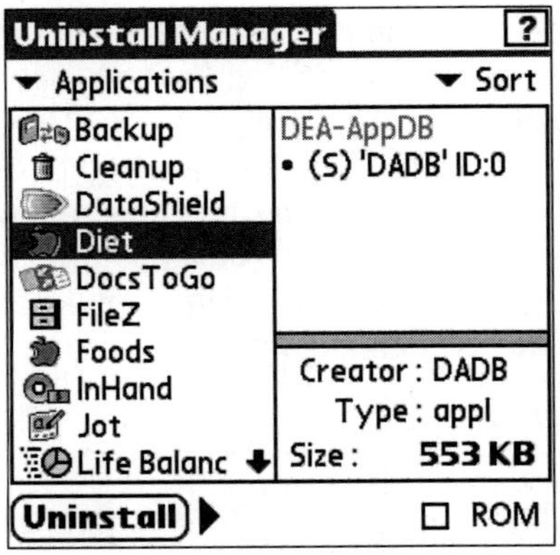

FIGURE 15.13

Uninstalling an application with Uninstall Manager is as simple as selecting the application and tapping Uninstall.

Summary

Although I wouldn't exactly call the Treo experience "life altering," I hope this chapter has opened your eyes to some other interesting uses of your Treo that can have an impact on your life beyond the obvious mobile communicator features. It's important to point out that I only scratched the surface in terms of what applications are available for you to experiment with. I selected a few applications that I found interesting, but by all means, please go out and explore the Treo software universe on your own. You might uncover that one application that truly improves your life in a new and unexpected way. Good luck!

APPENDIXES

PART V

IN THIS CHAPTER

- Common Upgrade Issues
- Performing the Upgrade

Upgrading to the Treo 650

If you're upgrading to the Treo 650 from another Palm device, there are some issues you'll no doubt want to consider. This appendix addresses some considerations for upgrading to the Treo 650 from another Palm device, including the Treo 600.

Common Upgrade Issues

The main consideration when upgrading to the Treo 650 is data on your previous device that isn't easily moved to the 650. A lot of your data is no doubt stored as personal information manager (PIM) data on a desktop PIM client, which means you can just synchronize your new Treo to move the data onto it. However, some data isn't included in the synchronization process, and you'll lose this data if you don't transfer it to your new device manually.

Following are the types of data you need to consider moving manually from your old device to your new device, along with a word about applications that might need to be addressed during the transition:

- *Favorites*—Favorites must be entered manually in the Treo 650. Unfortunately, there's no automatic way to transfer favorites from an older Treo or Palm device, so you must manually re-create each favorite on your new Treo. See "Create and Manage Favorites" in Chapter 7, "Using Your Treo as a Mobile Phone," for more details on how this is done.
- *Call log*—The call log is not included in the synchronization process. If there are numbers in your old device's call log that you don't have stored as contacts, make sure you create contacts for the numbers and then synchronize your old device. The contacts are then transferred to your Treo 650 upon synchronizing.
- *Email settings*—The VersaMail application is new to the Treo 650, so any email accounts you had set up on an

older Palm device have to be set up anew in VersaMail. Email messages cannot be transferred to your new Treo directly, although you might be able to forward important messages and receive them via the newly created VersaMail account. See "Create an Email Account in VersaMail" in Chapter 8, "Staying in Touch with Email," to find out how to create a new account in VersaMail.

- *Web bookmarks and saved pages*—Similar to favorites, there's no automatic way to transfer Web bookmarks and saved pages from an older Palm device, so you must re-create them manually on your new Treo. See "Create and Use Bookmarks" and "Save a Web Page for Offline Viewing" in Chapter 10, "Browsing the Wireless Web," to learn how to create bookmarks and save web pages on your Treo 650.
- *Ring tones*—There's no way to move ring tones automatically from your old Palm device to your new Treo 650. In fact, the only ring tones you even have the option of using on the 650 are MIDI ring tones that you might have acquired for a Treo 600. If you purchased these ring tones from an online service, you should be able to access them again and download them onto your new Treo. If the ring tones are unprotected, just email or beam them to your new Treo. See "Choose, Create, and Download Ring and Alert Tones" in Chapter 3, "Customizing and Personalizing Your Treo," for more information on how to work with ring tones.
- *Pictures*—Pictures must be moved manually from a Treo 600 to a Treo 650. Click the Treo Pictures icon in the Palm Desktop application to open the Treo Pictures folder and select the pictures to be transferred. Then click Media in Palm Desktop and drag the pictures from the Treo Pictures folder to the Media window. Perform a HotSync operation to finish transferring the pictures.
- *Expense data*—Unlike other Palm devices, the Treo 650 doesn't include a built-in Expense application. You'll need to export and save expense data from your old device if you plan to keep it.
- *Legacy applications*—Applications you used on an earlier Palm device might not be supported on the Treo 650. Be sure to check with the publisher of any third-party applications you use to check whether there is a new version that's compatible with the Treo 650.

> **TIP** You can also store your pictures on a memory card using your old device and then just switch the memory card to your Treo 650.

If you keep these issues in mind as you upgrade to the Treo 650, you shouldn't have too much trouble migrating to your new device.

Performing the Upgrade

The process of upgrading from an older Palm device to the Treo 650 can be broken down into a few basic steps:

1. Install the Treo 650 desktop software.
2. If available, update the software on your new device.
3. Synchronize your old device data to your new device.
4. Set up email accounts.
5. Transfer data from your old device manually.
6. Reinstall third-party applications.

It's important to point out that you must install the Treo 650 desktop software even if you're upgrading from a Treo 600. This is because the Treo 650 software is different and includes several new features you'll want to be able to use.

Step 2 might have you a little concerned because you have a shiny new device and I'm already recommending a software upgrade for it. Depending on when you bought your device and who your wireless carrier is, you might need to install a software update that helps solve a memory problem associated with the Treo 650's new nonvolatile memory system. The problem is one of efficiency, meaning that some Treo 650 devices have less usable memory than similar Treo 600 devices because of the changed memory system.

A software update for the Treo 650 helps improve the efficiency of the 650 memory system. To learn more about the Treo 650 memory system and its inefficiency issues, see "Understanding the Treo 650 Memory System" in Chapter 1, "Meet Your Treo." If you want to jump straight in and see whether an update is available for your device, visit this link on the palmOne website: http://www.palmone.com/us/support/downloads/treo650updater/. You might also want to take a look at Appendix B, "Conserving Memory on Your Treo 650," for more details on how to upgrade your Treo software as well as useful tips for conserving memory on your device.

B

Conserving Memory on Your Treo 650

If you happen to be one of the early adopters of the Treo 650, you might have run into the problem of your device's memory system not being very efficient. More specifically, the Treo 650's initial memory system was redesigned to be nonvolatile, and in the process became less efficient, literally costing users several megabytes of effective storage space. Although the issue has been resolved in newer Treo 650 devices, and a software update is available for older devices, addressing ways in which you can conserve memory on your device is still worthwhile.

IN THIS CHAPTER

- Update the Software on Your Device
- Move Everything Possible to a Memory Card
- Clear the Web Browser Cache
- Clean Up Your Email

Update the Software on Your Device

The first step toward squeezing the most out of your Treo 650's memory is to make sure you have the latest software installed on your device. I'm talking about the core system software, which is available only from Palm. Check the following link to see whether a software update is available for your device: http://www.palmone.com/us/support/downloads/treo650updater/.

This update can result in dramatic memory improvements if you have one of the earlier Treo 650 devices. For example, many Treo 650 devices sold through Sprint use the original memory system, which tends to waste precious RAM. By installing the software update, users have reported a gain of anywhere from 3MB to 5MB in usable memory, which is enormous on a device with such limited memory.

Move Everything Possible to a Memory Card

One of the key strategies for conserving memory on the Treo 650 is moving data and applications from the device's internal memory to a memory card. If you don't yet own a memory card for your Treo, now is a good time to look into getting one. Handhelds are somewhat like the desktop computers of old, in that they can never have enough storage space. A hefty memory card is the best solution for freeing up internal memory by offloading as much information as possible to the memory card. Information in this sense includes both data and applications.

Of course, not all applications can be moved to the memory card. Most applications installed on your device out of the box are fixed in internal memory, and even some third-party applications that you install yourself must live in internal memory. However, if you see an opportunity to install or move an application to a memory card, by all means do so, unless you have a good reason for storing the application in internal memory.

Follow these steps to move an application from your device's internal memory to an installed memory card:

1. If you aren't already viewing the main application screen, press the **Application** button to open it.
2. Press the **Menu** button, and then scroll down to select the **Copy** command. The Copy screen appears, where you select an application to copy.
3. Scroll to select the application you'd like to move to the memory card. Make sure the Copy To pick list is set to the memory card, and then tap the **Copy** button to copy the application. Tap **Done** to return to the main application screen when the copy is finished.
4. Of course, moving an application to the memory card requires deleting the original copy from internal memory. So press the **Menu** button and select the **Delete** command. In the Delete screen that opens, select an application to delete.
5. Scroll to select the application, making sure the Delete From pick list is set to Phone. Then tap the **Delete** button to delete the application. Tap **Done** to return to the main application screen.

> **TIP**
> To access the applications stored on a memory card, tap the pick list in the upper-right corner of the main application screen, and then select the bottom item in the list (the memory card). The application screen then shows only the applications stored on the memory card.

Beyond applications, offloading data to a memory card is also important. Fortunately, the Treo's design discourages you from placing MP3 music files in the internal memory—this is good because multimedia files can take up lots of memory. However, plenty of other types of chunky data can hog memory and are better suited for a memory card. For example, pictures, videos, and voice memos are great candidates for moving to a memory card, as they can quickly eat up all the memory in sight and leave your device struggling to find room to function normally.

To move data files from internal memory to the memory card, you can use the same technique used to move applications. The difference is you select data files in the Copy screen after selecting the Copy command instead of selecting an application. For more exact control over the files on your device, you might want to look into a third-party application, such as FileZ. To learn more about FileZ, check out "Manage Files" in Chapter 4, "Synchronizing with Your Desktop Computer."

> **NOTE** If you're using a picture as the caller ID for a favorite, you need to leave the picture in internal memory.

Clear the Web Browser Cache

Another strategy for maximizing memory on your Treo involves regularly clearing the browser cache. The cache isn't necessarily a memory hog, but in most cases you'd probably rather have your device's memory available for running applications rather than caching web pages, at least when you aren't actively using the browser.

Clean Up Your Email

One final technique for saving memory is regularly sifting through your email and weeding out unneeded messages. Email attachments can sneakily eat up memory without you realizing it. So make an effort to go through your email from time to time, paying close attention to any attachments or long messages.

INDEX

Numbers

Symbols

A

B

E

F

L

M

O

P

Q - R

T

U

V

W

X-Y-Z